THE GODDESS IN THE MIRROR

THE GODDESS IN THE MIRROR

An Anthropology of Beauty

Tulasi Srinivas

Duke University Press
Durham and London 2025

© 2025 DUKE UNIVERSITY PRESS. All rights reserved
Printed in the United States of America on acid-free paper ∞
Designed by Dave Rainey
Typeset in Garamond Premier Pro by Westchester Publishing Services

Library of Congress Cataloging-in-Publication Data
Names: Srinivas, Tulasi, author.
Title: The goddess in the mirror : an anthropology of beauty / Tulasi Srinivas.
Description: Durham : Duke University Press, 2025. | Includes bibliographical references and index.
Identifiers: LCCN 2025013320 (print)
LCCN 2025013321 (ebook)
ISBN 9781478032779 (paperback)
ISBN 9781478029304 (hardcover)
ISBN 9781478061502 (ebook)
Subjects: LCSH: Beauty, Personal—Social aspects—India—Bangalore. | Beauty, Personal—Political aspects—India—Bangalore. | Feminine beauty (Aesthetics)—Social aspects—India—Bangalore. | Beauty shops—India—Bangalore.
Classification: LCC HQ1220.14 S656 2025 (print) | LCC HQ1220.14 (ebook) | DDC 363.72/99—dc23/eng/20250615
LC record available at https://lccn.loc.gov/2025013320
LC ebook record available at https://lccn.loc.gov/2025013321

Cover art: Bhaven Jani/Alamy Stock Photo.

For Popsi

Contents

ix		A Note on Translation
xi		Acknowledgments
xv		**Prelude** REVERIE
1		**Introduction** Beauty, Myth, Recognition
31	**1**	**Alluring**
63	**2**	**Radiant**
94	**3**	**Hot**
120		**Interlude** NIGHTMARE
124	**4**	**Wounded**
151	**5**	**Fortunate**
179	**6**	**Fluid**
214		**Conclusion** Mirrors and Masks: An Anthropology of Beauty
225		**Postlude** DREAM
229		Notes
241		References
267		Index

A Note on Translation

As with my previous work on Bangalore, I attempt to place this work within the context of the multilingual cityscape of Bangalore. In fact, it is so similar that I "borrowed" some sections of this note from my previous work (2018).

In the beauty parlors that I haunted, I heard constant and endless talk in many different languages—Hindi, English, Tamil, and Kannada—combined with a Dhakkar street language that was a potent mix of Hindi-Urdu or Tamil-Kannada combined with English, depending on the linguistic origins of the speaker and audience. This linguistic and cultural diversity is not easy to represent. It needs to be tracked through its moves, imaginations, sites of encounters, and permeabilities and vulnerabilities. I have employed different methods to make the reader aware of this rich linguistic and cultural field, including dense descriptive interludes, reproduced stories, and explanations of narrative constructions, and I have used ethnopoetic notations in an effort to evoke the intensely elaborate linguistic and imaginative poetics of the area.

To denote language, I use italicized lettering at the first use of an Indian-language word, and occasional speech patterns to evoke the dialectical difference from Standard English. Usually, when quoting a client or beauty worker, I give the source language in text, and then for clarity, I translate the non-English words and indicate the source language within parentheses; so, often the Hindi, Urdu, or Sanskrit words appear within the body of the text followed by the English translation with the source language within parentheses, such as *yaar* (Hindi = friend).

Occasionally, I use a Sanskrit, Hindi, or Kannada word that is well known to specialist scholars, so I merely translate in parentheses without references to language of origin. In yet other cases where the word has filtered into the English language, I do not translate after the first usage, nor do I italicize, as with pajama.

In contrast to standard academic transliteration of Indian-language terms, I have usually elected not to use diacritics on the assumption that this is an ethnographic text and those who do know Indian languages will not need diacritics to correctly pronounce the word. Rather, I render transliterations as close as possible to what will result in correct English pronunciation. Thus, I render both ś and ṣ as sh; for example, *shakti* (spiritual power) rather than śakti. In direct quotations from authors who have used diacritics, the diacritics will be indicated as in the original; in these cases, the reader will notice, for example, spellings of Shiva as "Siva" or Vishnu as "Visnu." I have indicated Indian-language terms (except for proper nouns) with italics. Many terms in this book are shared across Indian languages with slightly different pronunciations and thus transliterations. Throughout this text, I will use the Sanskrit transliteration for proper names (Sita, Savithri), since these are closer to the vernacular pronunciations used by my collaborators in Bangalore.

Last, I retain the name Bangalore for continuity throughout the text, since that was the city's name when I began fieldwork. However, in keeping with many place names in India, it has since reverted to its precolonial name of Bengaluru.

Acknowledgments

As with all creative endeavors, this book owes its life to several people and many places.

First of all, I thank my friends and interlocutors in the parlors of Bangalore. My friends from Sophia High School who have become the elite of the city allowed me to "ride along" with them when they went to the parlor for their beauty treatments and patiently bore my intrusive presence. My other interlocutors, who did not know me initially, were hospitable and offered their time and thoughts as I watched them work. They welcomed me into the parlors, answered my idiotic questions on beauty treatments, and more intimate questions about their lives and work, and they did so with a patience, candor, and good humor that was humbling. None of this work would have been possible without them.

Many institutions also helped along the way. My own institution of Emerson College, where I have inherited and taught a general education course titled "Gender in a Global Perspective," enabled me to collaboratively read and think about beauty parlors all over the world with many smart and dedicated students. I also owe thanks to my colleagues at Emerson in the Women's, Gender, and Sexuality studies core, including Claudia Castaneda, Erika Williams, Nellie Sargsyan, Yasser Munif, and Jennifer McWeeny, and to Dean Amy Ansell, among others.

A decade ago the Kate Hamburger Kolleg at Ruhr Universität, Bochum, Germany gave me the time and space to look through my field notes and find these threads of beauty. Still later, at the Radcliffe Institute at Harvard, while working on the first book of the trilogy, *The Cow in the Elevator: An Anthropology of Wonder*, the possibility of writing a book on beauty parlors floated into view. Several years later, Anthea Butler told me about the Women's Study in Religion Program at the Harvard Divinity School, which she claimed my project was "perfect for." Many of the gender scholars I admired had held it, including Lindsey Harlan, Paola Bachetta, Tracy Pintchman, Vijaya Nagarajan, Amy Hollywood, and Rosalind Shaw, many of whom are my friends and mentors. In a delightful windfall, Harvard also offered me the senior Colorado Fellowship for 2022–23, though for another work. But it was *this* book that was completed at the Carriage House, as I watched the wild turkeys forage on the Divinity School lawns.

At Harvard, I am grateful to the director of the Women's Studies in Religion Program, Ann Braude, and my fellow fellows Kinitra D. Brooks, Jordan Katz, Rahina Muaza, Xhercis Mendez, and Elyan Jeanine Hill. Professors Frank Clooney, Janet Gyatso, Martha Selby, Arthur Kleinman, and Michael Puett also made me feel at home. Swayam Bagaria, a colleague at Harvard who generously read the whole book in the spring of 2023 despite the pressure to publish his own work, offered many helpful suggestions on storytelling and narrative that I am forever in his debt. My divinity school students Joe Archer, Anna Guterman, and Nathalie Folkerts and my teaching assistant Sunitha Das read iterations of this work and helped me think of the goddess in new and intriguing ways as we worked through our course titled "Goddesses and Ghosts." Additionally, the students in the Department of South Asian Studies at Harvard, particularly Poorna Swami and Seton Ullhorn, all supported me in ways large and small. I owe Poorna, a Bangalorean herself, a debt of gratitude for finding me a photographer in Bangalore, Richa Bhavanam, whom I could trust to act as my eyes and take photographs when I could not. Seton read the manuscript diligently and patiently created the first bibliography for this work.

Additionally, I thank Deepa Govindaraj for sharing her collection of photographs of the Miss Vegetarian Pageant in Bangalore and the Govindaraj and Goverdhan families for their recollections and photographs of pageants and fashions in 1970s Bangalore.

Indeed, to my surprise, I had many willing readers of this strange text. Andrew McDowell read fragmented notes as I began to write and convinced me that I did indeed have the makings of a book. Sarah Pinto urged me on, helping me think through notions of work and care when I fell into a well of despondency in year three of the writing and nearly gave up on the book altogether. Sudipa Topdar read sections of the work and offered ways of seeing beauty politically that had eluded me. As a historian, she also engaged me in ways of thinking and research on the history of beauty. Nell Hawley read and educated me on Sanskrit poetics and dramaturgy for which I am profoundly grateful. Annirudan Vasudevan talked me through the complications of reading Lévi-Strauss, and Marko Geslani offered me dynamic and fascinating discussions of Hindu thought, which kept me excited about writing this book despite its long gestation period. I am particularly grateful to Lawrence Cohen, who on a broiling hot summer afternoon spent several hours outside Sofra bakery in Watertown, discussing skin and trauma and generously offering me reading lists and creative thoughts on the writing. Finally, Tara Dankel helped me work through the manuscript with a care and candor for which I am ever grateful.

Many years of wrestling with the writing, largely invisible and in silence through the social isolation of the global pandemic, were made bearable by Joyce Flueckiger, Andrew McDowell, and Jack Hawley, all friends who provided me with the much needed inspiration to move forward, painfully slowly at this time, buoying my spirits with their cheery emails, reading lists, and Zoom chats. Vasudha Narayanan with her many wondrous photographs on Facebook enabled me to think of beauty in other, more productive ways, as a cosmological and theological quest. I owe a debt of gratitude to the late Gopal Karanth, who educated me not only on caste in provincial barbershops but also on the hairstyles and soaps of the 1950s. I will miss his educating emails.

In 2022, despite my friends' best efforts, I hit a wall of inaction, where I felt I could not move forward, that I did not have the vocabulary to parse what beauty did and what it was. Soumhya Ventakesan, who was wrestling (far more productively) with her own writing, became my thought partner and gave useful suggestions to move my work and life forward at this crucial time. Purnima Mankekar, who had a similar life trajectory of elder care, offered me invaluable advice over dinner in Madison, Wisconsin, and on the phone on balancing life and work, as did Ann Gold, who generously shared her writings on Sundari Devi, a goddess of beauty in Rajasthan. And at the same time, I managed to get back in touch with one of my childhood babysitters, a pioneer of feminist thinking and gender studies in India, Professor Uma Chakravarti, herself a Bangalorean, who has been called one of the mothers of India's women's movement. Her work on gender, caste, and widowhood in India, which I read as a graduate student, forms the strong scaffolding for this work.

Thankfully, as we emerged from the cocoon of isolation of the pandemic, an invitation from the South Asia Colloquium at Harvard University enabled me to share some of the beauty and storytelling practices I found in Bangalorean parlors, which at that time I saw as separate endeavors. But the thoughtful questions that the expert audience asked me gently pivoted me to the idea that these practices were twinned, and I turned back to the manuscript reinvigorated.

Finally, as *The Goddess in the Mirror* began to emerge, Ken Wissoker and his team at Duke University Press treated my procrastination and foot-dragging with patience. They always have treated me and my work with dignity, efficiency, and care. I am forever grateful for their support and for their finding of three perfect anonymous reviewers who made the manuscript far more readable and thoughtful through their invaluable suggestions.

Of course, none of this writing and storytelling, beautiful or otherwise, would be possible without my family. My mother, Rukmini Srinivas, is woven through the warp and weft of this book, as my memories of her begin the book and our life together today ends it. Her powerful natural beauty and strength, tall and graceful in her striking "temple" saris of vividly colored checked cotton and her cat's-eye sunglasses, is what I remember from my childhood. She was, and is, forever beautiful.

My sister and colleague Lakshmi Srinivas, who has always supported my writing and thinking, shared in the care of my mother and our pet parrot, Monster, when I wanted to work, often sacrificing her own desires for mine. And to Monster, who has, with his voice and presence, always lifted my mood and prevented me from allowing work to take over my life. He is the true natural beauty in my world. And last, to my spouse and partner, Popsi Narasimhan, to whom this work is dedicated, who has always given me the freedom of thinking and being. And I am more than grateful that Popsi has always found me beautiful and said so regardless of how I actually look!

Prelude

REVERIE

ONE BEAUTIFUL DAY . . .

I was daydreaming at my desk in Cambridge when a memory popped into my head of the first time I heard the term "beauty parlor."

Our family had decamped to the southern port city of Madras (now Chennai), where my maternal grandmother lived, to be guests at my maternal aunt's wedding. My aunt was the youngest at the tail end of eight siblings, and my mother, her elder by over two decades, was a guest of honor at the wedding, having missed her other six sisters' wedding celebrations.

My mother was and is a tall, distinctive-looking woman, with a flair for dressing. Educated, independent, and upper caste, she typically exempted herself from many bourgeoise preoccupations of dress and comportment. She never went to the beauty parlor or wore any makeup. Nonetheless, she always looked striking.

But that sunny afternoon, my aunts persuaded my mother to join the bride and her other sisters at a famous salon in the city, Eve's Beauty Parlor of Madras, to get their hair styled for the wedding. I remember my aunts excitedly talking about the "parlor," as salons were called in India. I wondered what a beauty parlor was and what it would be like. I remember too that my mother was not excited about the outing but had been persuaded by her sisters to go along. They left us cousins under the distracted care of uncles and fathers at the old colonial hotel where we were staying.

FIG. P.I. The author as a child, with her mother and the family dog, in Bangalore

Thus, I spent a glorious, hot afternoon with my sister and cousins, playing in the fountain at the hotel, catching tadpoles in a bottle, and getting thoroughly soaked. I remember looking up through the palm tree fronds at a lyrically blue sky. I remember the smell of my wet clothing, the fishy stench of the slimy green algae that covered the pond. I remember my sheer delight in contemplating my new and now ruined patent leather shoes and how they squeaked, oozing water with every step.

Later that evening, as I sat on the edge of the fountain in my wet dress and shoes, a tall woman walked up to me. She looked distinctly familiar but different, strange, glamorous (though I did not yet know that word). Her hair was pulled up tight and smooth in a French roll chignon with one yellow rose pinned at the side of the bun. Only when she called my name did I recognize this stranger as my mother and then only by the sound of her voice.

Stunned by her uncanny transformation, I burst into tears.

Beauty is truth's smile when She beholds her own face in a perfect mirror.
—Rabindranath Tagore, "On Beauty," 1955, quoted in George Santayana, *The Sense of Beauty*

It is said that analyzing pleasure, or beauty, destroys it.
—Laura Mulvey, "Visual Pleasure and Narrative Cinema," 1975

INTRODUCTION
Beauty, Myth, Recognition

TELLING BEAUTY

"Teen Deviyaan"

March 12, 1999. Bangalore, India. A sweltering summer afternoon.
 Radhika, *my friend from secondary school, a successful fashion entrepreneur, was anticipating a relaxing afternoon at the Lotus, a luxury salon-spa in central Bangalore. Her gleaming chauffeured car rocked gently on the potholed blacktop roads as we drove to the salon. As we entered, her cell phone burst into a Hindi love song, her signature ringtone.*[1] *Radhika yelled an invitation into it in a combination of staccato English and Hindi considered uber cool by some Bangaloreans.*
 At the entry to the salon, we were greeted by Rina, a young woman from the Northeast of India, who was often misrecognized as "Chinese" in Bangalore, wearing a green jacket, the uniform of the spa. Rina offered us cold bottled water. Radhika noted to me in a sibilant whisper, "Her real name is Lumlang! Her spa name

is Rina. . . . So bad, no?" Before I could respond, Lakshya, a middle-aged beautician with a gentle expression, also from the Northeast, came through the velvet curtain and welcomed Radhika fondly. She was ready, holding a tray with a bowl of mixed hair dye. "Madam's color—Revlon Luminista Brown and Buttercream Ash," she announced.

Lakshya tilted a leather lounger into a reclining position, and Radhika kicked off her sandals, stowed her many cell phones, and flung herself into it with a happy sigh. Lakshya snapped on a pair of gloves and ran her hands through Radhika's hair, appreciating its soft and silky lengths: "Very healthy hair madam has." Radhika knocked on the wood handle of the lounger to dispel the envy of the evil eye, as Lakshya began painting Radhika's long hair with the dye, folding foil carefully around each section of hair.

Soon, the two other women that Radhika had invited on the phone waltzed in, blowing air kisses. Dressed in white, draped with diamonds and pearls, they were clearly the elite of Bangalore. Tara, recently divorced, was a minor celebrity in the city who ran a modeling talent agency, and Aseema, the wife of a Hyderabadi aristocrat, was a successful interior design consultant. They too quickly flopped onto the loungers, greeting the beauticians familiarly, and asked after their families. Lakshya was joined rapidly by two more beauticians, Jimphong, an "eyebrow specialist," and Tanya, a manicurist. Tanya brought in a rolling bin holding a rainbow array of nail polishes. Aseema started rattling through it: "What shade shall I get, girls?" "Get a nice hot pink. Mine is Vagina Blush," Tara said, lying back to get her eyebrows threaded by Jimphong, her excited tone a sharp contrast to her relaxed position. Tanya too offered suggestions: "Madam, do Nude Night or Pussy Galore! Very popular colors."

Tanya stripped Aseema's fingernails of old polish, soaked her hands in a soapy solution that smelled of rose, and began to carefully clip, clean, and file each nail. As she bent double over Aseema's hands, bringing her eyes close to each nail to ensure perfection, she entertained the assembled women with a story, a complex narrative of marriage, blindness, and betrayal. Listening idly, I realized that the story was about the mythic Queen Gandhari,[2] one the heroines of the Hindu epic the Mahabharata. Gandhari was the mother of the evil protagonists, her one hundred sons. A teleserial version of the Mahabharata from the 1980s was being replayed on television in anticipation of an updated version, and Tanya relayed the latest episode. In the story, Gandhari is told that she will be married to the blind but ethically unimpeachable King Dhristharashtra and she binds her eyes to share his darkened view of the world.

Tanya's tale emphasized Gandhari's youth and beauty: her flawless skin, her lustrous hair, her sweet smile. The women in the salon interjected with sighs of envy. Tanya spoke of the rich silks and jewels Gandhari wore and of the velvet bandage she tied around her eyes once she was engaged to the blind king. Radhika, a fashion expert, noted hotly that the costumes were "all wrong." Then Tanya's voice rose as she described how Queen Gandhari foreswore all visual and aesthetic pleasure to become the ideal wife to the king and the matriarch of a clan of a hundred sons.

Radhika, Aseema, and Tara were enthralled despite being familiar with the story. Tanya emphasized that Gandhari never "for the rest of her life" took off her blindfold, relying on the magical television of her aide's reports to transport her to the battlefield, where her beloved sons fought in the fratricidal war. There were many tongue clicks of dismay at Gandhari's wifely and motherly plight. Tanya added playfully, "Ayoo, madam. I could not do for my husband!"

Tara exploded from her lounger, "Why should you? How stupid, na? At least if she could see, then she could help the king and see her sons in the war." Aseema, like many Muslims in India, culturally familiar with the Hindu epics, offered an explanation: "She wanted to be full patni-pativrata style [Hindi = wifely devotion]!" Radhika chimed in with her social commentary: "I can't imagine marrying a young girl to a blind old fart like him! Didn't they have any sense in those days?"

After Radhika's hair had been foiled into a neat ziggurat, Lakshya left the room. Fleeing the intense chemical smells, which were making me nauseous, I followed. I found her in the beauticians' "break room" at the rear of the salon with a young Tamil girl named Selvi, who was employed as a cleaner. They were drinking water and kneading their aching elbows. Through the curtained doorway back into the treatment room, I could hear the rise and fall of Tanya's voice as she told yet another story from the serial.

Sensing that Lakshya and Selvi were discomfited by my presence, I awkwardly turned to leave, when in a corner of the break room I spied a faux oil lamp in an alcove and above it a series of photographs and images: a stupa-like temple tower; the image of a stone yoni, the labia of the goddess, captioned in Hindi and English, "Sri Kamakhya Devi Temple, Guwahati, Neelanchal, Assam"; a calendar image of Lakshmi, seated on a lotus surrounded by gold foil; and a small statue of mother Mary with a crucifix around it. Lakshya caught me looking at the images and said with some sadness that she was from Guwahati, though she had not been back for many years, and Kamakhya was her family deity. Selvi watched quietly.

Radhika's timer went off, and Lakshya, Selvi, and I hastily returned to the main salon. Lakshya shampooed Radhika's hair and blow-dried it into a lustrous curtain. Tara said appreciatively, "Hair looking soo good! Totally shandaar

[Hindi = beautiful]!" Aseema added admiringly, "Full apsara[3] mode... to-tal!" waving her hands to ensure her hot-pink nails dried. When Radhika was done, they all stood in front of the salon's wall of mirrors admiring themselves.

There was a moment's quiet. I absorbed the frozen, silent tableau reflected in the mirrored wall. Radhika, Aseema, and Tara stood front and center. Behind them, holding hair dryers, mirrors, and brushes stood Lakshya, Tanya, and Jimphong. Just beyond the circle stood Selvi, with her mop and bucket. I spied Rina in the waiting room with the bright and noisy street as backdrop, and in the opposite sliver of the mirror, through the parted curtain of the break room beyond, I could just glimpse the lamplit Kamakhya Devi image. Radhika caught my eyes in the mirror and, gesturing to her reflection, jokingly said, "Teen Deviyaan [Hindi = three goddesses]!"[4]

Beauty Matters

This was what I came to understand had happened that day in retrospect. In the moment, I was completely overwhelmed by the experience. As Radhika and I got into the car to leave the Lotus, she asked me why I looked "so sick." I realized that the chaotic sights, smells, and sounds of the parlor had left me feeling unmoored. My field notes, usually so meticulous, were a jumbled array of words and phrases, of impressions and emotions. The cacophony of conversation, some about nail polish colors, others about the stories of goddesses and queens, was a confused babble. The images of women in their foiled hair pyramids and manicure baths, gossiping loudly about the sexual lives of people whom I did not know and probably would never meet, was for me like entering a bawdy play in the third act, not knowing what had happened before. The endless ringing of cell phones with their many signature Bollywood tunes, and the buzz of the timers, added to my jangled nerves.

I also felt physically ill, revolted by the unfamiliar smells of the parlor—the stench of burned hair, body sweat, and expensive perfume mixed with the chemical smells of hair color and nail polish, rose soap, strawberry wax, and incense. The impact of these mingled smells was so violent that I could not even describe it as an odor; rather, I experienced it as a physical punch to the gut. Hence, my dive into the break room to recover, where the beauty workers were clearly startled by my sudden entrance. Everything was happening so quickly around me, with different workers engaging in different unfamiliar procedures. I was terrified, in my uptight and prudish Brahmanical way, that in the midst of this chaos, one of Radhika's friends would suddenly strip down for some sort of intimate wax, and that would be the last straw.

I described this vertiginous feeling to Radhika. "How do you stand it?" I asked her, miming nausea. She found my description of the strangeness of the salon hysterical and fell onto the leather seat of her car, giggling helplessly. "My God! Sooo funny you are! What world have you come from?" she said. "Haven't you been to a parlor before?" I confessed I had not, other than a few brief visits many decades prior. My mother had also not been a parlor habitué, and I had little experience with it growing up. In the United States, I could not afford salons for beauty treatments, only venturing in occasionally for haircuts. Radhika was aghast. "WHAT KIND OF GIRL ARE YOU?!" she yelled at me.

I sat back in the plush vehicle and peered through the tinted windows at the hazy city beyond. Was *this* what beauty was? Was I less of a woman for knowing so little about it? As the car rolled on, questions swirled in my brain. Two stood out as anthropologically valuable: What in God's name was going on in that parlor? And how was I going to find out?

Self-Reflections

Before we left the Lotus, Radhika said briskly, "Okay, ready? Shall we go?" As the women checked themselves in the mirror one more time, I saw myself reflected behind them, watchful, overwhelmed, and nauseous, yet ready with my notebook and pen.

On the surface, I was not the best person to write this book. In fact, beauty was the furthest thing from my mind when I started the "fieldwork," as anthropologists call this intimate participant observation study, in 1998. I had returned to Bangalore to study ritual creativity in modern Hindu temples (T. Srinivas 2018). My work at the temples was fascinating, but at times, the male-dominated and rule-bound world of the temple unnerved me, and I went looking for my female school friends with whom to blow off steam and reclaim some parts of myself. Many, like Radhika, had become the elite of Bangalore. They were entrepreneurs and civic leaders, often required by their social networks to be at various "chatterati" parties covered by the celebrity pages. When I went to their homes unannounced, I would invariably be met by a maid who directed me to the beauty parlor, or a fashionable restaurant, spa, or boutique, and I would follow. That is how I found myself at the Lotus and in hundreds of other parlors, salons, and spas in Bangalore, watching my friends, other women, and later, queer and gender-nonconforming people as they threaded, colored, waxed, depilated, bleached, injected, packed, and painted their faces and bodies.

Beauty has always been a thorny subject for me. I was constantly chided, never by my parents but by well-meaning friends and relatives, for going out in the sun and getting "dark," for having messy curly hair, for biting my nails. As all my friends seemed to know, being well "turned out"—with waxed arms and legs, fair and glowing skin, smooth, shiny hair with the "right" highlights, and perfectly arched eyebrows—was indicative of being elite and powerful in Bangalore. It was the sign of being cared for and of being worthy of care.

But like Ursula Le Guin, I was troubled by beauty when I encountered it in the flesh. In her essay titled "Dogs, Cats, and Dancers: Thoughts About Beauty," Le Guin (1992, 165) sees beauty as a game with rules "controlled by people who grab fortunes from it and don't care who they hurt," making people "starve and deform and poison themselves" in slavery to artifice. I shared her beautifully voiced concerns about selfhood and its complex relationship to the bodies we occupy, if ever so briefly, when we look in the mirror:

> I know what worries me most when I look in the mirror and see the old woman with no waist. It's not that I've lost my beauty—I never had enough to carry on about. *It's that that woman doesn't look like me.* She isn't who I thought I was. . . . Who I am is certainly part of how I look and vice versa. I want to know where I begin and end, what size I am, and what suits me. . . . I am not "in" this body, I *am* this body. . . . But all the same, there's something about me that doesn't change, hasn't changed, through all the remarkable, exciting, alarming, and disappointing transformations my body has gone through. There is a person there who isn't only what she looks like, and to find her and know her *I have to look through, look in, look deep. Not only in space, but in time.*
> (Le Guin 1992, 165; emphases added)

Looking deep across decades, I realize that even early on, my discomfort with beauty practices felt like a failing in my Bangalorean milieu, but after decades of feeling and being told, in some cases explicitly, that I was unbeautiful and of feeling a desire to be perceived of as "groomed" yet being acutely ashamed of that desire, I had made peace with my oppositional relationship to beauty practices. My positionality as an upper-caste, heterosexual, cis-gender[5] (by which I mean someone who identifies with her assigned gender at birth) Bangalorean woman granted me privilege, but I was uncomfortable with it and uninterested in compounding it through visible aesthetic markers that signaled beauty. This was reinforced by my everyday life as a graduate student and then a faculty member in American academia. With little money and no privilege except higher education, there was no assumption that I would maintain a meticulously groomed appearance, even if I had had the resources to do so. In fact, the liberal academic ethos valorized natural aging and makeup-free looks. Too much concern with appearance was viewed as shallow, if not openly narcissistic.

Nonetheless, though I knew which camp I felt more comfortable in, these two approaches to beauty clashed. What in the academic world was viewed as evidence of living a life of the mind was perceived by my well-groomed friends back home in Bangalore as a lack of self-respect. They tended to remark on every photograph I uploaded on social media, commenting unfavorably on my graying hair: "Can't you color it?"; my clothing choices: "Are you blind?"; and my lack of makeup: "Why can't you wear some nice lipstick? You are letting yourself go, fully!" They seemed to view my carefree aesthetic as a form of insanity, an unbelievable carelessness.

But to their dismay, I had no interest in doing anything about it. Parlors and salons were alien worlds to me—unheimlich, uncanny, and strange. I was shocked by the painful and brutal processes, the easy objectification of bodies and selves, and revolted by the oversharing of intimate bodily details. Everything was oddly disorienting, from the technologies used, to the strange smells and leakages of the bodies in the parlor and the skill of the workers at ignoring these leakages, to the storytelling that harkened back to a mythical time but seemed to be interpreted in new and strategic ways.

Now, this may strike many as an inopportune moment to talk about beauty. The political landscape is poisonous, and we are a riven people. But I can think of no better time to talk of beauty, to hold it as a human desire and ideal, and to think about why women feel that they can never be beautiful enough and simultaneously that they are to resist and reconstruct the moral. As we war against each other, turn back the clock on women's rights, and move toward autocracy, perhaps a conversation on beauty is what is needed to remind us that what makes us human is the striving toward the beautiful and the divine.

When my disorientation turned to curiosity about the world of the Lotus, the most obvious resources I had for making sense of it were political and academic. But was I, as Laura Mulvey suggests in the epigraph to this chapter, seeking to destroy the pleasure of beauty by analysis, because I did not wish to master its intricacies? As a feminist, I had long ascribed to the idea that beauty was a form of oppression. When Radhika preened in the mirror and insisted, "Must be pretty, no? What's the use of being a girl if you are not beautiful?" my gut instinct was to think of her as a victim of the patriarchy, though a less "victimized" victim would be hard to find. When Western feminism is asked what beauty is for, it replies that women pursue beauty for men's approval and the resources that go along with it. Women,[6] feminists argue, are not only constantly trying to live up to ideals of beauty and subject themselves to painful procedures to do so but also the beauty workforce is exploited, invariably made up of women on the margins who worked at these salons for low pay (Banet-Weiser 1999; Bartky 1990; Hesse-Biber 1996). Thus, feminists, particularly in anthropology, have typically offered critical readings of beauty and beauty salons around the world (Black 2004; Furman 1997; Liebelt 2023; Ossman 2002). This colored my reaction when the project began. In fact, one Indian sociologist of my acquaintance, whose smooth arms, perfectly tweezed eyebrows, and sleek hair marked her as parlor habitué, noted pithily that my study of beauty would be "useless" as parlor work was "so frivolous."

My experience, however, was that Bangalorean women did not beautify themselves solely to be the "objects of the male gaze" (Mulvey 1975). To dismiss them as "frivolous" was not simply misogynistic; it derived from a Christo-colonial understanding of what *should* be studied based on a moral hierarchy of knowledge in which women's embodied knowledge ranked as negligible. As Susan Sontag (1975, 119–22) put it starkly in her essay in *Vogue* magazine, "A Woman's Beauty: Put Down or Power Source," "by limiting excellence (virtues in Latin) to moral virtue only, Christianity set beauty adrift—as an alienated, arbitrary, superficial enchantment." It would seem that beauty has always been suspect in Christian thinking and continues to lose prestige in academic circles due to an unlikely alignment between Christian ethics, colonialism, and feminist critiques.

When I turned to philosophy, the resources provided to understand beauty were helpful and yet not. One strand of thought, coming from the Greeks through Kant, views beauty as morally valuable and purposeful, allied to aesthetic judgment, truth, and taste (Kant 1987). The poet and Nobel laureate Rabindranath Tagore, following this traditional line of thinking, suggests that beauty is "truth's smile," when "she" is reflected in a "perfect" mirror, significantly conflating beauty with gendered female virtues. More recently, classicist Elaine Scarry (1999) has argued in her manifesto on beauty that experiencing beauty impacts us in ways that can assist us in achieving justice, or rather, that beauty's impact instructs and inspires us in ways that enable us to respond to injustice. Scarry's descriptions of beauty, drawn from the *Odyssey*, speak to the overwhelming nature of seeing something or someone truly beautiful; where beauty comes upon one "like a wave" causing a "radical decentering" of self. It "quickens," "adrenalizes," and makes life "worth living" (Scarry 1999, 24–25).

Beauty's force makes one pause and catch one's breath in a moment of suspended delight and wonderment, all located in its perception which, according to Scarry, pivots us to a Deweyan ethical action. This is the idea that ordinary life and aesthetics sit on a continuum, forcing us to imitate and replicate such beauty and perfection through laws and institutions (Scarry 1999). One might be tempted to argue that beauty's subjectivity makes it a difficult starting point for justice. However, what such philosophy makes grudgingly clear is that beauty is *real*, with real and powerful consequences. Beauty *is* power, and its privileges are immense. Thus, we have to contend with John Costonis's (1989, 15) accurate prediction: "We are condemned to come to terms with aesthetics, whether we like it or not."

But what of beauty's pursuit? None of these philosophical thinkers, valuable as they are, illuminate what happened that day at the Lotus, in the quotidian moment of beauty's making. Therefore, it seemed what was needed was not yet another philosophy of beauty, not an application of Western philosophy to Indian mores, but rather *an anthropology of beauty* that dignified not only what the women did in the parlor but what they said they were doing and why. Thus, in the following pages, I follow in the footsteps of Alfred Gell (1998, 17), who first thought of an anthropology of aesthetics and wanted to "wrest" the anthropological study of beauty away from the "soggy embrace" of philosophical aesthetics. And doing so requires us to explore the relationship between difference, as the structural fracturing of the modern subject, and differences, as a multiplicity of the sociopolitical as classed and casted identities, to contend with varying registers from the aesthetic to the overtly political where beauty's power resides.

Unfortunately, however, the anthropological sources did not precisely fit this project either. Traditionally, anthropology has divided thinking about beauty into two categories. The first is the magical in which beauty is a gift of enchantment achieved by powerful decoration, capable of elevating the ordinary into the divine (Strathern and Strathern 1971; Taussig 2012, 44). This emphasizes beauty's multisensoriality and cultural embeddedness. The second is the mundane, where beauty is understood as a set of practices that acts on the embodied subject and, as such, enables an analysis of gendered subjects' desires and body images as projects of self-making, embedded in transnational and locally mediated "beautyscapes" (Holliday et al. 2015 in Liebelt 2023), expanding in recent years to include the medicalization of beauty standards (Jarrin 2017; Plemons 2017). I found, however, that what are considered two distinct and separate anthropological understandings of beauty are interwoven in Bangalore: the magical and mundane come together in the parlors. This slippage between gift and practice meant that beauty was doubled in everyday life: first, as a natural attribute, a divine gift that was magical in its power (Taussig 2012) and then as a culturally determined goal to aspire to, since certain practices allow one to appear "naturally" beautiful (Liebelt 2023).

As the years passed, I explored these understandings of beauty and found myself at more and more parlors (outgrowing the attendant nausea) as I waited patiently for someone more appropriate than me to write the book on Indian beauty that I needed to understand the dynamics of the Bangalorean parlor. But I waited in vain. It seemed that my sociologist friend was right. No one was interested in studying "being, becoming, practising and doing femininity," particularly in the Indian parlor (Skeggs 1997, 98). In the meantime, what had once been a baffling site of frustration became thoroughly intriguing to me as I began to make friends in the parlors among the clientele and the beauticians, and make sense of what was happening within it.

Then, one snowy winter's day in Boston, while watching a movie where the heroine went past a salon, hesitated, and then entered, I realized that it was up to me to write an ethnography of beauty parlors in India. What had originally seemed to me like a negative—my total lack of familiarity with parlors and beauty practice, my visceral revulsion—was actually an asset. Approaching beauty ignorantly forced me to look at it differently, as it were. I needed to enter the parlor and decipher the practices precisely *because* I was a stranger to them; after all, moving from unfamiliar to familiar and stranger to friend is at the very core of the ethnographic enterprise (Powdermaker 1967). But another concern raised its ugly head. I was not thought of as a gender scholar, and I had never been thought to be politically "cutting edge." Gender scholars were the radical, the politically active, the "cool kids" of anthropology. I did not fit here either. What were my bona fides? Why was I, an ethnographer of religion, studying gender? These fears would paralyze me from time to time.

But in fact, as I continued to pursue beauty through the parlors of Bangalore, ethnography turned out to be a lifeline. Ethnography enabled me to document a moment in time where the Indian beauty industry was metastasizing. My connections in Bangalore, the many people I knew, allowed for detailed observation of women undergoing beauty treatments from "vampire facials" to laser waxing and showed not only how beauty functioned as an intervention in the problem of the aging or unbeautiful body but as an intimate experience between beauty worker and client. The women clients whom I followed initially, who populate these pages, were the elite of the city. They were the people who were idealized and who everyone else, including the beauticians like Lakshya, Jhuma, Tanya, and Lumlang, aspired to imitate. Similarly, participant observation allowed me to notice the subtleties of beauty practice. It made me sensitive to the value of pedagogy, as women around me learned how to embody the beautiful as the broader society saw it. Recent Indian economic growth has brought with it new and highly globalized ideas about the "ideal" female body.

The dramatic increase in the visibility of women with slimmer bodies and higher cheekbones, false eyelashes and Western-style makeup in public spaces (including billboards) and popular media (such as Bollywood and lifestyle magazines) indicates that the physical appearance of the Indian female body is increasingly imagined to be an indicator, and facilitator, of socioeconomic success.

Interlocutors who became friends, like Lakshya, Tanya, Mary, and Lumlang (whom I met later), made me consider the hidden lives of the workers that I met. Parlor workers were typically migrants from provincial and lower middle-class backgrounds who catered to wealthier upper-caste clients. The distance in terms of education, income, and social standing between beauty worker and client was generally insurmountable. The bodies of client and worker were layered with various meanings in terms of class and socioeconomic positions, but meeting frequently and working on the body in collaboration led to intimate and personal relationships between beauty workers and clients that occasionally transcended caste and class.

Watching women in the parlor over time enabled me to adopt a "critical realist" position where the body is seen as both real, as a physical and biological entity, and at the same time socially constructed in terms of narrative and bodily practice (Collier 1994). It also allowed me to distinguish beliefs about social reality from *actual* social reality.

Finally, a deep longitudinal ethnography over a decade and a half in a city that I knew intimately but that was constantly evolving allowed me to complicate and contextualize beauty's symbolic, transactional, and affective dimensions, teasing out how its dynamics serve as a medium through which new, unexpected, and strategic configurations of power and meaning could emerge. Anyone who has gone through the haptics of fieldwork knows the thrill of discovery, the sense of "this is what the question is." Such a long-term ethnography reminded me that it is not always clear when fieldwork begins and ends, what the questions might be, and where one might land. An anthropology open to unexpected encounters, juxtapositions, and serendipitous research questions was to be cherished.

Although many of the women in the Bangalorean parlor were Hindu, as my afternoon at the Lotus so clearly showed, the parlors were multiethnic, multilinguistic, multireligious, and variously classed and casted spaces, where a diversity of voices, inhabitations, and ontologies were at play. My previous work on Bangalore had demonstrated that this urban pluralism was further complicated by Bangalore's position as the software capital of Asia, where a large international population and many foreign expats and NRIs (non-resident Indians) with global ties to the United Kingdom, Europe, the United States, the Middle

East, and Singapore also live (T. Srinivas 2018). The women in the parlor were comfortable with the complexities of navigating this cultural tapestry, though they operated with certain strict notions of how one should comport oneself in such complex cultural spaces.

However, most of the stories told in the parlor were Hindu myths with which many Indians, regardless of their religion, were familiar. I realized as beauty clients and workers spoke of the ideal women in Hindu cosmology—the goddesses, apsaras, and other heroines—with a fondness and familiarity where my expertise in Hinduism, which I never anticipated being an asset in a space like the parlor, proved invaluable. I remembered that as a child I had been fascinated by Hindu myths and had pestered my parents, relatives, and neighborhood maids to tell me the stories endlessly. My parents bought me the popular graphic novel series *Amar Chithra Katha* (Hindi = Immortal Pictorial Stories), and I read them until I knew them by rote. Branching out, I went to the library and took out books on Greek myth. Keeping track of the various characters and their intersecting stories was like following a cosmological soap opera. I found the dramatic tales of gods and humans fascinating and deeply moving.

However, as my interest in anthropology grew, my interest in myth diminished. In the contemporary anthropology of my time, the study of myth seemed old fashioned and outdated, a vestige of an earlier, troubled era for the discipline. But when I stumbled across goddesses, apsaras, and other heroines in the secular space of the parlor, I felt a jolt of joy and recognition sweep over me. This was where the myths were hiding—in plain sight! I started noticing how often Indians, Hindus primarily but others as well, spoke about myths as a reality in their lives. In the parlor and beyond, they used mythical tropes and ideals to imagine the future, rehistoricize the past, and fabricate selves. It was, I realized, time to reinvigorate the study of Hindu myth, not as a stand-alone intellectual project but one woven into the ethnographic study of beauty and women's selfhood.

The Beautiful City

The story of beauty and the parlors in Bangalore starts with the growth of the beauty industry in the city, which really got underway in the 1980s, when Bangalore developed a reputation as a beauty capital in the niche circles, where beauty was a profession and preoccupation. Prasad Bidapa Associates,[7] a modeling agency that trained beauty pageant winners and movie industry hopefuls, gained renown throughout India when several of its protégés won international pageants and global modeling contracts. Other imitators followed.

By the late 1990s, Bangalore had become the premier destination for beautiful and ambitious young people from all across the country. The city, previously sleepily tolerant if slightly conservative, was suddenly host to crowded fashion shows and parties run by the modeling agencies, where models danced in the briefest of clothing. Billboards (known in India as hoardings) all over the city displayed larger-than-life images of men and women selling everything from cars to condoms to soap.

The modeling agencies, in turn, were catering to the advertising needs of a burgeoning beauty and "personal care" industry in India that was globalizing. The French cosmetics giant L'Oréal was the first to enter India in 1994, followed quickly by German cosmetics giant Benckiser and then Revlon in 1995.[8] By 2021, the beauty industry in India was the fourth largest in the world at 1.1 trillion Indian rupees (approximately US$16 billion) and expected to grow to 2 trillion rupees (approximately US$24 billion) by 2025,[9] making it ripe for franchise opportunities.[10]

This spectacular trajectory has been fueled in no small part by the growth of cities like Bangalore[11] as information technology and biotech hubs, where talented young software and bioengineers, many of them women, have flocked in the thousands to get lucrative jobs and live the good life (Heitzman 1999; T. Srinivas 2018; Upadhya and Vasavi 2013). Besides providing new avenues for making money, opportunities for social mobility and aspiring middle classness have also been important factors in these professions' popularity in recent years, and bodies that were beautiful and well groomed were textually (through Bollywood movies, advertising, and social media) linked to notions of socioeconomic success, cosmopolitanism, and even professionalism. Thus, image consciousness, primarily to land jobs and secure deals, led to a democratization of beauty practices. Rising incomes and shortage of time meant that what was previously done domestically, such as hair and skin care, was now outsourced to the local parlor. Business boomed, leading to ever more parlors opening and more beauty workers migrating to the city.

The profession of beauty worker in Bangalore needs to be understood within the context of related professions, such as coffee baristas, gym trainers, and those employed as salesgirls in shopping malls in urban India (Baas 2020). Such professions are generally thought to be open to provincial, aspiring middle-class workers, but they require highly specific, on-the-job training to cater to urban customers and require education through enrollment in diploma courses at commercially run training institutes in the city. As more beauty parlors opened, beauty institutes struggled to keep pace. The need for qualified workers grew every day as more parlors opened up.

FIG. I.I. A small parlor called Choppin in north Bangalore

In 2004, a research firm based in the city of Pune, Value Notes Database, studied beauty parlors in towns with over a million inhabitants and concluded that by rough estimates, India had sixty-one thousand beauty parlors in these towns alone. Since then, the beauty industry[12] in India has been expanding at 13 percent year on year, far surpassing the overall economic growth rate. The beauty business is so profitable that it has even caught the attention of global and national private equity firms.[13] Thus, in every village, provincial town, and neighborhood of India, salons and spas, known collectively as "parlors," abound, catering to different classes of clientele. As one client proudly noted, "in every nagar (township), every locality, every layout, every chawl, every village in India, there'll be a beauty parlor for us ladies."

Indeed, as Menaka, one of my interlocutors, confirmed, by the late 1990s, less than ten years after the tech boom hit Bangalore, there were "literally *hundreds* of new parlors." Walking through Bangalore in the early 2000s, I often saw painted banner advertisements for salons and spas hung crookedly all over the city, on walls and fences, and from trees the names of the parlors advertised redolent of an overt femininity: "Lotus," "Senorita," "Petals," "Blow," and "Rain." Newspapers were littered with color advertisements and discount coupons for hair and skin care "packages" at local parlors, alongside matrimonial

FIG. 1.2. A storefront converted into a neighborhood parlor called Posh Salon and Spa

advertisements for "fair-skinned" brides. Parlors were listed and reviewed on Yelp and Google and other customer service sites.

Menaka was an avid parlor goer, and she classified the parlors in Bangalore into six different types based on price point and image: "garage parlors" (small and affordable, catering to maids and recent migrants, they were usually in the garage of someone's house), "auntie parlors" (individually owned and housed in a few rented rooms or a small apartment or bungalow, these were local parlors where the beauticians knew the clientele and treated them like kin), "corner-wali types" (neighborhood parlors individually owned and run by women that were slightly more expensive and had better treatments and trained beauticians), "franchise parlors" (located in stand-alone bungalows or shops, these were more expensive, catered to a middle-class clientele, and were part of a national or global franchise, with trained beauticians and an efficient anonymity), and finally, "spa types" (located in sylvan settings, offering "exotic" treatments, some of them medical and therapeutic as well as aesthetic, these were the total-immersion experience where the staff were highly trained and pampered their elite clientele). With Menaka, Radhika, and others, I visited all of the above, traipsing through a quarter of Bangalore's two hundred listed and reviewed parlors in the decade and a half of my research, settling down in some

FIG. I.3. A three-story franchise parlor with towering images of Western women on its glassed frontage

for many years of interrupted participant observation. I learned something new about beauty every single time.

BEAUTY TALES

Myth and Meaning

The way a particular ideal body is produced and reproduced in the Indian parlor cannot be attributed to increased spending power, consumerism, image concerns, or the ubiquity of parlors alone. Even that first time in the Lotus, one of the things that struck me most palpably was the way Tanya told the story of Gandhari, focusing on her elevated status, her beauty, the aesthetics of her life, and finally, her sacrifice in binding her eyes. In fact, it was *I* who had been blind to how women in the parlors, both workers and clients, continually wove the stories of goddesses into their own everyday lives, responding almost viscerally to the myths. These interpolated stories and their aesthetics, set against the consumer publics of global India, offered an interplay of factors that layered the way in which the Indian female body was interpreted and understood.

FIG. 1.4. A shrine at the reception desk in the lobby of a parlor with a small Indian flag

I suppose that this should not have been that surprising. It was a way to explain the extant world ("as is") and the subjunctive world ("as if") with the goal of negotiating the current world and bringing an aspirational world about via the imagination. Indeed, as David Shulman notes in his exhaustive history of the imagination in South India, unlike in the West, the imagination *is* reality to Hindu Indians; seeing in the mind's eye is as powerful as perception itself or perhaps even more so, for imagination is causative and is able to create new, future-facing worlds (Shulman 2012).

Nonetheless, I *was* surprised to find myth so imbricated in the conversation of the parlor. Undoubtedly, one of the reasons was the particular moment in which I began fieldwork, when the epic 1980s teleserial the *Mahabharata* was being replayed on television. It seemed like almost everyone watched it, and it was a good topic of discussion for the parlor as it created common ground and seemed to circumvent more politically charged topics, though I found that political themes, national and gendered, wound their way in anyhow. As my fieldwork continued into the second decade of the new millennium, more Bollywood blockbusters that replayed history and myth in creative, sometimes (to me) disturbing ways that seemed to aid a conservative agenda, were released. They focused invariably on beautiful renegade queens, disgraced goddesses, or outlawed female revolutionaries and their ethical quandaries, and they flooded the marketplace and the popular imagination not only with supposedly historical dress, hairstyles, and adornment (which were rapidly adopted in Bangalorean parlors) but also with the ubiquity of female beauty and expanded notions of the power of a beautiful woman in the world as a moral force. Guided by these media phenomena, it was not unusual that Bangalorean women reflecting on themselves in the mirror wanted to create beauty that was inspired by myth, and to fabricate moral selves that aligned with mythical values. Indeed, as Leela Prasad has observed, such stories "illustrate the multifarious ways in which the 'moral life' is experienced, imagined, and constituted" (Prasad 2006, 183).

This tendency was bolstered by the ubiquity of myth in the everyday life of Bangalorean Hindus, especially as represented in the classical epics. As A. K. Ramanujan notes, stories drawn from Hindu epics are universes of meaning in themselves. For the reader or listener, the epic is never a new experience (hence Ramanujan's aphorism, "No Hindu ever reads the *Mahābhārata* for the first time") but an old one brought to life again, like a memory (N. Hawley 2022, 26). Through rehearings and retellings of stories from the epics, listeners experience a fully developed alternate world that is internally consistent and, crucially, that is being offered as an alternative to reality, one in which suffering exists, yet virtue overcomes all suffering (what J. R. R. Tolkien [2008] elegantly calls a "eucatastrophe," a catastrophe that ends in happiness). Thus, Bangalorean women told mythical stories not only to negotiate the moral requirements of everyday life but also to think about the divine female in relation to their own lives and the lives they wanted to lead. I came to realize that the women of the parlor existed in a spectral landscape, where concrete, mundane everyday life was spiked through with imagined spaces and fantastic emotions, allowing them to not only dream of better futures but to hope and at times even to act and transgress in the everyday. In the site of the Bangalorean parlors, myth and beauty were adjacencies, acting in concert and on each other toward the building of new subjunctive ethical worlds.

So, in the parlor, the mundane world of beauty practice and the fantastic world of the myths constantly interrupted and built on each other, interdigitizing toward what I will call "edge work," work that ruptures boundaries and strategically explores limits. This edge work of storytelling and beauty practice sat on the boundary between the political and the social and often contradicted or adumbrated the dominant caste, masculine, heroic, nationalist narrative, instead offering a "countersystem," an "alternative way of looking at things" (Ramanujan 1991, 53).

Because of the centrality of myth in the parlor, I found myself pushing back against the current attitude in anthropology that the mythical moment is passé and that myths are best analyzed as evidence of some other cultural phenomenon. Myths have been defined by the famed anthropologist Bronislaw Malinowski as a "primitive charter of moral wisdom" (Malinowski in Dundes 1984, 199), a set of rules or codes of conduct that enable the social functions of the culture to flourish. Malinowski (1926, 28) writes, "The myth comes into play when rite, ceremony, or a social or moral rule demands justification, warrant of antiquity, reality, and sanctity." For him, myths authorize and act as an imprimatur for the normative, a societal covenant as it were.

Emily Hudson (2012), in her work on the epic literature of the subcontinent, specifically the Mahabharata, would seem to agree. She argues that there is a defined relationship between ethics, aesthetics, and religion in classical Indian literature and literary theory that offers an ethical covenant. The Mahabharata, the epic myth of fratricidal war, where the Bhagavad Gita forms a central part, is considered to be a major transmitter of *dharma* (moral, social, and religious ethics that is also seen as one's duty), perhaps the single most important concept in the history of Indian religions. The fratricidal story itself, as Hudson (2012) argues, "disorients" the readers, or listeners, through a focus on the continuous problematic relationships between ethical self-formation and subjective suffering in varied contexts, and constantly reconstructs dharma (duty) and *satya* (truth), through the positing of ethical conundrums that get resolved in various ways based on each character's inclinations, contextual choices, and abilities. What Hudson sees as "disorientation," the women in the parlor saw as creative license to tell and interpret the story in the contemporary moment, thereby offering polysemic ethical possibilities to the audience and rendering the story and its characters unexpectedly alive and relatable.

For Claude Lévi-Strauss, the other great student of myth, however, content, context, ethics, and truth were distant concerns. Rather, Lévi-Strauss argued that comparing myths and the motifs within them across cultures allowed anthropologists to see their structural similarities, whereby one could conclude that myth was both timeless and timely, allowing for something very new to become something very ancient through a fabricated story, creating a distinctive cultural form (Geertz 1980, 9). The grammar of myth, its structure and patterns, Lévi-Strauss (1955, 428–30) argued, was laid out in mythemes, binary pairs of opposites that structured the story, thereby bringing order to chaos. Through his obsessive study of myths from all over the world, Lévi-Strauss believed that he had discovered some "universal human truths." Of course, this universality was shot through with the assumptions of the Christo-colonial project. Nonetheless, Lévi-Strauss's theories of myth have haunted anthropology for decades, contributing in no small measure to the study of myth being hidden or ignored (Badcock 1975; Carroll 1978; Dundes 1997; Godelier 2018).

But neither of these approaches seemed to adequately describe the usefulness of myth in the parlor. Alan Dundes, a folklorist, comes closest to the Bangalorean women's perspective in his study of myth. He argues that myths are simply popular "sacred narratives" where the human world and the divine are united. Myths for Dundes (1984) are not regulatory but explanatory, detailing how humans came to be the way they are. In that sense, for Bangalorean women, myths are the ultimate elaboration of truth, an ideal that speaks to reality. In these women's tellings, myths are not Malinowskian charters, justifying the world as it is but rather anti-charters,[14] *living revocations* that afford women the possibility to recall the characters in the myths to rework and negotiate the expected outcomes detailed in them toward radically different horizons. Telling these stories, I argue, allows women to speak strategically, to interact with the myths and reinvoke their ideals but also to subversively refuse, use, and negotiate ideas, aspirational values, and idealized characters to (re)construct selves both as raconteurs but also *as women*. So Benjamin's remarks about storytelling—"the storyteller joins the ranks of the teachers and sages" (1968, 14)—holds true, but in unanticipated and often quietly revolutionary ways.

In the following pages, Bangalorean women recast myth as a strategic tool for physical and ethical self-fabrication, sometimes knowingly and sometimes unknowingly. Myth here offers a polysemic possibility of an ethics with which one crafts a life. Indeed, I argue that these new tellings of well-worn stories offer challenges to our understandings of narrative theory and theories of culture in general (Scott 2016).

For as A. K. Ramanujan presciently tells us, women's tales—narratives spoken by women about women—offer alternative forms of storytelling that "present different selections, viewpoints and solutions," "different finite provinces of reality," forming a "counter system" to the everyday reality that the women face. Women's tales are reflexive, a dialogic response to the masculine-oriented heroic theologies and philosophies of Hinduism. As the following pages show, they steadily parody, invert, share, and overtake, face and deface characters, themes, and motifs; and they transgress and propel stories in new directions, often in opposite ones than those that were intended. And, as I found, storytelling is an art at which the women in the parlor excelled.

Beauty Work

It is no accident that the stories women told in the parlors were stories of beauty starring ravishing and seductive apsaras, goddesses, and heroines. Beauty is, in fact, a central ethical category in Hinduism through its association with *rasa* theory, a traditional Indian philosophy of aesthetics. The term "rasa" has a variety of meanings (among them "flavor," "taste," "juice," and "essence"), but in aesthetics it is understood to refer to an emotional experience produced by art (Schwartz 2004). The idea of rasa was codified in the ancient text known as the *Natyashastra* (200–500 CE), a compendium of knowledge on dramatic performance (including music and dancing) (Pollock 2016). This text argues that eight distinct rasas—the beautiful (*shrungara*), the comic (*hasya*), the pathetic (*karuṇa*), the furious (*raudra*), the heroic (*veerya*), the terrible (*bhayanaka*), the odious (*bhibasta*), and the marvelous (*adbhuta*)—can be aroused in audience members through skillful performances. Later commentators acknowledged a ninth rasa, the tranquil (*shanta*). Together, these comprise the *navarasa* or nine aesthetic experiences, but it is accepted that beauty is the foundational rasa. Ethnohistorical accounts of beauty (shrungara) note its centrality as "the substance of aesthetic experience" in the codex of rasa aesthetics (Coomaraswamy in Shukla 2015, 6).

Shrungara can be brought about by alankara, which are modes of decoration of the body, often mimicking the divine body of the gods (Comeau 2020a and b). While shrungara and alankara are both process-based experiences that produce beauty, saundarya is the effect, the resultant beauty. Saundarya is an attribute of the goddess, understood as linked to the feminine mythic essence, embodying the inscrutable and powerful female force, the shakti.

Simply put, beauty is telling—ethically and morally. In Hindu cosmology, the presence of beauty is one of the key signs of domesticated and valuable female divinity, moral worth, purity, and virtue. Goddesses, apsaras, and virtuous heroines all are beautiful. When beauty is absent, it signals the demonic, the dangerous, and the chaotic. Unruly goddesses, demons, and evildoers of all kinds are ugly. The quality of *saundarya* (beauty) and the practices of *shrungara* (appreciation of beauty) and *alankara* (beautification) are allied in the Hindu imagination as evidence of auspiciousness, a domesticated state, and goodness. But being that goddesses in Hinduism can also be a hot and seductive beauty, a dangerous allure, an untamable, erotic overflow, and finally, a transcendence. The idea of beauty thus encapsulates the ambiguity and ambivalence of the goddess within it affording a plurality of ontologies for everyday women (Flueckiger 2006; Kinsley 1988).

FIG. 1.5. Another shrine at another parlor with a crucifix, an image of the infant Jesus, and Devi alongside some Chinese Tibetan symbols of luck

In fact, as the cleaner at the Lotus, Selvi, explained to me several years after I had met her, beauty was ungraspable (Tamil = *itavika mudiyade*), evanescent, and elusive, yet when it could be provoked, caught, and curated in a body, it was an all-powerful force, capable of transforming worlds and selves, just like the divine feminine. Moreover, the diversity of women in the parlor, all from different classes and castes, religions and regions, languages and ethnicities, and gender and sexual orientations, all concerned about beauty, suggested that beauty work (Kannada = *kelsa*) mirrored the multiple forms of the feminine divine herself (Biernacki 2007; Kinsley 1988).

Invoking rasa theory also ties into a significant difference in ideas of ethics and selfhood between Hinduism and the West. McKim Marriott has suggested, drawing from Louis Dumont, that Hindu personhood is "dividual"; unlike Western individuals who are encapsulated, autonomous beings, Hindus are caught in a miasma of humor-based relations. Their bodies and souls, the argument goes, are porous. I do not think this quite captures what is going on, however. My work suggests that the women I interacted with in the parlors of Bangalore had neither a "dividual" self that was entirely porous and divisible, nor an individual self that was entirely bounded and discrete (Marriott 1990).

Nor were they somewhere in the middle, on a journey of inevitable progress toward individual selves (Englund and Leach 2000, 229). Challenging these notions, I draw on theories of ethical personhood (Lambek and Strathern 1998) to argue that women's subjectivities are "multiauthored entities" (Finlay 2018) that are constructed as composite in the parlor as women work on their bodies in intimate encounters with other women. My interlocutors are partible persons who have a composite self, made up of fragments that they stitch together. Women's selfhoods are porous and need to be protected from pollution and dirt, but they are also oddly impervious to external influences. They draw from multiple sources to stitch themselves together, always raveling and unraveling, fabricating their selfhood as they go, disallowing some ideas about beauty and enunciating others. Indeed, rather than seeing women as known entities (even to themselves), I argue that they are only seen and recognized in intimate relations with others, crafting selves as they go along, creating a shared idea of who they are. So instead of asking whether we are known, it may be more fruitful to ask whether we have arrived in collaboration with other people with whom we have relationships, intimate and not, at a conception of ourselves that we recognize. Thus, Bangalorean women are acting as much as being acted on in constructing their selfhood, using various influences and experiences to craft a composite self that is contingent and flexible yet fleshly.

As such, the parlor offers us another illustration of what I termed in the first book of this Bangalorean trilogy a "creative ethics," where the ethical (as the morally valuable) and the strategic (which includes the morally questionable) are braided together (T. Srinivas 2018). The ethos of Bangalore is best encapsulated, I had argued, by a Kannada exhortation, "solpa adjust maadi" (Kannada=please adjust). This "adjustment" is a creative circumvention of an obstacle: a hack that by its existence enables a future, and it can be applied to any challenge, small or large. Creative ethics is an "anthropological imagining of doing rather than philosophical thinking," which offers a way for locals "to get beyond the tedium of habit, the 'uncanny of everyday life' (Das 2015), where a broader understanding of 'new regimes of living' inheres in the category of experience (Collier and Lakoff 2004)" (T. Srinivas 2018, 30–31). Creative ethics allows for the building of a future amid the precarity of the present. In the parlor, creative ethics becomes an aesthetic ethics through the expectations of and aspirations to beauty.

Interestingly, while the women of Bangalore recognized and articulated their connection to the feminine divine constantly, they rarely used indigenous or Sanskritic terms for beauty. They were not versed in aesthetic theory or interested in how beauty functioned in the construction of the self. Rather, they used terms such as "pretty," "ultra glam(orous)," and "super cute" as complimentary and discretionary phrases that spoke to a contemporary discourse of beauty. Even in talking about mythical beauty, they often applied contemporary language, calling apsaras "too beautiful" or mythic queens "slim and glam." Thus, beauty was telling not only in the relations between selfhood and divinity but also in its language, gesturing toward the natural bricolage of the modern and the mythic that took place every day in the parlor.

The Endless Story

In listening to the beauty workers telling stories, I was reminded of the fables of *Panchatantra* that I read as a child. That work makes frequent use of frame narratives to link the stories together. The form of these stories is endless, one story weaving into another in a perpetually unfolding telling. Many stories are of adventure; others are bawdy love stories, drama, and tragedy. Sometimes the nesting devices are as simple as the repetition of a phrase that links two stories together. In other cases, they are more complex: the characters within one story start to tell another story, or a new story spins off from an older one to tell us the backstory of the lead protagonist in what we might today call a prequel. At other times, the stories wind forward toward what we might think of as a sequel, or we hear of the adventures of a minor character as a whole new tale, with its own cast of characters and its own landscapes. Thus, the mythical landscape becomes populated through these interlinked and nested stories. At the core of each narrative typically lies an ethical riddle, which is solved by following threads through the maze of words. This threaded form, like a tapestry where colors are woven together to create meaning, is so common in Indian oral and written storytelling that it is almost invisible to native audiences; a fugitive power. As the story dives into and pulls back from deeper layers, it creates loops within the frame narrative, demonstrating the connection between the present and the past, the mythic and the literal, the personal and the cosmic.

The version of this endless story that most people in the West are familiar with is the Orientalist fantasy of the *Arabian Nights*,[15] which is thought to derive from Indian storytelling and which serves as a useful metaphor for understanding the stories women in Bangalore told. The teller, Princess Scheherazade, wove her endless story at night to postpone an existential threat to her life. She deferred inevitable death at dawn by leaving the story at a tantalizing edge as it unspooled into yet another story, a masterpiece of storytelling.[16] I argue that the endless narratives in the parlor are also survivalist, allowing Bangalorean women to craft selves, to see their lives in both retrospect and prospect, to form ethical horizons, and to link aspirationally to divinity. But these are no simplistic renditions of a putative ancestral past. By mixing "intention and accident" (Cavarero 2000, 1), multivocal tellings of mediated myths are stories of self and the "primacy of life" (M. Moran 2017, 298), and they act as a reflective soundtrack to a world in which women live stories and are their authors as well. These tellings act as a talismanic territory from which to act in the present, not as in the name of progress, as Walter Benjamin might say, but in the spirit of "actualization" or the "suddenly emergent" (1999, 461–62). In the following pages, I seek to explore this selfhood as it is crafted in the parlors and identify the inclinations, the desires, and the cultivations that make these women who they are.

On Method

Scrolling endlessly through texts on WhatsApp, I finally located the one that I was looking for. It was from a beautician in Bangalore and included photographs of her client's facial, which I wanted to share with a fellow anthropologist of India. As my colleague looked through the pictures on the phone, it chimed with goodnight messages from Bangalore, adorned with hearts and flowers. When she handed it back, she marveled at the thousands upon thousands of texts and messages I had saved from beauty clients, beauticians, priests, and other Bangaloreans: "You have fieldwork at your fingertips!" she remarked.

Although I began fieldwork in person in Bangalore in the mid-2000s and spent years visiting parlors and interviewing dozens of beauticians, managers, and customers, by 2016 I often kept in touch with my interlocutors via the WhatsApp platform and other social media when I was not in Bangalore. Because of robust fieldwork connections in Bangalore, and the ubiquity and accessibility of phone technology in India, when the pandemic hit and my elderly mother's care regimen became more intense, confining me to Boston, I began to communicate regularly with my interlocutors on WhatsApp. When a particular fruitful conversation happened, I simply took a screenshot of it with my phone. Technologies such as these suggest that we need to not only write and read "against culture" (Abu-Lughod 1991, 137–39) but also to think about place and positionality differently, as being more porous to flows of goods, telecommunications, and ideas, a collection of "experimental and discursive spaces" in which people situate themselves "physically and imaginatively" (Hastrup and Olwig 1997, 3 in D'Alisera 2004, 7).

Doing digital fieldwork, I found myself literally in two worlds. I spent half the Boston night virtually in Bangalore, listening to the koels singing and crows cawing and hearing the blow dryers in the parlors and the election megaphones in the streets as I spoke with beauty workers. Messages from workers and friends came through at all times of day, wreathed in rainbows (indicating hope), glasses of wine (indicating relaxation), flowers (happiness) and hands pressed together (which meant thank you but was also sometimes used to indicate prayer), or images of deities. As the emoticons and memes on offer became wider, so also my contacts' use of them broadened. Messages now had personalized gifs where my friends endlessly twirled, showing off a new dress or hairstyle, or permanently batted their new eyelashes or applied lipstick. They shared photos of themselves pre–and post–beauty treatments and sent selfies and screenshots of prices and services. They liked and hearted certain salons and followed them on social media platforms. At the other end, I was wading through this river of data mostly at night when they were at work, and my days in Boston became exhausted stumbles through work and life.

Generally, questions of fieldwork still center on the characteristics of the fieldwork site itself (Gupta and Ferguson 1997a). However, the effect of new communications media on fieldwork cannot be ignored, especially in the wake of the pandemic. The sounds of incoming texts, messages, chats, and memes and the endless chiming and ringing alerted me to the fact that my cell phone was becoming my field. I was torn about this. On the one hand, I knew that the algorithmic architecture of social media platforms was a powerful tool for reproducing normative identities and intimacies, programmed to create a self-reflexive bubble. On the other hand, in thinking about media not merely as an object of study, as has been posited before, but as a new ground for fieldwork and a new methodology, I realized, as Patrick Eisenlohr (2009, 9) notes, that the more mediated we get, the more the medium fades away, making the technology seem as natural as embodied interaction. Thus, the immediacy of the data, the constant availability and the whittling away of temporal and spatial distance through technology has begun to make the field constantly present in a way that it was not in decades prior.

This is not always positive. In my case, it was not unlike trying to drink from a fire hydrant, drowning in streams of information about beauty that came unbidden, pinging late at night into my phone. The data were rich because my interlocutors were already habituated to social media, which depended on deeper, faster, and richer flows of affect, attention, and expression, rendering communication into private capital and reshaping their intimate relations. In fact, this way of doing fieldwork mimicked the way beauty work was done in Bangalore—partly in real life, partly virtual, all ruptural. Ruptural of time and space, and most of all, of attention. Thus, this book also serves as a meditation on ethnographic fieldwork in the twenty-first century, an invitation to reconsider our tools and methods and to recognize their limitations.

Representing this new fieldwork, with its ruptures, anxieties, uncertainties, and inaccuracies, requires a shift in writing to include more communications like texts, gifs, images, and words from the field. I thought that privileging interlocutors' communicative styles meant writing a meta-text of texts within a text, and so I began to consider what the text really is and what the writing of it means. The staccato rhythms of communication across oceans and the cadence of abbreviated typescript were both incredibly efficient and yet often dropped sentences and even whole thoughts. Moreover, the tensions between orality and textuality were immanent. If the world of the parlor was a world invested with endless story, how could I represent those fragmented stories and the meandering, looping nature of them?

This and the many other challenges of this project have led me to think deeply about who I am in relationship to this work. The politics of representation sees selfhood as a struggle around positionalities (Hall 1991). In this work, my positionality has been a preoccupation. As I continued to do fieldwork in the parlors, I became wary, concerned that I was ventriloquizing women who were of a different status than I was, a cultural inauthenticity and violent grabbing of voice that was deeply troubling to me. To avoid this, I include beauty parlor vignettes that reflect and refract the dynamics of the parlor, deploying and intensifying images from my field notes and diaries.

I find that in many ethnographies, defining one's positionality has become a rote confession designed to counterattack the danger of essentializing or ventriloquizing a marginal Other. This often reduces the author to a singularity, but the point of positionality, it would seem, is to do the opposite: to bring forth a nuanced identity both social and political, "to build those forms of solidarity and identification which make common struggle and resistance possible but without suppressing the real heterogeneity of interests and identities" (Hall 1995, 225). As ethnographers, we need to think about our positionality not as a defensive measure but as a dialogic act that assigns agency to the act of enunciation, sometimes through a recognition of the appropriation, or even the theft, of that which belongs to an Other. The question of dubious ethics has haunted our profession and our process since its inception, and engaging in twenty-first-century ethnography pivots them into focus in a way that cannot be ignored.

But ethnography can also be transformatory—a braided twine of time and place, subject and language, that turns the techne of representation into an agent of transformation rather than a mere medium of expression. Thus, enunciation of a nuanced position is not only necessary; it is ethically urgent, allowing for an unsettling of fixed identities and inversions and reversions in the positioning of the agent as subject and object in the field, as my interactions with the beauticians and clients demonstrated. This unstable equilibrium demands a translucent critical practice to ensure its health, not a fixity of enunciation but a fracturing of established positions to develop structures of power to speak orthogonally to the people whose habitus we study.

My wariness about representation extended across the technological and human connections of fieldwork. Therefore, this ethnography is also haunted by the idea of integrity in the face of the acquisition that ethnography requires. For ethnographers take images and ideas and offer a representation of them, sometimes compassionate, sometimes not. Being sensitive to such intimacies across cultures and temporal distances, despite limited knowing, is a form of solidarity. Understanding, as Édouard Glissant (1997) says, allows us to "share the unknown with those whom we have yet to know," a poetics of blind relationality that is key to the ethnographic enterprise.

The Form of the Text

As I have mentioned, when I set out to write this book, I followed in the footsteps of Alfred Gell. Writing an anthropology of beauty, however, at times felt evanescent in itself. It reminded me of Birgit Meyer's contention about religion, that it is "an unseen reality" that affects how we think about and represent it. Meyer (2020, 9) writes, "For me, the intriguing thing about studying religion is that it involves a sense of an unseen reality that is held to exist and yet can only be sensed and rendered present through special techniques. This calls scholars to grasp the ways in which such an unseen reality, a professed transcendent, becomes tangible through practices of mediation, the issue being 'how to capture the wow.'" This, I found, is true of beauty as well. I wondered how I could capture its wow. Yet, in writing these interactions into chapters, I found that they fell serendipitously into attributes of the goddess's power that Bangalorean women sought to emulate: allure, radiance, heat, woundedness, fortune, and fluidity.

Chapter 1, "Alluring," tells the story of a local Bangalorean beauty pageant winner of the 1970s—Miss Vegetarian—in order to trace a microhistory of the beauty industry in post-independence India. It coalesces around the creation of the mythical *Bharatiya nari*, the ideal Indian woman, who showcases upper-caste values and is both modest and alluring in imitation of the goddess. The question the chapter raises is how allure, though an attribute of the goddess, raises the problem of recognition for women in the nation.

Chapter 2, "Radiant," explores some of the technoscientific processes of beauty, including depilation and skin lightening, building toward an athwart theory of beauty that emerges from the diagonal links between beauty and the fair skin attributed to mythical heroines. Fair skin is thought to be a characteristic of upper-casted and classed bodies and seen as evidence of status. Focusing on the potentially explosive dynamics of colorism in a caste-based society, where some are deemed "untouchable," this chapter alerts us to the inequality and opacity rife in the parlor, evidenced in the intimate relationship between "fair" upper-caste and classed clients and "dark" tribal and marginalized workers. Through the retelling of the story of Draupadi, the heroine of the epic the *Mahabharata*, set against the narrative of Dopdi, a tribal woman, this chapter explores the complex workings of social violence, particularly against marginalized, darker-skinned women in contemporary India. In thinking through the forms of life that women inhabit, I argue that the patterns of practice that they engage in reinforces and subverts caste hierarchies and ideas of female domestication.

Chapter 3, "Hot," details the sensual category of heat, which defines the presence of the goddess and her *ugra*, her excess. Through an understanding of heat as a quality of power and sensuality, the chapter details heated interactions with the goddess as "leaky" and "bloody." Further, the chapter discusses the sensible and sensual register of the olfactory presence of migrants whose bodies offer a scent that is deemed "foreign" by Bangaloreans, interpreted as representing migrant women's sexual hunger. This chapter examines the intimacies of the parlor and the unwritten rules that mask those intimacies.

Interlude, "Nightmare," describes an encounter held over WhatsApp with Lakshya, one of the migrant beauticians from the Northeast whom we met at the Lotus, and her story of migration to Bangalore.

Chapter 4, "Wounded," builds on the story of Lakshya's migration to explore the political economy of beauty within the nation-state of India. It weaves together the myth of the dismemberment of Sati with the experience of displacement suffered by many beauty workers. Reflecting on sacrifice, the chapter moves from Bangalore to the Kamakhya temple in the blue hills of Guwahati, Assam, the home of most migrants from the Northeast. Tackling the question of labor and belonging through the politics of migration, the chapter details the legal construction of new regimes of citizenship in India, a dismemberment of the nation into fragmented parts, and its impact on Dalit and tribal women working in Bangalore.

Chapter 5, "Fortunate," describes the beauty processes inherent in preparing for a Hindu wedding. It reflects on the charged place of conjugality in Bangalore to argue that the notion of being fortunate, "bhagyam," is directly linked to marital status and the domestication of female power in the form of Lakshmi, the radiant, divine consort of the god Vishnu. Detailing myths of domesticated wives such as Sita and Savitri, both of whom are beautiful, chaste, and forgiving, the chapter unpacks the centrality of conjugality and savarna politics in understandings of contemporary Indian womanhood.

Chapter 6, "Fluid," follows my failed attempts to visit a queer parlor in Bangalore and ends up discovering an emerging space of digital beauty practice. There, I find new and dynamic queer resistances that speak to embodiment and sexuality in formative ways: in hijra cosmetic acquisition, a butch lesbian's discomfort with Bangalorean body shaming, and the sharing of myths of female asuras (demons) and queer divinities. Embodying gender-bending goddesses, such as Mohini, as the ideal and aspirational mythic figures of queer lives, trans celebrities in Bangalore tell stories of divinity that highlight transgression and divine capaciousness to make political claims for greater social inclusion.

In "Conclusion," we find ourselves with Selvi, who is getting made up to receive the goddess Amman. This experience of possession touches on many of the book's themes and thus provides a mirror to reflect on the lessons learned through the journey toward beauty. Selvi guides us in unpacking the meaning of beauty as edge work, a practice that gestures to what lies beyond the horizon of our imaginings.

Finally, "Postlude" brings us back to everyday preoccupations of care and intimacy and the question of recognition and imagination in a fragile world.

I think allure is something around you, like a perfume or like a scent. It's like a memory . . . it pervades.
—Diana Vreeland

Ayyooo . . . I love beauty parlors! I could live in a parlor, getting glammed up! . . . I'm shameless!
—Menaka

ALLURING 1

The Namesake

Menaka, a glamorous dancer and erstwhile celebrity in Bangalore, waltzed into Bloom, a posh parlor where we had decided to meet. She came from a well-heeled, upper-caste business family that had been settled in the city for several generations. Dressed in a deep-red ensemble of silk pants and embroidered tunic, Menaka wore chic designer sunglasses, her faux simple makeup emphasizing her perfect features. She greeted the beauticians of Bloom with a simpering smile and a wail. "Hazel, I desperately need my eyebrows neatened up!" she cried, pointing to a few errant hairs on her brow that were unnoticeable to me.

Hazel, a petite beautician with an efficient air, was from Guwahati, a city in the state of Assam in the Northeast of India. She brought a plastic tray with silver handles on which sat a spool of cotton thread and a tiny pair of gold scissors. Menaka pulled a stick-on bindi from her forehead and stuck it on the mirror. Hazel wound the thread through her mouth in a series of loops and went to work, her mouth close to Menaka's face as she pulled eyebrow hairs out by the roots in a process known as "threading." Within a few minutes, Menaka's eyebrows were perfect arcs, spotted slightly with blood, which Hazel wiped away with a rose-scented cotton ball. She then scissored the center of the brows perfectly and reaffixed Menaka's stick-on bindi. Hazel saw me watching her and added by way of explanation of her care in affixing the bindi in the center of the Menaka's forehead, "It's the third eye, no?" Menaka peered at her reflection in the mirror, "Thank you, ah? Sooo much better. Abbah!"

We went to a café nearby to talk. As we entered, many heads turned to watch Menaka. She was not unaware of the attention. She told me with a tinkling laugh that I was finally interviewing the "right" person about beauty and glamor: "Being glam is totally my game, baby! I know all the fundas [fundamentals]!" she said emphatically.

After ordering our coffees, to which she added "a yum choco pastry," Menaka spoke of her delight at relaxing in the local parlor getting various beauty treatments, how she knew all the beauticians "by name" and how they always "took care of her." She said that looking "glam" was a societal expectation of her celebrity status, which she insisted that she resented. Then she pushed her sunglasses to the top of her head, while smoothing her long tresses in a practiced flick, and told me casually how since it was a Friday, the day dedicated to Amman (the goddess), after her photo shoot for a national fashion magazine, she would stop by the local Devi temple to "check in" with the deity. The brief encounter with the goddess was enough to "reset" her and get her through the week. "She gives me solid power, T! I need to check in every Friday, no matter what, for a reset."

Later, as I was taking notes about her beauty regimen, she unexpectedly pivoted to the mythical yet again. She had been watching the old Mahabharata teleserial, which was being re-aired on television, as had the women at the Lotus. She knew the stories from childhood but was impressed with the television spectacle and its gripping storytelling, she said. She took a sip of her coffee and eased into the well-worn myth of the celestial apsara (nymph) Menaka, her namesake. I paraphrase.

> Menaka was a beautiful, seductive, and libidinous apsara, well known for her ability to captivate. She was tasked by the gods with distracting Sage Vishwamitra, who had commenced a heat-inducing penance (tapas) to gain immortality, which threatened to burn up the entire world. Menaka successfully seduced the sage, ending his earth-melting penance, but she unexpectedly fell in love with him and bore him a beautiful baby girl, Shakuntala. One day in a moment of lovemaking, Menaka let slip the truth about

her mission. *Vishwamitra was outraged by her deception. He cursed her to be forever separated from him and baby Shakuntala. A heart-broken Menaka left, never to return, and since she was cursed, she forgot her baby and the life she had led.*

Menaka, the celebrity, was angry at this turn in the story and chastised the celestial apsara: "How could she forget her baby? Curse or whatever! What kind of a mother was she?" *Then, pivoting abruptly, she turned, to my surprise, to beauty*: "All these apsaras—Urvashi, Rambha, Menaka—they are something, no? Glam and beautiful. They make these sagey types forget everything! The sages are supposed to be doing tapas (ascetic penances) and all, but they see one of these dames just walk past, and they come chasing after her with their . . ." *She mimed desire, tongue hanging out and panting. Then she added,* "These sagey guys were simply too frustrated, and when Menaka just looked at him like that . . ." *she flicked her eyes toward a young man at a nearby table in the café, who looked up eagerly, drawn by her charisma,* ". . . and dhamal (wham!)!" *Menaka slapped the surface of the table with the palm of her hand.* "He just fell for her!" *Then she added the takeaway:* "We should learn to be like that, no, T? Like these goddess types who have the smart guys fall here and there. What fun it would be!" *So saying, she batted her eyelids and licked the icing off her cupcake.*

Glamor and Allure

When Menaka asserted that her namesake apsara was "ultra glam," what did she mean? And for the purposes of this ethnography, what does her beauty have to do with the story? The tale does not suggest a formal marriage between the two characters Menaka and the sage, and the relationship transgresses human-divine relations, as the apsara is semidivine and the sage is human. Therefore, one might conclude that this is a connection born of the apsara's fatal allure, a sexual seduction, not a bond of consanguinity or affinity. However, the relations between men and women forged in the celebrity Menaka's mythopoesis are sexually charged and conflicted but also positive. To me, they are created in the violence of casted and gendered bodies, in men's anger and lust and women's supposed unbridled sexuality. Menaka, however, viewed them as passionate and romantic, resting in women's allure and glamor.

Nigel Thrift (2010) argues that allure is essentially a quality of captivation and that it gestures to an enchanted world in which value is generated through seduction. The effects of allure are immediate, perceptual, and emotional. Glamor, on the other hand, is the technology of this captivation, a beguiling affective force that is elusive and magical, expanding to include beguilement, enchantment, fascination, and seduction.

Reviving the idea of glamor allows us to analyze contemporary forms of feminine cultural production as being centered on allure, which produces a more magical, yet more calculated, aesthetic. Glamorous women like Menaka are constantly editing out details that can break the spell of beauty—blemishes on the skin, gray hair, sweaty armpits, and so on—and replacing these details with others that add richness and value, that enhance allure. Anything that speaks of wealth, celebrity, sex appeal, luxury, and look-at-me-ness speaks to glamor and creates allure. And glamor, according to my interlocutors in Bangalore, brings a woman closer to the divine feminine.

But as Lucinda Ramberg rightly notes, feminist theologians and religious studies scholars have tended to seek the vast power that the feminine is capable of not in glamorous apsaras, but in fierce Hindu goddesses like Kali (McDermott and Kripal 2003; Ramberg 2014). For example, Joyce Flueckiger (2013, xi) speaks of the ugra (fierceness) of the goddess Gangamma as "an empowering relationship in which their shared nature as possessors of shakti [female power] is asserted and performed." Feminist critiques of religions with a father god have argued that divinized male gods naturalize patriarchy, or, as Lucinda Ramberg (2014, 66) argues pithily, "when the gods are men, men are gods." So when goddesses are women, can women become goddesses?

In this chapter, I argue that both glamor and allure—powers that Menaka's story (both my interlocutor and the divine apsara) imbues the goddess with and are offered as a central vital attribute of womanhood—are the product of two intersecting forces that I chart in the following pages. The first are changing aesthetic practices, honed over centuries in India as a medico-therapeutic aesthetics that merged with industrial beauty in modern India to offer a mediated image of the "new Indian woman." The second is distinctive pedagogy of glamor that modern women learn through engaging these aesthetic practices. In overlapping the beauty of the divine Menaka and the human one, I explore the forces of allure and glamor not only as the product of modern, industrial conditions of beauty but also as an attribute of the divine feminine with ancient roots in the Hindu imagination.

As Menaka articulated it, allure is ambivalent, poised on the edge between attracting wanted and unwanted attention. And the problem and promise of allure, as Diana Vreeland, noted editor of *Vogue* magazine and adviser to Jacqueline Kennedy, argued, is that once it is established, it is pervasive, impossible to ignore, attracting attention and drawing people in to the person who is alluring, whether they seek the attention or not.

Sadly, gender violence—sexual harassment, rape, murder, honor killings, and other forms of violence—is also pervasive, everywhere in modern India. Women labor to look beautiful and alluring in the parlors but are always in danger of being accused of seducing men and thus being raped or murdered, paying the ultimate price for being seen as sexual. Thus, allure is symbolic of both ultimate power and a lack of power.

Yet women in parlors, clients and beauticians alike, said, echoing Menaka, that to look "like a goddess" was the objective, which I understood to mean alluring and powerful. But what, if anything, is the relationship between the presence of a powerful Devi and the social worlds structuring the everyday lives of women in whom she manifests herself? Feminist scholars have often argued that Indian women have been seen as embodying the nation, as the image of Bharat Mata, "Mother India," imagined as a mother goddess, the feminine in politico-religious imagination. Feminine beauty and the aesthetics of decoration and dress, such as being dressed in a sari with traditional jewelry, all became symbols of a good, chaste woman and a good moral nation (Bacchetta 1993; Ramaswamy 2010). The allure located in such beauty had to walk the fine line between attractive yet chaste and being overtly sexy.

I was surprised to find that in the beauty parlors, there was no talk of modern nationhood, embodied, attractive, or otherwise unless it was in the frame of the eternal constructs of myth. Rather, clients and beauty workers studied mediated images of modern Bollywood and Hollywood celebrities and more recently of TikTok stars to access notions of beauty and allure and how to "properly" engage them, depending on the image they wanted to portray—chaste goddess, seductive siren, virginal medieval queen, and so on. I trace the history of modern notions of beauty and allure in this chapter to invite thinking about relatedness between women, nation, and goddess in this context, where mirroring seems to suggest different strategic and historical ways of being alluring, all of which are, in fact, modern, and to contend with the moral slippage that such choices resulted in. I was given two utterly different answers to this question. The first came from young men in the city who watched, desired, *and* policed women's bodies, and the second from the beauty parlor habitués, whose aspirations were to be like goddesses, beautiful and alluring.

At Desire

I had planned to meet Menaka's niece Madhu at a parlor, simply named Desire, which was near her home. Tall and athletic, with shoulder-length auburn hair and a bright smile, she turned heads wherever she went in the city. She had unusual looks for a South Indian, with hazel eyes and a full mouth. She had been courted by the city's modeling agencies but refused, working for a city developer as his trusted aide. Just thirty years old, she had turned her intelligence and marketing skills to property development and was extraordinarily successful, earning a hefty salary in a few short years.

As with many middle-class women, however, she was late to our appointment, used to keeping people waiting. While I stood outside the parlor underneath a billboard that was surrounded by garbage but paradoxically advertised a sylvan spa resort, I ran into Rajeev, a young man who worked as a clerk at a local law firm. I had always thought of Rajeev as soft spoken, but as we talked about beauty parlors, he became animated. He pointed to the billboard that showed young women frolicking in a pool. "Girls nowadays have no shame," he said angrily. "Simply showing kundi [Tamil = bum] and all. This TV has spoilt them. They think it's all fun..." he trailed off, staring, as Madhu arrived.

She drove an unmistakable red Honda around the city. She pulled up fast and accurately and swung her long legs to the curb. As always, she was beautifully turned out, hair, nails, and skin gleaming, designer handbag on her shoulder. She flicked her eyes over Rajeev and decided he was of no consequence. Rajeev and I made plans to meet later. Madhu hugged me briskly and ushered me into the parlor with profuse apologies for keeping me waiting.

She said she had a loyalty program card at her local franchise parlor, Bodycraft, where she went "once a week" for beauty work, but Desire was where she came when she was in a hurry. She shrugged when I asked her why she went to the parlor so frequently and responded, "Just upkeep, na?" But after a minute, her pretty face twisted and she said sourly, "I think it's because everyone here, randos (random men) and relatives, all pass comments all the time! And I need an arm wax."

"Passing comments" is a unique Indian phrase, a genre of critique of the female body, which is not considered overt harassment but is understood to induce shame about the body and the self (Hindi = sharam; Tamil = vekkam) when a lack of self-care is noticed and commented on. When I went to college in the late 1980s, men would jokingly describe women as "hinde inda personality, munde inda municipality" (Kannada = in the back, personality, in the front, municipality), meaning that they were ugly, likening their faces to poorly built municipal buildings. If the woman was dark skinned, a favorite Kannada descriptor was, "Kathale nalli kansolla, photo nalli billolla!" (Kannada = Can't be seen in the dark and can't be captured in a photograph), or simply "negative!" a double-edged term that indicated both dismissal and a photographic negative which reversed light and shade. For women with bigger bodies,[1] the joking descriptors focused on the offending body part: "Thodai Rani" (Kannada = queen of the thighs) or simply the one word, "pregnanta?" (Kannada = is she pregnant?), which invariably evoked hooting laughter from onlookers.

"Passing comments" was seen by women and men in Bangalore as innocent "fun," easily dismissed, unlike the groping, touching, bum pinching, and other forms of bodily assault that they were subject to every day. Often, my friends noted that their age and privilege protected them from these assaults. "When we were young, God! These guys would pass you and brush your boobs or touch your bum! It was so sick! So my dad would drop us to college so that we could be safe. Now of course with drivers and all and also because we are old *buddhis* [crones], no one bothers us, thank God! They only pass comments." In most of the stories told, the source of the trauma was elusive, yet the comments were unforgettable. They were invariably and discomfortingly about a woman's body shape, her fat, her skin color, and her lack of beauty, the typical "fat, black, and ugly" discourse that has shaped public discourse and attitudes as well as women's inner voices (Smalls 2021). Lauren Berlant (2011, 80) has said about such anonymous trauma, that it "produces something in the air without that thing having to be more concrete than a sense of the uncanny—free-floating anxiety in the room, negativity on the street, a scenario seeming to unfold within the ordinary without clear margins, even when a happening is also specific." The public is threatening to women in Bangalore, filled with traumatic encounters that were rarely, if ever, articulated. Radhika made an important point about her friend Aseema who never was sexually harassed: "She never got touched, even by accident. She was too good looking and high class. Guys were scared of her. Only one time she got her bum pinched in a big crowd."

For women, all these anxieties about the public came to rest on their bodies, inducing a shame and fear, which was the precise objective. To be harassed like this meant and still means that one as a woman was not worthy of positive recognition. All the violences of groping, sexual catcalling, and "passing comments," spoken and enacted, were often blurred together into the generic category of "eve teasing" in Bangalore.[2] They created expectations and boundaries, determining what public and private spaces Bangalorean women could frequent, and how they could dress and behave in these publics.[3] Behavior beyond the prescriptive was considered provocation for any violence.

When, in 2017, several thousand women were publicly groped at the New Year's Eve street gathering that took place annually in Bangalore,[4] the Karnataka Home Minister Mr. G. Parameshwara was quoted in the *Guardian* newspaper, arguing that "unfortunate attacks" happened because women often dressed "like Westerners," by which he meant they showed some skin. Later, when held to account by women's rights groups in the city, he claimed to be misquoted.

Rajeev, the law clerk whom I had run into outside Desire, articulated a similar position—that he and his friends were the *actual* victims. They were receivers of mixed messages from women, who were demanding attention through their clothing or behavior, and then refusing the attention and saying they were assaulted. Rajeev felt angry at what he saw as an allure that provoked a reaction but simultaneously a refusal to "take responsibility" for the reaction. The objects of his gazing and illicit touching were inevitably women he saw as alluring, who wore "revealing clothes" and instigated a dangerous desire. An alluring woman was a "trap," as Rajeev and his friends noted, for she could also be a vamp, the toothed vagina, stealing power (in the form of semen), rendering men weak and powerless because of their desire (Alter 1992).[5]

But for the women, the gazing and touching were real violences that they mitigated in their day-to-day lives. I often heard older women give advice to those younger to be tough in the face of male harassment, especially when dealing with groups of men catcalling (Hawkins 2008, 2). I am sensitive to the popular Orientalist stereotype of non-Western men consumed by lust, so we need to treat this male voyeurism with suspicion, but in group settings, men in Bangalore frequently catcall women or sexually harass them in other ways to create homosocial bonds among themselves. When I accompanied women or went to the city by myself, I noticed men yelling out, "Sexy sexy," "*Beka ninge?*" (Kannada = Do you want it?) to women passers-by and receiving affirmation from other men. One of Madhu's grandaunts, Vijaya, was a tough athlete endowed with a large muscular bum, and she frequently slapped, shoved, or called out men who pinched her bottom.

When I was younger, I dealt with the threat of such violence by making myself small, slouching along and wearing oversize clothing to prevent such unwanted attention, but as I grew older, I, like Madhu's aunt, had little patience for men who sexually harassed me or other women.

Women who are alluring do not create a moral space but rather a territory of feeling of intoxication—a danger and an attraction rolled into one. Suffice it to say, to move in public as a woman in Bangalore, one must be toughened to one's objectification. The aspiration to a hardening, a toughness, what Gina Ulysse marks in Haitian public markets as a woman traders' "tuffness," is a threshold temporal and ideational moment of ethical subjectivity, marking the distinctions between worlds that we inhabit and we manage versus the worlds we want to build and inhabit and the kind of differential citizenship and authority that these two worlds demand (Ulysse 2002, 19; 2007).

Madhu's takeaway in navigating city spaces where she felt feminine yet often had her athletic physique commented on ("Is she a man?") was that she understood the public to be problematic, filled with "dirty men," the scene of a power struggle. She said she often "needed protection" and wanted to be seen as demure to counteract her powerful body. So she found a boyfriend who was also an athlete and had a big muscular body: "He makes me feel small and cute!" The son of a rich businessman, he gave her the expensive red Honda as a birthday gift so she could physically distance herself from the world around her. She said it made her feel "glamorous." She also found a job where she could pay for a monthly "package" at her franchise beauty parlor, for regular beauty work, "upkeep," and "pampering" so that she always appeared beautiful, "clean," and "well put together" with gleaming hair and nails, thereby establishing her superior class and distancing herself from the "dirty" public even further.

For women like Madhu, being alluring provokes attention, wanted and unwanted. The defining characteristic in allure's aesthetic value is both the focused attention and the deficit in attention it provokes. Its distracting effect is because allure pivots the viewer to their own desire, no longer focusing on the alluring subject but on their own wanting, turning the subject into object. This pivot inward makes allure distracting, imprecise, and ambivalent—in short, difficult to understand, like the goddess herself.

The Ambivalent Allure of the Goddess

I first met Mrs. Gowda with Menaka at Bloom, the local "auntie parlor" that they both frequented in the elite neighborhood of Upper Palace Orchards. Mrs. Gowda, a corpulent woman with a perpetually pursed mouth, was getting her gray hair colored a jet black, while instructing the "girls," as she called them, on how to behave: dress modestly, don't wear too much makeup, and so on. Mrs. Gowda was very light skinned and was always dressed in gorgeous silk saris and heavy gold jewelry, as befitted her elite status as the wife of a successful businessman. She seemed convinced of her perspicacity. Her voice was like a razor, cutting through the noisy atmosphere of the salon.

A few days later, Menaka and I visited the Banashankari Vijaya Devi[6] temple on the final day of Navaratri, the nine-day autumnal festival dedicated to the goddess. We had hoped for a quick stop in and then head to a family dinner.

The temple was filled with crowds of well-dressed women, singing songs of adoration to the Devi. Mrs. Gowda, who was near the front of the crowd, spotted us and waved, her diamond nose ring catching the light. Menaka said in dismay, "Abbah! Mrs. Gowda, super bhakt [devotee], has seen us! No chance of making it on time for dinner. She'll talk and talk!" Mrs. Gowda came toward us purposefully, her round eyes fixed on me.

She launched into breathless conversation. She was surprised to see us in the temple, especially me, she said. I understood she meant that she did not see me as particularly pious. She proceeded to underscore her own piety and regularity at the temple. She said she recited the famed Lalitha Sahasranama[7] (Thousand names of the goddess), a song of adoration to the goddess, every Friday and visited the temple "practically every day." She spoke of incidents of the goddess's compassion and grace toward her and her family. "I tell my daughters and granddaughters to come here to get strength from Durga Devi. She is Mother, no? Shakti . . . only she can protect us!"

Mrs. Gowda then grabbed me by the elbow and maneuvered me to the shrine, pushing other women out of the way. I heard Menaka moan behind me, "Ayooo! Gone . . . now! No chance of getting to the restaurant! I'd better call them." Mrs. Gowda said introductorily, "This form of Devi, Banashankari Devi, is popular in south Bangalore in Banashankari, there was an old temple there. But this temple has this shrine so everyone in north Bangalore can come here."

We arrived in front of the shrine, Menaka trailing us with her phone to her ear. Mrs. Gowda waved at the deity, as though introducing me. The deity was dressed in her incarnate form as Mahishasura Mardini, killer of the demon Mahisha (ignorance) depicted by a water buffalo. This was the final victory of knowledge over ignorance that the festival commemorated.

The iconography of the deity was terrifying. She was poised on the demon's chest, plunging a bloody trident into him, her other arms carrying weapons of war, her lion steed standing behind her, growling. The deity was dressed in a gold lace sari and was covered with glitter and gold jewelry, radiant with "glory" according to Mrs. Gowda. She emphasized that it was the allure of the goddess that drew the demon to his destruction seeing it more as gender play than a defeat of ignorance. "She was too beautiful, too much! He couldn't look away!" she said.

Mrs. Gowda clutched my arm to prevent escape and launched into the story of the Devi[8] and her battle with the forces of evil, which I had heard many times before, insisting that as a scholar of religion, I should know "the truth."

> You know, Devi is a form of Parvati, the wife of Shiva, and she is also Shakti, the female power of the universe. And Mahisha was a deceitful demon [asura] who was a shape-shifter demon [rakshasa] and the son of Mahisha (a buffalo). He was ignorant, driven by greed and lust. But he cleverly obtained

a boon from Brahma that no man could kill him and he became very powerful. The gods—Shiva, Vishnu, and Indra—were worried, and so they hid in the mountains. They knew only a lady could defeat him, and so they created a goddess, Devi, through their combined energy.

She was born from the gods' mind. She could draw anyone to her like magic. She could get anyone.

Mrs. Gowda snapped her fingers to indicate the rapidity of Devi's allure.

She rode a roaring lion and carried all weapons like the sword and the trident for this purpose only. Mahisha was a fool, and when he saw the beautiful goddess, he became mad [huchchu]. He wanted to possess her, marry her [maduve] not understanding that she was the Shakti (source of all creation).[9] He tried to grab her, to kiss her [muttu kotta]. She smiled and allowed him to touch her. But then, badam!! Like that, she killed him with her trishul [trident]!

Mrs. Gowda mimicked thrusting a trident into the earth.

Menaka listened distractedly to Mrs. Gowda while texting on her phone but on the way home said, "The story of Devi always makes me feel wonthara [Kannada = indescribable]. Like you can be beautiful, and you can also kick these stupid gaandus [Kannada = men, assholes]!"

In scholarship on goddesses in the subcontinent, there is ongoing discussion of whether the presence of the goddess in the cultural imagination changes everyday life for women. What is the relation between theology and the social world? In other words, can relations between the gods be seen as epigrammatic of relations between humans? And in reverse, what does a reimagination of the goddess today, such as Menaka's reading of gendered retribution, imply for Hinduism's myths and values?

The most important canonical text that we have of the goddess comes from the portion of the Sanskrit *Markandeya Purana* called the *Devi Mahatamya*, or the *Glorification of the Goddess* (circa sixth to seventh century), which relates the exploits of the Great Goddess (Mahadevi) and her many manifestations within the framework of Puranic cosmology. In Shakta traditions, as opposed to Vaishnava or Shaiva traditions, the Supreme Goddess is called Śhakti, literally "power," or Devī, literally "goddess" (Brooks 1992).[10] The theology of the goddess presents her as alternatively menacing and benevolent, celebrating an ambivalence at the heart of goddess theology (Kinsley 1988; Halperin 2019)— Kali as the paradigmatic hungry "goddess of the tooth" and the ever-beneficent Lakshmi, or "goddess of the breast" (Daniélou 1991, 190–92). The goddess comprises a polythetic set of characteristics, as described in the *Lalita Sahasranama* and the Puranas (Clooney 2005), some of which emphasize allure and sexual appetites and others that emphasize her wifely devotion and demureness.

The pan-Indian Navaratri festival (the Nine Nights of the Goddess) that Mrs. Gowda was at, traces and enacts the myth of the Devi's battle with Mahisha, culminating in the Vijayadashami or tenth day of her victory over the forces of ignorance, which is the day we attended the festival. But forms of Shakti and Devi are ubiquitously worshipped over the subcontinent throughout the year. From the 108 Shaktipeethas, or seats of the goddess, to local village Amman temples dedicated to goddesses of protection against pox and illness (*gramadevata*), dotted all over rural India, forms of Devi are woven into the very sacred geography of India (Biernacki 2007; Eck 1998b, 2012; Ramaswamy 2010; McDermott 2008, 2011). In the ethnohistory of goddess traditions,[11] discussions of local and contextualized categories and taxonomies rooted in caste practices and aesthetics such as Sanskritic, village, and so forth fail to do justice to the complexities of the goddess tradition. Indeed, the forms of the goddess stress the existence of mythic modes of thought and the usefulness of gynemorphic images, even if they are merely devices of the imagination (Gross 1978; Pintchman 2001).

What clearly emerged in Mrs. Gowda's telling of the myth was the goddess's allure, her irresistible beauty, intelligence, and charm, for the story of her victory rests on the Devi's ability to lure the demon to his death and that the evil force and the uncontrollable lust meets its end at the feminine divine. The deity offers liberation through knowledge and allure and acts as a retributive force for the ignorant and ego driven (Gross 1978, 269). For Menaka, Mrs. Gowda, and the other women I encountered, beauty and allure were attributes of the goddess, powerful forces, which, when harnessed, could elevate one to goddess status and destroy the lustful and the ignorant.

When Menaka felt the urge to worship the female deity on Vijayadasami, the tenth and final day of victory of the Navaratri festival, she put it in twenty-first-century pop-feminist-therapeutic terms similar to the "self-love" mantra at the local salon as she got ready to go to the temple: "It's our time, T! Got to go and find the shakti [power] inside us, na? Make us more . . ." she simultaneously waggled her hips suggestively and tapped her head. And then while applying a deep-red color carefully on her lips, she added that the paradoxical nature of the goddess as creative and destructive, and sexual and virginal only added to her disorienting allure. "It's total, no? Shakti is full power, all kinds! When I went to Himachal they have Devis who can cure cancer, and Devis who make you ill also!" She pouted at herself in the mirror, examined her lips, and seemingly changing the subject abruptly explained, "I was *pucca* (fixed, loyal), a L'Oréal girl, and then this Color My World matte shade came out and it's so long lasting *and* vegan. Guess what the color is called? You'll never guess! It's called 'Goddess'!! Too LOL, no?"

But Menaka's usage of the goddess in secular pop feminist terms raises Rajeswari Sunder Rajan's question of whether goddesses could be part of the secular feminist project of recovering the agency of women in a male world (in Hiltebeitel and Erndl 2000). Her concerns suggest that secular readings of the goddess are bound to fail, as they alienate the vast majority of Hindu women who are religious, allowing the Hindu fundamentalist right to draw women into its fold under the sign of the goddess (Purkayastha et al. 2003). It seems, however, that Menaka's reading of the goddess as a postmodern individual feminine empowerment scheme suggests that the goddess can indeed afford women some measure of power in a hierarchical and gendered society like India. And beauty was one way to harness the goddess, even if it required applying lipstick.

The Eggplant Queen

Jayshree, Menaka's aunt, said she had no intention of participating in a beauty competition. A national tennis champion, at twenty she spent every waking hour intent on her training. She came from a Brahman family in Bangalore, when it was just a small sleepy town, and she had, she said, "no idea of glamor." But in the summer of 1972, Jayshree's sister Vijaya entered them both in a local beauty competition—Miss Vegetarian, Bangalore—as a joke. The beauty competition was the brainchild of a city promoter who felt that the vegetarian diet should be celebrated in modern India.[12]

When Jayshree advanced to the final round, someone took her aside and told her that the final beauty competition would have a swimsuit portion, and she needed to wax her body free of hair and to get it "fully bleached" for an even "skin tone." After checking with her sophisticated college mates for their recommendation on parlors, Jayshree visited the oldest one in the city, Eve's Beauty Parlor, a sister concern of the one in Madras my mother and her sisters had visited. Eve's was located in a pastel pink bungalow in the colonial cantonment of Bangalore. Run by an Indian-Chinese couple from Calcutta, the Kos, Eve's Beauty Parlor was, at the time, the epitome of stylishness.

At the parlor, one of the beauticians took Jayshree into a small private room where she bleached and waxed her entire body. They washed and dried her hair and set it under the dryer into the required glamorous beehive hairdo, in imitation of the 1950s movie stars, Bangalore being about twenty years behind cutting-edge

FIG. 1.1 The Miss Vegetarian Pageant 1972 with Jayshree holding number 9 on the left

fashion. The beauticians told her in order to win, she had to perfect her gait and to wear makeup, teaching her to apply kohl in the fish-eye shape favored by film star Madhubala.[13] *Under their instruction, Jayshree went to a local shop that sold "foreign" cosmetics and bought herself pink Lakme lipstick, which she applied gingerly.*

The day of the pageant, Jayshree wore one of her mother's elegant chiffon silk saris to the city's town hall, chosen for its enormous wooden stage on which contestants were asked to parade back and forth. Black-and-white photos of the event show the pageant winners, looking alluring in a 1970s style. Even among these local beauties, Jayshree stands out, with her statuesque body, beautiful face, silken hair, and radiant smile. Unsurprisingly, she won the pageant and was crowned Miss Vegetarian, Bangalore. The Kannada newspapers' headlines were ecstatic: "Dilruba Miss Vegetarian!" (Urdu = heartthrob). Excited journalists asked Jayshree what her favorite vegetable was. Her candid answer, "the eggplant,"[14] *struck her brothers as hilarious, and they teasingly nicknamed her "Badnekai Rani," the Eggplant Queen.*

Jayshree's participation in the Miss Vegetarian pageant of 1972 had roots in three different yet intertwined national operations: the forging of a modern Indian nation-state that created a much anticipated yet complex feminine citizenship; the creation of a "new Indian woman" (Mankekar 1999, 1993, 551) with radical ideas of sexuality, cleanliness, consumption, and beauty; and the rise of India's beauty industry with its new "materialities of care" based on industrialized medicines and cosmetics (Buse et al. 2018).

Indeed, the fledging state of India was specifically imagined in gendered terms, as Bharat Mata, Mother India (also a goddess), who was depicted as a beautiful woman with long, flowing hair, mapped onto the cartographic territory of a modern Indian state (Kinsley 1988; Ramaswamy 2010). Allied to this poetic imagery of Bharat Mata was her human counterpoint, the imagined Bharathiya Nari, the new Indian woman, understood to be both beautiful and modest, dressed in pure white and carrying the flag of the new modern state of India, an inspiration to the emerging nationalist movement. But existing alongside this discourse of modernity was the consistent tension of preserving Indian "tradition," identity, and culture, which was mapped onto the bodies of Indian, read Hindu, women, leaving women with the ethical conundrum of how to dress and how to behave.

Returning women from postmodern India to a mythical landscape of apsaras, goddesses, queens, and heroines, as Menaka and other women did, offered ways of understanding Indian womanhood and their ethical problems through interlinked and nested stories. At the core of each mythical narrative lay an ethical riddle, solved by following threads through the maze of narratives, which the women in the parlors did, tracing characters and their development. These nested stories of characters and their evolution often demonstrate connections between the present and the past, the mythical and the literal, the personal and the cosmic—forming an endless story, as it were, with a vast cast of characters, each of whom offers different ontological states and ethical choices, making the linking of seeming tradition into the everyday postmodern ways of being that the women inhabited.

Purnima Mankekar (1999, 105–6), in her pathbreaking study of the reception of teleserials like the *Mahabharata* in 1990s Delhi, shows that the "new Indian woman" became an icon and a majoritarian identity that straddled this sociotemporal paradox between modernity and tradition, by asserting women's place in the home, away from the public, through a managed ethnic, religious, and gendered identity.[4] In contrast, for Jawaharlal Nehru, independent India's first prime minister, modernity was not about reinstating a traditional womanhood in India but about implying a notion of equality in which adult men and women would have a sense of dignity and self-reliance. Nehru supposedly sought to establish a nationalism based on equal opportunity for people of every backward group "race, and creed," which included women of "lower caste" and class status (Dirks 2001). In the newly minted republic, the idea of a public in which women participated fully and wholly as equal citizens in public life held much romantic promise as an attunement to, if not an arrival at, modernity (Breckenridge 1995). Part of women's participation in the Nehruvian public realm of the new India was through capitalist consumption, particularly of new toiletries (for hygiene) and cosmetics (for beauty), as well as through learning emergent pedagogies of self- and family care through the pages of new women's magazines.

Cosmetics and the Modern Indian Woman

In 1918, decades before the building of Nehru's dream of a modern India, the noted tycoon Sir Jamshedji Tata started a soap manufacturing factory in Cochin, Kerala, followed two decades later by the Mysore Sandal[15] soap company in Bangalore. As in Zimbabwe, where Burke notes that global capitalism brought new ideas of cleanliness, the rise of commercial soapmaking created a different kind of modern middle-class Indian woman citizen, one for whom new ideas of self-care, sexuality, well-being, domesticity, hygiene, and aesthetics were visible signs of a postcolonial, modern society (Burke 1996).

Indian women took to the new Indian cosmetics eagerly, for, until then, cosmetics were imported from England and remained out of reach for the average middle-class consumer. By 1950, several new national factories were producing soaps, talcum powders, and cologne, marketing them to the Indian public as essential to cleanliness and loveliness, thus nudging out traditional cosmetics, such as coconut oil and soap nut powder. The most popular brands of soap were Lifebuoy and Lux, Pears glycerin soap, the verdantly green Cinthol, and the red Rexona (which smelled strongly of carbolic acid). In addition, there were talcum powders and creams in Indian-inspired scents, including jasmine and sandal that replaced the nostalgic fragrances of lavender and lily of the valley preferred by the British. The jingle for Lifebuoy soap in Bangalore, "*Yelli idde lifebuoy, alli idde arogya*" (Kannada = Where there is lifebuoy, there is health), summed up these emerging materialities of care in an emerging nation. But these soaps and creams were just the visible manifestations of an enormous change in women's lives.[16]

Until the 1960s, women had eschewed the male domain of the local barbershop. Haircutting was thought to be impure, associated with widowhood, when women were often forced to shave their hair as a sign of the closure of their sexual lives. More important, it meant the pollution of being touched by a barber, who was not only a strange man but also one who was of an "untouchable" caste (Beteille 1965; Mencher 1974; M. N. Srinivas 1957). Barbers came to the home to shave male members of the household and the heads of widows, who bathed immediately thereafter to limit the pollution of being barbered. Women, particularly upper-caste married women, were expected to keep purity rituals and avoid the barber and haircutting. If they had a brush with people who carried pollution due to their casted bodies or occupations, such as the barber, popularly known by the Urdu term *hajama* (Hindi = nai; Kannada = shourika), they were said to be *mailige* (polluted), and ritual ablutions would be expected to be undertaken, despite attempts at strenuous reform by non-Brahman movements in south India (M. N. Srinivas 1957, 533).

However, with the emergence of the independent Indian working woman in the public sector industries of Bangalore in the late 1950s, haircutting and beauty regimens for women were normalized by the rise of the "women and children only" beauty parlor, of which Jayshree's choice—Eve's Beauty Parlor—was an early entrant. Until the 1960s, Bangalorean mothers styled their daughter's hair, oiling and braiding it. On festival and ritual occasions, they decorated their hair with strands of jasmine, hair jewelry studded with diamond pins, ruby plaques, and gold kunjalam (bells) in the traditional style known as the Mysorean *moggina jadai* (Kannada = jasmine plait) hairstyle. But with the emergence of the seductive mix of celebrity and consumer culture in the 1970s, every mother who wanted to be thought of as progressive in Bangalore and in provincial towns like Tiptur and Anekal in the exurbs of Bangalore took her daughter to get a haircut in the beauty parlor. These haircuts were in the style of the new film heroines—with a *fringe à la* Hindi film siren Sadhana or a short pixie cut associated with the blockbuster film *Bobby*, known simply as the "bob cut."[17] The turn to style and beauty consumption was seen as part of the new liberalized India where the economy was open to global influences and goods and where anxieties over caste pollution were seen as antiquated social mores.

The breakthrough that signaled this new focus on being beautiful was best captured in Liril, a new citrus-smelling body soap that hit the market in 1975. It had a memorable "fresh" advertising spot that spoke to Indians' emerging bold sexuality and paradoxical nostalgia for unspoiled nature (Mazzarella 2003). In the ad, beautiful young women frolicked under a waterfall, wearing green bikinis, meant to evoke refreshing bathing. These television spots became instant hits, not least for their alluring female leads who came to be known as "Liril girls." Lintas, the advertising company that had brought the Liril girls into people's living rooms, was both heralded and reviled for their "boldness." Timed to air during the family "must watch" television hours—before the blockbuster serial *Mahabharata*—these television ads reached a previously unreachable demographic. The Liril girls were seen as the unabashed, new Indian woman.[18]

By the early 2000s, the cosmetic and personal care industry in India exploded as did the new economy, with new shower and bath products, new toothpowders, pastes, skin creams, hair oils, makeup, and perfumes being produced and marketed at a dizzying pace, often with storylines and taglines about hygiene, beauty, allure, self-care, and modernity. Graphs of growth in these industries doubled every five years, and cosmetics giants started new packaging and product ventures to satisfy the hunger of consumers, who had sharp memories of domestic beauty practices that were laborious and often foul smelling.

The Domestic Practices of Beauty Care

We were sitting in the "hall" (sitting room) of Mrs. Gowda's bungalow in a posh neighborhood, surrounded by her collection of sandalwood figurines and original gold leaf Madurai paintings. The scent of a rich chicken curry wafted around us, and Mrs. Gowda occasionally paused our conversation to shout out directions to her cook while she happily reminisced about "beauty treatments" that she and her two sisters would undertake at home when she was a teenager: the trials of waxing with a homemade melted sugar wax and the hilarious failures of replicating hairstyles seen in fashion magazines with ribbons and pins bought in the local market.

Until the late twentieth century, Bangalorean women often made their own cosmetics, unguents, tisanes, infusions, treatments, medicines, powders, packs, and therapeutics out of seasonally grown herbs, roots, seeds, and flowers. Mrs. Gowda's mother had passed away at the age of ninety-two in 2016. She was renowned in local circles for her knowledge of folk medicine, skin and hair care remedies, and beauty potions. A sprightly old lady, she had thick, slightly gray hair that was neatly plaited; unusual, beautifully shaped hazel-colored eyes that she enhanced with homemade kohl; and soft, wrinkle-free skin that everyone commented on.

I had once accompanied Mrs. Gowda's mother to the *"grundige angadi,"* the local herbal medicine shop, where she asked the shopkeeper to weigh out certain roots, berries, and leaves to make what she called "Deepavali Ausadhi" (Kannada = Deepavali medicine), a rich herbal digestive concoction that she cooked and mixed with ghee to distribute as tiny pellets to her extended family before the big Deepavali feast. She swore it cured heart and stomach ailments. Another time, I watched as Mrs. Gowda's mother made an anti-dandruff hair oil by boiling cold-pressed coconut oil with hibiscus flowers and sprouted fenugreek seeds. In the winter, she made a warming body and hair oil for massage, infused with peppercorns. She was renowned in her family for making her own eye kohl, painstakingly collecting soot from a ghee lamp lit in front of an image of a goddess for several months, mixing with a paste of nandibatlu flowers,[19] ghee, and castor oil, said to be cooling for the eyes.[20] In my few conversations with Mrs. Gowda's mother, she had said, looking pointedly at my flat midsection, that she also had specific medicines for fertility and for pregnant women to ensure a smooth delivery and a healthy baby, as well as indigenous medicines to get rid of unwanted pregnancies.

We continued the conversation about homemade remedies and cosmetics several years later, as Mrs. Gowda got her hair dyed and nails polished at a neighborhood parlor called Yamira parlor. Mrs. Gowda was proud of her clear eyes, white skin and teeth, her long, dark hair that owed some measure to artifice, and her pink lips, "all due to my mother's recipes." She said her mother had had beauty recipes for skin masks and exfoliants, for hair loss and graying, for teeth and eye brightening, and depilation. She had also conceived remedies, as Mrs. Gowda whispered to me, for sexual dysfunction after "men-u-pause," as she charmingly termed it. But all the recipes had been lost when her mother died because no one had thought to write them down. Mrs. Gowda said sorrowfully, "We never asked Amma for her recipes... and now they are all gone!" She clicked her tongue in dismay.

Mrs. Gowda averred that her mother's generation did not visit parlors for the simple reason that there were none to visit, and in any case, women were often expert home beauticians and carers. Mrs. Gowda proudly told me that her mother's kohl recipe had been printed in one of the first issues of *Femina*, the women's magazine. She mourned that these folk remedies had been replaced with mass-produced "herbal" cure-alls and cosmetics: "It's all the fault of these cosmetic companies like Shanaz Husain[21] and that Baba fellow.[22] They want to make money on everything. My mother simply made cosmetics and medicine to give to people."

In 2016, the entry of global cosmetics giant Sephora[23] into Bangalore signaled that the Indian cosmetics and personal care products had matured as a market. In an irony that was lost on Mrs. Gowda, her granddaughter, a well-known model in the city, was featured in the main advertising campaign for the store. A photograph of her, applying Sephora's eye kohl, was all over the city, on billboards and in newspapers. Mrs. Gowda was delighted, pointing out the advertisement on a looming billboard as we drove by: "That is my granddaughter Lavanya! Her sister is Sukanya. Both are very pretty, big green eyes like my mother! Lavanya beat out hundreds of girls for the *kankappu* [kohl] campaign," she said proudly. The campaign, built on Mrs. Gowda's granddaughter's inheritance of her mother's unusual green eyes, paradoxically marked the definitive end of the era of Mrs. Gowda's mother's domestic beauty recipes.

"For All the Woman You Are"

The height of the Nehruvian dream of a modern India was in the 1960s, heady days for the new Indian woman. The first Indian women's magazine, *Femina*—which still graced the waiting rooms of several parlors—was written with this "new Indian woman" in mind. Published every two weeks, the tagline was (and still is), "For all the woman you are." Featuring articles on fashion, beauty, sex, relationships, current events (particularly related to women), celebrities, recipes, and profiles of accomplished women, it became enormously popular, catering, or so it said, to Indian women's limitless desire for modern ideas. Many copycat magazines emerged, including *Eve's Weekly*, *Woman's Day*, and *Woman's Era*. They were all huge successes. In fact, *Eve's Weekly*'s soaring profits allowed it to sponsor the first Miss India pageant in 1959. Some two decades later, Jayshree, as Miss Vegetarian, featured as a pageant winner in the magazine.

The rise of these women's magazines like *Femina* formed a part of the economic structural adjustment policy of the Indian state, with the goal of turning Indian women into modern consumers focused on their own embodiment and beauty. The magazines placed a premium on a specific beauty ideal: slim, toned bodies (yet with voluptuous curves), fair skin and shiny and smooth hair, fashionably dressed. That the Indian woman's body was quite unlike the ideal was a "problem" that could be solved through the right products or rituals.

Around the same time, a film magazine called *Star and Style*, home to the notorious gossip columnist Devyani Chaubal, debuted in India. Chaubal introduced a hybrid Hindi-English lexicon for her column to speak of celebrity embodiment, where she distinguished regularly between passionate *"badans"* (bodies) and useless, unsightly *"kachra"* (garbage) women, a language that Radhika and her elite friends still lapsed into, nearly fifty years later. This Hinglish vocabulary dominated beauty culture for decades, infiltrating beauty parlor waiting rooms through the ubiquity of the celebrity gossip magazines. Soon thereafter, *Stardust*, a rival celebrity gossip magazine with star columnist Shobhaa De, started *Neeta's Natter*, the "catty" column by De, an early version of celebrity scandal–ridden digital sheet TMZ, whose brand was a cartoon of a Siamese cat smoking a cheroot and wearing a diamond collar, the supposed epitome of urbane sophistication. De invented nicknames for celebrities based on their sexual appeal or physical characteristics: *"Garam"* (hot) Dharam, *"Lambu"* (beanpole) for the tall Amitabh Bachchan, and "evergreen" Rekha. *Stardust*'s unique language—a *Dhakar* street language constructed to describe sex and body scoops—made it required reading at beauty parlors in urban metropoles in the 1980s. I remember bringing home one of these magazines as a college girl aspiring to being part of an in-group of cool, young things and then being hilariously surprised when my father subsequently quoted a memorable line from *Neeta's Natter* to his bewildered colleagues.

These film magazines changed the discourse around and images of beauty work and female selfhood and embodiment forever. Featuring color photographs of the stars—caught exercising in Goa in the latest gym gear, glamorously dressed at a movie opening in London, or having lunch in Mumbai while wearing impeccable makeup—convinced the newly urban Indian women of the value of looking alluring. The copy spoke of romantic liaisons between beautiful people. It made the case, as it still does today, that glamor was allied with romance, power, celebrity, and money.

"Being Pampered"

Menaka and her daughter Radha, an upcoming starlet in the local film industry, met me at Yamira parlor, where the owner-manager, a middle-aged beautician named Lakshmi, had recently redecorated. Menaka and Radha were visiting for the first time after the parlor's reopening. The parlor was now a crisp black-and-white space, light filled, with gigantic color and black-and-white, high-fashion photographs of Bollywood celebrities—especially hometown heroine Deepika Padukone and Kareena Kapoor Khan. It smelled of new paint.

Menaka and Radha exclaimed with delight at the new interior. They stopped in front of each poster showing the Bollywood celebrities with windblown hair and arched eyebrows, pouting seductively at the camera. I noticed that the red border of the posters perfectly matched Kareena's bold red lips. The photo captured her kinetic energy and was alive with emotion and light. Above the poster hung a misspelled sign that read, "Yamira Salon: Any thang is possible!"

Menaka examined the close-up of Kareena Kapoor Khan intensely, particularly her hair: "I love her highlights, auburn, like. Can you do for me?" Lakshmi replied, "Yes, madam, why not?" Radha, on the other hand, was more concerned with eyebrow shaping, comparing one celebrity's face with another, commenting on Kareena's thin, arched eyebrows and Deepika's fuller ones. Radha pointed out to Menaka, "See, Mama? Kareena has used eyebrow pencil gel. Wonder which type? Do you think these eyebrows will suit me?" Menaka turned her attention to comparing eyebrows, suggesting that Kareena's face was "more open" because her eyebrows were sculpted thinner, whereas Deepika's thicker eyebrows were "more modern looking." Lakshmi chimed in with her opinion: "Everyone doing thicker eyebrows now, putta [Kannada = child]! You have nice thick brows. Will come

FIG. 1.2. Headshot of Bollywood star Kareena Kapoor, set as Menaka's cell phone wallpaper in 2004

out well!" Radha then added, "I really like her eyelashes. I wonder where she got them. They look so real!" Lakshmi said, "London only! Or Dubai. Here in India, we don't have so natural-looking glam ones!" Menaka and Radha both nodded sagely.

For beauticians like Lakshmi and clients like Radha, being glam is a necessary, if difficult to capture, condition of womanhood. It is created by attention to beauty work, including minute changes to eyebrows, eyelashes, skin brightener, lip gloss, and eye shadow, among other treatments, as well as fashion choices and practices. Being glam is an ideal that beauticians and clients collaboratively work toward. Radha explained to me that being glam was a condition that enhanced beauty but that beauty was not required for glamor. Menaka disagreed and felt that beauty was a necessary condition. It was clear in this debate that glamor was enhanced beauty, and it highlighted a woman's capacity for allure and bewitchment. From Menaka, I understood that the goal of being glam was ravishment, a feeling of delectation and ecstasy that natural beauty could provoke but that women could enhance and control through beauty practices and aesthetic choices. This feeling of ravishment is the overflow beyond the innocent persuasiveness of beauty, toward the conscious bewitchment of the alluring.

When I asked what "glam" implied, Menaka suggested that it required, at the very least, an obsessive focus on the effect that body and face can create. Practices enhancing beauty such as regular waxing, threading, facials, skin lightening, hair coloring, manicures and pedicures, and hair and skin care were mandatory. But glam implied "extra," as Menaka said, such as professionally applied "natural looking" makeup, including possible hair extensions, fake eyelashes, laser hair removal, anti-wrinkle treatments, and more invasive treatments like plastic surgery and Botox. According to Menaka, "glam" is what the Bangalorean socialite circuit aspired to, what she called "page-six types" (from the celebrity pages of the *Times of India* newspaper). She herself, she confessed, sometimes got "glammed up" when she went to a dance festival or a modeling gig and that this involved an entire day at the salon.

One day, she detailed for me via WhatsApp the time and practices she undertook in the parlor to be glam for a recent celebrity party, which she called "D-Day." Madhu added that to look glam, one "absolutely needed" the right fashion and "tons of jewelry" of the "classy" kind. Glam, therefore, is an intentional crafting of a sophisticated and beautiful image. Cynthia Packert (2010, 48) notes, in her work on temple decoration and aesthetics, that beautification is important, for "love needs a beautiful, decorated environment to thrive. Where there is beauty, love and eros will blossom; in the absence of beauty, love will wither." A beautiful and opulent body, one that is glamorous and alluring, indicates the hoped-for possibility of romance and seduction. Menaka stated this emphatically while exhorting me to "take better care" of myself, which she equated with being glam and getting pampered. "You must, T! See me? Even if I have no reason, I'll go to the parlor and get glammed up! Makes you feel good, na? Maybe even gets me a guy!" Menaka said happily, settling into a salon chair at Yamira. "Anyway, guy or no guy, I *love* getting pampered. Ask anyone. Sometimes I come here simply for myself to get pampered even if I have nowhere to go, no modeling, no get-together, nothing! There is too much tension in my life, so I'll come to the parlor, get a nice head massage, mani-pedi, and henna wash and all that, and relax *fully*! It's my me-time for just myself. It's *so* worth it, you know?"

Menaka's pleasure in getting pampered and looking glam begs the question, Is beautification an "art of disguise" where women cover up their defective

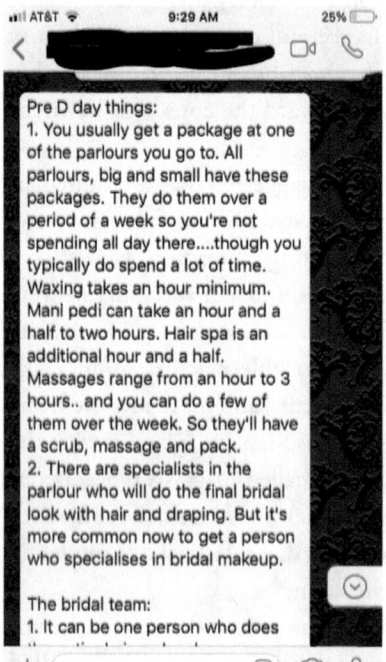

FIG. 1.3. Madhu's WhatsApp text with details of beauty rituals before an event like a wedding

bodies (Bartky 1990, 71), or do they beautify themselves as a form of self-expression and self-care, to be desirable and desiring (Cahill 2003, 45)?

The Pedagogy of Beauty

I realized in watching Menaka and Radha's analysis of the celebrity posters at Yamira that one can learn the aesthetic qualities and processes that make one alluring through mimicking the beautiful and glamorous in a conscious espousal of modernity and show of sexual sophistication that renders women high status in a status-conscious society. Middle-class women such as Radha and Menaka see celebrities as the ideal embodiment of cutting-edge fashion and beauty, and the degree to which they themselves are intoxicated by the posters is an acknowledgment of the power of such allure.

For Menaka and Radha, the posters of Deepika and Kareena can and should be read as a manual. The autogenesis of the posters distinguishes their minute, yet significant, details, leading the women in the parlor to look repeatedly for what they can learn about the beautiful image and how to re-create a satisfactory surrogate from the posters. But I was puzzled: What distinguishes the right details from the wrong ones? What makes for "correct" beauty?

The way Menaka and Radha understand the posters is as an image chronicle from which they draw lessons on how to lead the viewer's eye toward the conclusion of allure, through minute details of eyebrow arch, lash thickening, removal of facial hair, lip enhancement, and so on. Radha asserted that none of the details should be overwhelming, lest they "take over," and "anyway [she insisted], you don't want people to know." Menaka highlighted bindi placement and lipstick color as "very important" to gently lead viewers to the desired effect of allure.

Many clients make the case that the earlier one is exposed to the power of beauty work in manufacturing allure, the better one can achieve the desired effect. In fact, women like Menaka create an embodied form of an ethical subjectivity. The beautiful and alluring woman is a good and respectable woman, one worthy of care and love. She is the epitome of high status, exhibiting just the right amount of radiant, hairless skin and glossy hair, dressed in much admired clothing. Her bodily representation suggests that ethics expand from her body to the body of the nation-state making for an ethical society, forming a great and good Indian nation, the image encapsulated as Bharat Mata. For women like Menaka, to be alluring was to be ethical and worthy, and the sooner one learned these practices and skills, the better.

Menaka said wistfully, "I pestered my mother to go to the parlor when I was twelve, but she said I was too young. At thirteen, I told her I was going with my aunt, but I went off all by myself." She said she felt "good" about her decision because without going to the parlor, she would have never known about "maintenance," which she believed kept her youthful allure intact for longer and made her both noticeable and ethical. "See, T, if I don't go to the parlor, no one will give me a modeling contract, and then what will I do? Also, my women's group, na? I have to meet people, politicians, business guys, and all. Can't go looking like shit! They'll think I'm some useless person. Who will give money, then? So I go to the parlor, get nicely done up, and go and they give and give. Hundreds become thousands, and thousands become lakhs!" she trilled happily.

Alluring Problems

As I followed Menaka, Madhu, and Radha to the parlor, I found that women threaded their eyebrows into perfect arcs and wore glittery bindis to showcase their eyes, yet they frequently averted their eyes during personal interactions, looking at the ground. They wore bright lipstick but covered their mouths when they giggled for fear of looking wanton. Rajeev's pet peeve was that in imitation of Bollywood heroines, women often wore backless sari blouses and draped saris to show off their bodies. "Sari used to be modest dress," he grumbled. Yet these same women, he said, cried foul when a man catcalled them. All of this, however, spoke to a need for sexual modesty and appropriateness, particularly for middle-class clientele of the parlor. Privacy and modesty are safeguarded in India through practice, dress, comportment, and proxemics signifying a woman's innocence and moral worth in spite of her allure. The objective is to look alluring without being seductive, the latter of which connotes sexual promiscuity and adventurousness, and to be a good woman, an ethical subject, yet capable of attracting attention.

Of course, the danger is that this simple moral dichotomy between good and bad girls, which in the West is presented as the Madonna-whore syndrome, seems to suggest good equals purity and bad equals sexuality, but in reality, both men and women in Bangalore see the practices of allurement in complex ways, indicating an interwebbing between allure and moral positioning. Allure is multifaceted and ambivalent, shifting between assent and dissent, seduction and decorum.

The Allure of the Historical

Mythical and modern aesthetics provided the logics for glamor in the parlor, allowing Indian women to be both ultra glam *and* Indian, transecting two selves that are seen, theoretically at least, as mutually exclusive, radically separate. Interestingly, sartorial choices, mythical or modern or a combination of the two, offered choices that inflected glamor.

According to Menaka, for marriages, festivals, and family parties, "full ethnic looks" with "designer *ghaghra choli* or *kanjeevaram* saris with strappy blouses," "dewy makeup looks," "heritage jewelry" including traditional *maang* hairpins and bangles, and a mandatory bindi worked together to create the mythical Indian woman that everyone agreed was "the best": alluring yet modest. On the other hand, Western party wear with short dresses, leather pants, and crop tops were often worn to clubs, bars, "cool parties," or "posh restaurants," where one knew the partygoers and could be reasonably assured that they would not be judged for "being sexy." But Radha, being younger, had a different opinion: "I can wear jeans with crop tops for a party or anywhere, actually, if I go in our car. But nowadays with Indian fashion becoming so glam, we don't need Western fashion like that anymore. I actually wear jeans and

FIG. 1.4. Beauticians threading eyebrows in a small "auntie" parlor

Western dresses when I want to feel comfortable, not to look glam! I much prefer Indian saris with a new style like backless blouse or one that is scooped, or a fancy ghaghra (skirt) with a choli! Looks much more glam, 'romantic ishtyle!'" she said, in gentle mockery of a provincial accent to cover up her discomfiture at using a populist phrase.

By "Indian" in this context, she clearly meant Hindu, so I asked about Muslim women. Could they be glam and Indian, too? "Yes, of course," she replied instantly. Muslim women could also "go ethnic" by following the same simple rules, though their choice of attire and jewelry would denote fictive royal Mughal aesthetic roots rather than mythical Hindu heroines.

But I still had questions: How did these mythical beauty standards come into being? How were they "created"?

Menaka, Lakshmi, and Radha informed me that these religiously based "ethnic looks" had come into fashion in India after Bollywood had rediscovered the royal historical romance genre in the early 2000s. These films expanded on mythical romances, like *Jodhaa-Akbar* in 2008 (a costume drama detailing the romance between Hindu Rajput princess Jodhaa and the great Mughal emperor Akbar), *Padmavat* in 2012 (the overly embellished period debacle, starring Bollywood superstar and Bangalorean Deepika Padukone as

Hindu queen Padmavati), and *Baji Rao Mastani* in 2015 (a magnum opus of the love story between the Peshwa Baji Rao and the heroine Mastani, also starring Deepika Padukone). The costumed clothing in these period dramas, the rich embroidered silks, the ghaghra cholis with transparent netted dupattas that showed the entire midriff, and embroidered saris with bustiers were all deemed both traditional and ultra glam by the audience. Thus, the jewels and clothing, often created by Indian designers like Tarun Tehliani and Manish Malhotra, had leaped off the screen and into haute couture Indian weddings. Designers created a range of "queenly" clothes, allowing middle-class consumers the pleasure of playacting at being the emperors and queens from these spectacles, indicating an opulence and allure premised on an aloofness from the everyday. These then spilled over, in more affordable choices and materials, into provincial markets.

Then, over the past two decades, a generalization of style had occurred in Bangalore and in India as a whole. There is no one style of aesthetic expression that is now regnant. Rather, rigid hierarchies have broken down and a whole series of styles coexist. A kind of aesthetic pluralism has become dominant. Fueled by rising incomes and falling prices as well as more efficient methods of distribution and new product sources, something like a state of aesthetic abundance has been reached from which women, and increasingly men as well, choose alluring looks. I discovered "full ethnic" looks in different modes based on a fashion-consumptive cryptohistory of Indian kingdoms—Awadhi, Rajasthani, Bengali, Mughlai, and Tamil dancer style—which, with many other styles, offered an aesthetic smorgasbord to choose from for weddings, religious festivals, and the like.

Soon after our trip to Yamira, I accompanied Radha and Menaka to a designer showroom. Radha had been invited to wear and promote a ghagra choli set (which included a huge embroidered pleated skirt and blouse) from a famous designer at her cousin's wedding, which would be a huge celebrity affair. She was there to be fitted. She chose a gray ensemble covered in natural pearls and pink embroidery that "showcased her abs" from just below her breasts to her pubic bones, and her smooth hip muscles, which she claimed to have "worked hard on." Menaka approved of the choice, but she insisted Radha add a net dupatta that was supposed to cover her midriff but in actuality covered nothing. "Will look good, sweetie." Then turning to me, she added, "Don't want some randos thinking anything.... Dupatta looks cute but also can cover her, no?" she said watchfully. Radha twirled gracefully in her new *ghagra* (skirt) and abbreviated blouse, showing off her expanse of cleavage and midriff in a stylized mirror, while a photographer got close, snapping pictures.

She then posed in front of the mirror, pouting suggestively, with her fingers in a peace sign, and took a selfie. She was pleased with the resulting image and added, "I don't want to look too sexy!" Menaka agreed, okayed the image, and suggested she upload it to social media, which Radha did immediately with the hashtags #Deepikawannabe #Ultraglam #Desigirl. Within minutes, her post had garnered thousands of hearts.

Menaka's Misrecognition

When Menaka and I met again a few weeks later, she was back at Yamira for yet another beauty treatment. She returned to the story of her namesake, the apsara Menaka.

> *Dushyanta, the king of Hastinapura, went hunting in a forest and chanced upon a group of young women singing and playing amid the trees. Among them was a radiant and alluring young woman named Shakuntala, Menaka's daughter. King Dushyanta fell instantly in love with her beauty and followed her and her friends back to the ashram of Sage Kanva, Shakuntala's adoptive father. He courted Shakuntala and married her in the "Gandhara style"!*
>
> *Soon after, Shakuntala became pregnant with his child, but Dushyanta had to leave the forest and return to Hastinapura to take care of affairs of state. He asked Shakuntala to join him after the birth to become his queen and gave her his royal signet ring which would guarantee her entry into the palace. The ring was a token of recognition.*
>
> *A few months later, as Shakuntala was daydreaming of Dushyanta, the anger-prone Sage Durvasa arrived at the ashram. Lost in her daydream, Shakuntala failed to be adequately hospitable to him, so he cursed her to be forgotten by the person she was dreaming of, as she had forgotten to look after Durvasa.*
>
> *Soon after, Shakuntala lost the king's signet ring while bathing in a stream. Later, Shakuntala's royal baby was born, and she named him Bharata.[24] She was delayed for several years from leaving for the capital, and when she arrived at Dushyanta's palace with her young boy, the king failed to recognize her and treated her shabbily. Shakuntala was heartbroken and left the city to return home to the ashram with her son.*
>
> *But miraculously, a fisherman then arrived at court with the king's signet ring. When questioned by guards, he said he had found the ring in the stomach of a fish he caught from a stream—the very stream where*

Shakuntala bathed. Instantly, Dushyanta recognized the ring and remembered Shakuntala. He journeyed to the ashram to bring to the capital his "true wife," as Menaka termed it. They were reunited, and she introduced him to their son, Bharata.

"Bharata is where we get the name for Bharat. India," Menaka reminded me, linking beauty, misrecognition, and the nation in one fell swoop.

The point of the myth, immortalized by the Sanskrit poet dramatist Kalidasa in the drama *Abhijñānaśakuntalam* (The recognition of Shakuntala), is that the beautiful heroine was forgotten despite her beauty and allure because of a powerful curse. Misrecognition is the pivot around which the narrative tension of the play is built. But this misrecognition enshrined Shakuntala more firmly in the cultural imagination. Recognition, particularly after the tragedy of misrecognition, pivots the narrative toward affirmation of a better self, a morally upright personhood, an ethical trope that invests many ancient myths and stories and also contemporary political discourses of identity. Indeed, feminist readings of the myth suggest that Kalidasa introduced the curse and the token signet ring to excuse the king's caddish behavior in forgetting his forest liaison (Panjwani 2000).

Menaka, however, briskly recast the myth to have a more instrumental and instructional world-affirming end. In her telling, Shakuntala was forgotten because of her fading allure and lack of self-care. She saw in the story a parable for women to "take care of themselves," otherwise "everyone will forget you." A self-confessed "parlor addict" who was "hooked on" the techne of *shringara*, or beauty rituals, Menaka was quick to note that it would not have made sense for Shakuntala to be forgotten as she was "so pretty." "The problem," she diagnosed, "is that she forgot to take care of herself. She thought her beauty would just stay!" She emphasized the point: "If you don't do maintenance to look glam these days, you'll be forgotten, just like that by husband, friends, everyone." She snapped her fingers to indicate the sudden frailty of memory. For Menaka, Shakuntala is twice forgotten, misrecognized, cursed to be lost by her royal lover *because she loses her beauty*.

Beauty and allure have temporal limits, and Menaka saw the myth as instructing women about the dire consequences of throwing away their gifts through negligence: the loss of power and status, being forgotten, being indigent, being rendered marginal and erased. "When you are feeling and looking glam, you have to work *phataphat* [Hindi = speedily]! Hook a guy, get a contract, whatever!" A narrator like Menaka makes the myth recognizable as a life script, not as a charter for living that certified social arrangements, as Bronisław

Malinowski would have it, but as an interdiction, an anti-charter that strategically allowed for autonomy. In this sense, Menaka's understanding of the usefulness of myth afforded a real-time critique of Malinowski's normative theory of myth as offering information about how a society should function. For her, myth and its telling was endlessly creative, poetic, malleable, and appropriate to the everyday, encapsulating the ability to create an ethical and beautiful selfhood. For Menaka, the Shakuntala myth was no social critique called to life by the telling of the story of a social order in which women needed the recognition of men. Rather, the myth was revelatory in the sense that it was a reminder to all women to be careful of the draining of their looks as they aged, for beauty, enhanced by embodied care, was one accepted avenue by which social recognition and the access and success of crafting beautiful bodies and ethical selves that followed it was gained.

Menaka marshals the Shakuntala myth as the affirmation of allure in the search for access, status, and recognition as a modern Indian woman. But this also suggests something more complex about myth, that women offer the stories of the goddess as templates of beauty and how to be beautiful but also reinterpret these stories to construct a meaningful self-narrative. They draw on narratives within the culture to gain social and cultural recognition and to inscribe themselves in culturally accepted plots. This strategy is aptly described by Margaret Somers (1994, 606): "We come to be who we are (however ephemeral, multiple and changing) by being located or locating ourselves (usually unconsciously) in social narratives rarely of our own making." Judith Butler (2001, 26) makes a similar point when she says, "The norms by which I seek to make myself recognizable are not precisely mine." As Butler rightly notes, this "dispossession of perspective" haunts the singularity of the story of self. Stories from which we draw our self-narratives are rarely of our own making. They rely on the constructs of the social world within which we inscribe ourselves. Indeed, these constructs form the structure of the stories we tell. By using these constructs, the mythological archive becomes an exteriorization of internal states allowing both for an illustrative amplification of the women's ethical questions and ground on which to construct a telling of the self. So narrative practice lies at the heart of self-construction (Holstein and Gubrium 2000, 103). While the social narrative provides recognizable plot points and character frames for a self-narrative, it is the women who turn them into scripts for selfhood, knitting myth and interiority into a whole.

Living to tell the tale here is understood in the most basic sense as an act of women's survival, not only as the object of a story but as its curator as well. In that sense, this idea of myth shares its form with that most ancient of storytelling forms—the endless story—immortalized in the West in the Orientalist trope of the *Arabian Nights*. The telling of the endless story in fiction was often a strategy of female survival and a lens by which the ontology of both being a woman and the divine feminine are illuminated. I argue that these survivalist narratives allow Bangalorean women to craft a self in the beauty space, to see their lives in both retrospect and prospect, to form ethical horizons, and to link aspirationally to divinity.

Women like Menaka deploy articulations of their personal search for meaningfulness through self-narratives and myths that ossify around beauty as a resource for identity construction and Goffmanian impression management. But the question that remains is, does myth merely describe acts of recognition, or can it go further and provide recognition? For Menaka, as for many women in Bangalore, recognition by society affords one access and power, and it is rooted in being alluring, in caring for one's body and remaining youthful. Over FaceTime, Menaka looked appraisingly at my graying hair: "Looks good on you, T!" she said. "But for me, no way, haan? I cover it up, like that!" And she snapped her fingers to indicate the rapidity of her response.

I remembered that first day at the café, when Menaka finished her coffee and chocolate pastry, picked up her phone, ran her hand through her hair, tousling it, and popped her Chanel sunglasses on her face, suggesting that our meeting was ending. "Are YOU ultra glam?" I asked her hesitantly, expecting a negation. "Of course!" she shot back, tossing her head. "Can't you tell, dahling?" she chuckled.

Rejuvenate. Brighten. Radiate.
Cut. Colour. Cure. Culture!
—Bounce Salon, "Our Story"

All ladies like skin to be fair.
—Layla

2

RADIANT

Touch and Glow

I was waiting at Touch and Glow, a parlor in an upscale suburb in north Bangalore, for Madhu, the real estate developer and sometimes model. Layla, a young, beautiful Gurung tribal beautician from the Northeast of India, was washing her hands while waiting for Madhu to arrive. Madhu had booked the "regular" facial and "skin brightening" treatment that she had every six weeks. The parlor was close to her office, and she could stop by between work appointments.

Madhu arrived in her conspicuous red Honda and took a practiced selfie, pouting in front of the purple billboard that stood in front of the salon. The billboard advertised a skin cream, with an image of a beautiful lotus flower with a droplet of water on one of its pristine pink petals. I had seen similar advertisements elsewhere in Bangalore. The copy on the billboard exhorted women to "find the goddess within!" a clear link to Lakshmi, the fabled goddess of wealth, whose seat is the beautiful and fragile lotus flower.

Madhu entered the salon, and I asked her about the billboard. She responded, "The ad on the hoarding? I modeled for that skin luminosity cream! I totally used my Insta to push it, and they paid me so little! But it's not a bad phyto luminosity cream. And anyway, e-v-e-r-y-o-n-e wants the glow, right?" I looked at the billboard again. The Lotus Phyto Cream promised a "blemish-free" complexion. Madhu continued talking, adding that in India, brightening one's skin was a necessity because of the pollution of Indian cities: "Sun and the pollution totally clogs your pores and makes your skin dirty and dark, you know?"

As if on cue, Layla began Madhu's facial. She turbaned Madhu's silky hair away from her face, dipped two cotton balls in cucumber water and covered Madhu's eyes. She cleaned Madhu's makeup off with micellar water that smelled of cherry and then cleansed Madhu's skin with a milk cleanser, paying particular attention to any blemishes or pimples, which she dabbed with sandalwood and witch hazel paste. She touched the skin on Madhu's cheeks and commented on its softness and fairness. Then she threaded Madhu's upper lip while she set a steam machine to open Madhu's pores. Layla then bent double over Madhu's face with a magnifying glass to remove blackheads with a stainless-steel tool. This took some time. Afterward, she closed Madhu's pores with a cotton pad dipped in rosewater. She kept up a running commentary throughout so that I could follow what she was doing.

After a few minutes, she applied a thick coat of "brightening" cream and let it sit for five minutes. While waiting, she massaged Madhu's shoulders, neck, and decolletage with some more brightening cream and her feet with a richly scented balm. "Why so many brighteners?" I asked. Madhu rolled her eyes at the ridiculous question: "Makes the skin look good! And the brightening facial makes my skin glowing and . . ." she tailed off. "Fair?" I asked. She looked discomfited but said reluctantly, "I don't care for fair or dark; it's just better . . . keeps the skin shiny, light, hydrated, with a glow!" Seeing herself as liberal and modern, Madhu had clearly been upset by the politics of the color question. Layla jumped in, "No one wants to be dark, no?" There was a heavy silence. Layla added, "Dark skin, like patchy-patchy, is not nice, madam." Madhu spoke up, "If I have dark patches on my face at a photo shoot, then finished! People will think I'm simply useless! They won't book me as a model at all! Even skin tone, no?" Layla nodded, adding, "No, no, madam, we'll give you total glow only!"

After this interaction, I wondered why was Madhu upset by my questions around skin brightening? Why is dark skin "not nice" and evidence of being "useless"? My thoughts veered, trained as I was in the West, to the structural inequalities of colorism and race politics. Madhu's discomfort with the discourse of color and race gestured toward the popular but mistaken conflation between race, color, and caste in India as well as toward a well-intentioned liberal critique of color and casted politics.

But Madhu was not alone in her desire to lighten her skin. Even reputable newspapers made the hidden case for skin brighteners as combatants for air pollution: "Our skin is exposed to pollution, dirt, dust, sun rays, and the cruel climatic conditions almost daily. All these factors prompt dull, dry and imperfect skin. However, the dark spots and bluntness [sic] on our skin can be diminished by using a good quality skin brightening cream." Skin brightening, a code for the lightening of skin and body hair, seemingly to combat rampant pollution,[1] was the order of the day.

According to Bangalorean women, radiant skin is supposedly a defining attribute of the goddess Lakshmi and other domesticated and beautiful goddesses. Lakshmi is the golden goddess of wealth, the consort of the protector Vishnu. She is radiant, domesticated, and the personification of the Brahmanic Vaishnavite auspicious goddess. This chapter investigates both the complexity of the cosmological category of radiance said to be an attribute of goddesses like Lakshmi and Saraswati, its earthly manifestation as light and bright skin for Bangalorean women, and the complexities and recognitions of caste and race woven through this discourse.

The following pages will unpack the central historical misunderstanding of caste and colorism and the slippage between them that is concretized into a code where light skin is seen to represent "higher"[2] savarna castes and thus be more morally valuable and darker skin represents "lower" caste or Dalit individuals and is less morally worthy. Colonial-era discourses of the raced and gendered Indian body as inferior have combined potently with caste discourses of hierarchy, crystallizing into a modern secular concept of the overlapping of race and caste in a moral hierarchy (Jaffrelot 2005; Prasad 2020; Banerjee-Dube 2008). Neoliberal India is not only racist, casteist, and color-conscious in unique ways, but this hierarchy is further complicated by class. The class-based discourse suggests that smooth skin, like bright skin, is evidence of greater moral value. The slippages between all these categories—caste, race, class, color, and divinity—not only serve to underscore color politics and exclusion but equally to emphasize the putative connection between lightness and smoothness, coded together as "radiance," and goodness and beauty, all seen as physical attributes of the goddess and moral virtues of women. Radiance (Kannada = kale) is seen as a *moral* value indicating goodness and superiority and is evidenced in smooth fair skin. Thus, I take the women's discourses around fair skin and their linguistic usages of "glow" and "brightening" to think about what fair smooth skin is and does in the contemporary social worlds of Bangalore, what kind of *moral and casted economy* it enables.

As I said earlier, when I began to frequent beauty parlors, it was mainly to escape the confines of the Brahmanical and largely male authoritarian world of the temples. As a feminist scholar educated in the West, I saw the goal of beautification as part of an oppressive heteronormative, capitalist, and patriarchal culture that could become internalized, often imbuing the female subject with unending insecurity (Liebelt 2023). But I also noticed that accepting neoliberal consumer discourses of the beautiful body seemed to obscure other social hierarchies. As Yamuna, a sociologist and gender scholar in Mumbai, said without irony, "Caste is not happening in the parlors, na?"

Yamuna was not entirely wrong. Although caste "was happening," it was unseen because no one at the parlors spoke openly of it. Parlors and salons were seen to be secular and modern spaces where caste did not intrude. Yet caste politics and casted bodies were an indelible part of parlor life as they are of all life in the subcontinent. The aspiration to be fair, linked to being upper caste and living an upper-class, luxurious life, is supported by people of all classes, castes, and skin tones.

The Question of Fairness

From matrimonial advertisements in the newspapers to elderly women advising young women to apply pastes and unguents to make their skin "whiter and smoother," an aspiration to light skin is everywhere in India.[3] Having a "wheatish complexion," as the matrimonial advertisements would call it, is a sign of being less desirable. Unsurprisingly, the fairness cream industry was estimated to be worth US$432 million a year and growing by a whopping 18 percent in 2010. It has only doubled in the past decade. The popular pink tube of skin bleaching paste, Fair & Lovely (recently renamed the more politically correct "Glow & Lovely"), has dominated the Indian cosmetics market for over fifty years, capturing more than a 50 percent share of the lightness cream market.[4]

Indeed, as Anaka Kaundinya states in her study of Fair & Lovely's effect on Indian women's psyche, the skin lightening creams were seen as an "elixir of improbable existence." The tube promised that the dark skin that relegated women to being "underachievers" would be banished. As she suggests, "Fair & Lovely, by being at the helm of a new industry of promised quick fixes, had poised itself as our messiah; and we would take any chance we got to escape

FIG. 2.1. Billboard advertising Fair & Lovely skin cream in the outskirts of Bangalore

our pathetic, seemingly pre-decided fate—that of failure in love and work."⁵ Today, Fair & Lovely is voted as the eleventh most trusted brand in India.

The toxic trail of lightening creams across the world continues to grow. In June 2017, research firm Global Industry Analysts released a report projecting that global spending on skin lightening will triple to US$31.2 billion by 2024. India and China have the highest estimated growth rate, but robust markets exist across the Middle East, Africa, Latin America, and the Caribbean—in Jamaica, Rwanda, Ghana, Pakistan, Mali, Nigeria, and more.

And their growth metric does not take into account the many skin and hair treatments for radiance in local parlors all over India. Fair skin, now known in politically correct language as "nice complexion" or "skin tone," is allied with smoothness of skin and hair. Practices of skin lightening and brightening, allied with smoothness of skin and hair, form the ground on which gender and caste play out and where the moral economy meets the sexual economy.⁶

Being fair is a valued attribute for men and women alike in Bangalore but more so for women. Mrs. Iyengar, Madhu's grandmother, frequently commented approvingly on women's light skin color: "*Nodu yeshtu fair aagi iddale! Gauri thara ne* [Kannada = See how fair she is! Just like Goddess Gauri]!" Most middle- and upper-class women in Bangalore guard themselves from the darkening rays of the sun, refusing to go out of the house on sunny days. One of Mrs. Iyengar's granddaughters said that she had stopped competitive swimming because her grandmother told her she was "becoming too black"—"*Kappagagi aagodu* [Kannada = becoming dark]." As sunscreen began to flood the Indian market in the 2000s, Mrs. Iyengar warned her granddaughters to use it daily to "keep their skin nice and fair." On Fridays, the day dedicated to the goddess Lakshmi and to the *sumangali* (Sanskrit = auspicious married woman), she would bring her granddaughters, who were proudly light-skinned, to the puja room after her worship and bless them each: "Someday, may you be the Lakshmi of someone's house!" She fondly called the youngest granddaughter, the fairest of them all, "a little white cat" (Kannada = billi poonai) in admiration.

Color Lines

In modern Bangalore and India at large, colorism has been overlaid onto caste, coalescing into the current popular understanding that dark skin is associated with Dalit castes[7] (Kukreja 2021).[8]

Of course, this also has historical antecedents (Banerjee-Dube 2008). Indeed, the hierarchy of colorism existed in precolonial India, though it arose not from morphological factors like skin color but from a theological idea from the Rig Vedas known as *varna* (literally "color") that was no less toxic, that the various castes came from various parts of God's body which were colored differently and shaded light or dark. For example, Brahmans were believed to have emerged from God's head, which was yellow, and hence they were given a prime ritual and social position in the hierarchy but not necessarily an economic one. Moreover, this did not translate into race or skin color. Even today in South India, many Brahmans are dark skinned, and some Dalit castes are fairer skinned, inverting the expected racialized color hierarchy. Caste and varna were not complicit with each other but existed in a dynamic and sometimes conflictual relationship (M. N. Srinivas 1962). But caste as a social fact was rarely mentioned in precolonial India, and it was the British who converted the complex ranking of the caste system, where race cut across caste and tribal lines, into a solidified hierarchical system of rankings, concretizing the slippage between caste, colorism, and race, making caste what it is today (Dirks 2001).

Thus, by the nineteenth century in India, race, color, and caste had become inseparable. A racial apartheid developed where "black" Indians were often given menial jobs and banned from certain public spaces, while "light skinned" Indians were deemed trustworthy and given responsibility within the colonial administration. This reinforced the idea that white races were superior. The economic system began to favor "upper"-caste people, and soon class inequality became part of the poisonous mix, visible in the interracial conflict of the Abraham family, two Dalit brothers who lived in southern India in the mid-nineteenth century, married Eurasian women, and became wealthy as distillers in the local community (Malampalli 2011). This caste-based colorism did not fall away even when Indians converted to Christianity, Islam, and so on. Caste remained.

So in contemporary South Asia, fair skin is interpreted through both a caste *and* a class lens. The assumptions are that fair skin is the marker of savarna upper-castedness and elite economic status, a symbol of wealth and prosperity, and the ability of the leisured classes to stay indoors, as opposed to peasants who must labor in the tropical sun, as well as being upper caste, a doubled status indicator. Understandably, then, Dalit activists and historians rightly make the case that their oppression is rooted in racial politics and that the central goal is the humiliation of the lower castes (Guru 2009). Dalit scholars see many parallels between Black slavery in the American South and their own oppression, enslavement, and disenfranchisement, particularly in South India (Paik 2022a and b; Yengde 2023).

As Janice Boddy (in Masquelier 2005, 175) notes in her study of dervishes and dark skin in Sudan, dark skin was seen in colonial countries as a sign of degeneracy, a symbol of essential atavism, bestiality, criminality, and dirt. In other words, there was a conflation of dark skin with moral depravity. In fact, dark skin was seen as a tainting, spreading a moral darkness through the body. Similarly, in modern Bangalore, dark skin is allied with dirt and being unclean, which the rigors of caste-based pollution and dirt, *asuddha*, emphasize. Dirt as asuddha is considered to be "deeply embedded in one's substance and nature" in contrast to *suddha*,[9] which suggests embodied, spiritual, mental, ritual, and social purity[10] (Lamb in Masquelier 2005, 207–8). Thus, taxonomizing skin "tone" was a major Bangalorean preoccupation, where "tone" was a code word for a nuanced understanding of skin color as diagnostic to caste, race, class, geography, and ethnicity.

This modern color line follows Indians everywhere, even into the virtual world. On Facebook, a Bangalorean woman confessed in her status post that her "dusky skin" has made her the butt of jokes and insults:

> Like many dusky-skinned Indians I've been taught all my life to be ashamed of my skin colour. I was regularly cautioned since childhood to avoid the sun, never wear black, use skin whitening products, drink milk and do all sorts of other nonsense to achieve fairness. I was once gifted with a tube of "Fair & Lovely" for Christmas. I once succumbed to the pressure and bleached my face till it was raw and bleeding. I've

been the butt of jokes, which I learned to laugh along at even when the punchlines felt more like punches and less like lines. I've been called a crow, black devil (in Mandarin), the N word, gorilla... the list goes on. The sad thing is I tolerated all of it... even thought I deserved it.

In this world, attempting to get fairer skin can be a matter of survival for many women.

A "Glow-Up" at Face

I met Radha at a boutique to shop for cosmetics and natural skin care products on her way home after a facial at a very posh salon named Face! While wandering around the boutique looking for a particular facial scrub that Radha liked, I noticed products made with shells, honey, donkey and cow milk, placenta cream, collagen drawn from various hoofed animals, and eye cream from plant chlorophyll "for vegan anti-cruelty types."

Radha examined each jar carefully. Her skin looked moist and plump, and her lips were a shell pink. She was thrilled with the result of her facial and asked me to take a photograph of her in the small boutique garden so she could post it on social media. She chose a corner where the foliage highlighted her green dress and posed with hands under her chin, tilting her face to the sun. The light left a dappled shadow on her shining skin. She looked young, carefree, and beautiful. She titled the photograph "Glow-up!" and added a sun emoji.

Menaka and Radha talked about "glow" constantly, describing it as a particular type of shine and reflection, parsing it into its component parts: color distribution, evenness of skin texture, and facial attractiveness. Menaka often admired my pale Boston-winter skin when I arrived in Bangalore, complimenting my "rosy cheeks" with "Yeshtu billi aagu iddiya" (Kannada = How white you are) and "pinku, pinku!"

However, after a week or two in Bangalore, rushing around in the tropical sun, she would bemoan my tanned skin, offering generously to take me for a facial. Menaka said that facial radiance creams could "only go so far," and one needed a "good skin whitening treatment" regularly. She noted that it also bleached the fine hairs on the face, making them blend into the whitened skin, and thus removing the need for expensive laser removal or painful and time-consuming facial threading.

But Radha, being a starlet, was even more discerning than her mother, Menaka. She liked her skin "glowy and clean," she said, but was careful that she did not look "oily and shiny" because that looked "sweaty and gross," evidence of a lack of care. One state could easily blur into another if the light hit a person the wrong way, or they were not careful about applying makeup.

One day, Radha told me of her daily skin care regimen, a dizzying process of washing, exfoliating, toning, peeling, moisturizing, and hydrating: the ten-step "Japanese method."[11] She said,

> In this method, it's all about feeding the skin, okay? First, you cleanse with micellar water, then you double-cleanse with like a milk cleanser to get rid of all the dirt, makeup, and the oil, and with Bangalore pollution the cotton pad comes out black! Then you wash and exfoliate, and then you use a nice skin toner spray. I use one with rose petals. I keep it in the fridge for extra tightening and cold freshness. After that, you moisturize twice with a nice cream with antiaging properties. Like, you know, L'Oréal antiaging or something. I make sure to get that serum when I go abroad, like retinol-A skin cream ampules and hyaluronic acid masks. Have you tried it? Nowadays, I also go for a chemical peel every few months. Then I put some extra eye cream in refrigerated silicon eye pads and sit before bed in my lounger with them or else I get dark circles. I then drink one big glass of warm water with lemon before I go to sleep. That's all.

Radha's skin care practice has the air of a Sisyphean project about it, with the gel masks, double and triple moisturizing, and refrigerated silicon eye pads. However, one of her friends, a famous South Indian movie star known for her under-the-covers romps with several prominent politicians, described Radha's disciplined skin routine with admiration as "too good!" Radha also noted the feedback she got from strangers: "When I started the Japanese method, I did it on Insta, and my followers increased by twenty thousand!"

Skin care, as a phenomenon that invites unlimited expenditures of money, energy, and time, has exploded exponentially over the past five years in Bangalore. Menaka and Madhu educated me about vitamins, antioxidants, peels, and acids, although they noted that now with micellar water for cleansing and goat milk–based soaps, even they "can't keep up." Skin care requires constant research and consumer trials to ensure one is getting the best care and the latest product. Beautification requires time and expertise, and it threatens to slip away if one does not devote enough time and energy to its pursuit.

At the same time, Madhu explained the promissory force of these biotechnologies if used regularly: "They help you look glowing! It's not just fair anymore, haan? Fair skin is okay. The aunties all like fair skin, but nowadays everyone who is hip wants 'glowing' skin, the kind that babies and pregnant women have, you

FIG. 2.2. Two cleaning ladies from the Northeast sweeping and mopping the parlor

know? Shiny, healthy, just with that light! JLo has that glow!" Madhu, who had just turned thirty, emphasized the importance of "looking good" or "being glowing" for success in her business, for flourishing as a top-flight professional who could not afford to look "low energy."[12] Regular skin care promised "radiance" and "naturalness," both code words for youth. She said she "indulged in facials and laser skin care regularly," particularly in "hygienic parlors," to prevent her from "becoming a dirty, old hag!"

Aging Beauty

Becoming old and losing their youthful glow was considered an existential problem by Menaka, Madhu, Radha, and other clients. They all agreed that as Indian women aged, their skin became thicker and darker, often in patches around the chin and eyes that they found very disconcerting and unattractive. Menaka put it succinctly: "No matter what you do, after a certain age, your skin starts to look old. You get discolorations and wrinkles." As Susan Sontag (1972, 286) puts it in her essay, "The Double Standard of Aging," growing older is mainly "an ordeal of the imagination—a moral disease, a social pathology—intrinsic to which is the fact that it afflicts women much more than men." Day by day as a woman ages, the horizon of her potential recedes. So to reclaim herself, Sontag asserts, a woman must "disobey convention" (1972, 285).

Menaka looked in the mirror every day and mourned the almost imperceptible loss of her unlined fair face and slim body, seeing in her aging face a humiliation and increasing lack of value. "No one cares for an auntie!" she said to me. When I asked why she focused on her skin specifically, she was clear that skin betrayed age more than anything else. One could stay slim and color one's hair, but it was hard to disguise aging skin. "It loses that glow, T!" she said mournfully. Then with a shake of her head, as though casting off her problems, she firmly picked up a bright red lipliner and applied it, adding, "No matter! What to do?"

Sontag (1975, 287) writes, "Beauty, women's business in this society, is the theater of their enslavement," and "only one standard of female beauty is sanctioned: the girl." Critics of beauty culture, like Sontag, argue that women are not permitted to change with time, are not allowed to cast off their smooth innocence, beauty, and docility in favor of wisdom, competence, strength, and ambition. Thus, women like Menaka are caught in a crisis of their imaginations, pitting their rapidly aging bodies against the expectations of eternal girlhood and desirability.

As long as women are broadly objectified, beauty functions as value and its absence as lack. The beauty industry exists largely to solve this "crisis of the imagination," as Sontag (1975) puts it—the ambient fear that one will be less beautiful in the future, that some terrible consequences will result from a lack of effort and attention. I wonder what Sontag's words mean for beauty as a tool of self-cultivation for Bangalorean women over their lives. If we think of a moment of beauty as a conjunction of aspiration, societal approval, divinity, and self-recognition, does it become more infrequent or altogether absent as women age? Bangalorean women who spoke of beauty were clear that their power came from an adjacency to beauty and that beauty was synonymous with youth as well as divinity. "After all," as Menaka avowed, "goddesses are always young." This is why smoothness and radiance, both attributes of agelessness, are also attributes of the beautiful woman and of the divine goddess. The ethical subjectivity of Bangalorean women, their sense of moral worth, is increasingly tied up in being beautiful and as youthful as possible, an anxious position that the beauty consumption industry caters to. Using beauty as a resource to approach the divine while also navigating the world suggests a difficult balancing act for women, one that grows progressively more difficult as they age.

Gauri, the Radiant Goddess

"Goddesses are fair!" Swapna, a retired beautician and parlor owner from Bangalore, stated emphatically. *Then she told me the origin story of the value of fairness for women:* "See, even Lord Shiva made fun of Goddess Parvati because when she is Kali, she was dark and hairy. He said she was too dark, black she was. He said he didn't like it. When he made fun of her like that, she became angry, and she prayed to Lord Brahma to make her fair. Immediately, she became light and fair with smooth nice hair, so we call her Gauri [Sanskrit = the light one]. We have Gauri habba, that is why. But we ladies are not like that. We cannot immediately become fair by praying to Brahma!" *She chuckled. "It all takes time!"*

In Swapna's theology of illumination, one that many Bangalorean women share, modern Hinduism seems to parallel Christian missionary doctrines that see God as light, truth, and glory. In Hindu thought, the goddess is radiant, light, and fair skinned, epitomized in Karnataka by the Kannada goddess Gauri, whose name literally means "the white one/the brilliant one." Another form of this idea is the radiant goddess of wealth and plenty, Sri Lakshmi. Light is the idea that captures the divine essence. As the light of the world, Lakshmi gives light to the world, the light of life and prosperity. Female divinity is seen as *hiranya garbhe*, the radiant womb, the illumination of fecund plenty. It is no accident that Lakshmi is radiant, for she also gains effulgence from being allied with gold, the radiant promise of prosperity made material, the benefits of her luminary reception. In this popular theology of illumination, light begets light.

Like the goddess, the woman of the house has the power to attract wealth and prosperity into the household and prevent poverty from crossing the threshold (Nagarajan 2018, 58). But Lakshmi does not just arrive; she has to be "welcomed." Flueckiger (2020, 5) has described the way many Chhattisgarhi female householders light clay lamps (*diyas*) and set them outside doorways at dusk to invite Lakshmi to enter and protect their homes, mirroring the illumination and radiance of the deity.

Light is the active quality of a heavenly goddess, offered to her by the Brahma, the ultimate source of light, to satisfy her consort, Shiva. Here, what radiance provides is a theology of illumination that lights up surfaces and, in a deeper sense, offers grandeur, beauty, and glory. While the goddess is light in her essence, she also expresses that light in creation, in grace, in miracles, in the light of heaven, and ultimately, in sheer radiance. This language of light (and darkness) relates to morality in Hindu thought.

It is useful here to consider Georg Wilhelm Friedrich Hegel's discussion of the term "shine," which comes from the verb *scheinen*. Hegel believed that art involved schein and that it was associated with the etymologically related "schön" (meaning beautiful). Eighteenth-century philosophers tended to associate shine with illusion and deception, particularly in discussing the way that painting provided a three-dimensional illusion of reality. But Hegel equated the term "schein" with "wesen," meaning "essence," maintaining that this remained hidden behind a veil of schein, only revealing itself through emergent processes. Powerful responses to shine or brilliance can be observed in diverse ethnographic contexts, as can the notion that it manifests emergent essence. Howard Morphy (1998) has described how, in Aboriginal Australia, the shimmering patterns in bark paintings are seen to manifest and emanate *bir'yun*, the spiritual powers of the ancestral beings held in the land. In Papua New Guinea, Michael O'Hanlon's (1989) work on aesthetic practices records a traditional (pre-ritual) practice of greasing of the body with pig fat to create the shining, glistening skin thought to indicate spiritual power and physical well-being. For Evans-Pritchard (1940), writing about the Nuer of Africa, the shine of colorful body art traditionally expressed the health and virility of the person.

Thus, the association of shiny, radiant skin with the more than human in terms of health and divinity seems to have wide cultural resonance. Oddly, however, despite the social focus on radiant and fair skin as an attribute of the goddess, Hindu texts do not support such a narrow view. In fact, many of the goddesses and gods in Hindu myth are described as having skin as "dark as the night sky" or the "fathomless ocean," an inky darkness that suggests a rich blackness. *Shyamoli*, meaning "of dark color" in Sanskrit, has been used to define the dark goddesses of the pantheon, of which there were many (Mishra 2015, 729). Draupadi, a lead protagonist of the *Mahabharata*, is called Krishnaa, the female form of the Dark One, yet she is acknowledged to be a beautiful, alluring, and powerful queen (N. Hawley 2022, 220). Similarly, Parvati, the consort of Lord Shiva, is described as both bronze and extremely beautiful. Finally, Kali's very name translates as "the dark one." Darkness in these ancient Sanskrit texts is cosmological, as mysterious as the night sky. It is considered beautiful, immense, and grand, suggestive of the cosmos and the sublime. Therefore, the focus on acquiring fair skin as an attribute of the goddess is not only a modern misinterpretation of the aesthetic form of the goddess, as influenced by colonial racial hierarchies; it is also clearly inspired by Christian epistemological quests focused solely on Enlightenment-style illumination, as opposed to the divine darkness of enduring mystery.

But darkness and mystery endured in the telling of the stories as well. In the stories of myth that women like Madhu and Radha told and listened to in the parlor, where one story linked to another and characters bled across stories and through the intersections between one story and another, I realized that the stories were nested, one within another like a series of Russian dolls. Each story drilled further down into the characters' abilities, kinship, karma, previous incarnations, and so on. With these nested stories, motivations became mysterious and storylines became blurry. Without helpful character and plotline Wikipedia pages, it was hard to keep track of storylines and characters and their relationship to one another. Although the broad outlines of the myth were familiar stories that most women knew, I found that the narrative arc of one story tended to blur into another and the finer points get lost in the telling. Mystery was thus an enduring part of the nested stories and more importantly of their telling.

I was irritated by the fact that the distinctive details often faded, the telling was imprecise in my thinking, and these "problems" were brushed off by the women as being of no consequence. Would the stories not be mistold? Would the outlines of the myths not get blurred and confused? When I nigglingly tried to keep the story within the confines of a rational telling where the illumination of the narrative and the character were central in a Enlightenment style, the women withdrew. I was puzzled until I realized that part of the creativity of the nested stories was that new details emerged in each telling, giving the women agency to reinterpret the story as they willed it. They could tell into being a reality that did not quite exist and all could be reinterpreted toward a new, more contemporary reality.

Unfair Beauty

In the past decade, there has been growing resistance to the idea of bleached skin, both by women in India and among the South Asian diaspora, though none seem to reference or even know about the dark beauty of the goddess.[13] This resistance is constructed as a political campaign that alludes to, though never directly implicates, race. In 2013, the actress Nandita Das, always described as "dusky-skinned" in the tabloids, started a campaign called "Dark is beautiful" in alliance with the Women of Worth feminist group. Her slogan—"Stay Unfair, Stay Beautiful"—targets lightening creams as deepening women's lack of self-worth. Other resistance and activist groups have targeted skin lightening creams in social media. Being in favor of fair skin has been recast by these groups as being "old fashioned" and backward, if not overtly racist.

None of this seems to mean much, however, in the parlor, where "radiant" skin is the order of the day. Moreover, Madhu gestured to another knotty problem one day as she got her face lightened. "It's not only the skin glow, T," she abjured. "It's about being waxed also. No point getting fair skin if everyone can see dark hairs on it. You got to be smooth, too!"

"The Society of Smooth"

An advertisement for a parlor in the local paper in Bangalore put it succinctly: "Waxing is a F#3@ing pain! From your brows to your toes and everything in between, bare it all. Ladies, welcome to the Society of Smooth!"

"Only guys should have body hair," Madhu said firmly. "Otherwise you look like a porki!¹⁴ And nowadays, we have good technology to take care of that problem! Waxing, threading, even hi-tech laser!" An essential aspect of radiance for women in the parlor was smoothness. According to beauticians and clients alike, smooth, light-skinned bodies contributed to a cultured goddess-like feminine radiance, curing the ills of being human, dark skinned, and hairy. The franchise salon Bounce's "motto," visible in their ubiquitous advertisements in local newspapers and on the walls of their many franchise establishments, elucidated this connection clearly: "Rejuvenate. Brighten. Radiate. Cut. Colour. Cure. . . . Culture!"

Conversations around brightness were often full of tips for better and cleaner depilation: skin dermabrasion, tweezing eyebrows, and threading away wayward chin and mustache hairs—to make oneself ever brighter, smoother, and more recognizable as a woman and therefore more desirable. Smoothness is so akin to the feminine body that men in North India who are perceived as being overly feminine are referred to derogatorily as *chikna* (Hindi = hairless, also a synonym for a girl), a deep questioning of their maleness.

When I described hair removal techniques in the parlor and how painful they seem, my mother recounted how her aunts, many born in the late nineteenth century, used ash from the cooking fire to get a grip on their chin hairs, giving them a sharp and painful tug to remove them. Mrs. Iyengar and Jayshree, the Eggplant Queen, noted domestic techniques in their childhood and teenage years that included rubbing one's body with turmeric paste, which was a natural depilatory. However, it left a yellow trail, which Jayshree thought looked uncouth and which she associated with the backwardness of village life.

Nivedita, my feminist scholarly friend, pointed out that in North India, particularly in Delhi where "Punjabi women" were often "hairier," turmeric paste was mixed with kaolin clay colloquially called "Multani mitti" (Hindi = the mud of Multan) and used as a depilatory and skin lightener all in one. She added, "In the villages around Delhi in the 1990s, when I went to college there, I used to see women's faces were raw in their mustache area and between their eyebrows, they had rubbed the paste so hard." I too remembered when I was growing up in Bangalore that I would see older South Indian women with yellowed faces, particularly on their chins and foreheads, caused by the turmeric root paste.

In 1972, when Jayshree went to Eve's Beauty Parlor for the Miss Vegetarian contest, she was part of a wave of new urban clientele who sought commercial waxing for depilation rather than using home remedies. Many of her friends went to the new salons to get their eyebrows threaded and bodies waxed. Some even attempted chemical depilatory creams such as Nair at home. They reported back that the chemical stench of burning body hair was "awful." Waxing thus became the most popular alternative, with many innovations in the technology—self-warming wax, flavored and scented waxes, and single-use strips—replacing the old sugar waxes and cloth strips of Jayshree's time.

In the early 2000s, laser hair removal clinics began popping up in Bangalore. Many of my friends, who were then in their thirties and forties, were tired of a lifetime of waxing and went in enthusiastically for the new technology, though they complained about the expense. They invariably used it for their facial and underarm hair, preferring old-fashioned waxing for the rest of their bodies. By the early 2010s, the cost of laser removal was cheaper and the technology was more ubiquitous. Many of Menaka's friends went in for the full-body treatments, which took several weeks and still cost a significant amount.

When Radha, Menaka's daughter, started to get laser hair removal in 2013 and complained about the pain and cost, Menaka laughed and pointed out that she was privileged to have access to treatments that were hygienic and lasted for life. "Think of your ajji [grandmother] rubbing turmeric root paste on her body every day to get rid of hair!" Menaka said pithily. Radha shuddered, "I'd never do the turmeric paste, all yellow, yellow! Yuck!"

"Silky Smooth Skin"

Every Bangalorean woman I spoke to used the word "smooth" or its synonym "silky" when speaking of the desirable body. Uniformly, smooth skin denoted a body that was feminine. In contrast, rough skin, meaning the texture of the skin itself as well as the presence of hair, was thought of as unwomanly and also uncouth. The following description of an advertisement for a depilatory cream analyzes this fear of the unsmooth: "A woman brushes past her male colleague. He recoils when he apparently feels the hair on her arm against his skin. From the look on his face, it would appear that his arm has been grazed by jute or twine, not just touched by hair. The woman looks ashamed as she is mocked by his companions. The ad is for a hair remover" (Mani 2008). In Bangalore, unsmooth skin and unsmooth hair were both evidence of unwomanliness. Beauticians and clients alike echoed Edmund Burke, who felt that smoothness was an essential characteristic of beauty and that it encouraged tactility, which was almost as important as the visual to allure and appeal. As Menaka put it, "skin must be fair to look at and smooth to touch, no?"

In contrast, rough skin with cracks and blemishes was a sign of a "porki," an uncared-for body, associated with the working poor and lower castes. Menaka nagged her daughters to "apply Nivea cream!" every night on their elbows and heels, with the threat, "You want cracks?"

Smooth, fair, tight skin and silky hair are central to a radiant embodiment. One can get a sense of the immediacy and size of the stakes by looking at Madhu. When I admired her silky hair, she said smiling, "keratin treatments." Her skin is smooth and flawless, rich and creamy looking. "Peels," she informed me, "and regular facials, skin treatments." Her nails are squared off, the cuticles trimmed and painted a pearly pink and creamy white: "French manicures this time, but I think next time I'll go for a deeper color. This is for spring!" Her eyebrows are a perfect arc, rising at a thirty-degree angle from her nose, to end in a fine thread of hairs just in line with her temple, standard for the ministrations of Bangalore parlors: "Threading every three weeks!" Her upper lip and chin are smooth and denuded. Not a hair on her arms or legs: "Full body waxing last week!" Madhu said that her boyfriend appreciated her waxing herself thoroughly: "He says he loves how smooth I feel!"

Desire emanates from this structure of sensuality: an integrated union of affectivity, motility, and perception where smoothness is the desired object, part of beauty. Madhu also believed that this quality of smoothness and brightness made her "more pretty, more girly." The qualities of smoothness clearly gave Madhu a somatic, sensual pleasure of touch that could be experienced and recalled, integral to her idea of herself. Tropological touch and the tactility of the practices in the parlor raise several questions about nonvisual aesthetics. Somaesthetics, an aesthetics of the body, critically reinserts the fleshly body into aesthetics. Defined as the "critical, meliorative study of the experience and use of one's body as the locus of sensory-aesthetic experience and creative self fashioning" (Shusterman 1999, 302), it offers an understanding of this obsessive focus on the smooth body.

Menaka suggested that the obsessive focus on hairlessness as an aesthetic had increased in the past decade to include pubic hair due to access to Western pornography, matched by the enhanced skill of beauticians and the changing technology of the wax itself. "No one has hair anywhere down there in those porno videos, and so boys expect that when they see Indian women... and like good *Bharatiya naris,* these girls all go take everything off... like e-v-e-r-y-t-h-i-n-g! So silly they are!" She said she found the aesthetics of being "totally hairless" alien and disconcerting; "'Cause I'm old, na?" she laughed. She confessed that she herself was "crazy" about removing hair on her arms and legs when she was younger, fearing comments "from other *girls*, not from boys." But she felt that young women today were less concerned with the evaluations of same-sex peers and more attuned to "what boys think." This story within a story pointed to changing mores around body hair that Menaka and her daughters navigated. As beauty rules changed, they felt tremendous pressure to keep up.

Several years later, Madhu, who was about to be married, noted that the bridal makeup package that she was looking into included bleaching of the vulva to "make it fair." Although a regular Brazilian bikini waxer, Madhu was irritated by the new trend of lightening women's vulvas and speculated that this trend stemmed from pornography, "where most actresses are white." "Now not only the face, you have to be beautiful and fair, *down there*!" she said crossly. "This is when beauty becomes a mind fuck! Sorry for the bad language," she added apologetically. "I'm just super annoyed with people's, I mean men, marketers, corporate houses, their obsession with the woman's vagina being white and pink."

Bringing Lakshmi In

Smoothness, like brightness, is a moral value. Smoothness is an attribute of the radiance of the divine feminine and of women who are or are willing to be domesticated. In India, women with rough and tousled hair are thought to be unwell, either menstruating and therefore polluting, or alternatively and more troublingly, mad or possessed. During my research, whenever I appeared at my marital family home after riding in an autorickshaw from one of the temples in Malleshwaram, my naturally curly hair would be windblown. My sisters-in-law and other women of the family, caring as they were, would invariably comment on my hair and try to smooth it out. "Come in.... Why is your hair so khasa pasa [tangled]? Poor thing! Working too hard! Need a comb? I have some nice hair oil." Tousled, unkempt hair was for these women a crisis, needing immediate rectifying, for as Gananath Obeyesekere (1984) notes, women's unkempt hair is often a sign of mental illness, possession, and madness.

Women like Menaka and Radhika would also comment on my tanned skin as I raced from one fieldwork site to another in the searing summer sun: "Oh my God! How can you stand being out in the sun? It's so hot. Look, fully burnt you've become!" Radhika said solicitously, "Next time, tell me and I'll send the driver so you don't have to wait in the sun." Tousled hair, tanned skin, unsmooth clothes were all evidence, I found, of an "untethered," undomesticated, and potentially licentious woman, whose free sexuality would threaten the patriarchal order of *biradri* (brotherhood) which underlay the casted familial and lineage structure. This made tousled hair and rough skin dangerous sexually, deadly to the social order, and in need of immediate domestication.

The social costs of feminine roughness were brought home to me after Mr. Gowda (Mrs. Gowda's husband) saw me for the first time at my in-laws' home. That day, I breezed in after a day in the sun watching a temple procession. I was dressed traditionally in a sari with a caste mark and all the accoutrements of upper-caste married status. Yet Mr. Gowda took objection to my appearance, asking my mother-in-law loudly in my presence, "Why is she so dark, your first daughter-in-law? Dark and thin! Couldn't you find your son a better, fair bride?" Then with a particular focus on my hair, he pointedly asked, "Is she unwell?" which I took to be a question about either my menstrual cycle or mental health.

When I did not deign to answer his nosy questions, he took to chastising me, ending with a summative declaration of my unfitness to the assembled group: "They say daughters-in-law should be like Sri Lakshmi, bringing prosperity to the family . . . but this one!" This absence of bridal propriety was meant to be a cutting insult for an upper-caste daughter-in-law in a Vaishnavite Brahman family like mine. Having marked me as unfit, he proceeded to tutor me on the "proper" wearing of the sari, presumably to make me more womanly. I understood that, for him, the rough curliness of my hair and my tanned skin were associated with dangerous incivility, sexual license, and brutishness. He felt he was protecting my in-laws from social ridicule by instructing me in how to be smooth and goddess-like. In divine iconography, disheveled and flying hair does indeed indicate the demonic and untethered female outside of male control. Apffel-Marglin (1985, 54), in speaking of Devadasis, or women dedicated to the goddess, notes that "single goddesses are often represented iconographically with loose flowing hair, which signals their celibate state." Indeed, it may signal even more their liminal and dangerous status. An early medieval ascetic text, for example, warns mendicants not to beg from a muktakeinoe (a woman with loose hair), a term that could indicate either that the woman has recently engaged in sexual intimacy or has her period (Olivelle 2011, 326). Further, as my

FIG. 2.3. Two beauticians from the Northeast styling hair in a franchise parlor

interaction at my in-laws' house demonstrated, the alignment of sexual license and loose hair were interwoven in contemporary South India. My tangled hair made me a bad wife.

Mr. Gowda therefore was not wrong for urging me to be "like Sri Lakshmi"—well dressed, plump, fair, and prosperous looking—as it was an aspirational goal for most married South Indian women. In his article "Creating Sacred Spaces," Stephen Huyler (1993, 174) writes, "For most Hindus the guardian deity of the home is female. She is envisaged as a caretaker, nurturing and benevolent. Having many names, she is most often referred to as Lakshmi, the Goddess of prosperity, fertility, and abundance, the supreme provider and protector of the family." The goddess Lakshmi, consort of the great god Vishnu, is believed to bring prosperity and auspiciousness to the marital home in the wake of her entry. Even in the early 2000s,[15] Bangaloreans still kept their front doors open at dusk and lit lamps (despite clouds of mosquitoes and deafening traffic noise) to lure the goddess of prosperity into their homes. And married women (Kannada = maduve madidavaru) who aspired to be like a goddess and associated with beauty and divinity, with upper caste and class status, and with the morality of the good and the great aimed to be fair and smooth, bringing Lakshmi into their very bodies and selves.

Draupadi's Hair

Layla was waxing Madhu's "side locks," which I learned was the Bangalorean term for female sideburns,[16] after applying a keratin masque on her hair, when they began discussing a bowdlerized version of the myth of Draupadi, the long-suffering wife of the five polyamorous Pandava brothers and heroine of the *Mahabharata*.

A central act of the epic, a nail-biting, intense episode that features Draupadi and is the impetus for the entire fratricidal war that the epic traces, had been telecast the previous night in the ongoing *Mahabharata* teleserial. Madhu and Layla had both watched it, and it had made an impression on them.

In the episode, which is known in the Sanskrit text of the *Mahabharata* as "Draupadi Vastraharanam" (Draupadi's disrobing), Draupadi is staked in a game of dice by her eldest husband, King Yudhistira, who has already gambled his own life and kingdom away to his cousins, the evil Kauravas. Yudhistira loses this hand as well and thus his wife. In an incredible act of violence, his brute of a cousin, the evil King Duryodhana, leader of the Kauravas, whom Madhu describes to me as "an orc-like guy," demands that Draupadi be brought before him so he can presumably rape her before the entire royal court.

The violence of the act is increased in the Sanskrit text because Draupadi has her period and is in seclusion, dressed simply, her hair in a single plait versus the elaborate hairdo she would have worn as queen (N. Hawley 2022, 215). Madhu shuddered as she told the story. Touching a menstruating woman, who is also a queen, to demean her was the ultimate immoral act.

But Draupadi's strange civil status, being married to five husbands, seems to offer justification for her abuse: "The Scriptures prescribed one husband for a woman; Draupadi is dependent on many husbands; therefore she can be designated a prostitute. There is nothing improper in bringing her, clothed or unclothed, into the assembly" (*Mahabharata* 2: 65, 35–36). Through no fault of her own, her sovereignty and selfhood as a woman and as queen are at issue.

So Draupadi arrives, dragged by her hair, bleeding, and is thrown at Duryodhana's feet (*Mahabharata* Book 2, Sabha Parva, Section LXVII, 21–23). As Nell Hawley (2022, 216) notes in her brilliant reading of the *Mahabharata* text, the focus of the telling is on Draupadi's casual clothing and disarrayed hair, underlining her vulnerability. Indeed, in the Sanskrit epic, Dushshana, one of Duryodhana's brothers, plays on her vulnerability, her clothing, and the untethered hair: "I don't care if you're bleeding, Princess, wear a single cloth. Or wear nothing at all. You were won in the game of dice—You'll be our slave, And with slaves, well, we take our pleasure as we please."[17]

FIG. 2.4. Makeup artist advertising bridal makeup on WhatsApp showing change in skin color through before-and-after photographs

The Sanskrit epic makes explicit that Draupadi will bear the full force of the loss at dice and will become the sexual slave of the Kaurava brothers, "wearing nothing at all in their house," her social suffering visible to all. Her torment and her resulting anger come through clearly in the text (N. Hawley 2022, 225).

Despite her vulnerability, dishevelment, and fear, Draupadi is beautiful and queenly. She demands, with "withering looks," to know from Yudhistira how he could have staked her, having given up his own freedom and rights to become a slave. Yudhistira is silent, unable to respond. Dushasana begins to pull at Draupadi's sari to disrobe her, to shame her yet further. The looming darkness of men's sexual violence and the threat of brutal autocracy emerges in this scene. Draupadi is horrified, but unable to protect herself, she silently prays to the incarnate Krishna for protection. The idea of sustaining law (dharma) materializes itself as clothing, and as Dushasana yanks at her sari, more and more cloth unfurls, protecting Draupadi's modesty. Draupadi is infinitely clothed and cannot be publicly stripped. Tired, Dushasana finally gives up (*Mahabharata* Book 2, Sabha Parva, Section LXVII, 30–35).

Madhu noted that what was important was not that Krishna saved Draupadi, which is what the serial emphasized, but rather that Draupadi vowed to let her hair hang loose until she could bathe it in Dushasana's blood on the battlefield, propelling the story to the epic war. In the cosmological sense, blood and death has to pay for blood and dishonor. And to Madhu and other Bangalorean women I interviewed, this particular detail of Draupadi's hair being disheveled and loose during her assault and humiliation was crucial.

Interestingly, Hiltebeitel's (1988) reading of the text of the *Mahabharata* accords with the women's telling, arguing that Draupadi's dishevelment indicates her state of mind, the fear of potential rape that hangs over the scene, and the social disintegration that is occurring around her. Madhu agreed, making the point as her hair was being laboriously straightened: "As the queen, why would her hair be like that? She would have servants to make everything nice and smooth. But during the 'rape scene' her hair is all khasa pasa [tangled]. It means everything is gone! She can no longer be a good woman because this bastard Duryodhana is gonna rape her! This dharma-sharma is all *khatam* [Hindi = finished]!"

Madhu's mention of Draupadi[18] and her dramatic pronouncement that the episode signaled the end of dharmic life brings to mind the play *Draupadi* by Bengali playwright Mahashweta Devi, a middle-class leftist intellectual and artist-activist who worked with Adivasi tribal women and wrote the play in 1978. The short story pivots around the tribal revolt in the forests of Jharkhand against a system of land expropriation and exploitative labor practices. The narrative unfolds in 1971, a time when Naxal forces were surging and Operation Bakuli (a euphemism for Operation Steeplechase) was launched to "eliminate" tribals from the Jharkhand forests, mirroring the mobilization of the Indian army and police by the then Prime Minister Indira Gandhi against the tribals and Naxalites, in a massive counterinsurgency operation. Entire villages were razed during these "counterinsurgency" operations, leaving few survivors to recount the horrors they witnessed.

In Mahashweta Devi's rendering, Draupadi, the Sanskritized name, is shortened to a more tribalized and familiar Dopdi[19]—a doubling of the heroine in the fortuitous and yet elusive name, the narrator as one of the survivors of such state violence. In the plot of the modern play, a young soldier, Senanayak, a "pluralist aesthete," captures Dopdi Mehjen, a twenty-seven-year-old Bengali tribal woman, wanted by the police, just as Dushana captured Draupadi in the myth. The police inspector has an "irrational fear of black-skinned people" like Dopdi, believing them to exacerbate his diabetes.

In the play, Dopdi has a gender-specific vulnerability greater than Draupadi's menstruation—she is the widow of a Naxalbari revolutionary, shot dead in an encounter with the police (Munsi 2016, 13). Dopdi beats the local landlord because "his mouth watered when he looked at her," his lust apparent. Set

FIG. 2.5. Two beauticians coloring a client's hair

against the peasant rebellions in Naxalbari in northern Bengal, which sparked similar rebellions of landless and poverty-stricken peasants elsewhere in India, the play amplifies the statist narrative that Mahashweta Devi seeks to unearth and destroy (Spivak 1981, 381). There is a deep connection between the men's violence in the *Mahabharata* and the violence of the colonial desire to support an Aryan narrative in India, where the "accretive epic" of war dislodged tribal and indigenous claims to the land (Spivak 1981, 387). In the story, Dopdi is gang raped by the army men. She wakes from a daze and feels her arms and legs tied to posts. She has no gag but is incredibly thirsty. Her vagina is bleeding and her bottom and waist are sticky.

Placing itself within the narratives of exploitation of tribal women, the story centers the use of sexual violence to subjugate and discipline "dangerous" woman (Hiltebeitel 2011). The doubling of the Sanskritic heroine and the tribal one is an interdigitizing between center and margins, the counter of the tribal to the state.

Draupadi is put in a situation of *possible* rape, but in Mahashweta Devi's play, Dopdi, the wife of a single, slain man, gets multiply raped by the soldiers. Draupadi the queen is the pivot point for a violent contest between men and cannot be stripped or assaulted, but in Dopdi's case, the men easily strip and violate her. When Dopdi is attacked by Senanayak, she does not pray for salvation, to be clothed as Draupadi does; rather, she stands naked in her dark skin, demanding to be seen and recognized. Dopdi's essential unsmoothness, her rough skin and naked body, implies the lack of an aesthetic care, attributed to a sign of a lack of civility and therefore of moral virtue and worthiness. It offers the sheer impossibility for someone like Dopdi, a tribal woman on the margins, to achieve the smooth, bright skin that signifies the moral virtue of the goddess.

And yet, Dopdi turns her nakedness into a rebuke, pushing Senanayak to "counter" her, as in a police encounter of torture and beatings. The culmination of Dopdi's story, unlike Draupadi's, is not salvation from violation but a leaning into it, troubling the idea of gendered and casted recognition by the state, as decoupled and unrecognizable. Challenging the common practice of shaming and disciplining of women, this story turns Dopdi's nakedness into a tool of defiance. It highlights women's vulnerability to unlawful violence under the cover of security laws, particularly in the geographic and social margins of the nation-state.

The "Glow" of the Goddess

I found Menaka, her daughter Radha, and her niece Madhu waiting in salon chairs at Yamira. They were excitedly discussing the engagement and wedding plans of Madhu's cousin and their clothes for the various events at the wedding. The beauty parlor workers, Lakshmi, Raksha, and Shweta, arrived carrying bowls of warm wax and mixed facial bleach, which smelled acidic. Suddenly, Madhu stared at Menaka's face intently, and Menaka caught the stare. Madhu explained, "My God! I think you are getting gray hairs on your chin!" They both immediately squealed in shock and horror, and Menaka grabbed at the magnifying hand mirror. "Ayyooo! Yuck!" She then bridled, "Every day I come here to this place, and no one can tell me, or what?" She glared around at the beauty workers who looked discomfited.

To break the tension, Madhu asked Radha if she had been traveling for her modeling gigs. Radha nodded. Madhu said in admiration, "Good planning you did, Radha, last year during COVID *how you went to the parlor and got full laser! Now you don't have to bother waxing everywhere, na?" Radha agreed enthusiastically and said she would not have been able to manage without the ease of her lasered arms and legs. She urged Madhu to "invest" in laser hair removal. "Saves so much time . . . you don't have to worry about wearing a sleeveless blouse or anything!"*

Menaka was still tense as Lakshmi applied the wax to her face. She only began to relax as Lakshmi ripped off the wax and with it her unwanted facial hair. "Thank God! It's gone now, no? Please check, okay?" After checking assiduously for any stray hairs, the beauticians began slapping bleach on Menaka's face with small plastic trowels. They spread it evenly and covered her face with cloths dipped in cucumber water when they were done. The acrid smell of bleach and burnt hair spread through the salon. I wondered how the women could put such toxic chemicals on their skin.

From beneath a facial cloth, Madhu started telling us about an exhibit of paintings she had been to the week before. It was the exhibition of the year, held at one of the premier art galleries in the city and advertised with much fanfare. Apparently, the glitterati of the city had been there.

I started to tune out their conversation and was debating leaving when Madhu suddenly mentioned that she had bought one of the paintings, an image of the goddess Lakshmi, paying thousands of rupees for it.[20] It was an oleograph of a famous oil painting of Lakshmi by the nineteenth-century artist Raja Ravi Verma, who was a member of the Travancore royal family. Madhu said that his original paintings, most of them of mythological heroines and goddesses, sold to collectors at exorbitant prices, often millions of dollars and congratulated herself on her buy.

In 1888, the Gaekwad, a minor princeling of the kingdom of Baroda, commissioned Ravi Verma to paint a series of fourteen paintings on themes of the *Ramayana* and the *Mahabharata* epics. Influenced by European conventions and Indian theater, Raja Ravi Verma did a series, starting with Shakuntala. But soon thereafter, feeling a need to democratize his art and make it more accessible, he turned to oleography,[21] setting up the Ravi Varma Fine Arts Lithographic Press in Girgaum, Bombay. The first oleograph—the Birth of Shakuntala—rolled out on July 12, 1894, followed by images of the goddess Lakshmi and later Saraswati. For the first time, paintings of epic and Puranic stories, which had been restricted to the upper castes, came out of the temples and homes of the royalty and nobility.

Madhu noted that she had read in the art catalog of the exhibit of Ravi Verma oleographs that he often used a young Goan woman called Rajibai Moolgavkar as a model, idealizing her as the epitome of the goddess's youth, immortality, and beauty. In fact, most of Ravi Verma's models, including Moolgavkar, were plump, light-skinned women with dark curly hair, big eyes, and rosebud lips in the aesthetic manner of Hollywood flapper silent-film heroines. He famously set his muses in mythological settings, often in forests or in palaces, and lit them softly, the female body posed in vulnerable ways to invite the viewer into the narrative. His aesthetics cast the divine women in his paintings as "lyrical and sensual ideals" (McLain 2009). The paintings were "frozen tableaus" of mythological scenes and seemed almost to be plucked out of an "on-running spectacle" (Guha Thakurta in McLain 2009, 69).

The beauty of Raja Ravi Verma's paintings and the easy access to them made possible by the widespread distribution of the oleographs that he printed meant that these images were ubiquitous in middle-class and elite Hindu households in early twentieth-century India (Pinney 2004). His images dominated conceptions of womanhood, beauty, and female divinity from then on, even as his paintings were confined to museums and the homes of elite collectors.

In the mid-twentieth century, a common and valued craft among women of elite households was to decorate the Ravi Verma oleographs, sewing on chiffon pieces as saris and tinsel as jewels for worship in the family puja room. My paternal aunt was well known to be skilled at such crafts and decorated both Lakshmi and Saraswati oleographs. Sometimes, in wealthy households, real semiprecious stones and pearls were used as well. Such decorated oleographs had been rediscovered in the early 2000s, rescued from older homes, and given new status in neoliberal India. They were sold by savvy gallery owners as evidence of women's craft, commanding exorbitant prices by neoliberal entrepreneurs who wanted both connoisseur and feminist credentials.

I accompanied Menaka, Madhu, and Radha to several such "champagne showings" as they were termed, often in posh art galleries. They often dressed in "ethnic chic" for these events, wearing silk and velvet tasseled blouses and saris, or heavily embroidered skirts, and dupattas that would be suitable for a film premiere. They also pinned their hair with vintage hair ornaments, known as "temple" jewelry. Art collectors and socialites thronged these events, with many dressed as though they emerged from the paintings themselves.

"I couldn't resist!" Madhu said ecstatically, referring to the sequined oleograph of the goddess Lakshmi she had just purchased. "Like the images in Ajji's puja room!" By saying she could not resist the purchase, not only did Madhu underscore her value as a pious Hindu woman but also solidified her status as a neoliberal elite with good taste. Menaka added supportively, "Totally worth it! Anyway, it'll increase in value also!" Madhu then added as an aside to the room at large, "So beautiful this painting of Lakshmi is. She is standing on a lotus, wearing a red sari, and her skin is flawless! She's wearing all this shining jewelry and beautifully they have done the *buttis* [sequined decorations] on her sari. When you light the *diya* in the room, she simply glows! And the way he's painted her skin. Abbah!! So transparent. It's like a lamp is in her face!"

FIG. 2.6. Printed lithograph of the goddess Lakshmi, by Raja Ravi Verma

Menaka clicked her tongue in delight. "So nice you got it at the exhibition!" Then, in a seeming digression, she added, "That's where Radha wore my new gold backless blouse with that pink Mysore crepe sari for the opening.... I got that new Korean girl, Jyun, to do our makeup, like full natural, just with a nice kajal-style smoky eye! Everyone said she looked like the painting of Sri Lakshmi only!" Then she added to the beautician attending to her, "Don't forget to set the timer for the bleach, eh? We don't want our skin to be all yellow like last time!"

Brazilian Radiance

As the facial bleach set, Menaka added, educating me, "Now we have nice bleaches for down there! Gentle ones," she said. "But first you have to get a Brazilian, of course! Or else you'll be blond!" She slapped her hands together in delight, giggled, and said in self-admiration at her brazenness, "Toooo much I am, no, T?! Even I have tried it, you know. To see what it felt like. I felt so clean!" Radha mimed vomiting and exclaimed, "Mama, TMI! Too. Much. Information!"

Menaka then recounted her experience getting a Brazilian at a franchise parlor: how her beautician calmed her fears and helped her during the initial consultation, and how, just as the beautician had said, she had never before "felt so clean and free." Menaka joked that her beautician had "definitely seen more" of her than her lover had and exploded into a fit of giggles. Then she added that it had become "a habit," and she now went to the Yamira parlor and regularly had her entire body waxed. "Forgotten how it is to have hair down there really! So much easier just to wax and forget it off. Especially if you have your period and all. No messy."

During one of my visits, Mrs. Gowda confessed that her granddaughters Sukanya and Lavanya insisted on going to the parlor "every two weeks" for waxing. Lowering her voice to a sibilant whisper and keeping her eyes peeled for her cook, who was hovering in the background, Mrs. Gowda asked me if it was true that "girls nowadays shaved or waxed" their vaginas. I nodded seriously at her worried face but attempted to put her fears to rest by pointing out that most beauty parlors did so under the most hygienic and private conditions. She waved my comments aside. I clearly did not understand that her fears were not about hygiene but about her granddaughters' moral and sexual lives: "If they do all that, what else will they be doing?"

For Mrs. Gowda, waxing one's genitals is a sign of sexual license, for as she put it, "why else would they do all that?" An unmarried woman who beautifies parts of her body that should not be seen by others is courting a kind of misrecognition as "fast" or might be tempted to reveal these parts of her body in morally reprehensible ways. She may become careless. Lavanya, her granddaughter, giggled as she described her many intimate waxing accidents, and she covered her open mouth with her palm, a very Indian gesture denoting shyness and virtue. In India, women are not expected to laugh out loud with an open mouth, as it denotes a kind of abandon that is viewed as unseemly in "good women." As Mrs. Iyengar put it, while opening her mouth wide to demonstrate, "good girls from good families don't do like that!"

For some, therefore, pursuing smoothness can overflow beyond the moral boundary and, rather than making one virtuous, can make one morally dangerous, straying into a sexual economy where women are radiant but impure. Menaka told me, "This place called Venkat Center, some doc called Venkat and his family they do hair transplants and even do lipo so that you can have a smooth body! So many of the socialites get this stuff done so they can have a model's body. But they won't go here.... They'll go to London, Mumbai, Dubai, if they have the cash." She claimed that she knew for a fact that the Venkat Center offered vaginal rejuvenation or "tightening of the pussy," as she put it. "Feels good for the guy, so all these girls . . ." she dropped her voice another octave, "all these girls go there and get it all tight and nice!" Vaginal rejuvenation and hymen reconstruction are, Menaka claimed, the most valued surgeries in Bangalore. Madhu added scoffing, "See, the ideal woman is still like untouched, a virgin."

Indeed, despite the fact that smoothness encourages touch, for many Bangalorean women being untouched is the sign of a virtuous woman, of one who is sexually innocent and chaste. In a society where romance and premarital sex is frowned upon as a cultural import, politicized by the Hindutva government and its cultural apparatchiks as increasingly allied to Western debauchery and ideas of free sex and love, such "beautification" is seen by people like Mrs. Gowda as despoiling innocent young Indian women.

A few days later, Madhu said she had lit upon a new beauty practice that was sweeping through India, a lightening cream for genitalia called Clean and Dry Intimate Wash. It had been advertised on household televisions starting in 2012.[22] The advertisement showed a woman being ignored by her partner, followed by an animation scene in which the woman uses the product. The scene cuts to her playing with her boyfriend in the "after" scene. Described as "unique," the product is apparently designed to keep the skin "fresh and protected from infection all day" with the added bonus that it will "brighten darkened skin in that area . . . making it many shades fairer." According to Jhuma, this gestured to new directions in Indian sexuality where, she claimed, women, particularly "college girls," expected oral pleasuring and men were "put off" by dark vulvas. Madhu added a trenchant critique of modern Indian sexuality: "How did we get from like Kali and Durga who stood on top of guys and beheaded them and now everyone being allowed to bash us down there?"

Beauty at the Limits

For many women in Bangalore, beauty acts as a technology to enable them to mimic the divine and appropriate divine attributes such as radiance and allure through self-care rituals. This can go awry in a few ways. If a woman does not care sufficiently for herself, with an unsmooth body and dark, rough skin, she is viewed as wild, untamable, and sometimes unhinged. On the other hand, if a woman pursues fairness and smoothness with too much enthusiasm, she can be charged with sexual licentiousness. Overlapping with the hierarchy of casted and classed economies and embodiments, beauty practices fuse sexual and moral economies together.

In considering Menaka's and Madhu's elaborate care regimens, it would seem that they continually strive to make themselves into celestial women who deserve to be cared for, their very attention to themselves demands attention from others—boyfriends and husbands, beauticians, the social world, and so forth. Thus, the point in all cases is not that one ought to be recognized as a woman (in both Draupadi's and Dopdi's cases, recognition as women does not do them much good; indeed, it does them harm). Rather, the aspiration is to be recognized as woman who, like the goddess, is ultimately cared for and therefore elicits proper care, attention, and respect from others.

We must, therefore, ask how dirt, which is normally destructive, sometimes becomes creative.
—Mary Douglas, *Purity and Danger*, 1966

It is amazing how complete is the delusion that beauty is goodness.
—Leo Tolstoy, *The Kreutzer Sonata*, 1889

Not one, not two, not three or four,
but through eighty-four hundred thousand vaginas
have I come.
—Akka Mahadevi, "Not One, Not Two, Not Three or Four," in A. K. Ramanujan, *Speaking of Siva*, 1973

HOT · 3

Cooling Treatments at Glam

Menaka and her daughter, Radha, were in a big hurry. They had stopped by Glam parlor, a small neighborhood parlor, to get their hair henna treatment. It was summer and the sun was blazing down. "Henna is nice, cooling, nice color and conditioner," Menaka noted. She said with a gleeful smile that the smaller "auntie parlors," like "Glam," as she called it, were better and cheaper than the luxury salons for things like henna treatments and that they used purer local ingredients. We all entered the converted garage. Unlike the fancier Senorita or the Lotus, where the salon had a foyer, here the "waiting room" was a small section of the garage separated from the salon area by a frosted-glass partition and some plastic flowers in a plastic vase. The main salon was painted a pretty pink and had photos of Alpine landscapes and blonde women advertising Revlon makeup on the walls. The salon walls were lined with rolling bins with nail polish and hair care products. A small sink stood in the corner.

Menaka and Radha took their seats, and Preethi, the Kannadiga stylist and owner of the salon, greeted them perfunctorily and began mixing the henna in a plastic bowl in front of us. A young client, a college-aged girl in jeans, walked in, pushing through the glass partition. She had a bad acne breakout all over her cheeks. She announced that she was studying for exams and her hair was falling out in clumps. Preethi diagnosed the problem as "heat" (ushna)[1] and told the other beauty worker, a Tamil woman named Dhanu, to give the customer a head oil massage "for heat." Menaka agreed. "Nice massage will cool the body down. Then you can wash and do henna also."

Preethi had the henna paste ready and started painting it onto Menaka's hair. Radha was on her phone, absorbed. Dhanu heated coconut oil in a stainless-steel cup on a small gas stove in the corner and started applying it to the college girl's head with bare hands that were stained orange by henna. Once her hair and scalp were coated in the luscious oil, she began massaging the client's head and neck. The college girl began to moan with pleasure. Radha looked up from her phone, surprised, and shot me a quizzical look. The client sighed, moaned louder, "Abbah! So nice." Menaka looked at me. Radha started giggling. Preethi and Dhanu shot each other looks, and the latter finished hastily. The moaning ended. The college girl sat there, her head soaking with oil, her eyes closed.

Preethi completed Menaka's henna treatment and moved to Radha. As she leaned over Radha to grab her long hair, Preethi's big breasts grazed Radha's neck and back. Radha looked discomfited and smiled at me through the gap between Preethi's left breast and armpit. As soon as she was done, Preethi snapped two flowery shower caps on their heads. "Can go now, madam, if you want. Wash at home," she said and released them. I guessed that this was a routine that many of the habituated clients followed. Menaka paid, and we left.

As soon as we were outside, Radha began imitating the college girl's moaning, and she and Menaka broke out into laughter. Through her laughter, Menaka said, "Be quiet. . . . They'll hear you!" Then she turned to me and said, "So funny that was!" Radha said pithily, "Sounded porno." Menaka shushed her.

The next morning, Layla and I were walking to the Lotus for her shift. As we passed apartments and globally marketed luxury rentals, Layla spoke of the difficulty of finding accommodation in Bangalore for women from the Northeast. "They think we are dirty, madam, and won't rent to us thinking we are 'Chinese.' They say we eat dog meat and will have boys for sex and all."

The street curved, and at the bend, we passed a group of young men with pomaded hair lounging atop fancy motorbikes. Their eyes followed Layla. One of the men, who looked Kannadiga with a greasy pompadour and mustache, whistled a popular Hindu film tune, and yelled, "Arre, Chinku! Sexy sexy! Aati kya

Khandala?"[2] (*Will you come with me to Khandala?*). Layla stiffened and walked on, determinedly ignoring his rising catcalls. Pompadour man revved his motorbike and drove perilously close, attempting to scare us. I yelled at him in Kannada, including a few choice swear words. He veered away quickly. Afterward, Layla confirmed that the young man's reaction was common, that most Bangaloreans thought of her and her migrant friends who worked in parlors as "only good to bang": "They think we only work in massage parlors, madam!"

The parlor is a space of intimacy between female bodies. As beauty workers wax, wash, tweeze, and massage, they come into contact with their clients in ways that are meant to be tactile and pleasurable but can sometimes be uncomfortable on both sides. As we can see from the reaction to the college girl's moans, however, there are certain kinds of contacts and certain kinds of pleasures that are appropriate and others that are deemed not. Of course, it is the specter of sex that haunts the parlor. To maintain the illusion that beauty work is not sensual but diagnostic and technical, both workers and clients must strive to be clinical, to discipline their bodies, and to avoid slippages that reveal the true bodily intimacies afoot. The supposedly sexless intimacy between clients and workers, and between workers themselves, has been largely ignored in the scholarship on beauty. This chapter attends to this intimacy and to the policing of sexual and other indicators within it for workers and clients, to parse the structure and meaning of everyday work in the parlor and its underlying understanding of female selfhood.

As beauty work once took place in the home, close kin cared for one another's bodies in ways that skirted issues of who was touching whom and where. As such relationships moved into the parlor, they became veiled behind economic transaction and expertise. Of course, the Marxian idea that labor transforms selves into commodities to be bought and sold is nothing new (Cohen 1978). Neither is the assumption that ecologies and environments of work shape personhood in critical ways.

Yet parlors in Bangalore added another layer to the puzzle, that of casted touch, drawing our attention to the crucial yet subtle ways in which particular histories of gender, caste, race, place, and religion come to animate what could be glossed as purely economic actions (Besky 2013; Boyer 2005).

Despite this, clients frequently told me that the parlor "had no caste." Menaka said that in "her" parlor, the one she frequented in her neighborhood, "nobody cares about caste and jat, etc.!" On the odd occasions when caste was invoked, it was invariably to suggest that someone was "backward" for caste-ist practices, such as for being sensitive to the pollution of casted touch. For example, Menaka said, "I never go home and wash again after blow dry, etc. Some people do it because of the beautician's caste. So crazy, no?" Then she added explanatorily to her daughter, "It's because in the old days, if you went to the barber, na, you had to go have full bath because his touch was supposed to only be for widows. It was bad!" Radha screwed up her face in distaste. Then Menaka added, "When my grandmother was alive, we all had to do it. We would go to parlor, get hair washed and blow-dried, and totally set to go to a party. But then we would come home, and she would force us to wash it again, and all the blow-dry would go off. So we would try to pretend we had not gone to the parlor and run away to the party before she caught us!"

Regardless of these claims, it seemed to me that a concern for the difference between bodies rooted in caste-based practices of the pollution of touch was at the forefront of the relationships between workers and clients. Sometimes it came out directly. Radha told the story of how she was initially very uncomfortable in the parlor. She was just twelve on her first visit and hitting puberty made her very sensitive to her looks and body. Yet Menaka insisted she go to the parlor and get her arms, legs, and underarms waxed because the "sooner she got used to the pain, the better." Radha wanted to shave her legs at home, but Menaka insisted that would make the hair thick and deeper rooted, and waxing was the way to go. Menaka accompanied Radha the first time, spoke to the beauticians, and got her settled in, but Radha was still uncomfortable. She didn't want her eyebrows threaded like everyone else. "I liked my unibrow," she claimed. I had assumed it was her changing body being evaluated by other women that made Radha uncomfortable, but she corrected me. She said her discomfort was in *being touched* by "all these strange women." Embedded within this understandable discomfort of a twelve-year-old girl not wanting to be waxed by a strange woman, the question of being touched was key. Whether this was a caste-based fear of touch pollution, a strange preoccupation for a modern young woman, I could not immediately fathom. But before I could inquire further, Menaka waved her hand, dismissing in retrospect the sheer superficiality of Radha's objection. "How silly you were! Good thing I sent you. You got used to it, no?" Radha nodded. "Can't live without it now!"

Mrs. Gowda's twin granddaughters also spoke of their initial discomfort with being touched in the parlor, though unlike Radha, they were anxious to get their eyebrows threaded since they both had "bushy eyebrows" and wanted thinner, delicate brows. They had been "pestering" their mother to let them go to the local parlor, and finally when they were fifteen, she let them get their eyebrows threaded. They both spoke of how much it hurt and how strange the feeling was after, yet they both claimed it was "totally worth it!" Menaka said definitively, "You must get trained to get treatments in the parlor. Doesn't come naturally to our kids. They are so protected, so decent. But if you don't do it soon, then it only gets harder." Was a caste-based embodied ethic now transformed into an aesthetic ethics?

These pedagogic practices that Menaka outlined of "getting used to touch" revolve around the distinction I introduced concerning Indian selfhood. As I noted, my work suggests that the women I interacted with in the parlors of Bangalore had neither a "dividual" self that was entirely porous and divisible nor an individual self that was entirely bounded and discrete (Marriott 1976; Marriott and Inden 1976). Nor were they somewhere in the middle on a journey of inevitable progress toward the individual (Englund and Leach 2000, 229). Challenging these notions, I draw on theories of ethical personhood to argue that women's subjectivities are "multiauthored entities" (Finlay 2018) that are worked through in the parlor as women work on their bodies in intimate encounters with other women. Bangaloreans are partible persons who have what I call a composite self, made up of fragments that they suture together. Although it is true that women's selfhood is porous and needs to be protected from pollution and dirt, it is also fragmented, which enables them to draw from various influences. Thus, they are acting as much as being acted on in constructing their selfhood, drawing together influences and experiences to craft a composite self that is contingent and acts differently in different settings, still fractured yet holding together. So a concern with pollution has not faded away; it simply becomes coded in different ways.

Permeability is key. Hindus imagine themselves as having porous bodies that are encased in sheaths (*kosas*) that can be affected by the flows of various substances, such as food and drink but also bodily fluids, dirt and wind, unseen humors, touch, and even memory. What the body encounters enters it and makes its way to the soul (Kantor 2019; Lamb 2000; Marriott 1990). Sundar Sarukkai (2009, 41) writes that the skin is the organ of touch and tactility in both the Western and Indian traditions; but in Indian Hindu traditions, the skin has an important function, "that of encompassing and enclosing," which is inherently related to boundaries and therefore to morality (Guru and Sarukkai 2012). Ariel Glucklich (1994, 90) uses these characteristics to argue for an inherent relationship between dharma and skin since both of them have been symbolically conceived of as boundary. Skin thus becomes a "map of [the] character and moral disposition" of the person (Glucklich 1994, 100), and so the skin of both the upper-caste person and the "untouchable" (*achuta*) person carry with them moral logics and values, most particularly that of purity and impurity (Jaaware 2018, 55).

From birth to death, impurity is the shame to be feared. Touch (*sparsha*) can thus be dangerous, as contact is more than the mere physical. The haptic is the moral; pollution and impurity supposedly imperil the moral self of the savarna or upper-caste person. Indeed, the tactile is more primordial than the visual. The impact of touching is clearly felt differently by the savarna and by the Dalit person.[3] In the former, it is "associated with psychological feelings of revulsion, power, rejection and so on but for the latter it is associated with feelings of humiliation, shame" (Sarukkai 2009, 43). Aniket Jaaware (2018) argues that the operations of the metaphors and metonymies in the functioning of caste as system and caste as practice in India coalesce around the problem of "touch" and the nature of "untouchability" that savarna castes ascribe to Dalit bodies.

In the parlor, touch is ubiquitous and necessary. In thinking about touch in such a cultural milieu, we not only need to consider the staged intimacy between two bodies and the ideal of bodily aesthetics that they try to achieve but also the nature of the relationship of touch between casted bodies in terms of power and its subversion, particularly when a lower-caste body is working on an upper-caste body, as is frequently the case, particularly in expert and therapeutic relationships. Beauty work with its touching of other bodies across class and caste dimensions, its usage of chemicals and cosmetics, and its dealing with "impure" bodily fluids and excesses therefore not only transforms the client but also the worker through the interconnections across the bodies.

However, although touch is a key concept in the parlor, the rejection of the language of caste meant that clients had to find other ways to describe the sometimes uncomfortable presence of the other. Certain workers and clients were marked as bad, being lazy, or "being vulgar," a moral problem. The discourse and diagnosis often coalesced around smell.

Stinky Bodies

I found Lakshya waxing Menaka's underarms. She was stooped over the heated wax strips, carefully separating them. She applied them one by one to Menaka's armpits, waited until they solidified slightly and then ripped them out quickly to prevent pain. She examined each strip after three or four tries to ensure that she had used it thoroughly. After each pull, she placed a cool hand on Menaka's skin and blew on the reddened area to reduce the inflammation and pain. Menaka said she would see only Lakshya for her intimate waxes, "underarms and bikini," because she was "so careful." Lakshya exited the room after she finished the waxing to allow Menaka to change into her street clothes from the towel robe she was wearing. Menaka decided to confide in me her real reason. She said, "I only come to Lakshy, you know why? Because she doesn't have BO! The last girl I went to, no doubt she was too good in the waxing. So smoothly she would do. But, Abbahhh! The stink was too much!" She mimed being in another's personal space, drawing back, and wrinkling her nose in disgust. "Even if she stood away, she would smell so much it was terrible to come to the parlor. We stopped going regularly. . . . How long to hold your breath?" She giggled.

Many of the clients in the upper middle-class parlors I frequented commented on the body odor of beauty workers, and often it was indexed to "heat." Radhika's friend, Aseema, once observed, "Many Chinese girls stink! Must be their food. . . . Makes their bodies heaty, you know?" By "Chinese," women were generally referencing Indian migrants from the Northeast whose body odor was deemed "different," evidence of their fundamental "otherness," and diagnostically linked to their heated bodies. When I asked what they smelled like, many women rolled their eyes, as if to indicate the stupidity of my question. Some said, "You know. . . . They smell different, bad. Even their sweat smells different! Fishy!" Others replied, "Sometimes they smell of blood, you know, like when they have their chums [period]." And some insisted, "They just smell!"

The idea that bodily smells are linked to a moral hierarchy has long held sway over the Indian subcontinent, and considerations of difference in smell underscore the idea of difference and of the widespread exclusion of the caste system in general (Yengde 2019). The question of smellability and odor acts both as a marker of embodied difference and a rationale for prejudicial claims at the granular level and at the state level (Herzfeld 1988). In fact, it is a Brahmanical ideological premise that every caste has its own distinctive, hierarchically ranked "place" in the world and that the places inhabited by subordinate castes should not only be set apart but look, *smell*, and feel differently from those of the rest of society (Lee 2017, 470–71). This difference legitimizes inequality and is denoted by the sensual marking of bodies, a certain "foreignness of belonging" (Roberts 2016, 1).

In some ways, it makes sense that smell would be a dangerous and insidious vehicle for pollution. Unlike touch, it often cannot be avoided. It sneaks up on us, and once a person is aware of it, they have already come into contact with it and inhaled it, making it forever part of their self. Moreover, it speaks of the fleshiness of the body and particularly the distinctive category of heat.

Heatedness is a complex category in India. It is principally a quality of bodies. When diagnostic of bodies, heat (*ushna*) and cold (*sheetala*) are two fundamental and oppositional precepts of Ayurvedic medicine, seen as fundamental to the three humors (doshas) (Rastogi and Singh 2021). Ushna heat is a symptom of imbalance of excessive energy, which needs to be cooled down, else it is dangerous and unstable.[4] In Tamil, the term for madness is *pittam*, the Sanskrit word for bile related to heat (Daniel 1984, 91). Overheating is diagnosed through hair loss, increased sexual appetite, and digestive troubles, and it emerges as smells, noises, and leakages. The idiom of hot and cold is used to characterize types of people, places, times, foods, medicaments, temperaments, and bodily (and even mental) states. The goal of Ayurveda is the balancing of humors. When appropriately balanced, these qualities achieve a proper flow that "takes the form of health and happiness" (Leavitt 1996, 521). Thus, when a body is ushna or heaty, cooling remedies are sought, such as the coconut oil head massage and henna hair pack at the Glam parlor.

Heat as in *agneya*, or the power of fire, is a creative and powerful quality of the goddess, especially the sensual and healing goddesses that exist beyond the staid and pure ideal of the feminine. In South India, the heat of the goddess is transmissible as anger and as power, sometimes as a "forceful penetration" of the devotee's body which emanates in illness such as a pox (Nabokov 2000, 28) but also emanating as an abundance of *ugra* (righteous anger, excess), both sexual and not, that is so creative and destructive that it needs ritual management (Flueckiger 2013) of the goddess's heat as it overflows and threatens the world. The sensual heat of the goddess, her ushna, also makes her difficult to bear as a consort, as with the case of the goddess Tripurasundari of the Tantra tradition, where the management of her passions is at issue (Golovkova 2020; Lange 2022). Most of the Hindu women of the Northeast, and even some of the Christians, like Tanya and Mary at the Lotus, pray to the goddess Kamakhya, whose image I saw in the parlor and who is thought to be the dismembered vulva of the goddess Sati (Urban 2011, 16). When I asked Mary, a Christian beautician at Senorita salon, why she prayed to Kamakhya, she revealed that she had started to do so in Bangalore at the suggestion of the other girls from the Northeast who recommended it when she failed to get pregnant. After several months of prayer, she became pregnant and thus became a believer in Sati Mata. "So, on Fridays, I pray to Sati Mata and infant Jesus. Because of them I got my son!" she said happily. The sensual heatedness of the goddess suggests a focus on divine bodies as well as embodied, enacted, and situated practices of fertility and sexuality. Dirt and its ally in these parlors, heat, though usually destructive, can sometimes paradoxically be creative and generative.

Layla told me the day of our run-in with pompadour man that she was missing Assam, which would be celebrating Ambabuchi Mela, the festival dedicated to the goddess Kamakhya's menstruation, the source of her fertility. As the Brahmaputra River flooded and ran red, Layla said, the temple's deity, the Yoni (vulva) also ran red with blood,[5] evidence of the goddess's fleshiness, fertility, and "heat" (Hindi=garmee). Heat, then, is an embodied aesthetic sensuality redolent of the creativity and fertility of the goddess. It is an aura that surrounds and invests her divine body and overflows into the world as "excess," the source and seat of her uncontainable power (Flueckiger 2017). The heat of the goddess that Layla referred to permeates all embodied encounters with her, linking her with places, ecologies, peoples, and times.

It is not a far jump from fertility to passion and insatiability in Hindu cosmology. Thus, heat is also an evocation of an excess of passion that becomes dangerous, chaotic. Heat in the context of the parlor is multipronged, both ushna and agneya in one, indexing the sensual, both for the goddess and, more problematically, for the beauty worker and client. Heat is seen as overflowing from the body, emerging as sexual appetite, inattention, laziness, and general incivility, combined with problematic leakages and smells, blood and tears, things that are often smelly. These leakages are seen as moral trouble, gesturing to a fundamental sexual hunger, diagnosed as "vulgarity," that needs strict policing. It is not surprising, then, that the intimate touch of beauty work is often viewed as interchangeable with sex work in the minds of Bangaloreans. The two types of work are distinct in their expectations of bodily comportment and skill, in the types of care they give and pleasure they evoke. However, they are also both connected to the sensuality of heat. These interpolating sexual economies often overlap or connect as they did that day at Glam, mediating and indexing the moral personhood of beauty worker and client.

"Chinku" Girls

"Too hot!" was Praveen's diagnosis of women from the Northeast. "They are too hot, too sexy!" he explained to me. I had met Praveen, a young Tamil entrepreneur, who ran a series of copy shops and flower shops adjacent to Senorita beauty parlor, one day when he delivered a bouquet to the owner of Senorita for her birthday. Praveen rode a fancy motorbike and wore imitation Ray-Ban glasses. He had arrived in Bangalore some five years prior from Toothukudi, a provincial town in Tamil Nadu, determined to become a millionaire. In pursuing "business," he had encountered several girls from the Northeast in the parlors. According to Praveen, "Chinku girls," as he called them, had a "solid rep" (reputation) because they "deserved it." They sought attention, in Praveen's eyes, as they "did cabaret, sexy dance," and wore bikinis (which he pronounced "bikni"). He felt they were

"hot," by which he meant sexy and sexually licentious. As a final argument, he said that he and his friends had seen them in the massage parlors.

Although Ayurveda posits heatedness as the characteristic of individual bodies, it is also applied indiscriminately in modern India to social bodies. For example, Dalit and other "lower" castes are thought by my interlocutors in Bangalore, both clients and beauticians, to have greater unchecked desire and so are considered more heaty and also more polluting, whereas savarna are thought to be cooler and hence less desirous. This label of "hot" was inevitably used to describe women from the Northeast.

There are many factors that contribute to Praveen's understanding of the girls from the Northeast as being "too sexy." As we have seen, they are often misracialized as Chinese, and thus different, with strange eating (and likely sexual) practices. At the same time, they are viewed as being backward because they are typically lower caste, tribal, and provincial. Bhairavi, the manager of the Lotus, once said to me in reference to a worker's smell (who I later found came from Guwahati), "They are backward castes, no? SC (scheduled caste[6]) and ST (scheduled tribe) types," underlining the perceived connection between being tribal, Dalit, or lower caste and being uncivilized, savage, smelly, sexy, and wild.

Bhairavi claimed that rural migrants, particularly those newly come from "village life" like Selvi—who in actuality had migrated from Samayapuram, a fairly large town in Tamil Nadu (a distinction Bhairavi ignored)—had a tendency to be dirty because of their Dalit caste status and rural habitus. They saved bits of paper and plastic bottles, filled up the salon with "waste," and wiped surfaces with dirty, smelly rags unless she kept a close eye on them. "They are not hygienic like us in the city," she added virtuously. "In the village, it is okay to be like that, but here, we must teach them how to be clean and neat, madam."

The women of the Northeast also had a number of regional stereotypes to contend with on top of this prejudice of "being dirty." They were associated with blood and bodies through the story of Kamakhya, where the splitting of the corpse of the goddess permitted her blood to flow out of her body and vivify the earth (Caldwell 1999, 113). Also, the Northeastern tribes were seen as "different" because of their matrilineal cultures, some tribes famous for their head-hunting skills and consumption of meat and alcohol and their enactment of Tantric rituals where the consumption of sexual fluids and the use of alcoholic beverages and sacrificial blood were common (Sanderson 2006). Worship of Kamakhya, with her connection to menses, blood, and heat, was also transferred metaphorically to her worshippers, among whom many of the beauty workers I knew counted themselves.

According to mainstream Hinduism, menstrual blood is a highly polluting and dangerous fluid over which control must be asserted. In this way, the goddess violates a Brahmanic taboo, a transgression that sums up modern Hinduism's view of tantra as a whole as a practice steeped in black magic and sexual license (Urban 2018, 2010). In fact, Praveen mentioned this as we were talking about his "hot Chinku girls": "They worship all tantra-yantra, no?" This was an association that I, at the time, found strange but later came to realize was common. Praveen's easy slippage between tantra, dominated by powerful goddess figures, with the contemporary understanding of heat as being sexy, showed remarkable facility and flexibility, layering the modern understandings of the heat of sexuality and the heat of the goddess, another instance of the nesting of stories and ideas into a composite whole.

A more pedestrian reason for the association between migrants from the Northeast and dangerous heat is the ethnic conflation of Northeastern women with Chinese and Thai women and their stereotyping as hot vamps and sexy masseurs. It seems like no Bollywood gangster movie from the '80s was complete without a sexy dance number in a seedy dance hall, where the vamp, invariably played by actress Helen Richardson,[7] would try to ensnare the hero. In an era where bit players like dancers were invisible, Helen was a star, known for her scandalous dance moves and busty figure. Although Helen was Burmese, she was often mischaracterized as "Chinese."[8] This Bollywood vamp fantasy has commingled with the body logics of the intimate massage parlor. Once dominated by Thai migrants, migrants from the Northeast increasingly perform a range of coded sexual functions in these spaces. Thus, conflated migrant bodies are fetishized and rendered legible as sexually licentious, as "hot."

The similarity of intimate labor between beauty and sex work reinforces the slippage between them. Both involve tending to the intimate needs of others and encompass practices that promote the physical, intellectual, affective, and other emotional needs of others. Both are forms of intimate care.

When I spoke of the unfairness of this imprinting of migrant bodies as sexually available, Madhu explained, after rolling her eyes at my naivete, "Everyone knows of these Thai massage parlors and 'happy endings.' . . . Even guys from like Toothukudi!" she said, sneering at Praveen's provincial antecedents, after I told her about him. "These desperadoes[9] see movies and hear things on the internet. They now think any female from Thailand gives a good hand job and blow job. And you know it's about them looking Chinese. So anyone who looks Chinese they think is sexy and ready for sex!" Radhika agreed with Madhu's analysis. She explained the ethnic and racial stereotyping that conflated beauty work and sex work and the consequences for women workers. "See in

FIG. 3.1. Blow-drying at a franchise parlor

the sort of tourist industry now Bangkok and all have opened up. And everyone knows about Thai massage parlors. So now guys in India want that also. And these girls from Assam, Meghalaya and all have the right look! They look like Thai girls."

Of course, the fact that these women live marginal and precarious lives only increases their availability for objectification. As Catharine MacKinnon insists, the freedom that feminism should aim at is *incompatible* with subordination—incompatible with women being a passive object at another's disposal, or bargaining from a position of weakness. And she defines sexuality "as whatever a society eroticizes," which allows the erotic gaze to construct female objectification, drawing on pornography for its form and content, focusing on the "despised, the demeaned, the accessible, the there-to-be-used, the servile, the child-like, the passive, and the animal"(MacKinnon 1987, 53–54). Sareeta Amrute also describes the complex links between work and sex that imprint themselves on the bodies of women like Layla: "As women of lower caste and class backgrounds find roads to upward class mobility through pink-collar jobs, they simultaneously are increasingly sexualized" (Amrute 2015, 341). A migrant rights activist from Darjeeling named Meghna told me that Praveen's sexist and racist bluntness epitomized a problem that she viewed as "much bigger."

She said, "The 'Oriental' female body as the object of desire has a long and unsavory history. You know, even today in the States, men think that Asian women are better at sex, more compliant in life, and more wild in bed." This vision of the sexy Asian female body led to harassment and even abuse. Meghna explained in an email, "These women are expendable, you see. No one takes their complaints seriously because everyone thinks they are only good for sex. Even the cops think that they are deserving of sexual harassment!" Layla distilled the problem even more poignantly: "These men think they can do dirty things with us, and it doesn't matter because we are already dirty, that we are not like Bangalore ladies." This harassment becomes a vicious circle where the women get locked into service work of various kinds including sex work and that sex work or even the perceived affiliation with it leads to further marginalization.

Because of this, I realized that Layla's insistence that her work in the parlor was "not sexy work" was enormously important. Both kinds of work rely on similar forms of sensuality and sensibility emergent during intimate encounters with clients (Vijayakumar 2020). Sex work is seen in Bangalore as on a continuum with beauty work since both deal with, as Lakshya noted, "making clients happy." Layla's discomfort gestures to the possible blurring between the lines that formed the ground of Praveen's sexist labeling of all women from the Northeast as being sexually hungry and thus available for harassment and more. As Layla suggests, the flesh of the Other made emblematic through the figure of the "Chinese girl" is a suggestive canvas for overt sexual objectification, the right receptacle for highly charged erotic fantasy like Praveen's. Heat is the rubric through which this rampant female sexuality is understood. Chinese girls, according to Praveen and others in Bangalore, were heated by a hunger for intercourse.

One day, Aseema articulated the problem that emerged in the intimacy of beauty work, that when bodies are close together, the leakages of bodily fluids such as blood, sweat, urine, and pus can overflow from one body and affect the other. This is another connection to sex work, but it was also important in terms of the porousness of the body. Permeable selves were "connected to others through flows of substance" (Busby 1997, 275), and this flow of substances was seen as dangerous to the physical and the moral body. Indeed, I too became connected to the beauty workers through this flow of substances. Academics are not immune to the slippage between articulating what interlocuters think and our own thoughts. My resounding fear in speaking of caste, therefore, is that readers might assume my description of caste and prejudice in the parlor to be my own view, which could not be further from the truth.

"So Bad It Was"

As we learned at Glam, it was not just clients who dealt with unwanted smells, leaks, and excess. Beauty workers constantly confronted the unruly female body in the course of their work. Even though everyone pretended that clients' bodies were immune to dirt and heat, beauty workers told many stories of sodden armpits, leaky tampons, pus-filled acne, hair full of dandruff, greasy legs, stinky breath, and smelly feet. Layla, who was the waxing specialist, often refused to wax the underarms of certain clients. She would squirm and make excuses. One day, Bhairavi insisted she work with a particular client since no one else was available. Layla went, dragging her feet. She returned to the break room after half an hour and threw up violently in a bucket. "So bad it was!" Tanya concurred. "She is always so bad! Even her feet smell!" Other workers were more explicit: "Waxing her, I could smell her from across the room. She smelled like dead fish." "Thoooo! She was on her period and didn't say, and when I did her bikini wax, there was blood and dirt everywhere." Workers spoke of clients arriving dirty "on purpose."

Clients were not unaware of this judgment. Radha, Menaka's daughter, spoke about her first underarm waxing: "Mama forced me to go when I was twelve, saying I was ready. I was so scared of it. I was scared that I would smell and it would hurt and that the beauticians would be all judgy. I wore tons of deo and perfume and all. But they don't care. They've seen it all. They don't even look at you. I also learned not to meet their eyes when they are touching me. Makes everyone feel more comfortable." Another younger beautician at the Lotus, Gloria, noted that it was important to be modest and not upset clients regardless of the strangeness of their bodies: "You cannot stare, madam. One time, one lady, her mustache was so thick I started staring. Then Lakshya taught me. Don't do. Another time I was waxing one lady and she had three nipples! One was dripping.... Thooooo!" She mimed disgust.

Of course, the fact that they had seen it all did not mean that they felt comfortable with the excesses of the body in these intimate moments. Nor was it simply an issue of disgust. Interestingly, it was the workers who were more explicit about the pollution of beauty work. Layla, Gloria, and Lakshya talked about the client's refuse and how its removal was difficult and dangerous work. Jhuma was even more explicit about dirt and the aesthetics of disgust: "We remove all this dirt from clients, madam. We take out waxing, we cut hair, clean skin, nails, all we do. That's why we become sick so fast. All this dirt, madam . . . where it can go?" She gestured here to the stickiness of dirt, the pollution it carried, how it cut through the boundaries of the workers' bodies and infected them. Then Gloria, making a retching noise, added a final note: "When we do work, madam, it's like we are doing seva [service] for clients, making them glam. Whatever kharab [bad] is there, we take off. Sometimes it affects us also. Sometimes I feel like vomit!" Recalling my early nausea in the parlor, I felt I could relate to her revulsion.

Of course, these were stories of disgust, where revulsion serves to denigrate clients' heated and disgusting bodies, amounting to a condemnation of their excess. But the real fear is that clients' filth, and their excess heat, can and will transfer onto the body of the worker, making it unclean and potentially sick, thus increasing their marginality and abjection. In this way, filth, as Adeline Masquelier (2005, 12) notes, is reconfigured as sin. The workers' unbridled cynicism and disdain of clients' expensive yet filthy bodies merely underscored the social and economic inequality written into the intimate encounter.

Layla, Gloria, and Jhuma also spoke of the incidental leakages of fluids from clients' bodies and the need to manage them carefully: "Sometimes when they want wax and they have their chums, I have to clean the bench with Dettol." Layla gestured to her bum and said, "Sometimes full stain will come." Jhuma added, "This one girl always has pimples, and full blood will be there when I do threading." Layla also noted the dangerousness of leaks in a pandemic era: "Sometimes they have viral and full . . ." then gestured to the nose, indicating leaking. "Then we have to clean properly with COVID and all." For beauticians as well as clients, corporeality was inherently leaky, dangerous, uncontained, volatile, and uncontainable.

Bodily fluids demonstrate the permeability of bodies and therefore threaten the liberal, well-tended, elite client's aspiration toward status, independence, and self-identity. It also threatens health and selfhood of the worker. Fluids may contaminate or disrupt social and individual systems. Fluidity is interpreted as a threat to the integrity and stability of the subject and is therefore viewed with suspicion. Body fluids produce reactions of disgust and abjection generally, and as Grosz argues, bodily fluids relating to women's reproductive functions are treated as more dangerous and more disgusting than male bodily fluids such as semen because of the female body's metaphorical and material tendency to "leak." Women's bodies in particular have been constructed as uncontrollably liquid and formless and threatening in their potential to overwhelm boundaries (Lee 2018, 79). Associated with abjection, bodily fluids are a potential danger to the clean, proper, law-abiding social body.

The Refuse of Beauty

So too it seemed to me, with the refuse of beauty. One day, I was walking toward the Lotus when I saw Selvi and Gloria emerge with bags full of rubbish. They were tied at the top, but tufts of hair, toe separators, and used waxing strips pro-

truded. Selvi looked startled, then discomfited when she saw me. Gloria said, "We are just going to throw this rubbish. Not far, madam, here only." Then Selvi added, "Wonnu ille, madam . . . Kuppe than!" (Tamil = This is nothing, merely rubbish). I understood that they did not want me to accompany them.

The rubbish heap where they were headed was at the end of the street, but it could be smelled from where we stood. Somewhere beneath the mound of garbage that spilled into the roadway was a municipal concrete waste container. Used cosmetic sponges and cotton balls, empty nail varnish and plastic shampoo bottles, paper bags filled with food and home waste, used batteries that leaked chemicals, plastic "family size" Coca-Cola bottles, vials, rusted razor blades, cut hair, cheap sponge toe separators used in pedicures, some used nail files, a huge pile of blood-soaked sponges and bandages, along with some medical waste and syringes formed the bulk of the heap. At the top of the pile lay the body of a poisoned rat. A small band of crows poked through the waste. All of it sat in a puddle of oily black suds that smelled of human feces, blood, and decay. I watched as Selvi tossed the bags to one side, carefully obscuring them from view.

This moment reminded me of Sarah Pinto's brilliant work on Dalit midwifery and pollution in northern India. During the course of her work, Pinto became interested in the disposal of the afterbirth. However, when she inquired about it, Pinto's curiosity was deflected and evaded by the midwife, who made clear that her interest was "unseemly." Pinto potently asks what our understandings of offal as both locative and disgusting tell us about the body and the spirit, the implicit and the evaded. Her work makes clear that the afterbirth, the source of life, is transformed by the birth into abject refuse, dangerous in its abjection and therefore demanding to be disposed of quickly and efficiently (Pinto 2008).

Recalling Pinto's work while watching Selvi dispose of the refuse of the parlor made it clear to me that the refuse of beauty, like the refuse of natality, was abject, dangerous, to be stripped from the body and disposed of quickly and secretly. In fact, it almost seemed as though this dirt was not simply being removed but was being banished in the search for purification (P. Gupta 2022). I realized that beauty was a stripping away of something that was seen as not truly belonging to the body, in the way that the afterbirth, though a vital part of pregnancy, was reviled and discarded as all too human. Such liminal matter is thrown away almost guiltily before its pollution can threaten the illusion of the beautiful body.

Gloria noted the connection between the two types of bodily waste as well. Her mother was a nurse in their local polyclinic, and she was tasked with throwing away the blood-soaked bandages just as Gloria and Selvi threw away used waxing strips. The correlation between afterbirth, bloody bandages, and hair-filled waxing strips is the removal of that which is conceived of as excess, of overflow, the removal of which reveals the true, healed, and beautiful body of patient, woman, or mother.

But the removal of these abject objects merely transfers the pollution. Sara Dickey, in her study of maids in the city of Madurai in South India, suggests that the threshold of domestic space is believed to be porous, just like the body, and so maids who clean the home are policed as they enter and leave the home for what they might bring in or take out with them. The abjection of dirt is "sticky," adhering to anyone who is tasked with its removal (Adams and Dickey 2000, 462–63).

This made me think about another moment of intimate contact across caste. The nai, or local barber, has a long history as masseur of men, and the dai, or midwife, a similar history as masseuse of pregnant women. Thus, a person whose touch might be polluting in one context can be edifying or augmenting in another. This has often been described as a result of expertise, which renders the casted touch to be appropriate in its intimacy and sanctions the "low caste" touch of savarna bodies. Of course, beauty work also carries an expertise, and many women rely on credentials, such as previous experience in the parlor or training in a beauty academy, as a way of counteracting the dangerousness of their touch.

However, I wonder if it might not also be the case that it is when dirt (and presumably sin) must be transferred from upper caste to lower caste that such touch is sanctioned. Despite Radhika and Menaka assuring me that parlors "had no caste" and that non-savarna women touched and "looked after" them in the parlor, it was Selvi, Layla, and others from Dalit communities who cleaned the clients' savarna bodies and removed the dirt from them and from the spaces they inhabited, not the other way around. Workers such as beauticians and cleaners were portrayed as representing "the dirt, disease, and rubbish" of a disorderly outside world that employers were at pains to keep at bay in the parlor. Employers "pointedly contrasted" the workers' behaviors and bodies with the ideal cleanliness, order, and hygiene of their own homes and lives (Adams and Dickey 2000, 463). At the same time, it was these workers who made those lives possible by taking onto themselves the abjection of dirt and pollution.

As beauty workers crafted the ideal bodies for their clients (and politely looked the other way when they encountered evidence of their clients' excess heat), they were expected to discipline themselves or be disciplined. Mr. Dhanush, an aesthetician, worked as an instructor at Bodycraft Academy. He listed to me the skills that made students "good" workers—hair coloring, makeup techniques, blow-drying, curling, spa skin care routines, and so on. But he emphasized that the most important thing was "taking care of the client," being "clean and service minded." Dhanush added, "This means also simple things like wearing deo (deodorant) or perfume so that when you come close smell won't be there, wearing clean uniform every day, tying hair, and all." At the Lotus, Bhairavi complained to me, "Ayyo, madam. What to do? So many times I tell the girls, be clean, wear deo! Here, we only take trained girls after they work at another parlor, or they have certificate from an academy, only then we take them, but still I have to teach them!" Bhairavi warned her workers not to eat too much meat, onion, or mango as they "made the body heaty," increased other appetites, and caused unpleasant odors to emanate. "Who wants smell like that? Whushaaa, whushaaaa, when threading and all!" She pointed to the air from her nose and mouth. Then she smiled, and with a sibilant whisper, pointed to her crotch and bum. "Here also too much problem madam. They eat garlic and all!" Menaka giggled, "Durrum bhurrum, abah full farting only!" Finally, Bhairavi indicated that engaging in sex heated the body and caused leakages and smells: "Problem is, madam, if they go with boyfriend and all, body also becomes heaty, but how to say? This is why all these girls smell, no?"

Besides the policing of their sex lives, workers were constantly chided for being unclean, not washing hands, not cleaning floors or instruments correctly, being noisy and loud, unclean, and smelly, not wearing gloves or deodorant. Ushna bodies' leakages were also diagnostic of an overly desirous body, and so workers' appetites were policed in the parlor when they ate too much, farted, belched, their hair fell out, or they bled.

Workers were aware that ushna was evidence of difference, of leaky unhygienic bodies, and possibly of morally problematic sexual incontinence. They did their best to avoid such judgments. Layla, for instance, was very conscious of smell and the conclusions of ethnic, moral, and casted inferiority they produced. Haseena, a young Muslim beautician who specialized in hair coloring, said it was "even worse" for Muslim workers: "They say we stink of BO, madam, because we are Muslim, and we eat meat, garlic and all!" In an attempt to combat the stereotype, she wore deodorant and lots of perfume, which she bought in "smugglers markets" of customs-free goods that she could ill afford and which she "refreshed" every few hours.

"Too Vulgar"

The most disastrous outcome for a worker was to have her heatedness labeled as vulgarity. "Too vulgar" was a damning indictment of a beauty worker's character and work ethic. Bhairavi and other managers and owners used it to con-

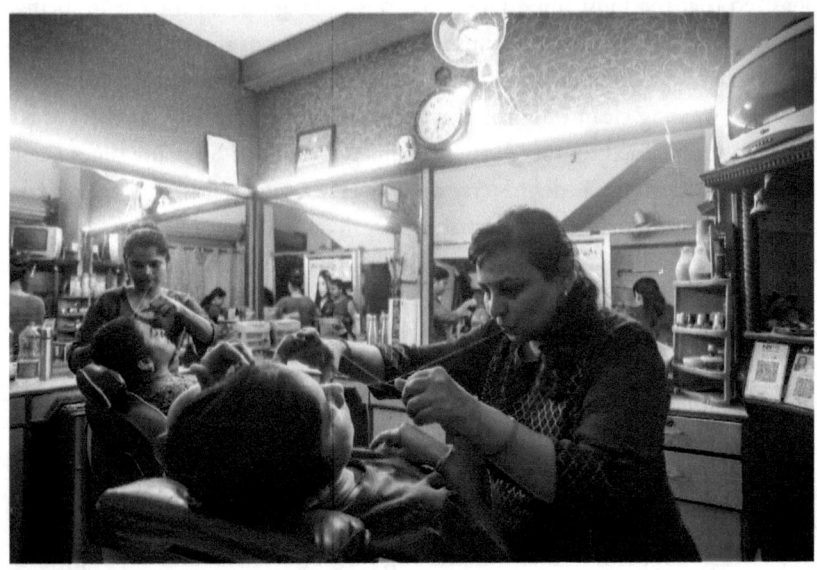

FIG. 3.2. Eyebrow threading at a small "auntie" parlor

note a worker who harbored an "erotic excess" that needed to be policed (Paik 2022b, 183). Here, the diagnosis of "being vulgar" acted as a coded disinclusion from the supposed Hindu moral world of feminine sexual and personal control. The idea of vulgarity was critical to the claims and counterclaims of upper-caste elites regarding the possibilities and limits of policing the boundaries of caste and sexuality. Parlor owners and clients used the discourse of vulgarity to shape a politics of overflowing eroticism and deviant sexuality that they believed ailed the bodies of tribal and low-caste migrant workers. At the same time, they legitimized an "authentic" female national subject as modest and sexually reticent (Paik 2022a). Vulgar women were seen as a threat not only to individual women but to the nation as a whole.

Indeed, taking care of female clients' bodies in Bangalore reifies class and caste boundaries in inexpressible yet durable ways. As Raka Ray and Seelim Qayum (2009) note in their study of domestic workers in Kolkata, labor relations between employee and employer or manager reveal clearly how employers, managers, and clients position themselves as middle or upper class through evolving methods of management even as workers grapple with the challenges of work and life in a classed and casted ecology embedded in relations of domination and inequality. Beauticians inhabit a similarly split world. Clients and managers see them through the lens of a modern erosion of "loyalty," a code for a "culture of servitude." In the past, the relations between employer and servant were based on loyalty and obligation, with the employer acting as patron to the servant and his family. Many mourn the loss of this world. Ray and Qayum (2009) argue that feudal imaginary feeds a feeling of nostalgia but also offers a mode of being for the Indian middle classes in the contemporary social moment. On the other hand, beauticians live in precarious real worlds of single-room apartments and rushed meals. The modern Indian imaginary clashes with the feudal one and a social order is still taking shape, whose contours are being uneasily filled every day. Vulgarity was the code used to categorize workers who did not abide by the loyalty expected by their feudally minded managers, and it denoted this abiding uneasiness and projected it on the worker.

Vulgarity took many forms, but it often involved the slippage of beauty work into sex work. A beauty worker might be wearing clothes deemed immodest. "Too vulgar!" clients often complained to the managers about migrants' bodies. "I don't want to see a free show when I come here, okay?" At other times, it might be a too lengthy phone call, presumed to be with a boyfriend. Bhairavi said of Northeastern girls, "They are too much sexy, madam. They grow up with boyfriend, girlfriend like that. Now they come to Bangalore. We do not do like that.... So they will always be on phone or wearing like too short." Sometimes it was the brush of breasts against the body in the act of performing a beauty service. Radhika once complained to me after an infuriating hair coloring session at the neighborhood parlor that the beautician kept leaning over her. "I don't want her boobs in my face," she sniped.

Clients sometimes found other clients at the parlor vulgar as well, but if they thought it, they were not as open about it. One day when Radhika and I were at the Lotus, a younger woman walked in to get her hair shampooed and styled. The salon hushed when she entered. The newcomer was dressed in a shortish white silk skirt and top that clung to her body. Even though she wasn't dressed in as risqué a manner as some other clients and her demeanor seemed relatively modest, her creased and fatty thighs were clearly visible in the short skirt. She wore expensive Louboutin high heels in pale pink and carried a matching Hermes handbag. She was clearly well-to-do but carried herself differently than the other women. I could not quite put my finger on what was misplaced. Radhika greeted her with "Hiiii, Tabu!" in a tone whereby I knew instantly that she wanted to keep the newcomer at a distance. All the workers

FIG. 3.3. Hair coloring at a neighborhood parlor

cast sidelong looks at one another, and only Layla got up to wave the newcomer to the sinks. Radhika cast me a glance and mouthed, "Tell you later." The newcomer, Tabu, was very chatty about her trip to Bali and the French Riviera for the summer holidays. She spoke to Layla about the weather, the food, and the resort amenities, ensuring that she would be overheard in the parlor. I noticed that Layla was not as forthcoming with her as she was with other clients.

After her shampoo was done, Tabu took a seat near Radhika to get her hair styled. Radhika greeted her with pleasantries: "All well? Good! Good! All well here, too. How is Rishi? Traveling as usual?" Tabu nodded and chatted desultorily. I noticed that many of the workers and clients kept glancing at her and at one another, and there seemed some unspoken tension in the room. After Tabu left, there was strained silence until Aseema broke it with "You see how she was dressed?" Instantly, the women all started talking. "My God! She's so bold!" "I simply didn't know what to do!" "Did you see how short her skirt was? So vulgar!" "How she said so calmly that Rishi was traveling. Look at that!" "Vulgar, she is!" I was mystified and asked Radhika what in Tabu's demeanor was so objectionable. Radhika laughed at me and said, "Oh god, T! You are such a sadhu-sant [innocent]! She charges!" Then observing my puzzlement, she clarified, "Rishi, her husband, doesn't make much money. He's a nice guy but total faltu! She was quite a quiet thing, wearing salwars and all, but then suddenly after he started traveling for work to Europe and UK and all, she started wearing fancy clothes and carrying name-brand handbags. Then we figured out she is an escort. She goes with married guys here there, and they give her gifts and money and all." Aseema snorted in moral and aesthetic indignation. "Vulgar! Her thighs ... she shouldn't wear such short skirts, but guys like her. She's sweet looking, na?" The judgment of Tabu was clear: she was morally problematic, coded as "vulgar." Everyone, clients and beauticians alike, knew enough to keep away from her. But Radhika suddenly said, in a bout of empathy, that she felt sorry for her and her need for money that her husband could not provide.

If such judgments were made, other clients would give the vulgar woman a wide berth, but workers could not. It was the workers who were responsible for stripping these vulgar women of their dirt and making them into the goddesses they imaged themselves to be. They did so with a smile, regardless of the asymmetry of the relationship. As Layla repeatedly put it to me, "We are STs, scheduled tribe, Bodo people, madam, so people in Bangalore think it is okay to be dirty with us.... For customers whatever, they come with lice or they don't clean, we have to clean! This is just our life."

And yet, despite these prejudices and difficulties, migrant women flooded into the Bangalorean parlors for work from provincial towns all across the subcontinent. Lawrence Cohen (2007b, 104), in his moving study of the murder of a young gay man in Delhi, notes that being cool and fashionable by living in the metropolis is the main factor in the pull of the big city on provincial youngsters such as the beauticians in the parlor. The world of beauty and fashion is alluring for small-town migrants like Lakshya and Tanya, Layla and Jhuma, and small provincial towns in South Asia are rife with aspiration and hope. "Computer institutes and English-language tutors have been joined by fashion and modeling schools. On the Internet, dozens of websites featuring the photos and biodata of many thousands of young women and men from India and Pakistan stitch these localized aspirations into a national and transnational scene of hope" (Cohen 2007b, 112). These aspirational geographies proliferate hope, and yet they also lure provincial girls and boys into the seamier sides of beauty. Girls dream of becoming Bollywood stars but end up as go-go dancers or sex workers. Their capacity to aspire for a better life despite the endless breaking and deforming of their dreams is rooted in poverty and desperation: their lack of recognition and dignity (Appadurai 2004, 65).

Satyavati's Stink

One day, after the odd interaction with Tabu, while I was watching Layla clean up the parlor, Tanya took the opportunity to tell the story of Queen Satyavati, "the great-grandmother" of the royal cousins in the Mahabharata, the episode of the teleserial that she said she and Jhuma had watched the night before. In Tanya's telling of the story, Satyavati was the daughter of a fisherman or possibly even a fish itself. The great Kuru king Shantanu met her one day by the riverbank. He had previously been married to the riparian goddess Ganga, who bewitched him with her beauty. Ganga had agreed to marry Shantanu provided he never questioned her. She proceeded to drown each one of their seven sons as soon as they were born. Finally, with the eighth son, Shantanu stopped her and saved his son. But Ganga explained that her sons were celestial beings cursed to be born on earth, and she was releasing each from their curse. Angered by the breaking of his vow, she left the final son, Devavrata, and ascended to heaven. Shantanu was devastated.

But after several years, he was by another river when he smelled an amazing perfume and saw another riverine beauty. This time, it was Satyavati, who stank of fish. But for Shantanu, consumed by the heat of his passion, her rank odor became a wonderful perfume. Shantanu proposed marriage to her. Her father knew that Shantanu's only son by Ganga, Devavrata, stood to inherit, so he made it a condition that only Satyavati's sons would inherit the throne. These sons became the fathers of the cousins who were the protagonists of the Mahabharata. Tellingly, when Satyavati married Shantanu, her body odor changed and became a wonderful perfume that could be smelled "nine miles away" (Shulman in Drobnik 2006, 411–26). Layla laughed at the end of the story. "Not bad for her, eh? She stank of fish but became a queen! We should remember Satyavati, no?" Lakshya quietly added, "She may have smelled bad, but she was good."

Tanya and Layla returned to Satyavati a few days later. In whispers, Layla complained of Bhairavi's and the clients' attitudes toward the workers as "too much" and vowed that she would go to Thailand to get her eyelids "done"—by which she meant double-eyelid surgery so that she didn't look "Chinese"—sooner rather than later. Tanya looked grim and said that she had started wearing perfume. "We are not like Satyavati. . . . We cannot marry a prince and hope our scent will change, madam! We must buy scent to wear," she said gloomily. This was the first time I had seen Tanya downcast. Jhuma came in suddenly and overheard the last part of Tanya's statement. "We are like Satyavati," she said emphatically. "We smell because of our work. Like she smelled of fish because her father was a fisherman, and she was with fish all day, like we are with this dirty work, but someday when we are free, happy, married, we will smell nice

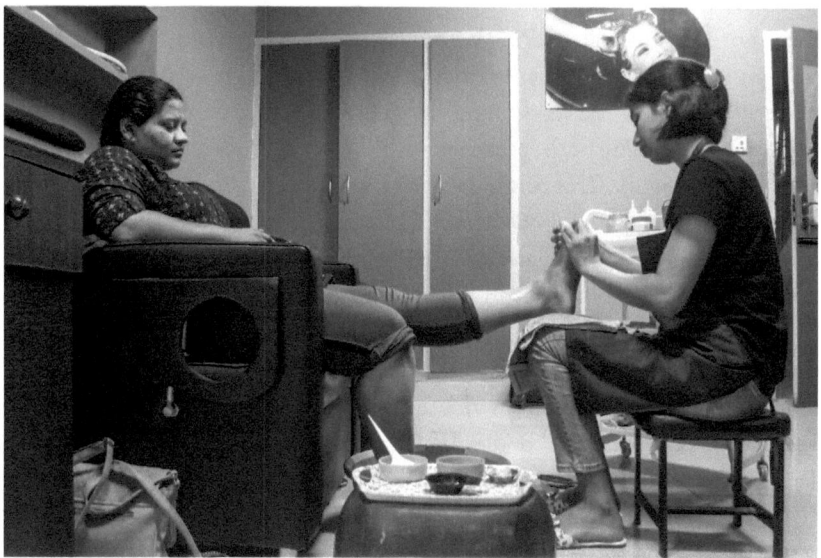

FIG. 3.4. A beautician from the Northeast gives a client a pedicure

and beautiful, like when she became queen and her scent became perfume!" Lakshya sounded determined and hopeful, but Tanya sighed, overwhelmed by the dirt and disgust that surrounded her.

Stories of Heat and Dirt

I have attempted in this chapter to unpack the intimate encounters of beauty in the parlor as the worker seeks to uncover the beautiful self of the client through practices that both remove and add to the body. Some encounters gesture to the dividual self, where the discourse of pollution is readily fused with modern discourse of hygiene and moral value. Others rely on myth and power and transformation. The fear of bodies, their smells and their sexual heat, is the evocation of the dividual body that is open to pollution, dirt, and abjection. This noise, stench, dirt, and passion threaten to overwhelm the delicate dance of intimacy at the core of beauty work. Various threads, moral and material, coalesce, rendering the workers' bodies "hot" and therefore ripe for harassment of various kinds. The hygienic world of the parlor and the Sanskritic world of Hinduism share an understanding that these forms of sensuality are at the limits of beauty; they threaten to overwhelm beauty with disgust and therefore need to be managed, policed, and sanitized.

Thus, the parlor, despite its often-sparkling newness, reinscribes the toxic hierarchy of caste through plaiting it, seamlessly and invisibly, into modern work, ensuring its longevity. Women, particularly Dalit women, have long been associated with the body and its cleaning and consequently understood to be prone to passions stemming both from their own disorderly bodies and the polluting nature of their work. This continues even in a modern space such as the parlor, where the exogenous often comes in a geographic as well as caste form. The slippage that occurs between material dirt and moral dirt allows for a discourse of vulgarity that encompasses any kind of uncleanness, observable or imputed. Policing the boundaries of bodies, another form of edge work, is necessary for cleanliness, both material and moral. Cleaning up bodies, removing anything considered dirty, is an ethical act. But the dirt removed necessarily attaches itself to the workers' "lower caste" bodies, impugning them as morally suspect and rendering them vulnerable, paradoxically, to moral critique. Thus, the caste hierarchy not only becomes reified through the parlor's work of beauty but, in aligning it with vulgarity and morality, places beauty workers at the edge of society.

The central problem in the parlors, however, is the physical intimacy between women inherent in beauty work and the ethical conundrums it creates. The intimacy of beauty encounters, which could slip easily into the realm of the sexual, as we saw with the unintentionally erotic head massage, is mitigated through comportment and expertise. Beauty workers try to ensure that they demonstrate knowledge and skill through their work and conform to ideas of cleanliness and good behavior to avoid leaks and smells. They attempt to evade the charge of "being vulgar" and to avoid being thought of as sexually hungry, a charge that they are often subject to based purely on their ethnic embodiment.

In a neoliberal economic framework, clients' bodies are divided from workers' bodies to promote an individualistic model of autonomous selfhood. But beauty work suggests that our bodies are neither dualistic nor autonomous; rather, beauty practices illustrate the fundamental intimacy of embodiment through which we are continually opened up to transformation with and through exchanges with others. The multiple trajectories of selfhood that emerge within the encounter offer a way into the body and the feminine self as "heaty," sexual, excessive, and overflowing and yet aspiring to be balanced, respected, and pure.

The fact that the parlor is idealized as a space redolent of goodness, beauty and luxury, a meditative coolness, epitomized by soft music, good smells, gentle care, and soft lighting makes problematic the sensual "heated" qualities of its inhabitants. Beauty work requires an alternative way of conceptualizing the relationship between bodies as intertwined in intimacy rather than separate and libidinous. The alterity and dirt of the other imposes an infinite ethical obligation on the worker to clean and beautify. Although the client too can suffer from heat and be judged for it, the ethical responsibility here is radically asymmetrical and precedes and exceeds the worker's subjectivity, as is always the case in capitalist service work (Lévinas 1981 in Grabher 2019; Joy et al. 2010). No matter how much a client smells, the worker must persist to carve a goddess out of the hairy, stinky flesh. Workers' bodies are disciplined in this space, not those they serve. Thus, here ethics and politics exist in an uneasy relationship, where ethics always requires more, a greater obligation of care.

I have argued that the Bangalorean female self is composite, made up of multiple parts, some porous and some not. Feminine selves are "constructed as the plural and composite site of the relationships that produced them" (Strathern 1988, 13). The composite dynamic self is, thus, created in encounter with innumerable others, and it requires a constant narration to lend coherence and consistency to the diversity of its lived experience.

As Layla and Jhuma told the stories of Kamakhya's menstruation, or Tanya spoke of Satyavati's smell, they made nuanced arguments for a located ethics of selfhood. Thus, storytelling performed the functions of making meaning in creating that selfhood. Workers wanted to see Satyavati's story as a positive illustration of her overcoming her bodily emanations and gaining agency through her excess, which was indicative in fact of her virtue. Yet they often had trouble envisaging how this was possible given the world they lived in. Nonetheless, the stories they told about the body, while undoubtedly about smell, heat, and sexuality, were ultimately about agency and the ability to create inhabitable selfhoods and worlds.

Storytelling is an essential part of religious practice, one way to embody and feel religion, but it is also a practice that makes women's experiences, and the telling of them, matter. Mythical literature depends on, incites even, perpetual acts of reinterpretation in new contexts, a process that embodies the very idea of appropriation (Barthes 1993, 119). Here, the telling of the story of Kamakhya's vulva or Satyavati's body odor is the working on of an oft-told story to make it useful for self-narration. Women persistently relocate these stories in new cultural geographies to reflect on the self at issue. This form of adaptation, relocation, and recontextualization proves an expansive one for Barthes; he argues that myths "ripen" as they spread (Barthes 1993, 149). But in Bangalore, the myth is never imported wholesale; rather, it is reworked to make sense of the narrative vis-à-vis the selfhood it aims to construct, and it undergoes its own metamorphoses, its own ripening, in the process. So myth is continuously evoked, altered, and reworked to offer meaning for bodies and selves.

INTERLUDE
Nightmare

Fifteen years after my first trip to the Lotus, my phone buzzed late at night with an appointment reminder of an interview I had set up in Bangalore. I had organized a WhatsApp video call to Jhuma, a beautician at the Lotus, who was now a manager at the new posh parlor called the Blow.

Jhuma lived in a house on the Dasarahalli metro line. On WhatsApp video, I saw that her window looked out onto a splintered tree, a pile of trash, and a gigantic electrical substation. The house opposite hers was incomplete. The lower floor was painted and ready for occupancy, but the upper floors had exposed steel bars sticking out of the top of bare cinder blocks. Like most of Bangalore, the incomplete landscape was built on the hopes of a tomorrow that might never arrive.

Jhuma told me proudly that she had become the manager of the salon in three short years, reporting directly to the owners. She managed the fifteen-odd beauticians and cleaners as well as the suppliers, accounts, and appointment books. She was so efficient and honest that the owners left the day-to-day running of the salon to her.

Suddenly, the doorbell rang. Jhuma answered it, and a shy-looking woman came in dressed in a cream sari. I recognized her as Lakshya, the woman I had met many years prior at the Lotus and then at Senorita. She joined the WhatsApp video call and greeted me with pleasure, asking about me and my family. Jhuma went away, made her some tea, and served it in wide-mouthed porcelain bowls, accompanied by sweet biscuits wrapped in brightly colored paper. They sat together on the divan under a photo of the Kamakhya Devi temple in Assam, their homeland. Jhuma and Lakshya seemed genuinely happy to see me and politely answered my many questions. I asked about their homes and families, and getting more comfortable, they spoke with pleasure and longing of their small provincial hometown: how one reached there by bus after traveling for three days by train to Guwahati, how they missed the hills and the cool Alpine weather, and how their aged parents continued to struggle. Then the conversation stalled again. As though it was a consequential decision, Jhuma said to Lakshya, "Talk to madam, no? About how you came here.... She is *still* writing her book on parlor ladies."

Lakshya started to respond, then paused. In that pause, I could sense her feeling her way around, trying to shape what she wanted to say next. At last, her shy affect disappeared and she abruptly turned so her back was to the phone camera. She lowered one shoulder of her blouse. "This is my story, madam . . . you can say."

I couldn't speak.

Lakshya's back was scarred with two wide wounds, furrows about four inches long, that looked as though the skin and flesh had been cut away by jagged knives. One furrow, the larger one on her shoulder blade, had a hollowed surface where the skin had been peeled back, seemingly with a blunt instrument, and was surrounded by thick, rounded, irregular clusters of scar tissue. In the depression, the skin had healed unevenly and the muscles of her back could be seen through a transparent film of flesh. Around the wound were fissures where the edges of the skin did not quite meet and where the reddish pink flesh and the whitish edge of the tendons running to the bone were visible like a living anatomic chart. The skin rolled into a cigarette-like coil on one side, where the cutting had ended abruptly. The wound looked angry and painful, the result of some terrible violence. The second scar was smaller but no less disturbing, with clearly visible raised white flesh that suggested hasty stitches around its edges. I realized that the contraction of the scar tissue was why she couldn't raise her left arm fully.

Lakshya said her village had been idyllic when she was a child, beautiful and green. Her mother stayed at home and herded goats. Her father had a job as a worker in a factory in the neighboring town, and soon her older brother joined him. Most of the people in her small village were landless tribals who worked in factories or on tea plantations. Lakshya and her two sisters would walk down the hill to a larger neighboring village where they had a Christian missionary school. There, she learned to speak and read English. She remembered the walk down the forested hill in the early morning, the elderly women of the village drinking steaming cups of green tea on their front porches.

But after the Indian government cracked down on labor agitation and political resistance in the region, many of the young people around her became radicalized anti-state actors, partaking in one insurgency after another. Roving bands of young men held up army traffic on highways as a protest against the state-based violence against them. Some, according to the state, even engaged in arson. Lakshya's brother, an impressionable young man who wanted to see a better world, joined them and left his job in the factory. Her father was devastated and forbade the family from speaking of him ever again. "He is a useless fool!" he used to shout. But Lakshya's mother used to meet him in secret and give him packets of food. "He is my son!" she would say. The happy family frayed. Her father became depressed and did not earn enough. Her mother sold the goats.

Lakshya was determined to build a better life for her family and, through her friends, heard of the opportunities in Bangalorean salons to earn huge sums of money threading eyebrows, a skill at which she excelled as a teenager. Lakshya's mother was worried that "parlor work" was code for sexual work in a brothel and she would be "spoiled" for life. But Lakshya had decided. Even though she did not have money for a ticket, she started thinking about how to get to Bangalore. Then her cousin told her about Ram, a fixer from Nepal, who arranged jobs in Bangalore for the "right girls" and who would front her the money until she could pay him back.

Ram came to her house and told her family that he would help Lakshya get the funds and it would not involve sexual labor. He swore on "his mother's life." Lakshya's mother was happy that she had found such a "good man" to help her.

Ram took Lakshya by bus (which she paid for with her small savings) to a small village just inside the Nepal border. It took them several days.

There, in a makeshift room in a small house, he sat her down on a charpoi (a wooden and string bed) and told her that they would do a "simple surgery." If she allowed the lady doctor to harvest the skin of her back, he would pay her the unimaginable sum of 20,000 rupees, more than enough to get her to

Bangalore and pay his broker's fee. Lakshya was scared of the pain but agreed. After all, she reasoned, it was not sex work.

The next thing she remembered was waking up on a straw cot in excruciating pain. She could not see her back, but she felt the stitches pulling on the flesh across her back. She had to sleep on her stomach for two weeks while a woman fed her dhal and rice every day. They rubbed some ointment into her back to help it heal. The first time the lady changed the cotton bandage, she had to tear it off since the pus had glued the cotton to her back. She wrenched out some of the skin and tissue with it, and the wound bled again.

After two weeks, Ram came to get her. He gave her 9,000 rupees and told her he had located a job for her in the Lotus salon in Bangalore. When she asked him about the rest of the 20,000 rupees she was owed, he said angrily, "I did this to help you and your family and now you are questioning me?" He threatened her, told her to take what he was offering, or he would sell her to a brothel in Katmandu and she would never see her parents again. She boarded the train to Bangalore the next day with her small trunk and a piece of paper with the address and phone number of the salon.

So saying, she turned back to face me and pulled her blouse back up.

Pleasure and pain, therefore, are not only necessary attendants of beauty and deformity, but constitute their very essence.
—David Hume, *A Treatise on Human Nature*, Book 2, 1740

Simply put, blood offerings are ends in themselves. They are pragmatic, material transactions and one cannot substitute a goat with thought or intention.
—Mark Elmore, "Bloody Boundaries," 2011

The Borderlands are physically present wherever two or more cultures edge each other, where people of different races occupy the same territory, where under, lower, middle and upper classes touch, where the space between two individuals shrinks with intimacy.... A border is a dividing line, a narrow strip along a steep edge. A borderland is a vague and undetermined place created by the emotional residue of an unnatural boundary. It is in a constant state of transition. The prohibited and forbidden are its inhabitants.
—Gloria Anzaldúa, *Borderlands/La Frontera*, 1987

WOUNDED 4

Vampire Facial

Menaka was anxious; it was her first time getting a "vampire facial." I asked what it was. Lakshya explained to me that it involved the application of a platelet-rich plasma, extracted from your own blood, after a microneedling of the face that aided the absorption of the platelets. Believed to rejuvenate delicate facial skin, this expensive skin care treatment had become incredibly popular among the elite clients of Bangalore. Mary, the microneedling technician, reassured Menaka that it "was nothing" as she rubbed a strong numbing cream over her face and slowly extracted a vial of blood from Menaka's arm. She placed the blood in the vial into a machine. And then she reappeared with a worryingly large array of needles to begin work on Menaka's face.

Meanwhile, Tanya, the manicurist, had removed Menaka's nail polish and cleaned and shaped her nails and was now carefully painting Menaka's nails a lovely pearlescent pink with iridescent dots. She was crouched over Menaka's hands as she dipped the brush in the pot and tapped off the excess lacquer. In an attempt to distract Menaka from the needling that was about to begin, Mary turned to Tanya, who had become the resident storyteller, and implored, "Tell no? Yesterday's story of Sati." Tanya laughed and launched into the story of the goddess Sati and her mythical sacrifice.

> Sati was the beloved wife of Lord Shiva, (the great god of the Hindu trinity). She had won his love through doing severe penance (tapasya). One day her father, Dakshya, who did not like "his son-in-law" Shiva, decided to hold a ceremonial sacrifice (yagna), but he did not invite Sati or Shiva for it. Sati decided to go to her father's ceremony anyway, but when she arrived, King Dakshya insulted Shiva in front of all the assembled gods, sages, and others. Sati was angered by the insult to her husband, but "because she was respectful of her father, she did not shout or scream." Rather, she channeled her anger inward, immolating herself in the heat of the internal fire that she called up.

Tanya explained that this fire was born of her penance and her purity. Before her death, Tanya added, she promised Lord Shiva that she would be reborn as Parvati (the daughter of the Himalayas) to marry him again.

As Tanya was telling the story, Mary tapped on Menaka's face with the needle array, drawing tiny streaks of blood along the soft part of her cheeks. "Hurting, madam?" she inquired solicitously as Menaka occasionally squealed in pain. Some blood got into Menaka's mouth and she yelped, "Ayooo! I tasted my own blood!" Mary apologized yet again but, after Menaka's insistence, continued. Layla, a younger beauty worker, also from Assam, brought Menaka a bag of ice to reduce the trauma to her face. Meanwhile, Tanya continued the story.

> After Sati died, Lord Shiva came looking for her and found her body. He was humiliated (apmanit hua) and mad with grief. He lifted Sati's body onto his shoulders and started to dance the tandav (the dance of annihilation). Lord Vishnu, realizing that Shiva's dance could destroy the world, took Sati's body and cut it into fifty-one pieces, each of which fell to earth chaotically "here and there." Wherever the dismembered pieces fell became a sacred place—a Shakti Peeth (seat of Shakti). Sati's yoni (vulva) fell at Nilanchal (the Blue Mountain), and it became a goddess, Kamakhya Devi. Around it was built the Kamakhya Devi temple.

Then, she added, "That's where all us girls go in Guwahati to pray to Ma!"

With microneedling complete, Menaka sat upright, clutching a towel dipped in ice water to her swollen face. Mary brought back the small test tube that held some harvested blood, separated into red blood cells and a yellow fluid, which she said was the "best part." Menaka said, "What all we do, no? Stupid we are!" I assumed she referred to the lengths that women go to for beauty. Tanya finished painting Menaka's nails and stretched out her back. "Done, madam!" She started to put the nail polish bottles and files away. Menaka admired Tanya's handiwork. "So nice.... I like the shining polka dots... chooo chweet!" she cooed.

Mary started patting the yellowish fluid onto Menaka's face saying, "This is the PRK, madam, from blood. This will help skin healing, becoming young only!" Menaka said enthusiastically. "So much I need.... Turned fifty-five last week! I'm becoming an old hag!" All the beauty workers clucked their tongues. "Ayyooo! No, no, madam! You are still so p-r-e-t-t-y!"

The connection between beauty and pain is so familiar that it has become a cliché, yet it hides a deeper truth. Beauty, though elusive, is grounded in wounding. Moved by the story of Lakshya's skin harvesting and the terrible scarring of her back, in this chapter I ask in what ways the political economy of beauty wounds women, both workers and clients, and inspires them to wound themselves. Cultural theorist Ravi Sundaram (2009) has argued that India has a "wound culture," best exemplified in its accident-prone roads, where mobility meets flesh (Solomon 2022a and b). The beauty parlor, however, is an unexpected and as of yet unprocessed site of repeated wounding. Focusing on the wounding that takes place in the parlor requires a rethinking of the beautiful, seemingly intact and undamaged, body that emerges from the parlor.

In the Hindi-English spoken in the parlor, the word for wound, *ghaav*, is a loaded term, as is its evocation in Kannada as *gayalu*. In addition to its literal use as a physical injury, wound is often used as a metaphor referring to a constellation of personal and social injuries, losses, pain, and grievances (Dewachi 2015b, 2). To be "wounded" is to carry lingering memories, pain, or histories of trauma, such as the loss of one's home or the death of one's loved ones, a grave injury to the self that requires some restitching and reconstruction. However, what I began to notice was that wounding seemed to both catalyze and constitute the relationship to beauty for all the women in the parlor. So here, I use the idea of the wound as an analytical framework to understand the multifaceted forms of physical, psychic, and social injury that attend to beauty both for beauty workers and clients alike (Scarry 1985). What kinds of wounds push a woman toward the parlor? Is violence to the body necessary and at what scale? In the end, is deliberate wounding transfigured by the outcome when beauty succeeds? Is suffering necessary for beauty to succeed?

I will argue that women use voluntary beauty wounding to overcome the unchosen wounding foisted on them by their worlds. In Hinduism, wounds and suffering are often the marks of pure, ethical womanhood that is sacrificed, always seen in relation to the unblemished man, the sacrificer—Dakshya, Vishnu, Rama, and so on. Wounding and sacrifice are relational and transactional but also as Mark Elmore tells us "an end in itself" where one cannot substitute one form of payment for another within the relational transaction. It thus behooves us to think about voluntary beauty wounding as agentive and powerful. In this chapter, I attempt to disentangle some of these elements through tracing five stories of wounding—the goddess Sati as Kamakhya Devi, the goddess of the northeast, as well as Menaka, Layla, Lakshya, and Madhu.

Despite the multiplicity of Hindu thought, I argue that the acceptance of wounds and wounding is the basis of Hindu female personhood, and wounding bleeds through the society affecting every woman, regardless of casted status. Traditionally, for Hindu woman, and in India more broadly, womanhood itself is viewed as a pollution, an existential wound that can only be overcome by lifelong work to become morally pure. Moreover, sexuality, childbearing, and other women's work are all bodily and morally polluting actions, and women bear the brunt of this pollution. Thus, being polluted and aspiring to purity is central and continuous wounding work for women, work that builds toward Hindu ethical selfhood.

The women in the parlor were united in telling the stories of their wounds, both mythic and real, as a mechanism of healing and creating agency. Moreover, they cultivated certain types of wounding in the pursuit of beauty. This meant that they did not see wounding as merely negative, though they sutured up their wounds constantly. This concept of suturing the self in the midst of life's wounding is significant for it suggests that a fragmented, complex personhood may have some transformative potential for a wide array of problems.

Important to this discussion of ethical selfhood is understanding the goal of human existence in Hinduism. Life is conceptualized as a process of perfecting oneself as a religious artifact through controlling natural processes and impulses via opportunities for refinement that allow karma to be worked through, creating an ethical self in its wake. Scholars have argued that women in India are powerful and agentive since they are evocations of the feminine power (shakti) of the universe, personified in the goddess Devi.[1] However, while Hindus believe that all women embody power and the indigenous concept of shakti plays a significant role in the self-understandings and self-perceptions of Hindu women, embodying shakti power does not guarantee, "in and of itself, the ability to exercise power and authority in socially and culturally meaningful ways" (Menon 2002, 140). For women in Bangalore to become truly powerful and generative, they have to remake the shakti energy within them in culturally specific ways that privilege moral actions (dharma) to overcome their karma, which gives them agency in the wider world. For women, beauty is important because it is evidence of this moral work being done, of a refined moral subjectivity emerging and imprinting itself upon the body (Biehl et al. 2007).

Layla's Wounds

I was walking with Layla, the young Assamese hairdresser, and Tanya, the manicurist, toward the Lotus for their morning shift. It was summer, and the trees were covered in dust; the roads were hot and the traffic relentless. As we walked, Layla talked about her village in Assam. She spoke of the beautiful green tea estates that terraced up the steep hills, the winding roads with lines of tall chinar trees, and the misty valleys where the goats grazed: "So beautiful it is there, madam. So clean!" She contrasted it to Bangalore: "Look, madam, Bangalore has become so dirty, dry, and hot!" she sighed. "It's my karma, madam, to come and work here. I was in Kolkata before and someone said go to Dubai, but I came here because people said Bangalore is like abroad, in India only."

Even though Layla was speaking about Assam in contrast to Bangalore, I felt that she was somehow talking about her own beauty and her feeling of being unhomed and unbeautiful in Bangalore. She said no one even thought of her as Indian, and she was seen as ugly. She added, "All ladies in Assam are beautiful. Nice skin, soft hair. They don't need to go to the parlor!"

When we entered the Lotus, Tanya slipped past the manager, Bhairavi, at the front desk. Bhairavi shot me a brief smile and then growled at Layla, "You are late! What happened?" Then without waiting for Layla's answer, she barked, "Go get ready! Clients will be here soon!" Gesturing at Layla's beautiful chestnut-colored waist-length hair, she said, "Tie your hair!" Layla disappeared and returned within minutes in her uniform with her hair neatly tied back to clean the stations. Tanya flicked her eyes over to her sympathetically after Bhairavi disappeared to chivvy other workers.

Soon, clients began arriving for their morning appointments. Tanya started a pedicure. As Tanya was bent over the foot basin washing the client's feet, she demanded a story, as Tanya had become the unofficial narrator of stories in the parlor. "So, what? No story today?" Everyone urged Tanya or Layla to tell a story. "Tell! Tell!" Layla began to speak. It was the backstory to the dismemberment of Sati.

> *Sati was a beautiful princess who was the daughter of Dakshya, a rich king. He loved his daughter and brought her up with the finest things. Her beauty*

was renowned throughout the kingdom. Layla said she had fair skin, long dark hair, and a perfect body. Dakshya was looking for a suitable husband for her, a prince equally handsome. But she had fallen in love with Shiva, a wild god with matted hair who dressed in animal skins and lived on the bleak snowcapped Mount Kailash, with his army of outcasts known as Ganas. Knowing that he would not even consider her unless she was completely pure, Princess Sati—her name meant Truth—did years of penance (tapas) and finally caught Shiva's attention. He fell in love with her, too.

At this point, the clients in the parlor all cooed happily, "Cho romantic!" Aseema said admiringly, "Shiva sounds like a total dude!" Manavi, the pedicure client, said, "Then what? His form is the lingam,[2] no?" Everyone burst into hooting laughter, a bawdy, sisterly camaraderie. Aseema playfully slapped Manavi on the arm. "Too much you are, man!" Layla continued with the story when the laughter died down.

But Dakshya was not happy with his daughter's choice. He was a devotee of Vishnu and could not bear Shiva with his matted hair and dirty clothes. He vowed he would get revenge....

After describing Shiva, Layla took a deep breath to continue, lifting her head from carefully filing Manavi's toenails. But at that moment Bhairavi, the manager, interrupted, bearing some sweet prasadam[3] from the famous Vaishnavite pilgrimage temple at Tirupathi. She stared at Tanya and Layla quellingly while offering the sweets to the clients. They fell silent.

Young, beautiful, and alluring with dark wide-set eyes, straight white teeth, a lean figure, waist-length chestnut hair, and a good sense of fashion, Layla seemed the epitome of aesthetic sophistication. The older clients liked her because she was softspoken and attentive, but the younger clients sometimes treated her badly, seeing her innate beauty as threatening. Layla had learned to be particularly self-effacing, attentive, and humble around younger women. Looking at her luminescent skin and bright confident smile as she greeted clients in the parlor, I was hard put to see her as wounded in any way.

But she carried deep psychic scars of the loss of home. She often spoke of her village, close to the foothills of the Himalayas, with longing in her voice. "People say it's backward, no-good place, madam; but so nice it is there." She spoke of walking on hilly terrain, slip-sliding on the tiny gravel of a moraine field near a tributary of the great Brahmaputra River. She told me often of the icy blue waters and misty green hills and valleys. Her home was the site of family, care, protection, love, duty.

In Bangalore, migrants like Layla had to accept being out of place, being othered and considered less than. This seeming disconnection between individuals' stories of their own painful lives and the political necessity of an abstracted out-of-place body invites a reframing of beauty as unjust, as a judgment that fails to "apprehend the lives of others as lost or injured" (Butler 2009, 1). Layla's displaced beauty was part of the loss and injury of migration. Layla spoke of how, when she first came to Bangalore, having to learn her way around a big city away from her family, combined with a lack of money, made her despondent: "Every night I used to cry, madam." I was particularly sympathetic to Layla's recounting of her move because I too spent a considerable time of my first year in America feeling untethered, othered, and in tears, missing home and feeling as though I was not enough. Layla put this sensation into words: "My body was in Bangalore, madam, learning parlor work, but my heart-mind [dil] was in Assam."

In the metropolitan centers of India, most people in service industries, whether beauty, hospitality, or retail, are from somewhere else. The reputation of migrants from the Northeast for being polite, skilled, and speaking good English[4] held them in good stead in most of these jobs. Nonetheless, Layla spoke of her marginalization in Bangalore as a sense of being ugly, out of place, and "stupid." Whereas Assam was full of power and beauty generated through ethical action over time that could transfer positive karma to Layla, the Bangalore streets with their houses cheek by jowl were alien and ethically impure and thus made her feel ugly and "useless." The ethical materiality of Bangalore was like a miasma, affecting her, and she felt like the negative energy was being actively transferred between the atmosphere of the city and its inhabitants. Cohen (2007b, 114) argues that provincial migrants like Layla come to big cities like Bangalore hopeful, aspiring to a better life, only to have such hope deformed by the exploitation of their everyday lives. What, then, does it mean to speak of beauty or ethics in the narratives and counternarratives of these migrant women's lives?

Layla said that when she first came from Assam to Bangalore, she was "too bigheaded of being cute" because "back home, boys liked" her and she enjoyed the attention. But once she came to Bangalore and heard people talk, she realized that her ethnicity made her "different," if not ugly: "I heard so many people comment about my eyes, saying Chinku eyes, why are your eyes so small? Or, why your skin is yellow? Things like that. It made me feel very bad."

Coming from the geographic periphery of the state, Layla was sensitive to her marginalization, feeling it viscerally as a loss of her beauty. She said that she felt out of place in Bangalore not only because people did not value her beauty but because she had "left her heart" in Assam and so was less beautiful and less strong, making explicit the connection between a powerful agentive selfhood and a beautiful exterior.

Wounded Geographies

Assam, home to a major global tea industry, has seen the rise of inequality over the past two centuries as colonial plantation economies based on bonded labor morphed quickly after Indian independence into a modern neoliberal marketplace with absentee landlords and rising exploitation (Besky 2013). Attempting to escape intermittent violence and lack of opportunity, many women and young men make their way via Kolkata to the major cities of India to work in restaurants, salons, and other service jobs. Those who stay are increasingly restive. Tensions between the native Assamese tribes and the Indian government over neglect of political, cultural, and economic issues, such as increased levels of illegal immigration from neighboring countries and the exploitation of tea industry workers, has led to the emergence of anti-state militias. These militias have attempted to revolt in a bid to change the exploitative landed and caste politics of the state and have engaged in attacks on trains, kidnappings, bombings, and murders. The violence has left the state economy in tatters. Further, conflicts over indigenous land rights, affirmative action policies on tribal status, and skirmishes between militias and the state have led to a near constant state of terror.

Midway through my fieldwork in July 2012, extreme violence broke out in Assam between indigenous Bodos and Bengali Muslims.[5] According to the government of India, 108 people died and nearly half a million people were displaced to refugee camps. Interethnic violence between tribal and religious groups over land is at the core of Assam's ongoing battles. Bengali Muslims were part of Assam's founding, but Bodos and other indigenous groups claim the land as theirs, creating long-standing disputes. It was after this conflict that the latest wave of beauty workers fled Assam and came to Bangalore. Of course, the violence did not stop.

Most recently, in May 2023, conflict erupted in the northeastern state of Manipur between various tribal communities. Over 224 people were killed and 9,000 fled as the state government ordered troops to shoot civilians on sight.[6] The proximate cause of the violence was a fight over an affirmative action measure by the state government. The state courts demanded special tribal status known as "scheduled tribes" from the government of India for one specific tribal group. This allowed one group among many guaranteed access to special governmental resources based on the affirmative action policy of upliftment. This was a surefire pathway to social mobility for the group chosen and thus a source of tremendous envy for those groups who were not.

Movement is of primary concern here, not simply in relation to migration and attempts to move across class barriers but also to feelings that oscillate between articulation and nonarticulation, between migrant women's recognition and misrecognition in Bangalore, and in the resultant relation to the barrage of images and discourses that reside outside them and to which they must respond. This pervasive experience of migrancy points to the limitations of anthropological models which aim to "give voice" to a community of migrants whose dignity lies not in words themselves but often in the recognition of what is not resolved and not known (for exceptions, see De León 2015).

Recently, the Assam government, in defiance of Indian state policy, listed all the communist cadres in the state on their public-facing website, inflaming simmering tensions.[7] The whole of Assam devolved into interethnic violence, suspicion, and fear, breaking out into riots.[8] Young men left home to protest state action with murder, arson, and homemade bombs, and the violence spilled into cities with significant diasporic populations, like Allahabad, Bangalore, and Mumbai. Rumors abounded on social media that Naga men had beaten up and tortured Muslim men in retaliation for the harassment that Naga women endured in Indian cities. Within hours, thirty thousand migrant workers from the Northeast[9] who worked in beauty parlors and restaurants across Bangalore left their jobs and boarded trains to Darjeeling, Gangtok, and Delhi. In fear for their lives, Jhuma, Layla, and Lakshya were among them.

The city came to a standstill. Restaurants closed, as did beauty parlors and other services. Menaka, who was blissfully unaware of the news, had stopped by Senorita for a henna hair color and was irritated by the sign on the door that read, "Due to unforeseen circumstances, we are closed until further notice." "Why are they closed? Ayooooo! Why did the girls all have to leave? Poor things! But ... still ... Now what to do?" But Menaka need not have worried. The workers soon returned, unable to survive in Assam without the regular paychecks on which their families depended.

Tribal ethnicity made Northeasterners unrecognizable in Bangalore. Feelings of unbelonging are in themselves constitutive features of indigenous Northeast[10] tribal identity (Schneiderman and Tillin 2015), and the long and uneasy relationship between India and China makes Bangaloreans, who are global in their consumption of international media, see Northeasterners as not even tribal but Chinese, an "enemy" within. This essential misrecognition as "not Indian" contributed to Layla's feeling of *unheimlich*, of being unhomed, strange, ugly, and "foreign."

Furthermore, the Northeast is an area of suture, where China, Tibet, Nepal, Bangladesh, Myanmar, and India meet. State boundaries have been redrawn continuously, almost dizzyingly, over the course of the twentieth century, making citizens into refugees and back again into citizens.[11] Additionally, peoples of the Northeast, often linked by tribal affinities and herding opportunities, have crossed the high valleys of the Himalayan foothills and the deltaic regions of the Ganga without worrying about national boundaries for centuries. Thus, the problem of interethnic and state-enacted violence was compounded by questions of citizenship rights. The state can make and unmake citizens at will, and inclusion is based on appropriate performances of ethnic, class, racial, and caste forms of belonging in which the dual relationship of recognizing and being recognized enacts and legitimates individuals' rights.

On December 11, 2019, at the height of the pandemic, the BJP-led government of India enacted a controversial policy—the Citizenship Amendment Act (CAA)—which changed the sixty-four-year-old Indian citizenship law to restrict paths to citizenship for refugees and "illegal" migrants. Controversially, the new law stated that all undocumented immigrants who had been working in India for a minimum of six years would be eligible to apply for Indian citizenship *unless they were Muslim*, a patently discriminatory move. In India's secular constitution, faith was never a metric of citizenship. Yet, with this new law, immigrants deemed illegal were to be deported or jailed. Historian Mukul Kesavan, speaking to the BBC, said that the law "is couched in the language of refuge and seemingly directed at foreigners, but its main purpose is a delegitimization of Muslim citizenship."[12] Opponents of the law stated that in a secular country like India, where the constitution prohibits discrimination on the basis of religion, the government making faith a metric of citizenship was illegal. Many lawyers joined the spontaneous protests against the law that sparked all across the country.

The increasingly right-leaning BJP government insisted that it believed in the rights of "rightful" citizens and, to determine who had the rights of citizenship, it created a National Registry of Citizens (NRC). To be included, individuals had to prove that they had been living within the borders of India by March 24, 1971, the day before neighboring Bangladesh became an independent country. As the news magazine *India Today* noted, the updated list for Assam alone left out 1.9 million people, Muslim and not, rendering them all potentially stateless.[13] Violent protests against the NRC roiled the region.

Many individuals whose citizenship was suddenly in doubt were women like Lakshya and Layla, whose tribal marriage and naming practices rendered them invisible to the NRC. Others were peasants who tilled the land but had no ownership over it and therefore no paperwork to legitimate their ties to their homes and forest; and herders, nomadic tribal groups who traveled long distances following their animals, often crossing state borders prior to their excessive militarization in the early 1970s. As Gloria Anzaldúa reminds us in *Borderlands/La Frontera*, the borderlands are spaces of precarity, and of prohibition, a fraught space in a constant state of transition, everchanging, and where transition is seen as natural, "a dividing line, a narrow strip along a steep edge." Which side of the line one falls determines one's entire life course.

Thus, the question of migration, illegal and not, is a serious issue, both for the workers in Bangalore and for the task of ethnography, as both must grapple with constant in-betweenness, allusion, and the unsaid. It suggests that knowledge may be half formed in the women's narratives, or lack of narrative. Their stories are necessarily incomplete and often incoherent, and fragmented stories can lead to fragments of anthropological theorization, pieces that mirror the women's own fragmentation. Biographies and temporalities in these fragmented, wounded worlds of migration are interlaced with those of invisible other forces, and these "registers fool with the ability of ontology, language, and history to recognize and/or recover a stable social subject" (Otero 2020, 87).

The beauty workers in Bangalore were told by state officials, whom they bribed, flirted with, feared, and sometimes (it was whispered), performed sexual favors for, that they had to place their case before an Assam tribunal and submit paperwork to prove their claim to Indian citizenship and scheduled tribe status. Otherwise, they would be deported or imprisoned in state detention centers. With this move,[14] villagers like Layla's father were now expected to produce "legacy papers," "link documents," "certified copies," "declared foreigner paperwork," "refugee certificates," and "Aadhar cards" or passports to prove their patrilineal rights of habitation.[15] The demand for legacy papers by the state meant that millions of impoverished people would have to battle the state and skirt police, all to stay in the only home they had ever known. After the existential wound of state unrecognition, Lakshya, Jhuma, and Layla expressed deep concern for their jobs and lives and the lives of those they loved. "How will we manage, madam?" Layla sobbed over the phone to me. I felt my heart squeeze hearing the fear in her voice. Then she added, "It's our karma, madam. Some bad thing we did in previous life. Now simply we have to suffer."

As Layla notes, the continuous wounding of state-based unrecognition had repercussions for notions of selfhood. The uncitizening of those on the periphery was seen by some as retributive karma for "bad things" done in a previous life. The women's worlds were built in part on this version of karma, of cause and effect, in which ethical responsibility was complex, diffuse, and fragmentary, often looping back on itself but nonetheless dramatically determining the course of their lives. Their understanding of ethics depended on a model of karmic cause and fragmented personhood when it came to explaining severe suffering. The concept of cause and effect woven through Layla's story is very telling. In some ways, her explanation was remarkably concrete, but the ethical story is complex because it combined various forms of misrecognition and dispossession. So she layered stories with different effects into her life to account for and detail the misrecognition and dispossession she felt.

For Layla and Lakshya, their personhood was not simply a fact but something to be navigated and worked on to force the state to heal the wound of disinclusion. They strategized in multiple ways to assemble the correct fragments into their own personhoods, including characters that might fuse with and possibly co-constitute their own bodies and spirits, such as Sati Mata and Bharath Mata, toward a hoped-for recognition by society and the state.

The existential wound of Sati's death and dismemberment, with which we began this chapter, continued to bother me. It seemed to suggest female self-sacrifice as a cosmogenic act that underpinned the power of the male gods, a fairly stereotypical if troubling reading. This led to a culturally defined canonical script of female suppression of ego (*ahamkara*), whereby shakti was offered as a template for appropriately refined feminine behavior (Menon 2002, 148). The Puranic[16] story of Sati's self-sacrificial death represents the ultimate existential wound. The prism of Shiva's stunned grief and the potentially destructive apocalypse that his grief unleashes on the world acts as a catalyst to Sati's dismemberment by Vishnu (Courtright in J. Hawley 1994, 31). This is the provocation for her transcendence, though it is fragmentary. The vulva is fragmented from her dismembered body and becomes its own form of the goddess—Kamakhya Devi—the foundation of Shakta and Tantra theologies (Hawley and Wulff 1996).

But Sati's sacrifice creates the moral geography of the nation of Bharath Mata herself. Fragments of her corpse falling to earth created the fifty-one peethas (seats) of Shakti worship, and so the Sati myth figures and configures the geography of Shakti worship in India. Through the landscape of India, where the pieces of her body fall, Sati is reborn, investing the geography with sacred life (Mukhopadhyay 2018, 4). As Diana Eck beautifully notes, "The divided body of Sati is the united land of Bharath [India]" (1986 cited in Courtright in Hawley 1994, 31). The mythical topos of Sati's corpse is based on a theological sacralization of the corpse itself that is central to Tantric worship and sacrifice and the understanding that Sati's corpse retains a surplus of life itself, a dynamic healing energy, the élan vital of the nation as mother (Urban 2010). Her self-sacrifice forms the sacred geography of the modern Indian nation-state. So, along with (re-)creating the world, Sati's grievous wound had created an ethical claim on the nation that seemed to be coming due.

The beauty workers at the parlor understood their affiliation with Sati as Kamakhya Devi on multiple levels: first, because she was the primary goddess of the Northeast and second, because of her wound, evidence of her sacrifice for her family. Anthropologists have written about sacrifice as an "intermediary between the deity and the human sacrifice"; the sacrificial victim maintains and/or repairs the cosmic order, creating moral conditions and ethical claims on the world and therefore establishing a social order (Turner 1992, 4; Valeri 1985, 65). For Sati, it is through facing death that eternal life is achieved. As Indira Arumugam notes, paraphrasing Marshall Sahlins, vitality and mortality are not contingent on human intentions and actions alone but come from elsewhere, from metahuman powers (Sahlins 2017 in Arumugam 2023, 4). Since in Hindu worlds, karmic debt creates a closed creative circuit, destruction is necessary for transformation, making Sati's self-sacrifice a necessary condition of the birth of the nation.

Worship of the fragments of Sati's corpse allows beauty workers not only to hope to get beyond their own karmic debt toward emancipation from the endless cycles of rebirth[17] but also to argue, as Lakshya does, that their devotion to Kamakhya makes them indubitably Indian, regardless of caste or religion. For the workers, these transductions between different ontological forms, worship, and citizenship are explicitly about what they see as a lack of justice (Keane 2016; Lambek et al. 2015).

It is no accident the beauticians come from the geographic margins of the state and the social margins of society and Kamakhya is their goddess. As Martínez et al. (2021, 4) say, "peripheral wisdom is not about some *other*, subversive knowledge"; rather, it is about resisting the urge to "extract meaning and assemble fragments into a whole." While epistemologically, opposition to the totalizing narrative of gathering the scattered body of Sati into a cultural and political whole might seem valid, ontologically the beauty workers felt that they, like Sati, were scattered piecemeal across the nation. Sometimes literally,

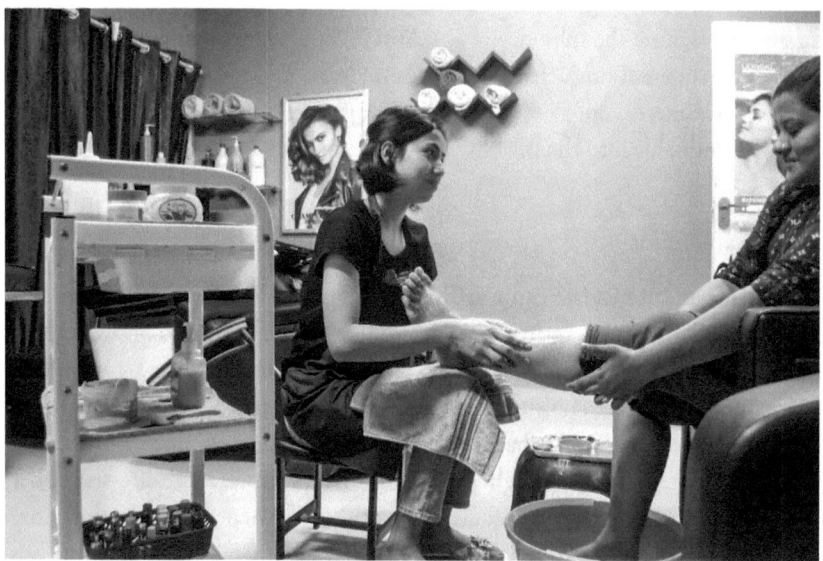

FIG. 4.1. A beautician from the Northeast works on a client's feet

as with Lakshya's back skin, which had been harvested from her and sold elsewhere. For them, then, the Yoni of the Kamakhya temple is emblematic of the dismemberment that the nation and their work demands. There is a paradoxical alignment between beauty and citizenship here, creating a transformation of the everyday world. Beauty is usually thought of as whole, harmonious and symmetrical; so for it to be applied to the disjointed and the fragment is a radical reconfiguration of what we consider beautiful. That the fragment of the goddess represents her wholly and the whole is beautiful, which makes the fragment beautiful and powerful as well as a representation of that which is lost and that which is beautiful that transcends the material and the everyday. As Ann Gold (2008, 175) notes, this idea that beauty is life-giving in an elemental sense, that it gives what makes life meaningful, is what renders beauty sublime. Elaine Scarry identifies this beyond-life quality—that beauty can in fact transform and transcend mundane life—which is ultimately an *ethical* act that makes sense of that which remains fragmented.

But where Layla comes from, one is brutally confronted by the limits of life. The way out, as Paul Stoller (2021, xiii) argues, is to tell a good story, while acknowledging "not knowing, unlearning, and the absence of knowledge." Telling stories of the constantly recurring sublimity of beauty via self-sacrifice and suffering is a strategy of survival, allowing beauty workers and clients to hope for and to visualize the subjunctive condition of wholeness, a mirror of the goddess's own reintegration. What Usha Menon (2002, 145) notes for Oriya women is true of Assamese women as well: "As embodiments of Sakti, women can transform the undoable into the doable, and the impossible into the possible."

Menaka's Wounds

Menaka's "vampire facial" came at the end of a long list of beauty treatments she had tried one after another in succession. When I first got to know her, she was in her late twenties, and I used to frequently find her with a cotton ball and toning solution, cleansing and toning her skin twice a day, a ritual that took an hour each time. At that time, she often visited the parlor for threading and facials. After a few years, when I began this study in earnest, she was in her mid-thirties and started to get facials and other treatments at the parlor more often. As she reached her forties, she started panicking, talking of nothing but her fading beauty. In her anxiety, she visited the salon at least once a week and had a monthly chemical peel and a standing hair-coloring appointment every six weeks. The repeated wounding of her skin and hair had its effects. She often returned from the parlor, her skin raw, hair an unnatural jet black, and wearing dark glasses. She would be unable to go out for a few days while she recovered, or, at a pinch, she would wear a thick foundation to cover her wounds.

We are familiar with the toxic combination of the global beauty industry and the embodied expectations of patriarchy setting impossible beauty standards in the West, standards that have gone global in the era of social media, and the accompanying psychic and social wounding that women endure in pursuing beauty (Etcoff 2000; Hesse-Biber 1996; Kaziga et al. 2021; Tate 2022). In Bangalore, home of the Indian modeling industry, these expectations, if one abided by them, were oppressive. They determined who was deemed the city's "*glitterati*," who was covered by the local press as "socialite material," what parties and influence one had, and accordingly, the opportunities that came one's way. For Menaka, who was a classical Bharatanatyam dancer, a part-time model, and a local celebrity, what beauty afforded her in terms of status and the wherewithal to open doors was significant. The fear of its loss was also about a loss of economic power and social influence.

As time went by, Menaka began asking me to bring her top-of-the-line "age-resisting" wrinkle creams and serums from the United States, along with cosmetics and micellar water for cleansing that were as yet not available in India. But as the Indian beauty industry grew and more of these beauty aids were readily available, her requests changed to newer technology of ice rollers, gold leaf under-eye pads, and shampoo that included strange ingredients like pregnant mare's urine or skin cream chock-full of hyaluronic acids and peptides to strip old skin cells and urge new, softer skin to grow. She urged me to try them, too: "We're growing old, T! Soon, it will all be over!" I had assumed she meant the battle to remain beautiful, but when I thought to ask her what precisely would be over, she looked discomfited and said with rising panic, "Everything, yaar! All over! No fun anymore." She then told me that she had stopped receiving gifts of saris from local sari shops, something that she had received as a model since her twenties. And her modeling gigs had started to morph. "Now I only get mother roles! Never mind... some role is better than no call only, na?" More important, I understood that the socialite pages had started overlooking her in favor of younger, emerging celebrities.

Menaka colored her hair with deep auburn highlights to cover the incipient gray. The ritual involved going to the parlor and sitting there, often for hours at a time, while her hair was foiled, treated, washed, and blow-dried. She told me how once they applied too much color and she got a "solid burning feeling on her scalp" and was scared all her hair would be burned away and she would be bald. So she hastily got the color washed off. Nonetheless, her wounding was continuous: the bleaching of her skin gave her burns, so did waxing, and once she told me in a whisper that vaginal waxing had torn her "down there," and she had to go to a doctor to get antibiotics: "Just my karma, T, to be so hairy!"

By her mid-forties, Menaka had started to put on some weight and began a daily exercise regimen of gentle walking, while she investigated liposuction and underarm pinning. In every WhatsApp call between us, she spoke about some beauty aid she had bought: a horsehair brush to prevent hair loss, a "totally natural" skin pack, a "tightening and brightening" skin care line that had mud from the Dead Sea, a Japanese kelp face mask, a set of black tar packs to remove blackheads, rose petal extract for firming, and on and on. She also started visiting medspas in London and Singapore for regular Botox injections and laser therapy for her underarms and face. She showed me the microscopic burn injuries from laser treatments, which I would not have seen or known had she not brought them to my attention. The vampire facial that I watched was the latest fad by which she hoped to keep aging at bay. It came after years of washing, cleansing, toning, facials, bleaching, threading, waxing, and Botox. With each passing year, I found Menaka discussing more invasive procedures.

In watching her chase one process after another, I realized that for many women beauty exists only as failed aspiration, a missed opportunity, a shadow that disappears as soon as we try to grasp it. What Menaka understood was that beauty is paradoxical; it flees as soon as attention is called to it. Very often, women's experiences of losing beauty are not coherent or linear, but they are wounding in ways that are largely inexpressible except through mourning that which was. Tim Ingold has called this tendency "the logic of inversion." "Through inversion," he argues, "the field of involvement in the world, of a thing or person, is converted into an interior schema of which its manifest appearance and behaviour are but outward expressions" (Ingold 2006, 11). So while lost beauty is seen on the exterior, women interiorize it as a fear, a failure to be beautiful, and this fear acts as a provocation to continue to greater and more radical beauty treatments to stay youthful and beautiful. Thus, the pursuit of beauty and its loss turns women inward, changing their interiorities, which in turn is supposedly reflected on their faces. Radhika met Menaka at an event sponsored by her company, and soon after she asked me, "What's wrong with your Menaka? Her face so hard.... She looks used and abused!"

For women like Menaka, intent on allure and radiance, beauty work becomes a boundless exercise of reconstruction, of chasing beauty through wounding practices as their beauty seems to stutter with age, and the depredations of time wreak havoc on their body, skin, and face. The women who pursue it most ferociously are not those who are unbeautiful but rather those who were beautiful at one time and enjoyed the power and status that beauty brought and are afraid of losing that power, like Menaka and many aging Hollywood actresses. Menaka was fighting for vitality against a ticking clock. She and others like her expressed that it was their responsibility to combat age with the tools at their disposal. When she went to Singapore to get fillers for her face, she bemoaned the fact that her face had "fallen" more than other Indian women her age: "What to do, T? It's my karma! Got to do something, no?" For her, getting fillers was ethical action to build her selfhood.

Beauty changes with age, and the wounds of beauty remain unhealed, left open. Beauty is always incomplete and unattainable, a source of frustration for women like Menaka. Complete analysis is not possible for beauty; rather, it rests in incoherence. We need to come to grips with this loss and the paradoxical wounding that women like Menaka engage in their pursuit of beauty. There is a sharp duality to this paradox—wounds are beauty, wounds lead to beauty, "one thing is another, but it can be both, and therefore neither" (Handelman 1998, 68). This creates a gap, inviting us to think of the status that women derive from it more critically. David Napier (1986, 5) says, "Our ability to recognize illusion depends upon the extent to which we accept some method of apprehending it." Indeed, for women like Menaka, wounds invite beauty in, and they are courted agentively toward apprehending beauty. Thus, wounding offers the possibility of an opening to beauty, and suffering is often seen as a pathway to the sublime by reconstructing the subject, endlessly, recursively, and mobiusly upon itself.

Menaka's ethical selfhood was built on the seeking of these wounds to provoke beauty. For as she averred, "if you are beautiful, you can do *anything*," implying both a courageous worldview and possibly an unethical one, depending on the emphasis one placed on the "anything" one could do. For Menaka, beauty allowed her to rewrite her karma, so her ethical personhood was not simply a fact, her karma not merely inherited, but something to be navigated and worked on via beauty. Her beauty, she believed, as did the women around her, was the outer manifestation of an inner ethical self, and so the more materially beautiful she was, the more morally valuable she could be. The loss of beauty for her was the loss of respect, goodness, status, and power. Thus, her panic at aging was inevitable, for it was not just her physical embodied self that she saw changing in the mirror but also the status and power she had as a result of it, and most important, her moral and ethical self was called into doubt. She felt an older woman might be respected, but she could never be a goddess.

Madhu's Wounds

Madhu met me at Bodycraft, the local franchise parlor where she went "once a week" for beauty work. She was in gym clothes and had an appointment to get her face waxed. While we were waiting, she recounted one particularly painful moment with her uncle that had propelled her to join a gym, work out every day, and to get more beauty work than before.

A year prior, she had returned home from college abroad where she had completed an advanced degree, studying marine mammals. But the rich food of the dormitory disagreed with her, and she "put on a lot of weight." At a family gathering a few months after she returned, her uncle cornered her in front of several family members and jokingly commented on her weight gain: "What's happened to you? You went to study whales and now you became one!" Madhu recalled her shock at his blatant attempt to hurt her: "He's such a bastard. He laughed happily after that!" The wound was so deep that she refused to go to any family reunions or parties for a year: "I decided I'm not going until I have a total makeover."

More often than not, wounds are inflicted by loved ones. The female body, with its particular nature and bodily cycles—menstruation, pregnancy, maternity, and lactation—its leaks and refusals, is often subject to the use of misogynistic disciplining in Bangalore.

FIG. 4.2. Madhu's response to her uncle, which she shared on WhatsApp

Madhu's mother, to whom she complained about the uncle's comments, told her firmly to ignore him and take the high ground. This was a prescription to be more "ladylike," more genteel. As Usha Menon (2002) notes, such refinement is the goal of Hindu women even when they unearth their *shakti* (female power). I eventually spoke to Madhu's mother who was clearly embarrassed that Madhu had spoken of her wounding so openly. "Nothing can be done since he is family," she said firmly. "She's got to learn to be classy. No point in focusing on the negative! It will only hurt more." In her mind, focusing on the wound only made the cut deeper. Thus, the only answer to the cut was to repress it, to suture it up and wait patiently until it scarred over. "You must learn to be tough; you can't be so sensitive," she told Madhu, who made a face. Her mother's contradictory instructions to "be classy" and yet "be tough" convinced Madhu that she needed to repress any negative thoughts and "carry on" regardless of the shame and anger she felt. Madhu's mother put it succinctly: this was an "everyday nuisance" for women in India—"If you are a girl in India, this is life, no? If you get upset by small things, then you'll be upset all the time." I often heard older women like Madhu's mother give similar advice to younger women to ignore their wounds and hope for the best. Being wounded by others is to be accepted passively, understood to be part of the female ontological experience.

But Madhu refused passivity. Instead, she focused on the anger her uncle's remarks provoked in her to regain agency, "my shakti," as she called it. Namely, she returned to the parlor and sought out deeper physical wounding to deal with the emotional wounding of being seen as fat. She told me of her experience getting liposuction in London, what she delicately termed, "body sculpting surgery": how she did research and saved money to go to the best plastic surgeon; how she convinced her parents; how excited she was when she and her mother traveled to London and stayed in a "cute" Airbnb apartment for two weeks; how the surgeon explained how he would use a huge syringe to suction fat from her thighs and belly with small incisions in her stomach; how much pain she was in after the surgery; how she took two weeks to recover and remove the tight bandages; and how much she "loved" shopping for "amazing" clothes in London after the surgery and during the European holiday they treated themselves to after. She said that when she woke up after the surgery, the surgeon showed her a "huge bottle" of yellowish fat he had dug out of her: "That was the first time I felt like, abbah, finally, I can look in the mirror and not see just my thighs!" She then said that she felt like the fat in the bottle represented the words that had wounded her, which was removed "like a poison" from her body. In other words, Madhu saw the fat in the bottle as something not of herself but rather something that needed to be taken away to reveal her *true* self. Ironically, Madhu's agentive action to combat the psychic wounding of her uncle's remarks was to demand and employ the physical wounding of liposuction and other beauty treatments to become the pretty woman she wanted to and was expected to be.

Madhu returned home triumphant after the liposuction surgery, and at the next family get-together, she wore her tightest jeans and a chic top. She said, "I had also straightened my hair with *Kerastase* treatments and started laser for my underarms and arms. It hurt like hell, but look now—so smooth!" She tilted the phone to her arms and showed me fair, poreless skin without a single hair. She continued, "Then I went on social and got tips for highlighting, definition and all with makeup. When I went for the family get-together later that year, uncle was stunned. He stared at me and called me 'superstar' and then asked when I'll get married. He's a total pedo[phile]!" she scoffed. "Then he started humming the tune to 'Pretty Woman.' But tomorrow, if I have hair on my arms or I put on a few pounds, I'm sure he'll say something stupid that hurts like hell!"

I asked Madhu's mother, a renowned beauty, what she thought of Madhu's approach to healing her wounds. She appeared on the WhatsApp call, glowing, her long hair tied up in a topknot and wearing a rich embroidered kaftan. She said admiringly that it was all Madhu's choice to have the surgery, the laser, and other "treatments." She said that she was worried and skeptical at first ("after all, she is so pretty anyway") but soon she saw how much confidence it gave Madhu. "Totally worth it! After the surgery, she came back and she became manager at the job and . . . Only thing left is two small scars on her thighs!" she summed up. Madhu looked pleased at the compliment of her judgment.

The idea of removing parts of the body that did not fit one's estimation of how one should be seen and othering it as something not of your own, like Madhu's fat in the bottle, came up one day in the parlor in the reaction of the women to the story of Sati's penance to marry Lord Shiva. Tanya detailed the many penances Sati did: how she went to the Himalayas looking for Shiva; how she found a place under a tree and went for days without eating or drinking; how she stopped speaking; how her body became rail thin; and finally, how Shiva found her and fell in love with her. At this point, Menaka stopped her. "Wow! Naturally, he fell in love. She was like on a super diet! She must've looked too good! Slim and trim! Like full gymming only." Aseema concurred, "I need to go on this *tapasya* diet . . . full! Gym not working."

It is no accident that the great goddess Shakti, in her incarnation as Sati, resorts to asceticism to garner Shiva's love (Hiltebeitel 2011). But after her dismemberment and rebirth as Parvati, she repeats the process to attract Shiva's attention yet again and succeeds. Nell Hawley (2022) notes that the classical texts remark on the goddess's mirroring of Shiva's own asceticism[18] and the fact that the embodied evidence of her asceticism makes her more alluring. She is thin but radiant with the power of the penance.

Following the story, Menaka announced to the parlor that she had lost fifteen kilograms when she went to Soukhya Spa for a month and went on a liquid diet. Everyone congratulated her. She told the group that while she hated the bitter gourd (karela) juice, it was efficacious and "melted" all the fat away. Manavi made an envious face, her henna-drenched hair in Layla's hands. Madhu said that Soukhya Spa was "very expensive" but insisted it was "totally worth it" because through the treatments, she had had an emotional breakthrough: "I felt free." Aseema summed up the ethical value of going to a spa: "Your good karma took you there. Must be your daddy sending you there." Menaka concurred, gesturing to the ceiling of the parlor and kissing her fingers, indicating the presence of her dead father: "Yeah! He knew I needed it."

The shared idea behind Madhu's body sculpting and the ladies' view of Sati's penance as a form of dieting was that these practices removed parts of the body that were alien to who they really were, and by removing the fat, the real person was revealed to them and to the world. What was valuable to Madhu's mother was the confidence that excising that part of her body gave Madhu. The lesson of Menaka's story was that the removal of the thirty pounds had made her feel freer, like Sati, more radiant, and more powerful. For Radhika, the surgeon's two tiny wounds were a way for Madhu to work through her grievance with her uncle's wounding words by suctioning them out of her body.

In the telling of Madhu's and Sati's stories, I realized that these parallel narratives allowed women to remain in the space of transverse irresolution, for if one's self is complex, then the path forward is not one of reconciling the parts but rather attaining an ease with the many different fragments. These fragments inhered, as did the body parts, the chemicals, the objects, and the memories, allowing women to see themselves as present in many different selves, in different places, each one piece redolent of the whole. Thus, the women did not fight the wounds but rather claimed them, courted them, as part of themselves that gave them power in an uncertain world.

Lakshya's Wounds

Lakshya's scarred back and the story of its acquisition haunted my dreams for months. Yet, as I knew from talking with migrant women who worked in the parlors, her physical wounds were merely an extension of the psychic wounds of displacement that they all shared. Nonetheless, working in a beauty parlor, making women beautiful day after day, seemed to me to be a cruel irony for Lakshya, for the question of beauty was fraught for her because of her scars. She hid her back like a deformity, being particular to always wear salwar suits or sari blouses with a high neckline that covered her back.

It was fashionable at that time for young women to wear low-cut or backless sari blouses, but I never saw Lakshya express a desire to wear such a style. Only once, when I was in the parlor and the girls were getting ready to go to Jhuma's niece's wedding party, did something untoward occur that brought this issue to the fore. Lakshya was planning to wear a beautiful watermelon-colored sari with sparkling zardozi work, but she could not find a matching blouse. Layla offered to loan her a blouse in the right color, but unaware of her scarred back, brought a blouse that was merely tied with some ribbons at the back. I saw Lakshya's face fall as she politely refused. In the end, she decided not to go as she could not find an outfit that she felt suited her and the occasion. It seemed that her scar and the wounding that caused it would continue to haunt her throughout her life.

Most of the workers did not know of her scars and often complimented her on her modest comportment despite her obvious beauty and expertise as a beautician. Only Jhuma, whom she had met in her first days at the Lotus, and

Radhika knew of her secret scar and protected it. I too had danced around the topic, afraid I would hurt her in speaking about it.

Although her scars would have surely elicited sympathy, Lakshya rarely spoke about or showed her wounds. Unlike Dewachi's (2015b, 2) Iraqi interlocutor, a survivor of war, who showed his wounds (supposedly acquired because of torture) to gain the sympathy of US officials and legitimate his claims for asylum, she was dignified and silent. The scar represented the peripheral, the unsayable, and the silence that surrounds such a gap typically makes us want to suture the skin of the narrative back together over the missing piece, the wound, toward a more complete picture, a more synthetic and beautiful one. But Lakshya was an exception; she refused to narrativize her pain and did not want to reconstitute her life or her fate around or through her wound. This silence, a failure of utterance, remits us to a cloud of the impossible, of unknowing, which reveals in turn that uncertainty rests as possibility. Lakshya's wounding made it possible for her to get a job and allowed her family back in Assam to live, but her silence begged the question: What happens when a woman is not able or willing to take control of her own wounding?

When I first met Lakshya over a decade and a half ago, she was in her early thirties, and despite the scar, she was energetic and fun. With her wide smile, hearty laugh, and efficient air, she seemed poised to go far. She was talkative in Hindi and an English patois, and we became friends (as much as the class divides allowed) as she joked about her job and the clients. But over the years, her body paid the price for the repetitive and unrelenting work of care. When I saw her again, four years later, I realized that she had traded in her original wound for an ongoing wounding, determined to build an expertise in beauty work. She had risen in her job, becoming the chief parlor worker overseeing the other "girls" of Senorita and then the Blushington and the Vive spas.

While successful and an acknowledged expert with a long roster of "ladies" who specifically asked for her, the change in her appearance was marked. She seemed to have aged twenty years. Her walk had stiffened as her knees had become swollen and painful, and she had a hollow cough that returned intermittently. She wore a thick cotton back brace and had got used to holding her hands a particular way while threading, which meant that the thread cut into her fingers repeatedly, and they bled all the time. Her hands hurt when she had to cut vegetables, pleat a sari, or do any other housework. She said to me while I watched her work, "My body is broken now" (Hindi = badaan toota hua hai). It was clear that beauty work wounded both worker and client.

Beauticians like Lakshya, Layla, and Jhuma spend years standing and doing repetitive tasks—stirring wax, twisting and pulling hair while blow-drying,

FIG. 4.3. Two trainee beauticians learning the endless work of blow-drying hair under the watchful eye of a senior beautician

and bending over eyebrows, feet, and hands. Doing the same tasks over and over again—standing, leaning over, pulling, bending, squatting—repeated for eight to ten hours a day, six days a week, for years without a break—took its toll on the body. As I got to know the beauty workers' stories, I began to index their pain and, through it, other unresolved wounds in their lives that they sought to mitigate through their expertise and self-discipline. As Lakshya labored over the following eight years, I watched her change: knees and elbows deformed, her fingers twisted with arthritis, her hands became spotted with burn marks from the hot wax, and she had a constant, ragged cough. Maura Finkelstein (2019, 75), in her illuminating study of mill workers in Mumbai, trenchantly calls their bodies an "archive of pain and exhaustion." Lakshya's seemed the same.

Lakshya tried various kinds of home remedies, rubbing warm oil and herbs on her hands and elbows and taking Dolo (paracetamol). All the pain remedies were temporary, but she never complained. Her pain was fundamentally unshareable across the abyss of class, ethnicity, and caste. Workers like Lakshya and Jhuma hid or ignored their damaged and deformed bodies, asserting their willingness and ability to work hard. At first glance, beauty work does not seem that difficult, and the beauticians' skill in conveying that is part of the appeal.

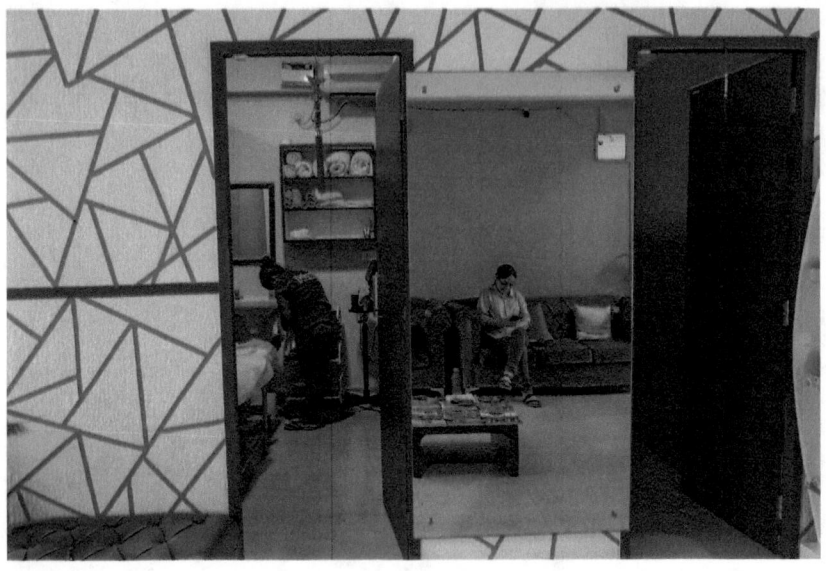

FIG. 4.4. A beautician taking a break and checking her phone in an upscale salon break room

Given the prevailing assumption by the client class that the working classes were prone to immorality and idleness, beauty workers had to frame their suffering carefully, lest they seem simply resistant to work. Acknowledging pain was often frowned upon, for it was seen as a discreet criticism of the parlor, and it suggested that the worker was weak. So workers like Lakshya hid their ongoing wounds and swallowed painkillers to prevent a breakdown.

One memorable afternoon, when Madhu had come to the parlor to get her underarms waxed, Lakshya could not bear the arthritic pain in her hands and broke down in tears, bewailing her broken body in the break room. "Only Kamakhya Devi must help me now," she wailed, holding her hands. The girls were upset and rallied around Lakshya, taking on her tasks for the day while she recovered. On other days, I watched the workers give each other empathic back rubs and pats on the shoulder to acknowledge the pain and continuous wounding. As Kleinman et al. (2001) note, the act of expressing suffering has profound political and perceptual consequences in creating connections between sufferers. There are different concepts of body at play between middle-class clients and working-class beauticians with different understandings of pain and wounding. In migrant communities, people's bodies are understood as "hard." Firm, untiring muscles promote hard work, and a tough skin is expected to develop, one impermeable to damage or hurt (Santo et al. 2023, 10). Migrant women are held to account in these terms, but sometimes the veil lifts. In these moments, Lakshya, the perfect caring employee with an impenetrable shell, was seen needing care herself. This made her feel frail and out of control, so she tried to hide it as much as she could.

Nonetheless, beauty and wounds were clearly on Lakshya's mind despite sublimating her scarring in the pursuit of expertise. One evening later that year, Lakshya WhatsApped me. She was sitting on the back veranda of the Vive parlor, cleaning her nails. After glancing around furtively to make sure no one could hear her, she asked me about plastic surgery in the United States for victims of traffic accidents. I knew she was thinking of her scar and decided to broach the taboo topic. I asked her about it and how working in a beauty parlor made her feel. She clearly had not thought about it so openly before but was willing to indulge my questions on that afternoon. She tapped the nail file on her nails and, after a brief silence, said thoughtfully and carefully, "Ladies are beautiful, madam." "So are you," I replied. And Lakshya *was* beautiful with her wide-set eyes, long hair, radiant skin, and gentle smile. But Lakshya said, "No, madam. See how short I am. See my nose . . ." Then after a brief pause, she added, "My back . . ." gesturing to her shoulder. "That's why I cannot wear backless blouse and all." I asked her what she thought would happen if everyone saw her back. She looked at me, the screen blue-lit behind her in the gathering dusk, her eyes clear, and then said, "I don't think, madam [the owner] would like. . . . Looks bad, no?" The trauma of her deformity haunted her as did the story of its acquisition. She asked me if it was true that American plastic surgeons could fix her back. I told her that they could certainly make it better. She said she had heard that doctors in London could fix burn victims' faces, and in Thailand they made new noses without scars, so she was hopeful that one day she could save enough money to go to Thailand to get plastic surgery for her back. But she never brought it up again.

Healing Wounds

Neoliberal economics combined with a right-leaning Hinduism and a nation-state apparatus that is plainly discriminatory is not only manifest economically in India; it penetrates the most profound layers of existence for women. It has led to the emergence of hyperagentic individuals who assume little reference to or support in institutions, who find answers and solutions to social and physical ills on their own, and who re-create the stories embedded in myth in nonnormative ways to think the unthinkable: that which is ineffable, nonarticulable, and wounded. Here, wounds are either sought willingly by clients in hopes of provoking beauty, such as with Menaka and Madhu, or they are the transverse products of state-based and social exclusion, such as for Layla, or they are the unexpected openings of migrancy and work that neoliberalism offers in the contemporary era. Wounding is the basis of the re-creation of self for these women. Workers like Layla and Lakshya, who were traumatized by forces beyond their control, attempted to achieve ethical selfhood through the repetitive wounding of hard work, conceived of as modern-day tapas. On the other hand, women like Menaka and Madhu, who sought out wounding agentively toward proximate concerns, often discursively focused on the suffering of past lives or the possibility of a future transcendence.

But the wound is also the origin of female ethical personhood in Hinduism, as the Sati story implies. In 2008, Roy Wagner argued that the concept of dividual personhood allowed for persons being composed of multiple subelements and that larger framing components and ethical personhood arose at various levels. So crafting ethical personhood involves dealing with wounds, either by ignoring them or by facing them head on and by choosing and choreographing an optimal set of ethical elements, including bodies, memories, affects, stories, material objects, chemicals, and the space between, forming a complex and contingent personhood.

The Final Wound

When I returned five years later to the parlor, which was to be my final time there, though I did not know it then, I noticed that Lakshya seemed to be determined to bury her wounds even deeper. She took more medications and worked harder, often spending fifteen hours in the parlor, six days a week. When I asked about her punishing schedule, she revealed that her father had a terrible illness (lung cancer) and her younger sister had to get married, and she had to save money for it. "When are you planning to go to Thailand?" I asked her, remembering her hope of reconstructing her back. She looked directly at me and said,

> No, madam. No money and no time. And even then, why to do it now? Now I am too old. Nobody cares about my back. Not like I will get married or anything. Why to bother? I will just be like this only.

Then, after a few minutes' silence, she added, "My karma, madam. Maybe in my next life."

Thank God, my daughter finally made up her mind to get married! Now her whole life is set.... He's good boy and will take care of her. I can die in peace!
—Radhika

Without makeup, how can you be a bride?
—Jhuma

FORTUNATE 5

Sita's Bhagyam

Mrs. Iyengar, Menaka's mother, often mentioned the goddess Sita, heroine of the Ramayana, to me in pointed ways. Sita, the long-suffering wife of the great god Rama, was, in Mrs. Iyengar's imagination, the exemplary wife: obedient, adoring, beautiful, and chaste. In the epic, Sita was abducted by the demon king Ravana and taken to the island of Lanka because he coveted her for her beauty (Kinsley 1988). Sita refused to give in to Ravana's demands, however, instead waiting for Rama to kill Ravana and rescue her, restoring his honor and hers as well. Her fidelity was her strength.

When I began this study of parlors, I was researching the temples in Malleshwaram, and I often arrived at Menaka's house in a sari and wearing my mangalyam (marital necklace) and all the accoutrements of my casted marital status. This was expected of me in the temples. Mrs. Iyengar, an older, married, Brahman lady, approved of what she saw as my cultivation of a modest persona. Occasionally, she would break into the Kannada song "Bhagyade Lakshmi Baramma" (Fortunate Lakshmi come here) in delight and offer me tambulam, the ritual gift of fruit and clothing that one offered married women.

Menaka would trill, "You are training to become a full auntie!" indicating my old-fashioned appearance and deportment. When I completed the Malleshwaram temple study, however, I took to accompanying Menaka to her salon appointments in my usual uniform of jeans, kurta, and a shawl. Mrs. Iyengar did not take kindly to the switch. She would pointedly note the absence of my mangalyam even though Menaka and her other daughters rarely wore theirs. "One should be like Sita" (Kannada = Sita tharage irribeku), she would intone, looking gloomily at my bare neck. Repeatedly telling the story of Sita's abduction by the demon king Ravana, which I suspect she likened to my abduction to the West for education, she would respond with many tongue clicks of dismay at Sita's, and perhaps my own, misfortune: "Poor thing! What a fate. To leave your home" (Kannada = Ayyoo Paapa! Yenu grihachara). Mrs. Iyengar's granddaughter Madhu, the successful developer, always rolled her eyes when Mrs. Iyengar returned to Sita as exemplary woman: "Oh my God! Again, Rama-Sita!"

A few days after Mrs. Iyengar had launched into yet another Sita story, I accompanied Madhu to the Bodycraft parlor as she got a bikini wax. She said it was in preparation for her boyfriend returning from a visit to London. She suggestively licked her lips. He had "fallen" for her across the gym, admiring her beauty, she said. "I just phasaod [Hindi = trapped] him," she said smugly. Madhu then brought up Mrs. Iyengar's story of Sita. "I don't know how you take it, T!" she said in solidarity. "I can't believe she said Sita was fortunate. Can you imagine? Ajji is really too much! Everyone usually says not to name your daughter Sita, right? Because she was kidnapped, they say it will bring bad luck. But Ajji thinks she was married to this great guy, so okay! So long as you are married, doesn't matter, right?" Single at the age of thirty, Madhu clearly felt the pressure from her extended kin group to be married despite her success at her job. Musing further about her own preferences in relation to Sita's story, she added flippantly, "Not a bad thing, island holiday for Sita. If I could bring my toy, I wouldn't mind a getaway. I told my guy, better be better than my toy. Otherwise, I'll need more batteries!" After laughing at her masturbatory joke, she continued, "And anyway, that Ravana . . . he didn't even touch her. Ajji says it because of her sowbhagyam, she was so pure! But what kind of guy was this Ravana? After taking the trouble to kidnap her, he couldn't even, you know . . . No balls!"

My field diary that day noted my surprise at Madhu's ready but odd comparison of her vibrator and her boyfriend, given that premarital sex, though ubiquitous among young adults in Bangalore, was still frowned upon and not talked about. But I was truly shocked at her suggestion that Ravana's reluctance to sexually assault Sita indicated a lack of machismo on his part. That Ravana was supposedly an ethical king who recognized Sita's wifely adoration, that Sita's bhagyam protected her from violation, and that rape was powerful violence was elided, if not erased, in Madhu's disturbing interpretation.

Bhagya.[1] Fortune. Conjugality. Rape. Vibrators and demon island vacations. My head spun.

It led me to ask myself how women in Bangalore understood fortune, or bhagya. The semantic field of bhagya as fortune is widely used in Sanskrit epic and religious literature as well as in most contemporary Indian languages, but its intersections with women's beauty and their recognition within society has not been sufficiently analyzed. How is fortune linked to beauty and to sexuality? Ideological polarity—between bhagya (fortunate, lit. "allotted share") and durbhagya (unfortunate)—plays a major role in defining the status of persons, particularly women, in the Hindu context (Carman and Apffel-Marglin 1985; Hann and Parry 2018; Raheja 1985). This is especially the case since women are expected to be pure and to carry the burden of caste purity (M. N. Srinivas 1977). A significant aspect of fortune for a woman is a successful marriage. In fact, I would disagree with Louis Dumont's (1980) claim that the binary of purity and pollution is the overwhelming structuring principle of social relationships in Indian casted society. For women, fortune and misfortune are the overriding metric by which women in Bangalore both judge and are judged.

Traditionally, bhagya was thought to be a divine gift, allied with women's beauty. It was a gift of grace from the gods, one's allotted portion based on one's karma. Radhika and her friends often pointed this out. After remarking that someone was "too pretty" or "really cute," they would crack their knuckles on their temples to rid themselves of envy and of the bad luck of the "evil eye" and say in begrudging tones, "She's lucky, haan? Good karma or what?" Young women are deemed bhagyashali (attracting good fortune) if they are gifted with beauty. Bhagya is thus intertwined with being fortunate, receiving a gift. When viewed through the lens of beauty, it is seen to be both prophetic, enunciating a possible future, and self-fulfilling of that future. In other words, a beautiful (bhagya) girl is imagined to have a fortunate marriage ahead of her, and of course her beauty conspires to bring about such a marriage. Unlike the usual anthropological focus on *mis*fortune, here we interrogate what the recognition of being fortunate offers for women in contemporary Bangalore. For women, bhagya seems to be located in being beautiful and thus being able to attract fortunate circumstances.[2]

The French thinker Luce Irigaray writes that female beauty is always about attracting the Other. According to Irigaray, in the West, beauty is almost never perceived as a phenomenon expressive of interiority, whether of love, of thought, of flesh. We look at ourselves in the mirror, as Irigaray says, to "please someone, rarely to interrogate the state of our body or our spirit, rarely for ourselves and in search of our becoming" (Irigaray quoted in Robinson 2000, 230). In this doubled consciousness, the beauty we seek is for others' pleasure but in time becomes a deeply meaningful practice for us as well.

For women like Radhika, Madhu, and Radha, beauty functions as a constructed surface decoration, a shrungar, which demands societal recognition but also affects selfhood. In studying the Hagen people's cosmetics and decoration, Marilyn Strathern (1979, 243) reflects that decoration is in fact a "disguise," and discovering the person underneath is a kind of "pleasurable shock." In Bangalore, by contrast, cosmetics, though applied superficially, are usually seen as "revealing" the beautiful person inside by covering up flaws that are thought to be extrinsic to the true self. Indeed, the growing beauty and cosmetics industry in India suggests that many women seek to reveal themselves and their beauty every day.

In the real world, as Mrs. Iyengar constantly reminded her granddaughters, beauty was the currency of womanly success through marriage. Marriage led to fortune since conjugality led to a rise in status and recognition. It is also linked powerfully with women's sexual continence and marital fidelity. Anthropology sees the social as "prior to the gods" (Ramberg 2014, 214), so conjugality has been seen in terms of social structure. In a casted and clan society like India, women are seen literally as "gatekeepers," maintaining the family's casted status through the performance of the household rituals and the cooking of caste-specific foods, and so forth so women's purity and sexual fidelity is thought to be of prime importance to group cohesion (Sengupta 2020). Thus, one type of feminine bhagya is supposedly derived from marriage and is a reward for women's sexual fidelity. Marital bhagya, known as *sowbhagya*, or fortune due to marriage, is formative to women's self-construction, and thus, widowhood has historically been a symbol of inauspiciousness (Chakravarti 1995). Generally, once women are married, they are thought to acquire sowbhagya—the fortune of conjugality coterminous with auspiciousness—regardless of individual circumstance, such as if the man was a wife beater or a loser.

Thus, sowbhagya, and bhagya more generally, are attached to womanhood and are conceived as forms of symbolic wealth that can be augmented or diminished as a result of personal choices that affect one's status (through marriage and otherwise). The more I thought about this wifely dynamic, the more I felt that traditional, idealized dynamic reverberate, disconcertingly, in my own life, filtering my world through its unrelenting lens. After all, Mrs. Iyengar's appreciation of me stemmed not from my individuality but from my marital state, which she saw as my selfhood. For her, sowbhagya was the key manifestation of my bhagya.

For Mrs. Iyengar, the mythical and Brahmanic male model of the sexual economy of marriage, where Sita's purity is exemplary and the chastity of women is central, is where the honor of the male clan and of the nation resides. One way it does so is by centralizing Brahmanic and Sanskritic goddesses like Sita and Lakshmi and marginalizing "folk" goddesses like Kamakhya and Amman. This displacement of the Devi not only establishes a rigid social hierarchy based in Sanskritization of the goddess but also subtly argues for heteronormative relations where women's roles are limited to wife and mother. As Lucinda Ramberg (2014, 215) states, "It establishes the secularity of sex and secures the state by displacing the Devi." This focus on female purity (as opposed to fecundity) sidelines some forms of sexual union and criminalizes others (Chakravarti and Krishnaraj 2018). The sanctions on alternate kinds of marriage and single women prioritize "ideal" citizens who are heteronormative in their sexual relations, modern yet religious in their outlook, and aspirational in neoliberal terms.

For Mrs. Iyengar's granddaughters, like Radha, a starlet in the film industry, who received her grandmother's wisdom on bhagya with a wry smile, Mrs. Iyengar's understandings of beauty and conjugality were "old fashioned" and somewhat problematic. Radha's mother, Menaka, explained to me that in the past two decades, as Bangalorean women became more independent, bhagya no longer evidenced itself in a "good" marriage alone. Radha corroborated this view: "If you have bhagyam, it's no longer like you have to have a guy. You can have bhagyam and be like a superstar! It's not just through your relationship, okay? We are all not like Sita, Sati-Savitris." In short, by critiquing established myths of wifeliness in combination with changing understandings of marriage, Bangalorean women like Radha demand a new recognition of their inherent bhagya, one that is not based on marriageability alone. Judith Butler (2004) writes that accomplishing recognition as a subject within a neoliberal conjugal frame, as is expected of Radha and many other women in Bangalore, depends on being able to "demonstrate one's ability to make these distinctions and to incorporate them as aspects of one's personhood" (Butler in Ramberg 2014, 217). This can result in alternate tellings of myth of heroines known for their wifely virtue, such as Sita and Savitri.

The alternate tellings of myth that Radha, Madhu, Menaka, Jhuma, and others engage in allow bhagya to be read in a broader sense based on the hermeneutics of telling. Storytelling in this sense allows a different morality to take hold, if not for the majority, at least for a few. For as M. N. Srinivas (1977, 223) noted some half century ago, contradictory theological and philosophical positions on women's freedom derive "thirdhand" from the sacred literature, as most middle-class and savarna groups are encumbered by a "bibliocentric view" of the society, though they might know little of the theodicy. Telling myths in counter-registers thus broadens recognition to incorporate emergent ideas that coalesce around neoliberal and sometimes feminist constructions of feminine desire and materialist longings. Women in this chapter accrue power through the telling of these myths, self-narrativizing in the process, and often becoming recognized as the moral center of their families. What is recognition in such circumstances?[3] Is emancipation ever a possibility? What form would it take? These rapidly shifting readings trouble questions of agency, desire, and ethics and in turn of the recognition of self and other that delineate the horizons of fortune.

Cosmetic Capital

One hazy May day, I was in an informal settlement named Lingarajapuram at the New Look Ladies beauty parlor. New Look occupied a small corner unit in a mall in a tatty yellow building off the Hennur Main Road, which was built over an enormous drain. The parlor was separated from the mall by aluminum-and-glass panels which bore photographs of Western women from the 1970s with outdated hairstyles, pink frosted lipstick, and blue eyeshadow. It consisted of two rooms and a few red plastic chairs. Two middle-aged Muslim women with the veils of their burqas thrown back were seated in them, desultorily drinking tea out of tiny plastic cups and chatting. One had jet-black hair and a pleasant expression, and the other had hair in shades of black and orange with gray showing through. I mentally dubbed her Tiger Lady. Another couple of women, one older in a yellow sari and the other a young woman wearing a light gray salwar, were seated in the other parlor chairs.

The woman in the salwar was named Preethi and confessed excitedly that Bhagya, the beauty worker in the parlor, was going to "do full makeup" for her so she could get some professional photographs to join a matrimonial website. Her mother, the lady in the yellow sari seated next to her, intervened quellingly, "Preethi was studying all this time. Already it is too late to find a good boy!" Bhagya rubbed talc on Preethi's eyebrows and instructed Preethi to hold her eyelids.

"*Illi kai haako* [Kannada = Keep your fingers here]," she said rather brusquely. When she was done with the threading of Preethi's eyebrows, Bhagya left and returned with a plastic case that held some well-used bottles of foundation and a bin of cotton balls. She smeared the thick foundation, which was a yellowish paste, onto Preethi's face covering Preethi's acne, patting it in as one would apply putty to wood. When Bhagya was satisfied that Preethi's skin was entirely covered, she dusted setting powder in a pale color that did not match her skin over her face.

Bhagya then quickly moved on to eyeshadow. The palette she brought out was so well used that some of the colors were totally worn away. She took some thick brown, yellow, and orange shadow on a brush and smudged the resulting shiny dust over Preethi's eyelids, adding mascara and eyeliner. Then she colored in Preethi's lips with a deep orange lipstick, which she also smeared on her cheeks and patted with a cotton ball. She declared, "*Aithu* [Kannada = Done]!" and brought out a small hand mirror for Preethi to admire her makeup. Preethi looked pleased at her transformation.

Bhagya stepped back and said to me quietly, "All girls want to get married. They think it will be like Hindi movie, full love, romance, dancing, and all. Before I got married, I also thought like that. But only after marriage, then I knew . . . with *beegaru* [Kannada = in-laws] life is very difficult, madam." Tiger Lady overheard us and was irritated by such truth telling. She said in a mixture of Urdu and Kannada, typical of Bangalore Muslims, "*Ladies ke liya shaadi se hi izzat hota hai!*" Preethi's mother nodded sagely and translated for me, thinking I didn't understand: "*Maduve idre sowbhagya, illadre aumana* [Kannada = With marriage comes fortune! Without it, dishonor]." She added, "Without marriage, how is a girl to manage? Our Preethi is very intelligent, good at studies, works hard, but . . ." She turned to the Muslim women and said, "*Masood, yane lucky nahi hai* [She is not lucky]." They nodded. "Even I, her mother, am telling this. With Preethi, I worry who will take care of her? What will people say?" Preethi looked upset but not surprised. Clearly, she had heard it all before.

The instrumentalization and democratization of bhagya or *masood* (luck) through beauty practices has led to a booming bridal beauty industry in India. A quick search for #bridalmakeup #India on Instagram will fetch over thirteen million results under the rubric of "curated Suhaag[4] (nuptial) look" with artists demonstrating their skills at contouring cheekbones, shadowing soft, "sexy" eyes, and achieving the flawless dewy complexion that brides dream of. According to the consultancy group KPMG, the Indian bridal industry was estimated (prepandemic) to be worth about US$50 billion,[5] with twelve million weddings per year, second only to the US industry, which is the largest in the world. As the COVID-19 pandemic dragged on through 2020 and then 2021, the Indian bridal industry carved out a significant presence on social media. Brides all over India shopped for their clothes and jewelry, makeup, and hairstyles online,[6] particularly on WhatsApp. Whereas Instagram serves as a discovery platform for retailers, WhatsApp is where customers communicate with family members and store owners[7] and where brides like Ami, Radhika's daughter who had suddenly decided to marry her American lover, and Madhu viewed possible "looks." "Can't manage without social these days" was Radhika's conclusion.

Bhagya and Beauty

Bhagya is a Sanskrit noun derived from the verbal root bhaj (to divide, to share, to distribute, to allot), used in everyday Indian languages to denote destiny—particularly a good destiny—and fortune, adjacent to if not allied with *feminine* auspiciousness. Men are rarely, if ever, thought of as having or needing bhagya. As a married woman dressed in a sari, when I was headed early in the morning to do fieldwork at the temple, I would be hailed by shopkeepers and vendors. They would beg me to buy their produce and wares, often giving it away at rock-bottom prices, seeking my bhagyam for their sales during the day. In a local practice known as "boni," young women's hands, particularly married women, like the goddess Lakshmi they represent, are thought to be abundant, transferring fortune from the woman to the vendor for the day.

Although underinvestigated, the concept of bhagya, and its links with auspiciousness and beauty, form the ground on which destined relations, particularly marital relations, are tied. In her study on ritual fasts (*vrat*), Susan Wadley (1983, 161) refers to bhagya as a "counterpoint to the karma doctrine": "In the vrat literature, the most common term for destiny or fate is bhagya. In these texts, karma quite clearly refers to actions, with specific attributions of human conditions due to actions. But bhagya is destiny, or fate. . . . [The concept of bhagya] presents a potentiality of 'luck' or chance or fate (understood as unrelated to past acts) that is not implied by either the classical concepts of karma nor the concept of karma found in the vrat literature" (Wadley 1983, 159, 161 quoted in Guenzi 2012, 44–45). Indeed, then bhagyam, and by extension the vrat, is a fragile, unstable state where failure is expected. In Vedic literature, bhagya is read as "good fortune" or "prosperity," and Bhaga, "the Dispenser,"[8] is a deity[9] who distributes goods and pleasures (Dumézil 1988). So bhagya in Vedic literature denotes the portion or share of fate that humans receive from gods, rather than the consequences they bring on themselves through their past actions.

Interestingly, however, the word "bhagya" is also used to denote the human vulva and female sexuality as "shared" by the clan. Therefore, the purity of the woman becomes the purity of the clan itself. Bhagya is a gendered attribute located in heterosexual conjugality. As a consequence, dayabhagya, as a concept enshrined in Hindu law, is the portion of fortune that one is entitled to by virtue of one's birth, inheritance, and blood (Copeman 2019). Fortune is thought to bring one to one's destiny, as one aspires it to be. In thinking about bhagya, what emerged was the distance between luck as experienced and fortune as ontological. The exegesis that women offer in thinking about beauty as bhagya thus refers to two levels of reality: the ontological level (the objective reality of beauty and fortune) and the phenomenological level (people's perception of their fortune). Catherine Guenzi argues that "bhāgya has two main meanings. In its broadest sense, bhāgya is 'the ineluctable rule of destiny according to which all human actions are predetermined' (R. Varma 1971: 766), that is, 'fate,' 'destiny,' 'time.'"[10] But the second, more popular meaning, as women like Tiger Lady used it, was in the sense of "fortune," "luck," and "wealth." Thus, the adjective meaning "endowed with bhagya" (bhāgyavān or bhāgyasālī) designates a person who is prosperous, fortunate, wealthy, and lucky. In the feminine case, a person endowed by luck to be beautiful is thought to be bhagyashali, or fortunate.

A focus on physical beauty as a valuable possession seems to reverse scholarly preoccupations about Hindu embodiment. Traditionally, the focus of Hindu theology (except in Sakta and Tantra female-centric traditions) has been the negation of the desiring body. These Sanskritic theologies all focus on the goal of liberation (*moksha*), best attained by asceticism, a rejection of the sensual body, which is seen as the seat of the delusion. The Upanishadic corpus states, "In this body, which is afflicted with desire, anger, greed, delusion, fear, despondency, envy, separation from what is desired, union with what is not desired, hunger, thirst, old age, death, disease, sorrow, and so on, what good is the enjoyment of desires?" (Maitri Upanishad 1.3, cf. 3.4). But in the parlors, desire, or at least the appearance of desire, was central to the construction of "bodily capital" (Wacquant 1995).

This has much to do with status. For established English-speaking, upper middle-class families like Madhu's, the history of belonging is fixed, never at risk. Thus, their place in society is firmly cemented, yet they are constantly seeking to move up in the hierarchy and guard their current position. Madhu's grandmother, Mrs. Iyengar, was very concerned that Madhu's disastrous engagement "to a driver," as she put it, would endanger the family's status. "They are not like us!" Mrs. Iyengar said firmly, distinguishing Madhu's fiancé's family and their class position from her own. Madhu was upset with her family for "putting her fiancé down." "He owns a taxi company; he's not simply a driver!"

she defended him to me after hearing the rumors. Traditionalists like Mrs. Iyengar, and even modern women like Madhu, discriminate based on caste and class, making it very difficult, if not downright impossible, for newcomers like Preethi, Lakshya, and Jhuma to gain a foothold and climb the middle-class ladder. Yet all women desire the transformation of their bodies into the beautiful and fortunate, as denoted by upper-class and caste bodies. Makeup helps.

Makeup is revelatory. It sits painted on the skin, but Preethi said it revealed the bhagyam, the fortune of the woman underneath. Interestingly, the Hagen tribe exploits the cosmetic paradox in exactly the same way. Strathern avers that what is ordinarily hidden is brought out into the open through facial decoration; the inner beautiful self made manifest. Decoration here is not about creating or enhancing physical beauty but a mechanism of the revelation of the self (Strathern 1979, 249). For the Hagen, then, superficial decoration is illuminating, and the skin is the point of contact between the person within and the world without. This is true also of the women in the parlors. Their skin is thus both porous to the person within, and yet it is decorated like an impervious surface without.

Marital Bhagya

I met Preethi three years later, and she looked worn out. She had taken a prestigious job in a biotech company and was earning good money but was still single, much to her mother's chagrin. Her father had had a stroke and passed away, and she was now the sole wage earner for the family. Preethi's mother was worried that she was "still not settled." I told Menaka and Radha about Preethi's desperate search for a groom and her mother's worry. Menaka was sympathetic: "Poor thing! Everyone will ask about her being single." Radha said annoyed, "It's such BS! Thank God Mumma and our family doesn't apply such solid pressure!" I asked why Menaka didn't pressure her. "I think it's because we are more open minded, you know? Education . . ." she said smugly, though she herself had dropped out of college to pursue a movie career.

Marriage in India is situated as a "civilizing, normalizing and propertied form" of social relations that "saturates sexual relations with moral, jural and material significance," particularly for working-class and lower middle-class girls like Preethi (Basu and Ramberg 2015, 13). Radha said with a wry smile that "girls are supposed to 'settle' into married life," and her own choice to become an actress was viewed by those outside her family as unusual, risky, and "very out there."

Radha was gesturing to "powerful gendered marriage imperative" for women in India, particularly among middle-class Hindus and Muslims (Lamb 2022, 25). Shabnam, Aseema's daughter who was studying in Paris and had an English boyfriend whom her parents did not know about, spoke of the pressure to "get settled" constantly. "Mumma is bugging me. She keeps saying, 'Doesn't matter who, we will accept whomever you bring home. Just get engaged and settled!' As if! But she keeps saying their friends are pitying them saying I'm not married. I feel bad!" Then she added, "The first thing Papa will say if I bring Caspar home is, 'Jannat [heaven, love], how can you marry a Christian boy? And what is this name? Is he a ghost?' You can just imagine! I'm waiting until he becomes partner in Barclays, then Papa and Mumma will feel better that I'm settled to a guy who can look after me!" The pressure to "get settled" to someone who earns well is exacerbated by the notion of being thought of as (un)fortunate.

Unmarried or single women like Preethi, particularly those whose earnings support their families, are invisible, and life outside marriage is "unthinkable" for them as the burdens of their economic precarity structure their lives (Lamb 2018, 49). Indeed, as Sarah Lamb's poignant work on single women in India shows, singularity in India is a terminal condition that is feared, almost as an illness, particularly among the non-Westernized, provincial middle classes. Women who are single do not have the protection of a male figure, they lack resources, and are made to feel, both by their families and by the society at large, like failures. Women like Preethi, who try repeatedly but fail to get married and need to support their families with their own income, are still seen as burdens. When I saw Preethi's mother after a three-year hiatus, the first thing she said to me was, "We have not done our duty. Preethi is still not married! What to do?" Preethi herself started feeling this sense of failure despite her success at her job. She refused to go to her cousins' weddings or familial celebratory events, making herself more invisible in the process. Wider assumptions in the public media insist that the "unattached woman is a problem to be fixed" (Pinto 2014, 247). Indeed, marriage "looms large" in anthropological study, coalescing around questions of recognition that parallel these women's concerns about beauty. Because of the fundamental domains it encompasses as a primary axis of kinship and property, as a mechanism for regulating caste, class, and religious endogamy; and a crucial locus of recognition and governance within community and state, marriage is, as Srimati Basu reminds us in her study of mediating divorce and marriage in Kolkata, an overwhelmingly powerful economic, social, and governing force (Basu 2012, 2015). Heterosexual conjugality is the dominant frame in which women can be recognized in South Asia as in many other parts of the world.

However, with the changes that neoliberal capitalism has brought to Bangalore and the new pressures of education and career, the notion of "being settled" as the ideal aspirational state is not as appealing to women of Radha's generation. Radha spoke of her aspiration to become a "total superstar," which involved being single (at least in public) and seemingly available: "The tabloids and fans are always trying to pair you with someone. The minute you get married if you are a girl, then they simply discount you as 'taken,'" she scoffed. "You stop getting jobs. The directors think you'll break your contracts to have babies. And they feel you won't be up for doing romantic scenes with your screen partners. It's changing but very slowly." Ami, Radhika's daughter, put it best in an argument with her mother about the "right age" to get married. Radhika insisted it was in one's early twenties when one could "have fun" and yet start a family in due time. Ami listened impatiently to her mother and then said defiantly, "What if I want to have fun but not be married?" There was silence in the room. Then she added, "What if I want to stay by myself and have a good career rather than a family? Why should I be tied down by a family when I'm young? Isn't it my choice?" Radhika looked upset but then said through gritted teeth, "Whatever makes you happy, Beta [child]!" Thus, the neoliberal notion of autonomous individual choice has to some degree exerted its force over some (admittedly, elite) women's lives in Bangalore. Ami and Radha both enunciated what they saw as the terrors of marriage: paralysis, stuckness, and of being held down. Marriage was framed as the abduction of will in the overwhelming wish for forward motion. Ami spoke of her desire for flight away from the burdens of care that marriage imposed on women: "I can't be like my mom, taking care of the family!"

When I spoke to my friend Nivedita the sociologist about marriage and how women's expectations of careers and life seemed to be turning away from early marriage and family, Nivedita set me right: "You are speaking about the secular elite of India for whom marriage is framed as a choice. But for most, or rather many, in India, marriage is not an option. They, men and women, just have to get married. Khatam [Hindi = Finished]!"

After a year, I met Preethi again just by chance in a mall, and she was with a delicate-looking young man. She looked startled to see me but then introduced me to him as Prakash, her "would be," her fiancé. He told me he was a "techie," an engineer, but a "dancer also." "My heart is in dance." Preethi had met Prakash at work. He was well spoken and, though not from their caste group, seemed to fit Preethi's needs. Preethi's mother emerged from one of the shops and beamed with happiness.

She was planning to move in with the young couple after their marriage. "You can call it arranged love, no? God only arranged it. It is her bhagya. He is a very nice boy. Family also good. When God puts two people together, what can we say?"

Romantic love in contemporary India, seen through the poisonous political lens of Hindutva, is foreign, derived from overt Western sexual impulses, essentially un-Indian in its freedom and therefore supposedly immoral (Mody 2002, 237).[11] But Preethi's mother's discourse of bhagya as her luck finding romantic love was evidence of a slow, creeping change in society to offer women more freedom. There is an uncanniness to love and marriage where a woman's ability to break through these traditions and live on their limit is a new definition of bhagya but one that still remains tied to physical beauty.

Auspiciousness

Radhika's daughter Ami was at Pretty Lady getting a trial run of her bridal makeup from a Korean makeup artist named Minjun who was known, or so Ami told me, for her ability to create "the perfect bridal look." Ami pulled out her phone and showed Minjun examples of the fresh look she wanted from a file she had saved. Minjun picked out shades of eyeshadow in browns and lilacs and spent over an hour shading Ami's eyes, drawing them out and making them look huge. She added a winged eyeliner, applied mascara, and then added a "brightener" at the corner of Ami's eyes and on her cheek "for a glow." After carefully applying three shades of lipstick to get the right delicate shade of peach they were looking for, Minjun finished with a setting spray. Meanwhile, Jhuma attended to Ami's hair, spraying the hair with a "high gloss" lacquer, and curling it into a princess look with a crystal headband. Ami looked like she had stepped from the pages of a Cosmopolitan bridal magazine. To finish the look, "make it like Indian," Jhuma placed a tiny glittery stick-on bindi carefully on Ami's forehead. Ami looked at herself in the mirror and twirled. The women in the salon all cooed over her. "Looking radiant!" was the general consensus. But then Radhika swept in. She took one look at Ami and said with authority, "Fine for the sangeet [musical evening] or reception." For the actual wedding ceremony, Radhika insisted that Ami had to be dressed "with full solah shrungar [the sixteen signs of bridal auspiciousness]." "Can't be party style, Beta," she abjured. When Ami threatened to throw a tantrum, Radhika was unusually firm: "Simply have to do for the wedding!"

The *solah shrungar* (sixteen auspicious decorations) is part of the Hindu ritual wedding ceremony, largely culturally North Indian but spreading to all of India via Bollywood. It is the ritual decoration of the adorned virgin bride who is offered as gift (*kanya dana*) to the groom's clan. The solah shrungar is believed to, as one wedding website put it, help the bride "transcend into the beautiful bliss of being married in India."[12]

Radhika detailed the traditional oiling and washing of hair and its decoration with flowers and jewelry. Saskia Kersenboom conjures up an image of the beautiful goddess Saraswati holding a veena and seated on a white lotus in a garden, while bees swarm to the flowers in her hair (1995), to describe the emulatable quality of the aesthetic of the goddess. Kersenboom explains, "The icons that continue to live throughout the ages are the images of the goddess; they set an example that is believed to be alive, active and efficacious for all women to follow" (1995, 89). The objective, as Radhika told me while discussing Ami's marriage, which was at that point completely hypothetical, was to re-create the bride in the image of Goddess Lakshmi, the bringer of prosperity (in which Radhika echoed Mrs. Iyengar): "She should be like Lakshmi coming to the husband's house!" Through the solah shrungar, the bhagya of the beautiful girl transformed into the sowbhagya (auspiciousness) of the bride. Essential components of the solah shrungar were the *bindi* (vermilion dot on the forehead), the *sindoor* (the placement of vermilion in the hair of the bride denoting her marital status), the *maang tikka* (hair ornament adorning the forehead), *kajal* (kohl enhancement of the eyes), *nath* (nose rings), *haar* (necklace), *kaan phhol* (earrings), *mehendi* (reddened henna hands) *choodiyan* (bangles), *bajubandh* (armlets), *kesar* (hair ornaments), *kamarbandh* (waistbands), *payal* (anklets and toe rings), *attar* (perfume), and *shadi ki ghaghra* or sari (dress). They are supposed to bring lakshanam, or beauty, to the fore and make the bride ready to receive the sowbhagya of marriage.

In 2021, when Ami announced her engagement to a young Californian living in London, Radhika was at first apprehensive and then threw herself into wedding preparations for a "fairy-tale wedding" in the "dream destination" of the Lake Palace in Udaipur. She began the process with elaborately designed digital "save the date" announcements a year in advance and review visits to couturiers in Delhi and Paris, florists in Mumbai, and sari weavers in Chennai and Punjab. "No need for jewelry. . . . I've been collecting since she was three years old!" The aspiration for a "fairy-tale wedding" combined with India's enormous young adult population has led to gargantuan growth in the bridal industry. The materiality of the wedding industry is terrifying in its enormity in what is in many ways a very poor country. But with neoliberal capitalism at its zenith in India, the ultrarich have taken to splurging on weddings with sun-drenched Grecian temples, Italian palaces, and French châteaus as backdrops, and featuring acts from around the world, including Beyoncé and Katy Perry.

FIG. 5.1. Radhika saved similar images of Bollywood heroines Deepika Padukone and Aishwarya Rai dressed in historical costumes and jewelry for Ami's wedding look

"With world travelers who have seen everything, there is always a scope to push the envelope," said Tina Tharwani of wedding planning company Shaadi Squad.[13] "The key here is to give a unique experience to everyone attending the wedding. The price there is secondary to what it comes for," revealed Devika Narain, who designed a distinctive pastel wedding for cricketer Virat Kohli and Bollywood actress Anushka Sharma in Tuscany.

A three-day wedding for the rich in India can cost US$3 million. Radhika said with a laugh that because Ami wanted a "pucca" (Hindi = full, lit. ripe) Indian "dream wedding," she had "gotten off cheap!" The aspiration for global wedding destinations has created a trickle-down effect and the middle classes of Bangalore now hire Rajasthani palaces and Sri Lankan resorts to host their nuptials. The pandemic slowed down the wedding industry due to governmental regulations on gatherings, but the industry rebounded spectacularly in 2022. Over US$46 billion was spent on weddings in the final two months of 2022 alone.

The solah shrungar is now a marketing tool in modern India to sell trousseaus and wedding jewelry to prospective brides and their families. Weddings are planned months, if not years, in advance, and couturiers, both Indian and Western, are hired to design ensembles for the entire family of the bride as well as the groom. In 2021, wedding jewelry sales stood at a value of US$78.50 billion.[14] Even middle-class families like Preethi's specify color schemes for the bride's and groom's party in their invitations so that the Instagram images have the perfect color composition.

Salons have also gotten into the game, offering "bridal packages" that focus on dressing the bride and designing makeup looks that match the outfits for the wedding. The bridal packages resolved the problem that multigenerational families faced in Bangalore. With many young women marrying outside their endogamous caste groups and religions and with greater cosmopolitanism and digital access to global bridal looks, many young Bangalorean brides, like Ami, wanted to have a more contemporary and celebrity-influenced look. But their families often wanted to stick to ritual and traditional elements. In response, wedding planners and makeup artists have created a five-day culturally North Indian–style wedding inspired by Bollywood as the template—a haldi ceremony where the bridal couple are anointed with turmeric and ritually bathed; a sangeeth musical evening in which Bollywood-style song-and-dance sequences are choreographed, practiced, and performed by the families and guests as a dance-off; a muhurat ceremony, which is the ritual ceremony with its circling of the sacred fire; and finally, a reception where the married couple greet guests and well-wishers. This can then be tailored with regional, familial, and caste and clan cultural requirements and budgets as needed.

As Minjun, Ami's Korean makeup artist, told me, "ordinary" beauty parlor wedding packages offer two different makeup packages, one for the ritual wedding and one for the reception party. The makeup package includes hairstyle, makeup, and dressing the bride for the two occasions.[15] But "most people nowadays had four- to five-day weddings." So Minjun was firm: "The bride must be ready with looks for a month of parties and events, madam, but definitely four to five looks for wedding are minimum—one haldi look (turmeric bath), one sangeet look (musical evening), one muhurat look (the Hindu ritual wedding itself), and one reception party look. Haldi and muhurat are full traditional, sangeet is North Indian, and reception is Western party wear which can be

FIG. 5.2. Radha's saved images of bridal looks by designer Manish Malhotra

long gown in gold like Kareena, maybe ghaghra choli like Deepika, but some older ladies wear Kanjeevaram for everything." Minjun usually asks the bride to bring in her many outfits and the jewelry she will be wearing so that she can suggest bridal makeup possibilities and hair "solutions" to help the bride. Minjun also noted the many makeup changes a typical bride needed during the wedding: "For sangeeth, we use nice full blue eyeshadow and lipstick, full foundation; for turmeric bath, nice light makeup; for muhurat, must have nice foundation, fair skin, light eyeshadow for daytime and natural-shade lipstick and for reception full glam look, with glitter and all." The makeup makes "visible on the skin" the bride's new "relationship with the world" (Strathern 1979, 254). Decorations like the bridal makeup traverse the bodily domain and then are bound back onto it. A "necessary shift," says Nancy Munn (1973, 57), "from interior dream to exterior reality, suggests the importance of binding the inner imagination to the outer, social world the inner self to the external social order." The decoration of bridal makeup over the days of the wedding act on the body, bridging the inner world and outer, transforming the brides from free, modern, young women to chaste wives and then back again to cosmopolitan party animal for the reception, enhancing bodily capital by traversing multiple ritual and aesthetic domains.

Radha found the bridal packages "simply awful," but she had saved images from the catalog of designer Manish Malhotra for bridal looks that she thought were "luxurious."[16]

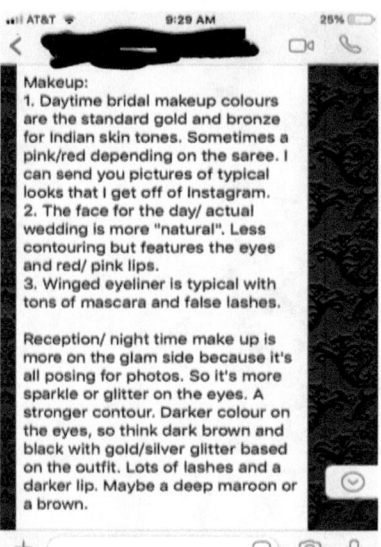

FIG. 5.3. Madhu's WhatsApp texts about bridal makeup

FIG. 5.4. Madhu sent me this image, classifying it as "too glamorous" but having the right tonal quality

She proclaimed loudly that she would "never" have her bridal looks done by neighborhood parlors. "They make your face blue, as they don't know how to match the foundation. And they put red eyeshadow on everyone!" But she added that she and her boyfriend planned to either elope or get a registered wedding, anyway, since she had acted as a bride and been dressed in the solah shrungar "so many times" that it "wasn't special anymore." Menaka interrupted hotly, "Who says? Of course you'll have a traditional, full wedding, and if you don't want a package, we'll get a specialist beautician for each look, okay?" Then turning to educate me, she said, "Nowadays, we get Korean and Thai beauticians in Bangalore doing amazing natural looks! Totally glam but like in an understated way. When you dress it up, it's like you look super! Beautiful but not like made up fully. Just natural." She detailed her expectations for her bridal makeup on a WhatsApp message and added an image that she claimed was "the right tone and palette."

The Good Wife

As Mrs. Iyengar said, Sita is the Hindu mythical exemplar of the good wife. Her originary myth connects her to the earth as mother. The Sanskrit used to describe her "ayonija" (not born of a womb) suggests a chaste virgin birth and highlights the agricultural connotations of the Sanskrit word Sita (furrow) (Kinsley 1988, 65). When, according to the epic *Ramayana*, Rama is banished to exile in the forest, Sita uncomplainingly follows him to a life of hardship, though a princess and used to living in luxury (Kinsley 1988, 65). When Ravana kidnaps Sita because of her beauty and holds her captive in the island kingdom of Lanka, she is unbowed and loyal to Rama (Richman 1991). Sita refuses Ravana's overtures of love, his offers, and coercion and waits for Rama to rescue her (Kinsley 1988, 73). Afterward, she returns with Rama to rule his kingdom, a chaste and beautiful queenly presence. Later, when Rama banishes her to the forest under some pretext of ethical kingship, she is quoted as saying, "I am not distressed on mine own account, O Prince of Raghu, it is for thee to keep thy fair name untarnished! The husband is as a God to the woman, he is her family, and her spiritual preceptor, therefore, even at the price of her life, she must seek to please her lord" (Kinsley 1988, 74). Her devotion to Rama is an ideal, the "quintessential exemplar to young Hindu girls" (Tobler 2001, 59) epitomizing the Sanskritic term *pativrata*,[17] which translates to "one who worships the pati," or husband.

Pativrata (sometimes spelled pativratya) as an ideology of chastity and loyalty is distilled in the idea of wifely obedience, of total loyalty to the patriliny, of bearing sons for the clan (kula), and dying before the husband in a state of wifely auspiciousness (Dhruvarajan 1988, 27–28). Sexual continence is important, as women are thought to be the "personification of sex," corrupting of men, and as such they present serious ethical impediments to men's sense of purpose and spiritual growth. Indeed, the entire society has a stake in women's purity and chastity. Protecting women is the injunctive claim of the men of her clan at the expense of her autonomy. Mrs. Iyengar had a series of sayings that underlined this injunction, such as "women should live in men's shadow" (Kannada = *Hengasaru gandana neralina irribeku*). She saw this as the natural order of things, a recognition of women's rightful place in the world.

Feminist Suma Chitnis (1988) argues that the ideal of pativrata is the root cause of women's disempowerment in India. Yet this pativrata Sita is a construction, a literary and theological device developed over centuries-long shaping of the mythical corpus. As Linda Hess (1999, 6) has powerfully shown in the story of Sita's trial by fire (*agnipariksha*), the tale changed over time from the original ancient text by the sage Valmiki, where Sita has "a healthy sense of her own self worth," to Tulsidas's text in the sixteenth century, where Sita is silent and obedient. But this story of Sita morphing into the good, obedient, and silent wife mimetically links cultural worlds.

The original story lives on in the goddess Pattini, a Sri Lankan version of Patni or wife, where the goddess is a shapeshifter who moves through the timelines of the myth, from a rampant Kali to a subservient wifely figure (Obeyesekere 1984).[18] The central question to be drawn out is, of course, the gendered articulation of virtue epitomized in the figure of the good wife. She forms one half of a God-fearing heterosexual couple, an example of Hindu dharma, in the image of the gods Vishnu and Lakshmi. Justice Hidayatullah, a famed Indian Muslim jurist, says, "Rama and Sita . . . are exemplifiers of right thought, right speech and right action under all circumstances. Sita represents compassion and grace. She suffers most but preserves herself with heroism, love and devotion. She is the ideal wife and is the model for our womanhood. . . . Ramayana, one of our classics, gives to our youth the fundamentals of our culture" (Iyengar 1983, 28). The Indian state and Hindutva apparatchiks, following such legal understandings, have held up Sita as the model Hindu wife, drawing from Brahmanical conceptions of conjugal relations and the control of women's sexuality through a double sleight of hand whereby they claim that Sita is ethically and morally superior to Rama and yet insist that she is also obedient to him. M. N. Srinivas noted as early as 1977 that "there was a basic contradiction in Sanskritic Hinduism in the conceptualisation of the conjugal bond," where the wife is literally "the moral and religious half of the husband" and his superior, but at the same time, "he is her superior" and, we should add, her deity (230). Thus, the conjugal bond is understood as necessarily asymmetrical and built on an ethical twisting that reveals itself in the concept of a woman's bhagya.

Radha asked me to explain how the goddess could be at the same time angry and obedient, superior and inferior. Menaka rushed in with an explanation: "See, she's one, but different avatars with different rasas [flavors], different emotions. Just like we are all women, but each one is different, na?" Anger and wifely obedience seem at odds with each other in the contemporary world, but both, according to Menaka, are just different facets of the goddess. And, of course, the defining attribute of the goddess, regardless of her avatar or her rasa, is beauty. "All goddesses are beautiful," Menaka said with authority. "Even Kali! I don't appreciate her beauty; I get scared. But others do." Radha looked skeptical but then brightened up: "I guess I get it. Lakshmi is like total wifey and she's beautiful, okay. But Kali is like super badass and she's beautiful, too, but like in a different way?" "Exactly!" Menaka averred, and then added a neoliberal twist, "Your choice who you like!"

Mirroring Vows

Radhika breezed into the Lotus parlor with Tara and Ami. They all wanted to have their hair colored and shampooed and a manicure in a hurry, as the next day was the festival of Karva Chauth, the celebration of the annual marital vrat[19] (vow) for the protection of the men of the clan, and Radhika had invited twenty-one close women friends and their husbands for the ritual and dinner at her home. They would fast all day from sunrise to moonrise. The fast ended when the women spotted the reflection of the full moon in a plate of water[20] followed immediately by the reflection of their husbands' faces in the same moonlit water. "It's very important for me, haan? I'm a total Sati-Savitri!" Radhika commented, only half-jokingly. "Shut up!" said Tara, delighted at the audacity of identifying herself with the epitome of wifely devotion. Radhika pretended to take umbrage: "Why? Do you think I couldn't save Rakesh from Yamaraj [the god of death]?" "Remember when he got bronchitis? He nearly died. Only when I went to the hospital he got better! Thank God!" In a symbolic gesture representing her marital status, she parted her newly washed and blow-dried hair and took a pinch of sindoor from a small box in her purse, placing it carefully in her parting (maang).[21] Tara replied, "No, no, you are total Sati-Savitri. Don't mistake me!" Radhika looked at me in the mirror and put on an exaggerated American accent: "You know when I went to a parlor in your stupid Boston, they said, 'Oh, madam, you are bleeding in your forehead. I got such a shock! Then I realized it's my maang ka sindoor!"

There are a number of marks of wifely auspiciousness in Hinduism. Here, Radhika mentions *maang ka sindoor*, kumkum powder in a bright vermillion that is placed in the part of the hair to denote marital status. In domestic puja, the gesture of putting kumkum on the foreheads, is also considered essential to mark a woman's status as married goddesses as well as to satisfy an important part of daily adornment without which many Hindu women "feel not fully dressed or incomplete" (Flueckiger 2015, 92).

The festival of Karva Chauth is said to celebrate suhaag, or the marital state of which the red sindoor is emblematic. Women are expected to dress in the solah shrungar, with marital jewelry and bridal dresses in auspicious colors of red and orange. Radhika wanted her hair colored and a facial for the inevitable photographs and social media posts that would be uploaded after the festival. "Better to look good, na? You never know what idiot will post a pic of you looking like shit!" Radhika said that her husband had been traveling for work a great deal and had had a series of small medical scares. She felt it was "better" she do a big vrat to "keep him safe" and had invited all her friends and their husbands to "keep the vrat" and fast with her. I was surprised at Radhika's celebration of the festival since she and her husband had had a "love marriage" and they seemed a very modern couple with equitable relations. But Radhika interpreted the vrat as keeping her husband alive and well: "He's my best friend, na?" In this she was not wrong, for the festival recognizes women's unsatiated desire for love. Womenfolk ritually are expected to ask each other if they are satiated at the culmination of the festival (Hindi = Dhapi ki ni Dhapi?), and they are expected to reply that they are satiated by the water they drink or the food they eat but are never satiated in their love (Hindi = Jal si Dhapi, Suhaag se ni dhapi). At the same time, the vrat implies that unbounded female sexual desire is channeled and protected within respectable heterosexual marital relations.

In response to my question about why she had to go to the parlor for the vrat, Radhika's response was seemingly simple: "We have to get ready, na? For the puja? Nobody will go for a puja looking like shit! You have to have nice hair, nice looks, be pretty, relaxed." When I asked if she was doing it for her husband, Radhika considered it. "For both of us," she replied. "Women should be like the goddess, na? Beautiful. And guys like it when they have a beautiful wife. And it's relaxing to go to parlor, sit, relax, get a nice shampoo and blow-dry, mani-pedi, vagera, vagera [Hindi = other things] before the fasting and puja."

Radhika had an image in her mind of how the good wife should look for the puja. When I asked her what she imagined, she showed me an image of the

Bollywood star Madhuri Dixit dressed as a bride. Then she added, "She's grown old now but still looks good, haan?"

In fact, the link between beauty and marital desire was strengthened after the vrat. During the multicourse dinner at Radhika's home, Radhika's husband, Rajesh, connected Radhika's beauty with her moral worth as wife and partner, with the somewhat drunken declaration to the gathered guests, "I am so lucky! She is my beautiful wife, my Sundari, my ghar ki devi [Hindi = Devi of my home]!" Radhika swatted his drunken declaration of love away: "He's such a fool!" but was clearly pleased. Later in the evening, I caught her failing, eating a sweet after her repeated insistence that she did not eat anything sweet during the vrat. She looked at me mischievously and added, "I'm no Sati-Savitri, okay? I've done the vrat. . . . Enough!"

Some might suggest that women who do the vrat are submitting to the will of their husbands or are buying the gods off with token obeisance. But many women insist they do this vrat because they see themselves *and* their husbands as one entity (Kurtz in Hiltebeitel and Erndl 2000, 183–85).[22] Radhika suggested the same: "I do the vrat not just for him but for the whole family. We are one, no? And to do the vrat is like 'girl power.' I invite all the girls and we hang out. It's not for the guys! It's for us!" I found this transmutation, this bending of a male-oriented ritual done by women into a "cool" feminine social activity, to be central to removing the sting of female disempowerment that the ritual carried.

On this particular night, after the puja, Radhika turned to her guests while distributing small silk bags with bangles, symbolic of marital status, and yelled, "Happy KC, girls!" They all yelled back "Happy KC!!" while embracing each other. Then, to me, Radhika said, "Sounds cooler, no?" She foreshadowed an episode of *The Fabulous Lives of Bollywood Wives* in 2024 where one of the husbands referred to Karva Chauth ("KC") as the Indian Valentine's Day. The Bollywood wives on the show insisted that doing Karva Chauth made their husbands feel "special," which they needed because they were "big babies." The lines became blurred between wife as servant as protector, and as empowered party girl.

Wrestling with Death

The "Sati-Savitri" trope of wifely devotion that Radhika used to describe herself was a conjoint evocation of two different goddesses, Sati and Savitri, both epitomizing wifely devotion, together to double the force of their pativrata. The day after the vrat, when I asked Radhika what she meant when she jokingly referred to herself as a "Sati Savitri," she launched into the Savitri story despite my assertions that I knew it well.

The Savitri story[23] of *pativrata* is enfolded into the *Mahabharata*[24] as a story of total devotion extending beyond life itself yet shot through with failures (*Mahābhārata* 3.277:3; Smith 2009). In Radhika's telling, a version unique to her in the details and elaborations, the emphases and elisions, I suddenly realized that Radhika was narrating the self, deriving power from it despite the patriarchal origins and focus of the myth. She deliberately wrested control from the narrative, gaining agency in the process.

In Radhika's version, Savitri "fell in love" with Satyavan, a gentle, learned man, the only son of a king and queen exiled and living in the forest. She learned that he was cursed, doomed to die within the year. But so strong was her desire that she married him. Despite this curse, Savitri joined him in the forest. One day, she accompanied her husband on a walk, where he suddenly collapsed and "just died." Yama Raj, the lord of death, arrived soon thereafter on his buffalo steed to harvest Satyavan's soul (atman) with a noose. Savitri watched and chatted with Yama Raj about her life. Yama Raj harnessed Satyavan's soul, got back on his buffalo, and was soon ready to depart. Savitri got up as well and followed him. She kept Yama Raj in conversation, walking ten paces behind his buffalo as he left with Satyavan's soul. So beautiful and wise was she that Yama was enthralled by the conversation and gave her three wishes (always excluding Satyavan's life) (Brodbeck 2013, 527). Savitri asked for various kindnesses for her frail in-laws and for others. Yama Raj was so impressed by her selflessness that he granted her a fourth wish; she wished for children, that she and Satyavan should have a hundred sons. Yama recognized he had been tricked. He was forced to release Satyavan's soul so that he could live to beget his hundred sons. Radhika concluded the story with a touch of cynicism: "It's because she was so pretty that Yama Raj talked to her and gave her wishes and all. You think he'd stop for an old bag like you or me?" In Radhika's telling, Savitri was triumphant in resurrecting Satyavan *because* of her beauty. Radhika was not entirely wrong. In the *Mahabharata* telling of the myth, Yama notes her loveliness and her auspiciousness, "look[ing] like a goddess, like Sri in human form, with a slender waist, broad hips and eyes like lotus petals" (*Mahabharata* 3.277:23–3 in Brodbeck 2013, 532).

But Savitri's beauty aside, delaying Yama Raj's task and outsmarting him enabled an existential moment of self-transformation for her, from widowhood to exemplary wifehood. In the story, Yama praises her as a pativrata, the perfect wife. Set in opposition to Sita, the wife of Rama and heroine of the *Ramayana*, who is seen as passive and gentle, Savitri is a model of wit and action. The Savitri story is the story of a woman who overcomes the cruel fate of becoming a widow through perfect wifedom, casting her as a "woman hero" (McGrath 2009, 106) and a narrative representation of the ideal Hindu woman. Fighting death through intelligence and wisdom becomes the romantic and powerful ideal of the model wife.

Although the myth may seem transparent in its misogynistic and patriarchal leanings, for Radhika, the focus was on Savitri's beauty, wit, and strategy. In engaging the myth, she induced a new narration focused on agency, not only positing Savitri as the ideal virtuous wife who protects her husband and their bond but also focusing on her cleverness and strategy, thereby bringing the myth into the contemporary. Finally, through her strategic negation of the wifely trope, when she claimed she was "not a Sati-Savitri," she moved the discourse from one of wifely victimhood and patriarchy to one of a protean feminism and agency, rooted in a negation of the cultural ideal of virtuous wifedom.

Ami, Radhika's daughter, on the other hand, interpreted the myth as embodying Savitri's seductive capacity: "That Yama was a total flirt. . . . He looked at her because she was beautiful! And she flirted back! Totally! Forget that her husband is lying there dead!" Radhika was aghast at such a self-centered interpretation of Savitri's behavior, which went against the marital ideal. "No, bah bah!" she said, hitting her head with the palm of her hands in frustration. "Savitri is fighting for her husband's life! You girls won't understand. I hope once you are married, you'll get it." For Radhika, Savitri's autonomy and independence in choosing Satyavan and in fighting for his life at a moment of vulnerability is notable, for it is proactive. At the same time, Savitri's pativrata can be read as a story of patriarchal revival in its most obvious and even literal sense. Savitri's life as a wife and potential mother of the lineage is renewed by his resurrection. Without him, she has no life at all. This theme of transformation and renewal is significant as it undergirds the recognition of women as wives and mothers while also gesturing to alternate understandings of freedom and choice that modern understandings of marriage or of singlehood entail. What I found interesting about the myths and the women's creative retelling of them was that they often held these two contrary meanings in tension. In one sense, they hewed to the patriarchal or caste discourse and its values; in another sense, they cleverly subverted that dominant discourse, often turning it on its head and garnering the women agency and a new selfhood through the narration.

Retelling Sita's Story

While Mrs. Iyengar waited in the lounge at Bodycraft to pick up Madhu, she told me about a mantra she would recite when she massaged hair oil into her children's hair: "The hair oil, we used to massage for girls and pray for luck [bhagya] for them to find good boy, get married, like that. We would say this shloka, 'Ahalya, Draupadi, Tara, Sita, Madodari, Thatahi pancha kanyam smare nityam, duswapnam thasya nashyathi [Ahalya, Draupadi, Tara, Sita, and Mandodari, these five goddess wives will chase the nightmares away].'" *She continued,* "And for the boys, we would bless, 'Ashwathama, Bali, Vyasa, Hanumanaschya, Vishnuschya, Kripastheya Parashuramaaschya, Saptha chiranjeevinam [Like Ashwathama, Bali, Vyasa, Hanuman, Like Vishnu, Kripa and Parashurama, may you be immortal like these seven heroes]!' Girls must have bhagya; men will be Chiranjeevi [heroic immortals]."

Soon after, Madhu arrived at Bodycraft sporting a huge diamond ring. "He proposed," she squealed delightedly. All the women in the parlor, clients and beauty workers, clapped and congratulated her. When asked about the wedding and details about the young man, Mrs. Iyengar seemed oddly reticent. I later learned that this was because of Madhu's fiancé's ownership of the taxi service, which Mrs. Iyengar classified as demeaning.

After she spoke to everyone, Madhu sat down to get her hair washed. She said she was irritated by her grandmother's fixation on Sita: "So this Sita stuff that my ajji was telling you about . . . works for the guys, right? They all want to be the first in, first out, and have the girl on call!" Although Sita was a goddess, Madhu said she found her "annoying" as an ideal type. I was amused by her reaction, given the Hindutva rendering of Sita as goddess incarnate, the pious and virtuous wife of Lord Rama. Since Hindutva's rise in India in the 1990s and its growing popularity under the Modi government, India has been renamed "Rambhoomi" (the land of Rama), reasserting a muscular Hinduism known as "RamRajya" (the rule of Rama), which is rooted in a poisonous disinclusion of all who are suspected of being non-Hindu (or not correctly Hindu). Madhu's take on Sita's supposed virtue was refreshing in this climate. "Goddesses are powerful, right?" she continued, looking at me for confirmation. "They say Vishnu is no one without Lakshmi, but then they say you must wash the guy's feet! I'm like, if she's the goddess of wealth, he should wash her feet, right?" Her conflation of Sita with Lakshmi followed a traditional collapsing of Vaishnavite goddess incarnations into the form of Lakshmi, but her reading of what was due to her as a goddess brought the ecology and power dynamics of neoliberal capitalism into view.

Recognizing Myth

Beauty practices in the parlor form the ground on which aspiration toward recognition occurs. With the neoliberal economy exploding in India, women's dependence on others' evaluations sways unsteadily between epistemic and moral contexts. As the society changes, members of the savarna castes feel the need for recognition because of the shift to class and wealth as markers of status, but the rising bourgeoisie also feel that the only real way to attain political influence, lucrative positions, and financial privileges is to gain the approval of the leaders of society. No longer do competitors display their respect for traditional aristocratic virtues of chastity and fidelity; rather, Bangaloreans have come to regard the demonstration of a debonair attitude, luxury, and fashionable dress as superior forms of demonstrating honor. As a result, the beauty industry's growth has doubled and tripled over the past five years. The wedding sector is the fastest growing part of the beauty industry, bringing gendered understandings of marriage to the foreground.

The concept of fortune, bhagya, coalesces around gendered practices of conjugality. But Bangalorean society is facing a major social challenge in the not-so-gradual intrusion of instrumental and economic modes of behavior into a public life traditionally protected by moral principles, creating the self-interested moral subject. At the same time, the goddess's identity is being rethought and her devotees' identity negotiated and refashioned. Taken as a whole, the choices made by women in the parlors reveal their attempt to push back against their marginality, the magnitude of which they have only recently begun to realize. To do so, they pursued new frameworks of reference that aimed to challenge, if not subvert, the hegemonic narratives of ideal wifedom that were promoted through the concept of bhagya. Thus, by highlighting new readings of sowbhagya wives like Sita and Savitri, women offer a new kind of epic frame for national and religious identity. As the myths are told, they morph and change, forming unexpected strategies for living in the telling and uncovering of new selves. Jacques Lacan suggests that acts of uncovering are equally acts of concealing, just as unraveling [selves, relations, stories] involves simultaneous reknitting. Here, a kind of understanding happens in the space of reknitting, interjecting knowledge not only in the tellings but also in the joints between the various stories and practices. Stories of rejection and acceptance are themes within the joints of the stories of marriage. These are iterations of a structure of feeling, of "something more," a recurring motif that keeps trying to tell us something about conjugality in modern India.

Maritally induced bhagya is a tautologically constructed idiom. If one is married, one is the inheritor of bhagyam; but to be married, one must have bhagyam. The fortune of a woman, her allotted share of life as determined by the gods and her karma, her ineluctable fate and her value as a woman, are all bound up with her marital position, though there is always the danger that she will end up in an unjust position in the social hierarchy—beleaguered by in-laws, bound to a useless taxi driver. The ontological realization that our social contract rests on recognition of the other in a deeply misogynistic world appears to justify the weight of needing honor and status offered as a moral consideration of respect, which is what the women seek. By insisting on emergent practices that seem to hew to the traditional but are reinterpreted through a new telling of myth, women often invert and celebrate that which is marginal or subversive, offering moral recognition in a different register. In doing so, they defend their own agency and find a legitimate place for themselves and their way of life at the local, pan-Indian, and global table. As beauty is conflated with virtue through fortune and being fortunate, women attempt to gain recognition as moral and virtuous actors in the world by becoming beautiful and telling moral tales.

We do not turn our eyes away from either beauty or violence; that we begin to hear what each says to the other; that there may be healing and hope.
—Grace Jantzen, *Foundations of Violence*, 2004

There is a goddess within each one of us.
—Author unknown

6

FLUID

Queering Beauty

Four years after I met Selvi at the Lotus, I lost touch with her. She had left the Lotus, and no one seemed to know where she had gone. Radhika told me, on a FaceTime call, that she heard that Selvi had "gone off" for a job in a new parlor in Shantinagar, a neighborhood in south Bangalore. I had already asked several of my friends about her and the parlor she was working at, but everyone I spoke to had simply echoed Radhika and said they did not know much except that she had "shifted" to a parlor in Shantinagar.

Ami, Radhika's daughter, who was home on holiday from college in the United States, suddenly swung into view on the call with Radhika: "What Mumma is not telling you is that Selvi went off to work in a lesbian parlor." Radhika yelled at her, "Shut up! Fool!" Ami, rolling her eyes in disgust, added, "My mother is such a homophobe; it's not even funny! Everyone knows about gay parlors in Bangalore, but she and her friends still act as though everyone is totally hetero! Sooo crazy!"

FIG. 6.1. Trans Studio: An LGBTQ inclusive beauty parlor in south Bangalore

With a final shrug and a sniff of disgust, she disappeared from view. But then she returned briefly to say, "Lots of young people from small towns come to Bangalore to come out of the closet. They used to advertise these parlors as giving 'yoni massage.'" She made air quotes with her fingers. "But now, there is no like, you know, problem being gay in Bangalore. So they just say 'LGBTQ-friendly parlor' or even 'unisex parlor.'" Tossing her long hair, she left once and for all. "BYEEEE!" Radhika returned to view and sighed, "These children nowadays . . . I'm gay, you are they . . . Arre Baba! But if they are happy, we are happy!" she concluded with a shrug.

After this conversation, I decided to try to find Selvi in earnest. But embodying the apparent epitome of Indian normativity, it was difficult for me to inquire into queer parlor life. Although I have always been aware of myself as a cisgendered, heteronormative, upper-caste person, I was made undeniably aware of these limitations in this moment as a fieldworker. When I began to tentatively inquire about LGBTQ-friendly parlors in the city, I often put my foot in my mouth, not knowing how to phrase such sensitive questions or if I should even be asking them. As it was in the temple and the cisgendered parlor, so also here I was out of place (Srinivas 2018). In fact, even more so. My embodiment and identity made me the ultimate outsider to queer worlds, for while I am committed to liberal politics, I am not marked by queerness. And even as I write this, I feel its inelegance, its incapacity to frame my outsiderness.

After months of uncomfortable inquiry about queer parlors, all of which expectedly yielded no result, I asked Sundari, a hijra[1] and queer activist, if I could join her at Trans Studio in the suburb of Jayanagar in south Bangalore. Trans Studio was a unisex parlor that was supposedly LGBTQ friendly. Sundari went there occasionally since losing her hijra Amma—a motherly guide and mentor—who had not only taught her about beauty but also taught her the ontology and politics of being hijra. Since losing Amma, Sundari had occasionally taken to going to the parlor to indulge in a head massage, shampoo, waxing, and other treatments, though often she "managed" at home with the help of other hijra women in the community.

Located on a tree-lined street off a bustling main road, filled with men's clothing stores, ice-cream shops, cafés, and restaurants, Trans Studio was in one of the few remaining bungalows in a street of apartment blocks. Close by was a big park where various fitness groups and walkers seemed to congregate, and an impromptu autorickshaw stand had evolved under the shade of a big tree. The sign advertising the salon hung crookedly on the outside wall, which also held an image of a Western man in a shirt and loosened tie with a book flipped open, advertising "L'Oréal Homme" products. The main salon comprised one large room with a further shampoo room and private treatment rooms down a hallway.

I arrived early, and while waiting just inside the door, I heard a phone caller who was audible in the parlor inquiring about facial hair removal by laser. The receptionist, a middle-aged woman, directed them to a laser clinic nearby: "We only do waxing and no laser." She looked up at me. It was clear to her that I was an outsider. I wondered what about me and my aesthetics had made that judgment so easy.

Whereas I had felt uncomfortable in the normative cisgendered parlor, my discomfort in the queer parlor was based on my very embodiment and sexuality. As a cis-het (cisgendered/heteronormative), upper-caste woman, I was out of my depth, and it was, I felt, apparent to everyone around me. The lady at the desk asked me in a businesslike tone, "Madam, what you wanted?" I told them I was waiting for my friend. They told me politely to wait in the "waiting room," a clear designation I was unwelcome in the main parlor.

I flipped through some magazines while waiting, and it occurred to me that rather than my embodiment, it was my notebook and sling bag, associated with activists and government employees, that the parlor employees were reacting to. Whereas my academic eye and persistent scribbling was sometimes the butt of jokes in the cisgendered and heteronormative parlors I had visited so far, here my bag and notebook took on a more sinister cast. It was clear they thought I was nosing around, maybe a journalist or a government employee trying to "out" a nonnormative parlor. This was not surprising given that I had arrived at Trans Studio at a moment when LGBTQ rights were being hotly debated in India.

In 2009, soon after I began thinking seriously about the beauty parlor as a possible site of study, the Delhi High Court had rendered a judgment on a local case and overturned a centuries-old anti-sodomy law, citing it as discriminatory. This ruling was celebrated by LGBTQ Indians all over India, and many gay rights advocates started speaking openly about their hope for equal protection under the law. Visibility did increase, especially in large cities like Bangalore, and there was a widespread hope that India would decriminalize homosexuality. But in 2012, during my next stint of fieldwork, the government of India expressed opposition to the idea of decriminalization, and many "out" and publicly visible LGBTQ individuals feared harassment. This proved a flashpoint, and protests and counterprotests broke out in many metropolitan areas across India, including Bangalore. This was the moment I had arrived at Trans Studio. It was not surprising that the beauty workers were suspicious of my unannounced entrance with camera, phone, notebook, and pen.

I meditated on whether attempting to find Selvi at this moment in Indian history was a big mistake. The questions grew more difficult the longer I waited. How could I get to the knowledge I sought without compromising or ignoring the situatedness of the knower and the subject? How did I figure out queering beauty in a way that was not rooted in my embodied and desiring selfhood?

It did not take long for the silent tension caused by my presence to grow palpable. I debated whether to leave. Just as I picked up my bag, Sundari walked in. She introduced me, and there were smiles of relief; my place in the world as "a friend of" was acknowledged. Chewa, a young beautician from Nepal, offered me tea, and we all settled down to chat. I felt welcomed and at home.

Situations like this sensitized me not only to my overwhelming privilege as a cisgendered, heteronormative, upper-caste woman but also to the fact that in looking for queer parlors in Bangalore, I was going about it all wrong.[2] It was not the spaces of beauty but beauty itself that I was looking for, and it was clear that queer beauty lay hidden further afield.

Shailaja's "Boycut" at Blow

Shailaja sent me a WhatsApp message: "here@ Senorita 😊." Her nausea was about how she had been treated by beauticians, she explained, during her quest for the haircut that she wanted. Several years earlier, Shailaja had walked into an expensive unisex salon named "Blow" and demanded a short haircut known as a "boycut." The hairstylists were reluctant to cut her waist-length hair short, but they did so. Shailaja was delighted, as the cut was the culmination of a decade-long desire to have short hair, which she realized in hindsight was also a quest to understand her queer sexuality. But, she noted angrily, the beauty worker cut her hair relatively short but styled it in way to make her look more feminine, with wispy bangs. Shailaja was upset. "I wanted military boy cut 😡!" she said using the emoji for anger and cursing. But then she added emphatically, "But I'm not a boy, okay? I'm totally a girl. I just like a boycut!"

Shailaja's story of her haircut struck me as remarkably similar to the way that women who were cisgendered used beauty work to unveil their "true self" (Arain 2023). For Shailaja as well, beauty work seemed to function as self-revelation. Just as cisgendered women like Menaka and Madhu came to the parlor to craft their femininity, so did Shailaja, except her understanding of what was feminine was more capacious, including a "boycut" hairstyle. As I pursued queer beauty through Bangalore, one question I asked myself was, what space is available for individuals like Shailaja who are seeking to embody beauty at odds with traditional notions of Indian feminine beauty?

Shailaja spoke of her body in remarkably truthful ways, inflecting her self-presentation as "ways of being queer." "My shoulders, see how straight they are?" she said referencing her square-shouldered torso. "And I don't have a waist. So I have a 'boy-like' physique, no?" she asked. I agreed that she projected a masculine look. "I'm very strong," she added laughing. "But people get confused by this. They say I'm not like a girl." In fact, Bangaloreans insulted her as "ombodu" (Tamil = nine) and "chakka," both epithets for transpeople. She added emphatically, "I AM a girl! This makes me very sad for my queer community to be insulted like this."

Shailaja noted that women from around Madurai (in Tamil Nadu, where she was from), where agricultural labor was relentless, "are robust with strong powerful shoulders, masculine cut of face, and strong arms and legs because of the physical labor." Thus, in Tamil Nadu, Shailaja with her "rough hair," brown skin, and "manly body" felt seen and recognized. Tamilian men fell in love with "masculine-looking women" not because they had gay leanings, as was glibly argued by liberal Anglophone Indians and Hindutva alike, but because their understandings of women could hold and be respectful of such difference. "There in Chennai, they really gave respect. They used to call me 'macha' [Tamil = bruh, also expert] 'guru' like that! I felt good. I felt like they could see who I was." In contrast to current understandings of gender and sexuality, Shailaja also gestured toward the queer resources of precolonial Indian culture, noting, "In India before the British, we were all so queer, no? I mean all our religious stories are all bursting with homosexual and gender-queer and trans-representation as gods and demons. Ardhanarishvara, Shiva-Parvati, all Hindu gods change their gender and sexuality just like that!" She snapped her fingers. "It's the British missionaries combined with Brahman heteronormativity that made us so scared of queerness, you know? Before that, Hinduism was full chill with being queer." "But now," she added, her face troubled, "nowadays with these North Indians thinking Hinduism is only masculine gods like Rama and all, all these other stories have been pushed aside. It is the story of Aryan violence against us South Indian, Dravida people, you know." Shailaja then detailed some of the violence that North Indians wrought against the south: "They make fun of us; Madrasi, they call us. They say we're short and dark. They force us to learn Hindi and have no respect for the ancient language of Tamil. They want to force us to worship masculine Aryan gods like Rama only, when we all worship Amman [goddess]." She ended hotly with, "It's just a different, local form of colonialism! They will never appreciate the way we are!" She echoed the feminist religious studies thinker Grace Jantzen who argued that *only* when we see beauty and violence in their totality with their inherent links to each other can we move toward a healing of both.

After contemplating the political violence of colonialism and contemporary North Indian chauvinism, Shailaja turned back to her boycut and her body, seeing them as a resistance and refusal of prevailing norms and a way of creating a more capacious understanding of being feminine: "I get my hair cut so short because I like it. When everyone sees me, *they don't see a weak woman*. That's why I cut it like that. That's also why I am studying martial arts. People think there is only one way to be a woman. When we say we are queer, then we must overturn expectations. To stand up for my queer community, I must queer everything, illya [Tamil = isn't it]? Even my own body."

In fact, I had wondered previously about Shailaja's haircut. Clearly, her boycut was performative and a conscious subversion of the feminine. As such, it was ethical and political as well. The purpose of this haircutting for Shailaja seemed to be to perform an aesthetic ethics in which shearing her long hair unveiled her more masculine, yet still female, self. In this sense, then, her subjectivity itself can be seen as an aesthetic practice, the making of the self an ethical art.

Shailaja said she had long felt disincluded by mainstream Indians who expected women to look and act a certain way: "They used to call me all sorts of curse words ... that get used for queer people, you know?" But then she added that she also felt disincluded in the nonnormative community because of class: "Queer people also did not welcome me because I came from lower middle class, you can say. I've read Marxism, so I know. Because being queer is thought like so immoral, no? It's like unstable. So most of the queer rights people, they are too busy cutting everyone. Most went to convent school and came from upper middle-class and savarna families, so there was discrimination there also. I was a lesbian woman, but no one wanted me, particularly in Bangalore, because everyone thinks they're so posh like."

Shailaja contended that the ethical act of queer inclusion was still relatively new and unstable in India, and hence, LGBTQ communities were still exclusionary. Carla Freeman (2014, 4) reminds us that "the kind of subject being mobilized, the nature of the labor they are performing, the feelings rallied and produced within this supple and unstable system, and the meanings these affects hold cannot be assumed to be consistent." As Svati Shah (2019) cogently argues, neoliberal governmentality's heightening of the gendered, classed, and urbanized self offers a unique opportunity to trace how modern power informs the self. And Shailaja invited us to turn not just to the political but to the aesthetic as well to consider the embedded ethics of such a self-fashioning, particularly in the midst of a crisis of migrant labor in South Asia as a whole (Shah 2021).

Conservative critiques of LGBTQ rights had framed the queer rights movement as a foreign policy ploy of Western governments intended to corrupt Indianness. Indeed, liberalized sexual politics were powered, in part, by critiques of homonationalism and Hinduism (Puar 2007). Discourses from both sides that suggested a conflict between being Indian and being queer had led to queer citizens like Shailaja feeling unhomed. But regardless of the critique, slowly but surely, as had happened with women in the 1960s and '70s, gender and sexuality became key to the consolidation of the transnationality and modernity of the "new" Indian middle class, visible in Bangalore. Nonetheless, a part of the project involved ensuring that queer Indians were "appropriately Indian" through gender and sexual governance and allegiance to what Shailaja saw as a North Indian Brahmanic culture (Rege 1998, 43). Shailaja found this rendition of queerness stiflingly problematic, and she sought to subvert it through her boycut, challenging the presumption that there is one correct embodiment, one way to be a woman.

Ironically, Shailaja also articulated an embedded critique that paradoxically echoed the Hindutva discourse of indigenous heteronormativity aligned with Hindu personhood:

This new Hindutva is all about Ram Rajya, the rule of the Aryan male god Ram. So many queers go along with them or maybe they don't understand. So they run around saying, "We are free, we are free!" Who is free? Hindutva is all about accepting *these* people so we can cut *those* people. Today, we accept Brahman English queers who speak all *tatatath* [she imitated what she thought of as a Western posh way of speaking], so that we can cut Dalit and Dravida women! It's all caste and class.

She continued,

> Like before we had feminism, no? And all these Brahmanical feminists all going to college in America were talking about upliftment.... They did not care about upliftment of our sisters in the Thirunangai[3] community in Chennai, therima [Tamil = do you know]?! So nowadays, it's all these Brahmanical queers from big cities, who have all studied abroad, in America and London, and they came here and say we are for equality and freedom ... everyone can be free, it is our human right!

She made a derisive face to show her cynicism at what she saw as Brahmanical hypocrisy.

Queering the Nation

Shailaja was right in pointing to class and provinciality as a metric of discrimination in neoliberal Indian queer communities, particularly in a global city like Bangalore. Elite urban queer subjects, who were plugged into international LGBTQ+ discourses, led the battle over gay rights in India. The classed hierarchy of recognition still meant that not all nonnormative subjects were recognized, and while some (cisgender middle-class metropolitan gay men and even women) were interpellated as "model capitalist subjects," others (historically marginalized and stigmatized transgender communities, for instance) lobbied the state precisely on the basis of their "backwardness" (Rao 2020, 25). As Svati Shah (2014, 636) notes, it is cities like Bangalore that are the ground for acceptance of queer subjects, and conversely, provincial towns have occupied a "special place in Indian imaginaries of sexual and gender subjectivity" as conservative spaces. Lawrence Cohen's essay "Song for Pushkin," on the killing of a queer provincial boy in a posh Delhi suburb, exemplifies this dichotomy. The wider speculations of the prostitution of young men from the provinces based on what he terms "the contemporary remaking of a persistent sense of India as a split world"—the provincial, supposedly uncivilized and backward youth, versus the capitalist, hungry, seemingly civilized city folk—and the unequal sexual economies that stalk such divided worlds (Cohen 2007b, 105).

The "campaign to decriminalize consensual gay sex," which arose from the legalization and then recriminalization of homosexuality by the Indian Supreme Court, led to a greater number of people declaiming their nonnormative gender identity and sexual preference in a range of cultural, social, economic, and political spaces. Kareem Khubchandani (2020) speaks to the emergence of queer nightlife spaces in Bangalore as spaces of critique of the dominant heterosexual order, following gay men "across borders into gay neighborhoods, nightclubs, bars, and house parties" between these landmark decisions. The greater visibility for the fight for equality led to greater visibility for queer Indians overall.

In 2015, there was a bill introduced in the Indian parliament to repeal the criminalization of homosexuality that had succeeded the year before, but it failed. Support and protest marches filled the streets of Bangalore, and Sundari took part in most of them. Every time we WhatsApped, she was busy leading a march, sitting on a panel, meeting with local politicians, and so on. There were exciting rumors that an LGBTQ couple had petitioned the Supreme Court to recognize their marriage. Sundari was buzzing with delight at the thought that no longer did trans and queer Bangaloreans have to hide in the shadows. In early 2016, when I returned to Bangalore, Sundari told me excitedly that a number of cities were hosting public gay pride events and protests, more public spaces had emerged in which to socialize, and a greater number of virtual networks had been created for the LGBTQ community as well.

Over the next year and a half, Sundari's WhatsApp messages were full of the ups and downs of LGBTQ rights in India and the struggles for recognition until finally, in October 2018, she texted me in delight a rainbow emoji and the happy news: the Supreme Court had finally ruled to eradicate the colonial-era law on sodomy, the infamous Section 377, calling it unconstitutional, claiming that it infringed on the fundamental rights of LGBTQ citizens' autonomy, identity, and intimacy. In fact, although it had been about a decade since I had started researching the terrain of queer beauty in India, it felt like a completely different moment in terms of gender inclusivity and visibility.

Sundari was unreachable for a few days, giddy with delight, as she celebrated with other LGBTQ activists, walking the streets waving rainbow flags of inclusion, doing interviews with the press, and partying. This moment of rainbow inclusion afforded Indians unprecedented queer possibilities (Shah 2019). "This isn't India becoming 'westernised.' It's India decolonizing," stated LGBTQ activist Shahmir Sanni's tweet on the historic Supreme Court of India judgment, as they spoke back to the critique that one could not be queer and Indian at once.

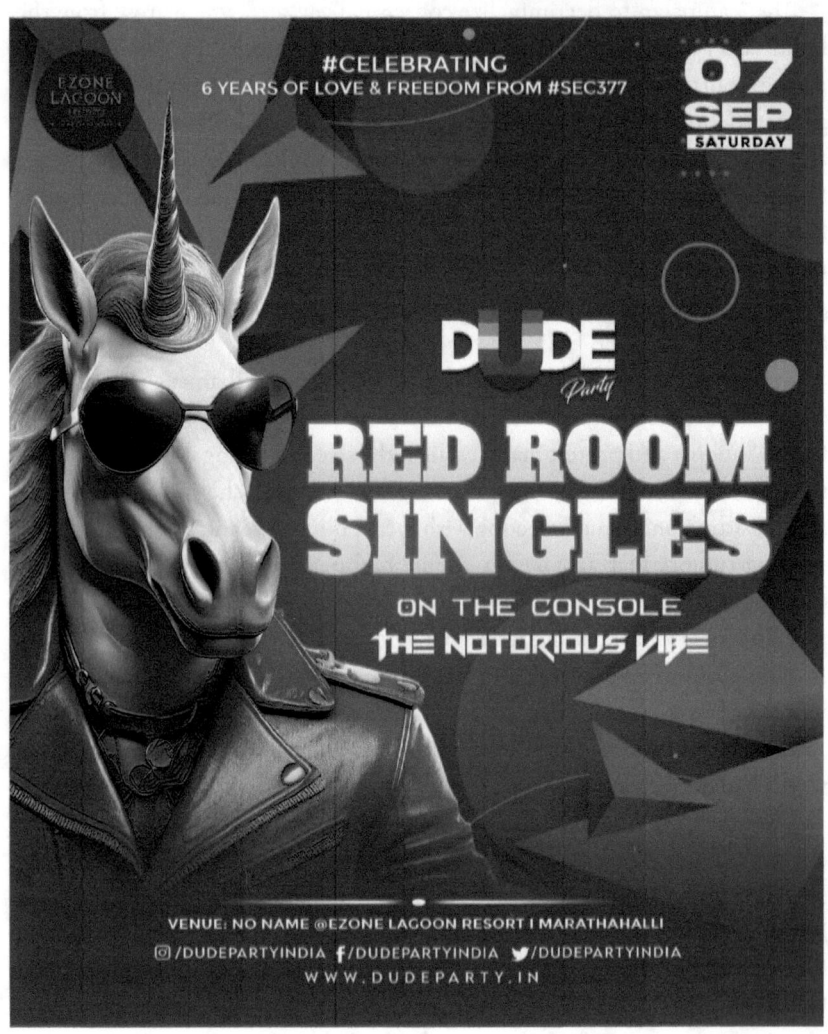

FIG. 6.2. Instagram invitation from Dude Party to celebrate the end of Section 377

Post 2018, more and more nonnormative Indians were visible in the city. Sundari said that Bangalore was now the acknowledged gay party capital of India, and the city became a crossroads where global capital met local and provincial talent. Queer Indians from the provinces who moved to Bangalore for work or education soon came out of the closet and met the queer global circuit of professionals who formed the new international middle class (Khubchandani 2020). Even though they were undoubtedly still subject to discrimination and harassment, the city's storied tolerance and its emergent queer-friendly spaces all marked it as an LGBTQ-friendly city. The next time I was in the city, Sundari waved delightedly at a tattered rainbow flag in a shop window.

But Shailaja was unconvinced, and she stuck to her argument of class divisions in the queer community. "Yes, that's okay . . . important," she said with a wave of her hand that denoted a movement forward as I told her of Sundari's joy. "But still, the community is divided. The posh lesbian and trans people use English only and dance in nightclubs in New York and Bangalore waving flags and all. But still, local hijras, Thirunangai, Aravani, and Jogappa communities are poor and struggle. Sometimes they are forced to beg and do sex work, and the police beat them! What can they do?"

Surpanakhi

It was clear that Shailaja's haircut was about a different kind of beauty, one that actively rejected typical feminine beauty norms. In a system in which so many women around me worked to find the goddess within, I wondered how Shailaja's rejection of makeup and typical female adornment figured in her idea of beauty. Was it a question of authentic embodiment or a political stance or both? And given her insistence that she was a woman, which female mythical figures would she cite, if any?

I waited. Shailaja launched into a story, an unexpected one: the narrative of the demon princess Surpanakhi from the epic of the *Ramayana*. Surpanakhi was the sister of the demon king Ravana and princess of the island kingdom of Lanka. While flying over the Panchavati forest where Rama, his beloved wife Sita, and brother Lakshmana were in exile, Surpanakhi spied the brothers out hunting. Shailaja said, "She really fell for the way Rama looked. . . . He is supposed to be tall and beautiful, illya?" Surpanakhi longed for Rama, for his shoulders "tall as towering mountains," and for his lips redder than coral, for his radiance, "glistening like the moonlight" (Hart and Heifetz 1988, 88). But Shailaja said that Surpanakhi knew that if Rama saw her in her demoness form, he would never make love to her. Shailaja added, "According to the story, Surpanakhi was like, really ugly—with a potbelly, wiry hair, long nails, big bulging eyes, and dark skin!"

So Surpanakhi, being able to shape-shift, imagined Sri Lakshmi, the consort of Vishnu, of whom Rama was an avatar, and so his natural partner over eons. Surpanakhi uttered a mantra and became a beautiful goddess, appearing "fresh as that of a young girl" and "softly clothed." As a "beautiful woman, her face shining brighter than the moon and more radiant than a rose, glowing," she then tried to seduce Rama. She expected her "sweet abundant beauty" and "perfumed honeyed words" of devotion to do the trick (*Ramayana Aranyakandam Patalam* 5 72: 2943 and 2861 in Hart and Heifetz 1988, 109).

Indeed, Rama *was* initially attracted to her, and according to Shailaja, he looked at her with interest, appreciating her limitless beauty. "He totally like lusted after her, okay? Not like he was so great!" But then he felt that something was not right. So he rejected her and chastised her for approaching him, saying he was loyal to his wife, Sita, who had returned, to Surpanakhi's surprise, from a bath in a forest pool. He then tried to set her up with his brother Lakshmana, piling insult on injury.

Surpanakhi was destroyed by his rejection. She left to hide in a cave, but she could not get Rama out of her mind. She was caught in a fire of suffering, of unrequited desire[4] (Hart and Heifetz 1988, 100). "She went crazy with love and spent all the night burning up," said Shailaja. The next day, Surpanakhi returned and watched Sita with envy. Sita's beauty was ravishing, legendary; her eyes were "like blue water lilies," her forehead "lovely as the moon," and her waist "thin like lightning." While absorbing Sita's beauty, Surpanakhi thought, "Beauty that remains with us, in our hearts has no flaw, beyond the limitations of its creators. My eyes refuse to leave her. . . . If I a woman feel like this, what must she be to others?" (Kampan's *Ramayana Aranyakandam Patalam* 5 72:2888 in Hart and Heifetz 1988, 97). Shailaja said, "Surpanakhi recognized that she wanted to be just like Sita but also to eat her up." It is no accident that Surpanakhi took on the shape of Sri Lakshmi, for Sita was supposed to be the incarnation of Sri Lakshmi born to marry Rama, an incarnation of Vishnu. Sita was Rama's eternal cosmological "type" as it were. So when Surpanakhi wished to devour Sita, there is a real question of whether she wished to eat Sita as rakshasas were wont to do to humans, or whether she simply wanted to inhabit her skin, consuming and thus becoming her.

Surpanakhi could not contain herself in her jealousy and attacked Sita, trying to kidnap her (or possibly devour her), a foreshadowing of her brother Ravana's kidnapping of Sita later in the epic. Lakshmana, Rama's brother, ran to Sita's aid. To stop the attack, Lakshmana cut off Surpanakhi's nose, ears, and nipples. Shrieking in pain and fear and her blood flowing through the forest, Surpanakhi retreated, destroyed.

Shailaja stopped her telling, dramatically adding, "Such a terrible story, no? This chopping off of her breasts and lips, cutting off her sexual organs, is so terrible. She was only saying how she loved Rama, and they are so violent toward her, those brothers! Surpanakhi is a Dravida[5] princess, and because she expresses her desire for Rama, the Aryan god, she is humiliated sexually." I asked Shailaja if we could understand it as a question of ethics: Does one's own desire articulated in the myth as a hungry lasciviousness allow one to inflict suffering on another? I pointed out that when Surpanakhi was overcome by desire for Rama, she attacked Sita and attempted to devour her. Shailaja demurred: "This is the violence of North Indian Aryan culture. Valmiki's *Ramayana* is from the North.[6] In Kampan's Tamil *Ramayana*,[7] Surpanakhi is just a woman who desires a man. It's her longing that is the story!" For Shailaja, the Tamil telling of the *Ramayana* showed Surpanakhi to be a southern woman, who was powerful but not beautiful, something she could relate to. In that version of the story, Surpanakhi was punished with mutilation because of her southernness and her supposed "ugliness" because she dared to desire a man who was Aryan, beautiful, and kingly.

I was intrigued by Shailaja's moral opprobrium and her reading of the assault on Surpanakhi as racism, articulating the embodied oppression of northern beauty standards upon a southern body. Kathryn Erndl argues that Valmiki's northern version of the story makes the comparison between Surpanakhi's ugliness and Rama's beauty directly: "His face was beautiful; hers was ugly. His waist was slender; hers was bloated. His eyes were wide; hers were deformed. His hair was beautifully black; hers was copper colored.... He was a tender youth and she was a dreadful old hag" (16: 8–9 in Erndl in Richman 1991, 69). Moreover, whereas Valmiki's Ramayana emphasizes that Surpanakhi lacks the valued qualities of purity and chastity and that is what leads to her failure to achieve her desire (Erndl in Richman 1991, 73), Kampan's Tamil *Ramayana* expressed sympathy with Surpanakhi's plight, making her human in her longing for Rama and in her fear that her ugliness would put him off. Kampan dwelled on Surpanakhi's awareness of her forbidding presence and her attempt to look beautiful by taking on another face, her futile attempts to talk to Rama, and her dismay when she sees the beautiful Sita and realizes the folly of her quest. Valmiki's *Ramayana* equates beauty with the good. As Rama orders Lakshmana to mutilate Surpanakhi, he calls her "ugly" and "unvirtuous" and "ignoble," clearly signs to him and to the audience of her lowly demonic selfhood. Kampan's *Ramayana*, on the other hand, focuses on Surpanakhi's feelings of unrequited love and of feeling undesirable, sentiments that contemporary female audiences can relate to.

Thinking through these various forms of embodiment and the narratives around them that Shailaja sensitized me to, I meditated on the fact that the discourse of gay freedom that I had happily accepted largely took place in political and legal realms and rarely spoke of embodiment. However, it was Shailaja's nonconforming Hindu body that caused her the most stress. Her reframing of the Surpanakhi myth was a powerful critique of what she saw as the alliance between Anglophone urban queer folk and the Hindu right and the types of beauty they embraced. She saw the erasing of her people's version of the story of Surpanakhi as an act of epistemic violence designed to crush the Dravida sense of self and to dehumanize their existence, in the same way that Surpanakhi was mutilated for being different and refusing to be held back by that difference. Recuperating Surpanakhi was a way to rupture the alliance and destabilize the postcolonial, modern, secular formation of the Indian state and the elitist and casteist formations of Indian society, a transgression in the most elemental form, stretching for something beyond those limits within which she was confined. It was also a way of calling out beauty spaces for being inclusive of some bodies and faces while rejecting others. Hafsa Arain makes a similar point about queer communities in Pakistan, noting that even after the gain made by the LGBTQ community in India in the late 2010s, for many, including trans men, butch women, and nonnormative people assigned female at birth, the negotiation of their identity, expression of gender, and balancing of globalizing LGBTQ discourses with preexisting South Asian forms of queerness has meant that their struggles continued.

Tellingly, the second time Shailaja wanted a short haircut, she decided to go to the local *hajama*,[8] or barber. She recounted her relief at finding someone who would give her a true "boycut." "See, he didn't care at all. He charged me 50 rupees and gave me a nice short haircut. With a head massage also. The hajama don't care: man, woman, whoever. They are thrilled a lady customer is coming to their shop, and they will cut your hair the way you want. So, this haircutting style is all about class and caste, not only gender.[9] These Brahman guys always say hajama is *achchuta* [untouchable], so polluting, no? So I'm proud to be polluted!" I was struck in this exchange by the fact that Shailaja had not sought out a queer-friendly salon to have her haircut but had instead simply found a space where she felt that her gender was irrelevant. As she pointed out, the barber was happy to have a new customer. This reminded me of the fact that Sundari only went to Trans Studio because she did not have anyone to help her at home. As I became more acquainted with trans beauty, I noticed that finding a physical beauty space could be a fraught enterprise.

Online chat boards and the comments section of social media posts were spaces where trans people discussed their experiences in parlors. One user, "Gender-Bai," asked about trans-friendly parlors in Bangalore. They confessed that they "passed" for a man, and their mother had given them a buzz cut to prevent them looking like a woman, but they needed to get up the courage to go to a parlor. Another user, "Acharya," replied that most unisex salons in

Bangalore were now trans friendly and did not discriminate. Gender-Bai replied, "Okay! I might just gather my courage and go to one.... It's just that the last time I went to a unisex Naturals salon in Chennai and after my hair was done, I asked them about shaping my eyebrow, and they said that's a service only provided to women and refused me." "Miz," another gender-fluid user, joined the chat and confessed that they were frightened of going to the parlor for a hairstyle since they were "before anything"—that is, they had not begun to transition. Despite having a Lakmé Salon and an Enrich salon within walking distance of them, both of which were "marked LGBT+ inclusive," they were "scared of the ground reality of going there." Another user responded to this thread, "I remember contacting the Lakmé Salon in Malleswaram last year in November they just assumed my gender i asked if they do waxing and they mentioned only for woman so I'm guessing need to pass as cis woman for me to ever go there for waxing in the future. With that experience i don't plan to go there in the future but it did force me to check out other options for hair removal and found electrolysis treatment need to now find one near me which is Transfriendly."

Trans activist Bi-Kool from Bangalore emailed me about trans studios and salons linking to a site that they said showed "exactly" the problem they faced as a transwoman: "Not to generalize, but those parlor wali aunty videos on YouTube have some element of truth to them. A traditional beauty parlor can be a space of judgment for anyone even a cisgendered woman. So for someone who identifies themselves as a queer individual or refuses to fit into the narrative of how a man and a woman should look, or wants to avail of any services that challenge the gendered notions of beauty, spaces are really difficult to find." In response to this dearth of trans beauty spaces, a nongovernmental organization (NGO), Project TransCreations,[10] has successfully set up beauty salons that are run entirely by the transgender community and offer a range of services including facial, manicure and pedicure, haircuts, full-body wax, and more at affordable rates. But they have yet to open one in Bangalore.

All of this led me to the conclusion that queering beauty required an acknowledgment of absence. I had been looking for presence while queer subjects felt that their bodies were unwelcome in spaces of beauty. Although truly inclusive beauty spaces might be on the horizon for the LGBTQ community in India, the reality was that those with nonnormative bodies and pleasures had not learned to be beautiful in a parlor, like my cisgendered friends and their daughters. Rather, they learned beauty surreptitiously, from actresses and singers, glamorous models and goddesses, and from friends and mentors with whom they could feel safe. They mentioned hijra "mothers" and trans "mentors" and "queens" who taught them how to be beautiful. In fact, the commercial world of beauty seemingly had no place for them. A transwoman beauty queen in Bangalore said to me sadly, "There is an assumption, you know, that if you are queer, particularly hijra, you cannot be beautiful. That all wrong, no?"

The Changing Queer Parlor

The problem, I realized, was that queer spaces did exist adjacent to beauty, but they were not analogous to the cisgendered, heterosexual parlor in which I was doing my research. Lesbian parlors, like the one at which Selvi worked, did exist and had existed in the shadows for many years. These, however, were not spaces of beautification so much as spaces of intimacy. They were spaces, as Naisargi Dave (2010) writes, for women to discover and embrace their sexuality in the late twentieth century. While creating community in many ways, these parlors were not spaces that focused on feminine adornment, on the ways in which one presented oneself as a beautiful woman.

I also came across many spaces where queer beauty was on display. As attitudes in Bangalore changed, more nonnormative queer Indians were visible in Bangalore. They came to celebrate their queer selves, though undoubtedly they were still subject to discrimination and harassment. One night, following Bi-Kool's recommendation, I arrived at a gay dance club, called Jeff's, near the old airport, for a Bollywood queens drag night. I was interested to see how a gendered traditional aesthetic would factor into the party, given that the events the group running it typically put on were much more standard Western aesthetic of an adult party: Halloween, Valentine's Day, and a Red Room Singles Stallion Party, and so forth.

Jeff's was a typical club, with a small stage on which queer acts performed, a catwalk that cut through the dance floor, neon strobe lighting, and loud music. The floor was packed with young men, many in muscle T-shirts and shorts, and some in leatherware, chiffon pants, and a six-pack. All seemed delighted to be there. Huge screens behind the DJ showed rotating neon-lit images of the blue sky, fireworks, the gay pride flag, and men kissing, mixed in with images from the floor of people dancing and strobe lights popping. The stage was marked by balloon bouquets in rainbow colors and the rainbow flag.

Young men rotated on and off the stage, dancing. As each man took to the stage, they were cheered on loudly. The floor was packed with glistening bodies, some dressed in party gear, glittering costumes, and masks. As Kareem Khubchandani argues in his book *Ishtyle* on the aesthetics of these queer parties, they demonstrate how brown queer bodies inadvertently become accents

FIG. 6.3. Zeesh dressed as an apsara for a party at KittyKo

themselves, ornamental inclusions in the racialized grammar of desire. The parties highlighted a different kind of labor, the embodied work these men do to feel queer and sexy together (Khubchandani 2020). This was certainly a site of beauty, but it was not a site of beautification. Neither were unisex or LGBTQ-friendly parlors, which as we have seen were not unproblematic. Where did the nonnormative go to learn beauty?

Then I realized that like everything else in Bangalore, it was online.

The Digital Parlor

I met Zeesh at the KittyKo nightclub at the LaLiT Ashok hotel in July 2012, when the LGBTQ community all over India was celebrating Indian Coming Out Day. The club occupies a space that I remember well. It used to be a Chinese restaurant called the Mandarin, which my family used to visit in the 1980s and '90s on rare occasions as a special treat. The LaLiT Ashok hotel was on a high ground, and the Mandarin was on the top floor with large plate glass windows, so one had a view of the lights of the city.

KittyKo had closed off most of the views to enhance the nightclub atmosphere and extended an open-air balcony for dancing. When I arrived, the party seemed to be in full swing, the strobe lights spinning, and everyone dancing to the pulsing music from the DJ booth. Lithe men ground up against one another in the small space, while others danced, bodies shining, rivulets of sweat on their brow, joyful, laughing. A group of women in tight leather miniskirts stood near a small stage, sipping drinks. Everyone seemed excited that the main show was going to be a drag performer named Zeesh. "Zeesh! Zeeesh! ZEESH!" they chanted while jumping up and down. Suddenly, a figure appeared on the tiny stage, dressed in a shiny black outfit with sparkly tights, a big golden tiara, and a full face of glam drag makeup. The crowd surged forward and held up their phones, snapping pictures. It was clear that Zeesh was a celebrity.

In a quiet moment at the club, I retreated to the lobby and perused their Instagram page: "Zeesh is a drag artist also known as Zeeshan Ali, born in Mumbai, who discovered their artistic journey when they shifted to Bengaluru. Arriving in the city as a closeted medical student, they are now a nonbinary drag artist, costume designer, and makeup artist." Like many Indians, Zeesh came to Bangalore to go to college. It seems that once in the city, Zeesh quickly abandoned their medical studies and moved into fashion. Gradually, their makeup tutorials on YouTube started going viral as well. They had apparently become a successful queer representative and beauty influencer, garnering lucrative sponsorships, party deals, and advertisements through their social media presence.

Bangalore had a lot to do with Zeesh coming out of the closet, as they told a group of admirers: "It's a cool city! I could be myself here!" The city offered freedom, not a set of rules or norms to be followed but sites, people, and resources for self-making through which individuals could rework and reimagine the self. Zeesh felt they could even exercise some choice with respect to what it meant to be a certain person and live a certain life. But as they noted painfully, even in globalized and digitalized India, people often struggled to fit in.

Like Zeesh, some had names that identify them as Muslim. Or even if they were otherwise privileged, upper-caste Hindus, individuals might struggle to fit if their English was not fluent or if they had consumer capacity but "bad" taste. Some individuals remained in the closet because they felt that they would not be accepted in what they saw as homonormative spaces. "Closets," as Srila Roy (2022, xv) reminds us, "can offer comfort and safety from several registers of judgment and failing." For Zeesh, drag ultimately gave them an outlet to deal with the wounds of being nonnormative in India.

Vogue India did an interview with Zeesh in 2019,[11] where they[12] were named "our very own Marilyn Monroe." There, they traced their evolving identity: "For the first year, I didn't even tell my parents I had quit med school. I just explored what I wanted to do for myself. I tried everything, styling, designing, modelling. And while I was researching, I came across, the 1990 Club Kids. Where people would completely transform themselves through costume and makeup. And that's when I started playing around with makeup." What Zeesh articulates here is the role of the internet in allowing them to discover resources to craft a beautiful self. First, their inspiration came from the past, but soon they were discovering makeup and beauty tutorials online, which allowed them to play with their embodiment without fear of judgment or harassment. Zeesh tried out looks both ethnic and contemporary. They imagined themselves as a demon (with white makeup and black horns), a magician (red waxen face and yellow eyebrows), a robot (metallic makeup and purple smoky eye), and a queen (ultra glam makeup with eyelashes and pouty lips). All of this was documented online. Zeesh felt that it was their mission in life to offer images of queer beauty and tutorials of how to achieve it for "other queer people to follow."

The more I dug into it, the more I realized that these digital forums, what I call the "digital parlor," were the beauty spaces I was seeking, the places where queer individuals learned to embody beauty. Zeesh was constantly creating and curating content on Instagram, their social media of choice. Images, short video clips, advertisements for upcoming performances, memes featuring a few seconds of their fabulous clothes or makeup all made it onto their page. Later, I found out it was not just them who posted content. Rather, they had a team for hair and makeup, a costumer, a promoter, a videographer, and a stylist. They saw the team as necessary "to be glam" but also to create the videos which they felt might reach a nonnormative young person in some corner of India. Listening to them, I realized that unlike Madhu or Menaka, Radhika and Ami, gender-fluid Bangaloreans did not acquire the tools of beauty visiting the parlor as teenagers but rather from queer mentors in their lives—in one case an older hijra who taught them sex and makeup tips, in another case a Bollywood celebrity off the pages of *Stardust*, and more recently, in online makeup and dress tutorials. In the nonnormative gender community, beauty had been taught and practiced in the absence of official spaces for it.

Like Zeesh, many trans influencers posted regularly about makeup, offering tutorial videos for the whole face, eyebrows, lips, highlighting, eyeshadow, tinting, skin care, and so on. They saw their role as pathbreaking and pedagogic, training others in how to apply makeup to support "gender-bending looks" that were taken up by men, women, and those who were both or neither. A recent Instagram post by makeup influencer Rahil, accompanied by a selfie mimicking a Bollywood romantic lead, read, "Gave up on love, fucking with them heartbreakers ✒ ♡" and was followed by a series of hashtags recording the makeup they used for their look, citing cosmetic companies like Mac, Lakmé India, and Estée Lauder India, and also Zeesh as an influence.

As I explored this space, I asked myself how use of the queer digital parlor differed from the way that ciswomen use the traditional beauty parlor. Madhu explained to me that there was actually little difference; the digital parlor was "just like the regular parlor!" In fact, once I was looking for it, I found that many of my cis interlocutors also consulted the digital parlor for the latest "look," which they then proceeded to deconstruct with the beauticians they trusted to replicate it "in a way that suited" their individual style. Madhu showed me a picture of a princess hairstyle, with loose curls and gold pins and other hair jewelry folded in, from a Deepika Padukone movie: "I like her hairstyle.... Looks so fab! For my cousin's wedding, I'm going to ask Jhuma to do my hair like this!" Oddly (or perhaps not so oddly), I found that Zeesh had the same image of Deepika Padukone on their phone, and they planned to do similar eye makeup—"hot, smoky, smudged eye like Deeps"—for a "party look."

In fact, this overlapping of queer and heteronormative standards of beauty often led to uncanny resonances among my interlocutors. As Radha's career as a movie star grew, she became one of the icons of the digital parlor, and my social media feed was filled with close-up images of her eyes and lips. Beauticians made viral tutorials on how her makeup could be imitated. At one point, Sundari, the hijra activist who was my guide to Trans Studio, showed me an image of lips she wanted to replicate, with a minute-long video tutorial on how to apply lipstick to enhance one's lower lip with gloss in the center. I recognized Radha's lips as the ideal Sundari aspired to.

Thus, digital parlors acted as an archive of beauty and a pedagogical tool in the queer world, as they did for normative persons. Beauticians and clients saved Instagram posts, Reels, and TikTok videos of makeup tutorials and their favorite celebrity images for later examination and replication. For example, Sundari said she had tried five different eyebrows in the space of two years to "try to find the one that suits my face!" She had saved images of Deepika Padukone's face and was growing out her eyebrows in preparation for getting her eyebrows done a few months later to be "full fashion." As she became a spokesperson for trans activism, she started to keep a look book on her phone of makeup and hair tutorials for each different event. She used the digital parlor as a pedagogical tool to teach herself how to dress and do her hair for different events and to match the clothes.

Others used the digital parlor to catalog and review new processes. In the mid-2000s, as laser hair removal clinics started sprouting up all over Bangalore, a flood of social media posts that sold laser hair removal as the "ultimate solution" were going viral. Zeesh wanted to get their arm hair lasered and showed me posts on their phone. By 2020, however, there were many posts of "lasering trauma" and "laser mistakes," which many clients and beauticians cited as the potential pitfalls of the technology. Individuals would comment, "Did you know, her armpits got burnt only! Full black!" or "That new clinic she got her side locks lasered and now she went bald!"

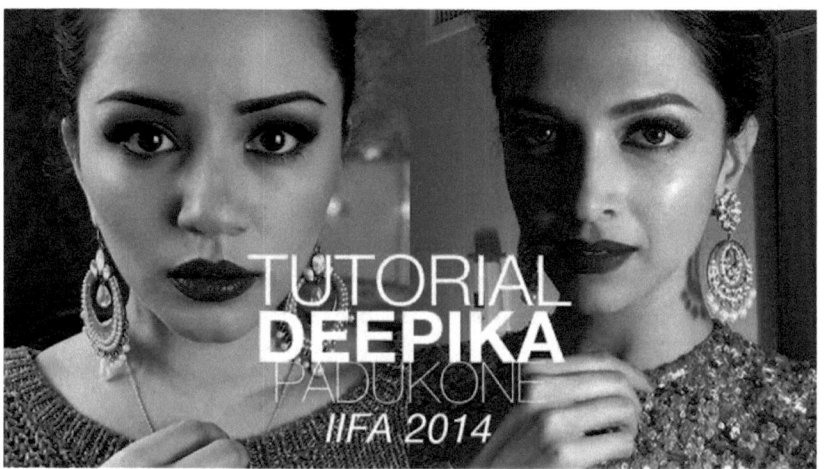

FIG. 6.4. Makeup tutorial to achieve Bollywood star Deepika Padukone's look

The biggest difference I discovered between ciswomen's use of the digital parlor and its use by the queer community was that LGBTQ individuals were more likely to use the tutorials to experiment at home, whereas the women I spent time with in the parlors were more likely to bring the look into the parlor to be reconstructed. Madhu, Radha, and Ami saved images of movie stars and celebrities to show their makeup artists and hairstylists what the aspirational ideal would be. Sundari, on the other hand, often saved the tutorials to try at home in the mirror with her other hijra sisters. This was partially because she could not afford a parlor regularly and partially because as a queer person, she still felt uncomfortable going to a regular women's parlor. But this too was changing. By 2020, just before the pandemic, Zeesh had a "glam squad" of stylists and makeup artists, who came to their home or hotel suite to dress them and were skilled in trans and queer makeup and dress.

Of course, not every queer individual searching for a way to create authentic embodiment utilized the digital parlor. Some, like Shailaja, looked askance: "They are all guys, no girls.... Some are trans and some are nonbinary and queer, but mainly it's guys who are excited about wearing makeup." She was wrong. There were plenty of women excited about the digital parlor tutorials and recommendations. Nonetheless, this trend tapped into a tradition of nonnormative individuals idealizing cis-beauty standards, as represented by female celebrities—actresses, singers, and models—but bending them to fit their own needs with the help of mentors and peers.

Sundari's Lipstick

I had met Sundari, a hijra, queer rights advocate, in 2010, when she was speaking at a panel to educate the public about LGBTQ rights and the inclusion of hijras into trans communities. It proved serendipitous, as I was slowly becoming interested in the queer parlor.

I left Bangalore soon thereafter to return to Boston, but we traded phone calls and WhatsApp messages, and when I returned to Bangalore in 2012, I found myself in her "office," a small room in a no-name office building. We were surrounded by other trans and queer Bangaloreans, engaged in the work of advocacy. She was warm and welcoming, opening up about her life and education mission.

As we talked, Sundari stood in front of a mirror by an open window touching up her makeup, her bangles tinkling. She wore a plum-colored sari and was getting ready to go to a local politician's office. She held a small pocket mirror in her left hand as she carefully traced the outline of her lips in a hard plum-colored lipstick. She was educating me on her toilette as she applied the liner: "I wear outline first and then I fill in the color with Lakmé lipstick," she said. Applying makeup was, she said, central to her self-expression, and she said she learned it from watching the Bollywood superstar of yesteryear Rekha, who was known for her skillful and alluring makeup. "She always went outside [the lip line]," Sundari said as she filled in the color. "Made her lips look much bigger."

On the green wall above her were pasted centerfold images, which I recognized from old *Femina* and *Stardust* magazines: Rekha, dressed in a gold kanjeevaram sari, long fake eyelashes and winged eyeliner, a thick plait adorned in bridal ornaments, a stack of gold bangles, jasmine in her hair. Sundari commented on Rekha's feathery eyelashes: "I heard her eyelashes are made of real cat hair or something. She gets them in Dubai. She must be sixty-plus but so beautifully she has kept up!" Sundari looked at the image adoringly. She said that ever since she was a little boy, she wanted to be beautiful like Rekha. "Rekhaji tho behad khoobsurat hain, na [Hindi = Rekha is amazingly beautiful, isn't it]?" Then she added she had bought the plum lipstick because Rekha frequently wore the shade and had mentioned it in an interview. She touched Rekha's lips in the poster and pouted her own in the mirror.

"My parents thought I should be like a boy," she told me, pivoting to her own biography. I got the feeling that she had told the story many times. "I grew up in Maddur. I played cricket and all with other boys and I did well in school. But I used to work also and secretly I took some money and bought lipstick and kajal, and I would apply it on at night when everyone was asleep because always I like makeup. My father caught me and beat me until I nearly died. They locked me in a room for a month so I would change, and they shaved my head. But finally, I escaped and came to Bangalore and joined the hijras. They welcomed me. My hijra amma, Savitri, took me in and looked after me, showed me how to be, helped me. I owe her my life only!"

Vaibhav Saria, in their pathbreaking study of the hijra community in a provincial town in North India, argues that hijras, who represent a third gender that might be categorized in the West as nonbinary or gender queer, have traditionally been seen as erotic ascetics (because they exist transversally to the traditional life stages of Hinduism) (Saria 2021). While they are accepted in religious literature, they are socially ostracized, often living in small communities, surviving through begging and sex work. Sundari said she had been a sex worker for a short time but soon found her vocation in advocacy for the community, liaising with government officials, politicians, and NGO leaders.

I met Sundari again in 2015, and by that point, she was well known in the city for her hijra activism, appearing at protests for equal rights and in television and print interviews. She had become *the* spokesperson for the hijra community. Her dress and comportment had become more cisgendered: she wore her hair long with jasmine strands and she had gone in for some plastic surgery to make herself look more feminine. She had also gotten married to a man and wore a black bead mangalsutra and gold bangles, signs of being married. As usual, she spoke of the plight of hijras.

She told me that just a few months prior, on November 26, 2014, the police had rounded up 150 hijras in Bangalore under the criminal code Section 377, the Victorian-era law prohibiting "unnatural sex," and deposited them in what is known as "Beggars Colony," detaining them there for many days.[13] The queer rights group Sangama, with whom she worked, had organized a protest at the town hall. Several hundred hijras demonstrated and created a racket accusing the police of discrimination. She chuckled at the chaos they created.

Sundari went to the protest wearing red lipstick, she said, because the police knew she gave "good blow kelsa," and she knew many of them as former clients. The visible presence of Sundari and her sister hijras and the coverage their demands received in the press forced the release of their queer kin from detention. Sundari told me that the police are scared to touch or detain hijras too long in the lockup because they see them as dangerous: "They are scared we will curse them. Sometimes I pretend to lift my sari because I know they are scared of what they will see. You see, they know God has given us unique powers, not like simple men and women, not bums and breasts only."

Like many of the people I talked to, Sundari moved easily between beauty, politics, and myth. She noted that there was a distinct place for the third gender, hijra, in Hindu sacred texts and traditions. For instance, the *Mahabharata* features Shikhandi, who fights as a man yet dresses and looks like a woman, and the great warrior Arjuna, who spends a year passing as a woman in the great epic.[14] Yet, despite the spiritual value given to hijra for their ability to inhabit liminal, nonnormative gendered space, Saria (2021) argues that figures such as Shikhandi are powerless to change social mores in which hijras are reviled and feared for their nonnormative status, especially in provincial spaces. Saria's (2021) claim that hijras lived orthogonally to society interrogates easy framings of hijras as marginal to demonstrate how hijras enable Indian familial life through a specifically religious idiom of erotic asceticism, arising in both Hindu and Islamic traditions. Hijras' existence is at once foundational and interventional in Indian society, rendering unfamiliar global ideas about how queerness works. Indeed, the figure of the hijra, as indubitably Indian and Hindu, emerges *as a moral presence* in Indian society, one that collapses the categories of Hindu, Indian, and queer. But most important for me, what Saria's work enables is a pivoting to focus on the hijra body, its aesthetics and desires, to demand an interrogation of the aesthetics of queer subjectivity in India. How can we think of the aesthetics of nonnormative bodies? How does beauty fold into this discourse?

Sundari was clear when I ask her what Shikhandi's existence proves regarding hijra life in the contemporary world. She argued that Shikhandi served to underscore the idea that the body of divinity is transcorporeal and permeable—that is, queer. So when we (meaning humanity) assign Shikhandi a normative form, we fail to appreciate the all-encompassing fluid form of divinity that is the womb of Hindu ethics. Because hijras exist transversally to traditional Hindu ethics, they have the power to evoke gods and goddesses by bending gender and social norms in dangerous and creative ways (Saria 2021, 26).

Sundari saw this as a redemptive idea and one that offered the aspiration of final perfection where the body is transposed and transfigured, shape-shifting into various forms, gendered, ungendered, and most important, queer and Other (Reddy 2019). This reminds me of Sarah Coakley's (2000, 70) meditation on theological queerness, where she writes that queerness "[gestures] to an eschatological horizon which gives mortal flesh its final significance, a horizon in which the restless, fluid, postmodern 'body' can find some sense of completing without losing its mystery," without "succumbing again to 'appropriate' or restrictive gender roles." Sundari would argue that all Hindus are caught up in this body, formed from it and sharing in its fruition, marking the possibility that the divine is continuous with the human world and is queer and inclusive in its essence. Thus, the potential of theological queerness is precisely fluidity rather than ossification. Although there is a yawning gulf in India between the potential and the reality, queer embodiment in Hinduism nudges theology toward this different horizon and holds potential to rethink the mysterious heart of religion and its troubling connections with modern selfhood (Saria 2019).

Sundari, however, had no need for a mythic quest. For Sundari, as a person who combined glam makeup with a carefully curated five o'clock shadow, just applying lipstick was a revolutionary and transgressive act and an "insubordination" of the rules of gender performance, an intervention into discourse for a critical purpose, a deliberate inscription and dissemination of nonnormative discursive subjectivities (Baker 2011). She understood it as artifice but also one that constituted a new queer feminine self, one who could do blow kelsa easily on heterosexual and queer men. She advised me to wear red lipstick: "Then you don't have to do any work. Men just fall! You should try it!"

After I got to know Sundari better, I told her I knew the manager of the new Sephora shop in the Forum Mall, and she could go there and pick up some lipstick samples. She beamed. Later, I learned from the manager that she had left with about twenty tubes of lipstick and several types of mascara to try.

Voguing India

I would learn that Sundari's approach was not the only way to combine the masculine and the feminine or utilize the oneness of Hindu spirituality to trouble the binary. Zeesh defined themselves as a "goddess." Through Instagram, they had charted their growth as a nonnormative performer, often switching between gender performances in real life and various drag characters on stage and screen. I met Zeesh and Prakash, their friend, at a local club. They tended to talk over each other with one ear out for what the other was saying so that they could cut in, and with the noise of the club where we met, I found the conversation confusing. When I asked them about makeup, however, they were eloquent:

I learned about how to apply makeup by myself. Watching videos on the internet and learning about '80s-style club culture. It's the idea that you can be whoever you want to be. Korean makeup videos are great ... also American ones. And of course, all the drag videos like RuPaul's *Drag Race* behind the scenes where they apply the makeup, some European MUA [makeup artist] shows and also some ladyboy videos from Thailand! Those are more for fun actually! And I love it because it's such a big FU to heteronormality. I love hyperfeminizing. Participating in queen culture and breaking the binary is so empowering. That is what allured [*sic*] me to drag in so many ways.

With regard to makeup and its potential for transformation, Prakash was clear: "Makeup is a form of self-expression. My body is my canvas. I use all the colors in my box and create these magnificent characters through which I can emote part of myself. Express, explore. Makeup gives me the power to showcase a side of me which I can communicate. That's fabulous!" At the same time, Zeesh said,

> Most people don't see the fantasy aspect of makeup. They are too conservative with it. Matching it to clothes or whatever. They don't see it as expressing. And nowadays, we can get all the makeup easily, not like before. And we can try at home. Just order on Nykaa or Amazon and in one day it will be there. But before, I used to try different looks and style myself. I used to make my own like crowns and flowers and costumes and do my own makeup and experiment. But now, I get lots of sponsorships and get makeup artists and stylists and all!

In an interview in *Grazia* magazine titled "Queen Culture," Zeesh was asked what beauty meant to them. They responded, "Beauty is an acceptance of what is and what it can be. Who and how you are right now and who and how you can be!" It was clear that beauty was aspirational for Zeesh and that playing with and reaching for different embodiments was associated for them with full authentic selfhood. In their 2019 *Vogue* interview, they (then still using the male personal pronoun) said, "Many people say he is playing with gender nowadays.... But you can be whoever you want to be! You can wake up today and be a queen, wake up tomorrow and be a king, wake up the day after and be an alien."

Zeesh was not the only one who felt that beauty practice allowed individuals to transcend the mundane and aspire to something greater. Bhanu, a young transwoman from a small town near Bangalore, had been working as a professional makeup artist in the city for several years. She said to me, "I use makeup to make a different person from who I am. It gives me confidence and motivates me to be a better version of myself. I think this is how my approach to makeup is different from that of most people."

Bhanu and Zeesh described the way in which makeup, such as lipstick and highlighters, could become a tool of both power and reclamation for queer communities. Such expressions were important for queer people, they said, not only to declare their identities but also to make their bodies a place they wanted to live in and be admired for. It reminded me of Sundari and the sexual and social power that her glamorous lipstick-adorned embodiment gave her. And I realized while listening to Bhanu and Zeesh that the red lipstick Sundari offered me was, for her, a technology of transformation.

Prakash told me about various clubs in the area where he danced, "I go to Jeff's, KittyKo, Drag Parlor, all the clubs, madam. I also dance Kuchipudi, Bharatanatyam also." At the same time, Zeesh was holding forth on how to ensure that fake eyelashes and acrylic nails did not fall off to Bhanu, who was adding in her advice, resulting in a cacophony of beauty. "Glue must dry half... then when you place it, you have to be so careful!" they looked at me for confirmation or rebuttal, and I said I had never worn either. Zeesh looked alarmed. "You never wanted to do nail polish?" they asked. I stretched out my hands with bitten nails: "Not really! I did try false eyelashes once and found them really uncomfortable.... My eyelids began to itch and hurt." Zeesh rolled their eyes and came back with a withering remark: "Well, to be beautiful you have to have some pain, no? You can't be beautiful and comfortable. Look at me.... Maybe you are simply a woman, you don't understand!" I was unsure what they meant by this remark. Did they mean I was already a cisgendered woman and therefore I did not need to contemplate how to be feminine? Or did they mean that as an unbeautiful woman and one who clearly was not fashionable, I failed at being adequately feminine? Or were they saying with my apparent politics there would be little expectation of my knowing these esoteric beauty and makeup tips? My internal monologue echoed Srila Roy's thoughts on her own positionality as someone who "failed" at heteronormative patriarchal aspirations, in her case of conjugality, and in mine of "proper" embodiment. She writes, "I also think I was embarrassed at my own failing.... And this sense of embarrassment was enough to cast me, in my own eyes, as a bad feminist" (Roy 2022, xv). I would add that in my case, my failures seemed to cast me as an unworthy woman, one on whom the pleasures of being feminine were lost. Zeesh had picked up on this failure and merely articulated it, though not unkindly.

Return to the Goddess

For International Transgender Day of Visibility in March 2022, Zeesh uploaded a video to Instagram titled "Mohini." Mohini is a goddess, a seductive enchantress form of the great god Vishnu, who maddens demons and gods with desire, often leading them to their doom. Mohini is a trickster, beguiling everyone she meets, alluring and beautiful. The form of Vishnu as Mohini the enchantress first emerges in the Samudra Manthana (the churning of the ocean) story of the *Mahabharata*, which I had of course read. Zeesh told me the story of Mohini's birth in their own words.

> The devas [gods] and asuras [demons] were fighting and they both wanted to get amrita [the nectar of immortality]. For that, they had to churn the Ocean of Milk [Kshira sagara]. They used mountain Meru as a churn, and they churned the ocean. The asuras wanted to keep the amrita, but Vishnu knew that. So he became Mohini, who was beautiful, and the asuras went mad with desire. Mohini tricked the asuras to give her the amrita, and she distributed it to the devas only. They say she is the true form of Vishnu, hidden like a maya inside him and only she comes out to save everyone. Sakkat power, no?

Zeesh's idea that the female form of Mohini lurked inside Vishnu's male god form was an innovative reading, since in the Sanskrit *Mahabharata*, Vishnu takes on the Mohini form at will. Zeesh's idea of Mohini as the goddess of deception[15] or maya who also leads humanity to a truth of being was an intriguing idea.

The video moved from a portrayal of Zeesh as Mohini in a white sari, gold jewelry, and bridal makeup, to a black-and-white video of Zeesh becoming the goddess by dressing in front of a mirror. As a final touch, Zeesh added a garland of jasmine and Grecian-style crown of gilded spikes. The caption of the video read, "It's crazy how sometimes a blessing can also be a curse. How beauty standards can be so flawed. And how humanity can be so easily coerced. Deception is the ultimate weapon. And the truth sometimes is too fragile to handle." As Zeesh draped their sari like a bride, they outlined their lips with their fingers. "Mohini the enchantress, the only female avatar of Lord Vishnu, is not only an epic story from Hindu mythology, but a modern-day personification for each of our brothers and sisters who don't think they belong. But for those who live in bodies they didn't choose, or identities they can't measure up to, living becomes an act. Life becomes a stage with the hope of a payoff that is looking right back at you . . . the irony." The scene then shifted abruptly to color. Zeesh as Mohini stood at the seashore as the waves lapped at her feet. The camera focused on her back as she walked into the waves. The camera panned from Zeesh's feet over their bejeweled body to their face with kohl-lined eyes. "The ritual of enchantment is really an extension of our truest selves, backed by the blessings of god. The seductress. The slayer of demons is tarnished by the expectations of society, and the perversions of artistry. What was divine is now derogatory. We live with it but only to set the record right. One way or another, we will prevail. Or perish. But not until we have cleansed society for her sins." The video ended with Mohini walking slowly toward the waves, her sari flowing behind her, her crown gleaming. As the screen faded to black, the word MOHINI etched in gold stood out.

I found Zeesh's film intriguing. Its aesthetics suggested a pluriverse of sources, some Western, some Indian, some ancient, some modern but all mythical in service of reimagining gender in India. Zeesh as Mohini implicated history to constitute contemporary selfhood, turning to the past in more explicit, even defensive, ways in the face of the threat of the present disinclusion. In doing so, they combined the image of Mohini with Western ideas of free love, self-expression, and human rights. Hauntings of this kind complicate easy assessments of the present as succeeding the past, or the global as decimating the local. However, neither are they uniformly transgressive nor nonnormative effects. Rather, there are multiple hauntings and mythical figures at play, overlaid with one another, with messier and more ambivalent creative effects.

Indeed, thinking of the "ambivalence" of the body or bodies in interaction reinforces Maurice Merleau-Ponty's crucial insights that come after and exceeds the current emphasis on how the varieties of language and history have reorganized (Michel Foucault [1977] says they have "utterly destroyed") the human body. Rather, for queer Bangaloreans like Zeesh and for women in Bangalore, telling myths and bringing them into the contemporary reasserts the primacy of the body, not merely the primacy of perception. What the word "perception," Merleau-Ponty argues, cannot usually include how the living body *consists of* interactions with the world and the determinations that the body makes. Living bodies determine desire and the feeding of those desires. It is both the edge of being and the creation of order. Zeesh's telling of the Mohini myth reiterates the body sense by which one understands the desires and feelings of the body and interactions with others and gives this body sense legitimacy through the divinity of Mohini.

The structure of Zeesh's narrative was a familiar mythical one, a story with a series of familiar references for the knowledgeable audience, and combined with the visuals, it formed a densely compact nest, spinning the myth into an ontological queer ethical universe. Here, the mythical worlds are not only a means of expression but also a method of interpretation. For Zeesh and others like them, not only do the words and images carry deeper meanings, but so did the stories that the words described. Zeesh and others seam together bits of energy and information to create meaningful worlds/meaning-filled words. And they do this visually as well as linguistically. Here, I turn to Martin Heidegger and the role of the poet, which is what Zeesh is, to travel to the edge of the abyss and bring some insight back. Poetry exaggerates the metaphorical axis of language and enables meaningfulness as resonance. Their main reading method was a type of hermeneutic by which myths are read not only as in the past and a rehistoricization of a past, an imagined made real, which is how the Hindu right sees myth, but also as prophetic signs of the unfolding of a divine plan, a future extant, which is how the liberal order sees the power of myth. So myth is not a charter for living but an anti-charter, a hermeneutic technology that leads in both directions—past and future.

In Zeesh's creative reading visualization and enactment of the myth of Mohini, prophecy and fulfillment are twinned, real to more real. Bangaloreans like Zeesh provoke these imaginings through what I term "edge work" of storytelling as everyday experiences. They speak powerfully to the dynamic, the unstable, tensile, indeterminate, vulnerable as places of emergence, elasticity, flow, transition, and creative transformation of what David Shulman (2012) beautifully terms "mind-born worlds." It is in this realm of the imagination of mind-born worlds that women's edge work resides and pushes forward as a reemergent aesthetic ethics, where ideas of selfhood are perceived and played with, tried out, and sometimes, though rarely, discarded.

Thus through hermeneutics, a new queer reading and expression of the myth builds its own legitimacy on the old myth of Vishnu as female Mohini the enchantress but at the same time supersedes it with the contemporary ethics of human sexualities to legitimize modern yearnings. This is a different exegetical expression of the mythical narrative that better suits contemporary queer needs. Prakash said that the video "gave people hope." Zeesh as Mohini at the ocean's edge at dusk suggested that a new dawn was breaking for queer people in India. Such hermeneutical flexibility of narrative allowed for a restructuring of power and ways of being in significant ways.

In the form of epic poetry of myth such as the Mohini story, we can hardly fail to be struck by the sheer number of stories piled one on top of another, with the frame story, here that of Vishnu, providing a rationale for the many stories to come and their proliferation, an excess of narrative as it were. Besides offering different points of view, these stories offer different explanations for the listeners. They may be expository as when the characters ask for more information to ground the story for the audience. Or they may be didactic, serving as attempts to teach a lesson, or argue a case, or persuade or dissuade characters as also the listeners. But at no point was a story told for no purpose.

And these selected storytelling techniques both narrative and visual offer a rhythm of telling: there is repetition of certain thematic elements and a dramatic visualization that is familiar. There are also standardized descriptions of women, repeatedly through the form of the stories, which clearly were clichés to give the narrator breathing space while keeping their audience entertained. These would also have provided for the listening audience, another pleasurable sensation, that of recognition and familiarity. A glance at almost any medieval Hindu work of imaginative literature is enough to show that whether Western scholars appreciated this form, the contemporary audience certainly did and does even today. Returning to the framing story and the voice of the primary teller is a looping mechanism that offers the narrative a threading that is compulsive.

I was particularly interested, as might be expected, in Zeesh's use of goddess imagery. In fact, Zeesh's online profile was filled to overflowing with his performances as goddesses—Southeast Asian, Grecian, Inca, and Hindu. I asked Zeesh why this fascination with goddesses. They looked taken aback and then answered flippantly, looking at their glam team, "Goddess? It's a drag term.... I am a goddess!" They threw their arms up and posed. In fact, they said, they felt that the goddess was the divine feminine in them that demanded expression: "She has to come out, na?" They loved embodying any goddess but felt a particular kinship to Mohini. "Why?" I asked. "Because Mohini is gender fluid. Because she is born from a god's, meaning Vishnu, a man's body. She has a man's essence in the form of a female. That's what I do in drag. And afterward when they see my performance, people are happy."

So if we understand the Mohini myth here as a narrative of queer selfhood, I ask if the impetus to tell stories is also an indirect plea to the other for recognition. Can we argue that these stories form choreographies of recognition that "revisit, survive, and (re)make culture and belonging" (Conquergood 2006, 354)? Telling the tale and hearing it changes one's ontology in significant ways, and it allows one to survive, particularly in an oral culture where theologies of living are always understood to be knowledge which one remembers (smriti) and hears (shruti). Zeesh marshals the goddesses as affirmation of the acquisition of beauty in their search for access, status, and recognition as a modern Indian woman. To be able to construct a meaningful self-narrative, they must draw on narratives within the culture, and to gain social and cultural recognition, they must inscribe themselves in culturally accepted plots. This is aptly described by Margaret Somers (1994, 606): "We come to be who we are (however ephemeral, multiple and changing) by being located or locating ourselves (usually unconsciously) in social narratives rarely of our own making." Judith Butler (2000, 26) makes a similar point when she says, "The norms by which I seek to make myself recognizable are not precisely mine." As Butler rightly notes, this "dispossession of perspective" haunts the singularity of a self narrative.

But it is not just the ingenuity of the fabulation that made these stories resonate through the spaces in which they were told and through my interlocutors' lives. I found that frequently, the tellers of the stories ended their stories not with the expected "happily ever after" but rather with "and afterward," as Zeesh did. This usage suggested that the story continued into their lives and did not end, but rather, we were in media res, in the center of a larger story, a story of human existence. They suggest that storytelling and narrative link us to an unbroken chain of human memory, where we agentively experience the same problems and attempt to solve them (with varying degrees of success) (Moran 2001). This idea of agency solves the suffering of life though the narrative and aligns with the complex consideration that a person may not only be the author of a story but its object as well. This perspective of the world sees the act of storytelling as creating an alternative vision of the future, rooted in narrative structure, that introduces the aspect of contingency to the present reality, including power structures, privileges, or identities. The story transports us into a world outside our experience, a world in which human and mythological creatures exist side by side, blurring the lines between imagination and reality.

Goddess imagery allows Zeesh to "dwell in possibility," to quote Emily Dickinson, both living in the real world, with all its challenges, trials, and constraints, and reaching for a larger vision of life. They do this, I think, by immersing themselves in the stories that cultivate their moral imagination. The idea of drag as a vocation enables Zeesh to make the argument for a different moral imagination, to "dwell in a different possibility," where beauty is essential to self-recognition.

In his book *The Ethics of Beauty*, Timothy Patitsas (2020) makes a similar argument: that by taking a "truth first" approach to life, the West tends to relegate the importance of beauty to second-class status, to see it as unnecessary or an add-on, when in fact it is essential to understanding both truth and life.

Zeesh noted,

> When I dress as Mohini or Durga, it is their story that I bring to the club, but I also bring myself to it. Because then I can show who the goddess

is. How she can come from me and my team's creativity, and also how I am only a small piece of her, no? She is fabulous; everything comes from her. She is man, woman, hijra, trans whatever you want to say... one minute this, next minute that. From these stories of her, we can say, Okay, now she is Durga on the lion, next she is Mohini dancing, coming from Vishnu, the sky, the earth, everything; she is everything! So then I can think, no matter if some people can't accept me, some others will accept me and my drag as Durga or Mohini or whatever, they can see who I am.

However problematic was the fact that Zeesh's illustrations were all idealized forms of Hindu divinity worshipped by savarna castes, their rendition of Mohini, and the story of her emergence, showed that the beauty in certain stories could defuse our assumptions and open us up to different ways of seeing the world around us. These can be stories, factual or fictional, of goddesses or of human others who have faced unbelievable suffering and gone on not only to survive but to flourish for the sake of the larger world. It is by seeing and contemplating lives lived beyond the odds—whether in fiction, myth, or history—that we reflect, imagine, and aspire to live and be beautiful. And this quest also provokes a different moral imagination to take root.

Yet recognition implies some familiarity and a reckoning. One must recognize what one sees as feminine from a familiarity with what the feminine is, as well as a reckoning of what the feminine implies. It is the very act of acknowledging value (Lamont et al. 2016). It is a collaborative process, where the viewing of a form, even a superficial viewing, sparks the familiarity of the known and leads to recognition. Zeesh as the goddess Mohini: Is the recognition of Mohini a recognition of Zeesh and vice versa? They seem to suggest so. But recognition is rarely understood as the simultaneous mutual apprehension of two subjects; rather, there is always an implicit hierarchy. This is obviously significant in terms of understanding empathy and respect, given the supposedly secular, plural, and democratic society that Bangaloreans inhabit, which presumes equity as an ideal, even if it is unattainable in a deeply hierarchical society like India.

But making one's body anew to align oneself, even if momentarily, with one's gender as one experiences it, as Zeesh does, and to elevate it to goddess status, seeking recognition, is a trenchant act of the imagination that implicates the body. And although both Shailaja and Zeesh use Indian religion and mythology to argue that India has always been queer, they mobilize these stories with seemingly opposite political agendas, one to dismantle the idea of feminine beauty and the other to entrench it. Thus, queer embodiment in Bangalore is diverse in its enactments, and it nudges theology toward this different horizon and holds potential to rethink the mysterious heart of religion and its troubling connections with modern selfhood (Saria 2019).

Transforming the Self

At the end of our interview, Shailaja returned to the ontology of being gender queer through the body of Ardhanarishvara,[16] an incarnation of Shiva where he splits himself in two, half-feminine and half-masculine. In a troubled voice, she said, "Where I grew up, there was a small Ardhanarishvara temple, you know? Half-man-half-girl-type Shiva temple. It was a big problem to dress the idol, they used to say, because they had to buy full sari and full dhoti, cut in half and stitch it so that the priest could put it on the idol. Dressing and other things is not easy for us in the queer community. . . . It takes trouble. Taking some from here, taking from there. We have to fight to be who we are."

Shailaja's haircut, like Zeesh's drag, is a technique of the self, a remaking of subjectivity—an aesthetic, existential struggle toward an ethics. It is beauty "edge work," occurring at the political edge of what constitutes a "good citizen" and how we think about bodies and selves.

Shailaja sees this re-creation of self as a battle. She understands that by stepping into the pollution of the hajama's barber salon, she re-creates herself in her queerness and resists oppressive Brahmanic narratives of selfhood as well as neoliberal, global, queer narratives of self. Her haircut does not construct an embodiment aligning with a certain ethics (Ambrosio 2008) but rather is a self-fashioning, an aesthetic ethics whereby the aesthetics itself shape the ethics or bring them into being.

For Zeesh, their embodiment does the same thing. Their drag, they say, is a work of art, realized in the makeup and styling, not the transcribing of some sort of platonic ideal of gender. This is edge work in gender, formed in situ, reconstructing how we think of beauty as aligned with womanhood. Zeesh's Mohini is a performative and ontological act of ethics, an aesthetics that speaks to their being, and it requires that they act with personal courage and develop a tolerance for uncertainty and vulnerability. This aesthetics ethics is the painstaking work of crafting an embodied self, through actions that derive meaning from cultural norms but also make use of the self's mutability and transformative capabilities to incite new ways of thinking about forms of transcendent experience that exist at the edge, beyond our horizons.

But Shailaja, Sundari, and Zeesh know that we cannot transform ourselves through a simple act of knowing, through critical reason or reflection alone, "but only by *risking* who we are, by... seeking out and testing ourselves in situations that illuminate the contours of our subjectivity, that destabilize our certainties" (Ambrosio 2008, 255). They play with and critique Hindu myth, yet use its imagery as a commentary on queer embodiment. Myth here is truly understood as an interdiction, a speaking back to a society and its pathologies. It is a lens that allows us to think of how we view ourselves and the other.

The stories of lust, betrayal, pain, love, and beauty that captured my imagination on the previous pages created a community defined by queer rights and the right to define a collective past (Das 1995, 15). As Zeesh, Sundari, Shailaja, and others transform their bodies, their ability to transform consubstantial acts of violence into acts of moral solidarity is the key for defining an abiding moral structure.

For to be unsure often means to not know what lies in the beyond, the undiscovered, the unthought.... We do not always know what we can be.
—Joshua Myers, *Of Black Study*, 2023

Beauty is not so much what you see as what you dream.
—Walloon proverb

When I look in the mirror, Amman looks back at me.
—Selvi

CONCLUSION
Mirrors and Masks: An Anthropology of Beauty

Through the Looking Glass

Selvi was difficult to know. She was reserved and treated me with such deference that it was difficult to break through the walls that she had erected between our perceived stations. However, one day, she invited me to her house in the informal neighborhood of Ejjipura (known colloquially as a "slum") for what I thought was an Amman (the goddess) festival. Looking at Google maps, I discovered Ejjipura was just a few minutes from the Bodycraft Beauty Academy, where I had met many aspiring beauticians in training.

I arrived in the tobacco-colored gloom of a dusty evening, following the blue dot on my phone. A small footbridge lay across the open drainage ditch leading into Ejjipura, and I was directed to Selvi's house by helpful neighbors. It stood on the edge of an immaculately swept courtyard with a straggly Moringa tree in a corner. Under the tree stood a chicken, tied by one foot to the trunk. It was scratching comfortably in the dirt but upon my entry became instantly alert. "Aromale"

(Tamil = My beloved), a haunting tune by the Tamil composer A. R. Rehman, was blaring from the loudspeakers in the courtyard.

Entering Selvi's home, in front of which was a patch of dry earth decorated with kolam,[1] I found her with her sister Suguna, draping a bright orange sari around herself. Someone outside started playing the mridangam drum, a staccato, hypnotic eight beat. Later, I learned that the drumming was by Selvi's kinsmen. The drums made one's blood run, they said. It brought the goddess.

Suguna explained that that evening, Amman the goddess would "come" (Tamil = varavaal) to Selvi, transforming her into an oracle for the community. As Suguna chatted with me, the sun set and the courtyard filled with people waiting to consult the goddess. Selvi lay down on a mat and placed her head in Suguna's lap. Suguna held a brass bowl filled with a rice paste mixed with yellow turmeric powder, and she started painting Selvi's face with it, making it glow like an orb. She then dabbed some kumkum on Selvi's forehead, a sign of her ritual auspiciousness. With the rib of a coconut leaf frond, Suguna drew patterns along Selvi's gleaming face. Called mukhathezhuthu, this face painting is an intricate art form. Suguna had learn to draw these designs from her grandmother who, like Selvi, had received the goddess. The accuracy of the design played a critical role in the transcendence, in the arrival of Amman. It was a question of the goddess binding (Tamil = pinnaippu) with Selvi, Suguna said as she carefully drew the intricate designs around Selvi's nose.

I made myself comfortable beside Suguna, taking care not to upset the assorted trays and pots of dye. Suguna painted wide black lines below Selvi's eyes, hollowing them out, and white lines from her forehead outward. A slow metamorphosis was beginning. I asked Selvi how she knew when Amman entered her. "They give me a mirror," she said. "When I look, I see Amman's face. Then the pain hits me in my stomach. . . . Badaam! Like that. It is terrible pain, like my body is breaking. The next thing I know, I'm sitting in the chair." She pointed to the courtyard, where a plastic chair had been set up under the shade of the Moringa tree and covered with a velvet carpet and strands of jasmine, as though for an important personage to occupy.

In the weeks leading up to the "day of the coupling," Selvi told me, she adhered to strict rules. She prayed every day and only ate food that she herself had prepared. Normally, Selvi didn't eat meat, but after the ritual, she would need protein, Suguna noted.

Almost immediately, there was an ominous squawking outside. Then Suguna added proudly, "She is so pure that all her predictions are 'perfect'" (she used the English word). Our conversation paused as Suguna began working on Selvi's eyes, deftly drawing jet black paisleys around them.

Half an hour later, the courtyard had filled up completely, and the crowd was thick and loud. Right at the front sat a local politico in a starched white dhoti, wearing a gold chain and carrying a purse under his arm, presumably full of cash. He was accompanied by a band of thugs. The locals had given the politico the only other chair in the courtyard.

Finished with painting Selvi's face, Suguna lit some incense in an incense burner, and the room became thick with smoke. Selvi lay motionless. Suddenly, she started mumbling and her eyes rolled back in her head. Then her body began twitching as though electrified. Almost intuitively, the drumming from outside quickened and grew louder. Suguna took a small mirror off the wall and held it in front of Selvi. Selvi's body jerked as though a current coursed through her. She stood up and rushed out the door into the courtyard. The drummers' beat, now loud and insistent, had an almost physical impact, the sound reverberating through my body.

As I followed Suguna outside, I saw the goddess sitting in the chair, her eyes charged, her legs spread apart. The Selvi whom I knew, with the polite melancholic air and soft voice, was gone. Yellow-faced, black-eyed, the goddess leaped to her feet and twisted and turned frenetically. The bystanders, now transformed into devotees, chanted, "Vandirka! Vandirka!" (Tamil = She has come! She has come!) and rushed forward to prostrate themselves before her. Two kinsmen held Selvi by the arms to prevent her from hurling herself on them. One man asked the goddess who she was. "Don't you know? Why do you ask?" she spat back. The drummers reached a crescendo of playing, and the rhythm seemed to seep into everyone's body. The goddess danced herself into a frenzy, flinging herself back and forth, her feet moving in a blur. Then suddenly, she stopped and swayed in position. The gathered crowd approached her, gingerly and reverentially, to ask their questions. She intervened in a land settlement, soothed the anxiety of an unmarried daughter of a family, and helped determine when an illness might be healed.

Finally, the politico approached her and asked a question about his success at by-elections. The goddess bared her teeth and roared at him, "You think you are a big man [Tamil = periya alla]? You will win if you sacrifice a black goat. But after you win, that's when the fun will start!" she said. It sounded like a threat.

Then, as suddenly as it began, the goddess fell to the floor writhing and then was utterly still. Selvi was helped back into the house by the drummers and laid on a mat on the floor. Everyone left and the courtyard became silent and still.

The next morning, I was back at the Lotus, and I glimpsed Selvi, silently bent over a client, carefully threading her eyebrows.

When I returned to Boston, Selvi's possession haunted me as a parallel yet obverse mirror that illuminated beauty practices in radical ways. The goddess's arrival brought together many of the themes that have animated this work—allure, adornment, sacrifice, power, pain, (mis)recognition, porousness, alchemical selfhood, and the power of narrative. Throughout these preceding pages I have sought to think about these themes *anthropologically*, following in the footsteps of Alfred Gell (1998, 17) in "wresting" the study of beauty away from philosophy. After watching and listening to women and others in the parlors of Bangalore for a decade and a half, I wanted to get beyond simplistic renditions of beauty as evidence of poisonous patriarchal socialization and see it as my friends and interlocutors did, as something complex, political, powerful, and possibly divine.

At the beginning of this book, I asked what beauty is. It seems a critical question in a postfeminist world. Watching Selvi, I realized that my question did not have a singular answer. Beauty is not a singular thing or a singular moment but a multiplicity, a series of alchemical transformations that are subject to normative rules and ideas of aesthetics that changed over time. In doing this work, I realized that first, beauty is a moment of pleasurable conjunction where alignment between the human exterior and divine interior is achieved. In that moment, the interior self was sutured up to the exterior, the face and body, which had been cultivated to conform to achieve social recognition. And this external self was constantly negotiating status via normative aesthetic standards. In that moment of magical alignment between interior and exterior, which is temporary and fraught, beauty is transformative for the subject and transcendent for the viewer. It is a rare experience but a consuming goal for most women.

Provoking beauty is like entering into spiritual possession; it is a bodily praxis and an aesthetic discipline, an edge work that is unthought, tentative yet powerful, work that ruptures boundaries and strategically explores limits that often contradicted or adumbrated the dominant Brahmanic, masculine, heroic, nationalist narrative, instead offering a "countersystem," an "alternative way of looking at things" (Ramanujan 1991, 53; 1999). This countersystem, that is an anti-charter, a living revocation, runs in opposition to quotidian virulent sexism normalized in the contemporary moment that is invariably diagnostic of a rising tide of fascism. So such edge work points, even in its tentativeness, as Joshua Myers (2023) insists in his powerful study of Black radicalism, to "what we *can* be" (my emphasis).

Pursuit of such a conjunction is one key aspect of what makes life meaningful for Bangalorean women, and it forms the horizon of their human becoming. It is possibly why there are so many parlors, so many products, and so many beauty workers. It is why, early on at the Lotus, when I asked the beauticians what they do, they said it was *jadu*, magic. But as I found, this magic of beauty and its pursuit was not restricted to biological women or the physical parlor but rather encompassed a range of gender-fluid people and a number of spaces in which beauty was interrogated and acquired including spas, medspas, barbershops, homes, and makeup trailers. Indeed, I argued that regardless of the diversity of women in the parlor, all from different classes and castes, religions and regions, languages and ethnicities, and gender and sexual orientations, all concerned about beauty, suggested that beauty work mirrored the multiple forms of the feminine divine herself. I learned that women's subjectivities are "multiauthored entities" (Finlay 2018) that are crafted in the parlor as women work on their bodies in intimate encounters with other women. My interlocutors, as I said, are partible persons who have a composite self, made up of fragments that they stitch together. They are always raveling and unraveling, fabricating their selfhood as they go. So, instead of asking whether we are known as women, it may be more fruitful to ask whether we've arrived, in collaboration with other people with whom we have relationships, intimate and not, at a conception of ourselves that we recognize.

Watching Amman inhabit Selvi, I was transported in my mind's eye to when I had first entered the Lotus and watched Radhika and her friends preening in front of the mirrors. Radhika had joked that they were "teen deviyan," three goddesses. *What I didn't realize at the time was that there was one goddess in the mirror—it was Selvi.*

Radhika and her friends looked in the mirror and knew when they had achieved the felicitous conjunction that marked transcendence. So did Selvi. Mirrors became a powerful motif for the work, evidence of the critical realism of beauty projects. The mirror represented the self that stood in front of it and the aspiration to see the goddess shine through. But the mirror also captured the self that one reflected to the world and the recognition that one sought. So mirrors afforded a form of recognition of a better self, a more beautiful one, an idealized, possibly divine, personhood.

I also learned through my journey that beauty is epistemological. It is a form of knowledge that women gain through practice in collaboration with other women. Its realized form is the goddess in the mirror. Watching Selvi in that evening gloom dance with writhing joy, overtaken by a divine self, I realized that beauty was about learning, about how to fluidly and seamlessly embody a different self, and it was achieved in community with the human, and the beyond human. Suguna, Selvi's sister, had spent years of apprenticeship learning the necessary techniques to invite the goddess, from face-painting to chicken-cooking, techniques she learned from the women in her family. She

FIG. C.1. Woman in a sari walking by a posh salon where the advertisements show sexy Western women

could not herself become divine, but her skill and knowledge were integral to Selvi's transcendence. The intimacy of the beauty parlor and its spaces acted as an archive and a laboratory for this same kind of embodied and expert knowledge. Madhu, Menaka, Radhika, Radha, Ami, Jhuma, Lakshya, Layla, Preethi, and others all learned, practiced, and mimicked various practices and processes together to try and provoke beauty, sometimes in themselves, sometimes in others. This understanding opened me up to broadening my thinking on what constitutes an archive and how it can be used, as well as the question of exemplarity and how we think of it.

Finally, I understood that the idea of beauty is tied strongly to uncertainty and precarity and the need for hope. Indeed, this entire trilogy circles around the idea of hope in uncertain times. Moments of perfect conjunction are rare. Women and gender-fluid persons struggle to hold on to beauty that slips away with time. Yet engagements with beauty practices, whether successful or not, train one in an appreciation of beauty. Experiences of beauty, whether brief or long lasting, when repeated over time, link the participant back to a moral imagination alive in Sanskrit poetics and drama, which emphasize the importance of beauty for moral development and thus train practitioners in the shrungara and alankara that evoke it. Here, the message of beauty is deeply tied to the medium of its expression, the nonmasculine body. Hence, to transform it into a set of propositions is to risk the fundamental crime of exegesis: reducing the richness of a particular experience that flows through the aesthetic universe and all its resonances into a series of banal generalities.

Most of the time, beauty is aspirational, ungraspable, evanescent, and a moment of failure for women. I often saw them look at the mirror with concern, their eyes worried, foreheads crinkled, when they felt they had failed to achieve what was in their mind's eye. Beauty was usually situated elsewhere, in a body other than one's own, in an ideal, both mythic and real and sometimes something in between. The mirrors in the salons reflected these repeated moments of failure, much to the women's chagrin. Thus, mirrors acted as frames of recognition, allowing women to recognize, and sometimes to misrecognize themselves in different ways, as human when they failed and as divine on the rare occasions they succeeded.

When the conjunction succeeded, beauty work allowed the goddess to appear and walk in the quotidian world. As I watched Suguna paint Selvi's face and recalled Selvi's own careful attention to clients' faces in the parlor, I recognized that beauty work is not only a space of dangerous intimacy between women but also between women and the goddess, which must be negotiated carefully at each encounter. Bangalorean women's lives are a constant oscillation between the hoped-for transcendence and the human desire for status, for love, and for life in general. I concluded that *beauty is a question of imagination and discipline enfolded together. The practices of beauty are about how we can align our embodied selves with our imagined selves.*

The second question with which I began this work was, What does beauty do? In pragmatic terms, beauty makes a woman valuable and sought after, affording them status in the social world. This is not only because it transforms them into a valuable object, something to be appreciated and cared for, as many scholars have argued. But it is also because beauty for Bangalorean women seems to represent female goodness, purity, and auspiciousness. Beauty, when it is achieved, aesthetically manifests on the outside that which is hoped for within the subject, the powerful, the divine, and therefore, also the ethical.

As to the ethical, in the parlor I found yet another illustration of what I termed in the first book of this Bangalorean trilogy a "creative ethics," where the ethical (as the morally valuable) and the strategic (which includes the morally questionable) are braided together (Srinivas 2018). Creative ethics, as I said before, is an "*anthropological* imagining of doing rather than philosophical thinking," which offers a way for locals "to get beyond the tedium of habit, the 'uncanny of everyday life' (Das 2015), where a broader understanding of 'new regimes of living' inheres in the category of experience (Collier and Lakoff 2004)" (Srinivas 2018, 30–31; emphasis added). I clarify that I did not necessarily like the creative ethics of the parlor, where I found the dropping into what I saw as the unethical and the retreat into the masculinist to be far too frequent. But it clearly afforded women, both clients and beauticians, the power of telling and of the choice to create their worlds. Creative ethics allows for the building of a future amid the precarity of the present. In the parlor, creative ethics becomes an aesthetic ethics through the expectations of and aspirations to beauty.

An appreciation of these aesthetics, both as practiced and emergent, creates an attunement to the various sentiments that form the rasas, and this training in rasa aesthetics cultivates the individual moral attributes of a person, their *guna*. Gunas, in turn, form the moral framework of the person, the basis for their ethical behavior. Thus, beauty is indelibly linked with ethics through the outward appreciation of rasa and the internal cultivation of the moral guna. For this reason, beauty in the parlors is practiced as a strategic negotiation and moral cultivation. However, these two goals often seemed to be in conflict, as strategic interventions and negotiations implied practical self-interest whereas moral cultivation tended to be thought of as disinterested. This sometimes led me to be ambivalent about beauty in the parlors, for even though I appreciated the women's self-empowerment and their cultivation of a powerful selfhood, I often recoiled at their blatant egotism, their strategic maneuvering, and their hunger for status.

Nonetheless, beauty is an embodied aesthetic category with profound moral weight, allowing Bangalorean women "to become divine... to become perfectly, to refuse to allow parts of [themselves] to shrivel and die that have the potential for growth and fulfillment" (Irigaray quoted in Jantzen 1999, 6). So we return at the end to the beginning to ask—What is an anthropology of beauty, and with what does it provide us?

What these practices of beauty enable, in alliance with narrative practices based in myth and indigenous concepts of ethical formation, is the emergence of ethical theory—an aesthetic ethics—that is deeply rooted in Indic culture and in the modern secular space of the parlor. It unearths and reinvigorates the plural aesthetic ethics found in epic *kavya* poetry that gives expression to beauty and the wonder of the human imagination. However, this aesthetic ethics is not without discomfort. Not only does it often recapitulate normative standards that are harmful and limiting to women; it also allows for the braiding of the strategic and self-interested into the ethical.

Moreover, as important as beauty is the question of its anthropology. This is the first full-length treatment of beauty in India, where practice and process play a key role. It is a work that takes everyday practices seriously in thinking about ethics and religion more broadly. What women do in the parlor, the beauty work and the telling of stories, makes use of the ethnographic sensorium, that "multifaceted and affective point of contact with worlds of inequality, hovering on the verge of exhaustion," while also harboring the potential for things to be otherwise (Biehl and Locke 2017, 3). It is this otherwise that is the space of subjunctive dreaming, both for anthropologists and their interlocutors alike. For these consummately expressive women, beauty offers an aesthetical corrective to the inherited, often oppressive, structures of their lives.

Selvi is a "myth dreamer," a person who can dream while awake when in the form of the goddess, thus bringing the subjunctive to life through her predictions (Obeyesekere 1984). Her myth dreaming invests daily life with meaning. Despite my initial perplexity, it is natural that women would tell mythical stories in the parlor. I was dogged by the question as to why gender and sexuality still sought validation in a historical archive, however mythical. We have investigated the spatial and racial logics of such a return, particularly for the vulnerable.

It allows women to rehistoricize the past and renegotiate the present toward a yet unwritten future. In a world dogged by precarity, offering futurity is an act of faith. Many secularists like me tend to see myth telling and its capacity to rehistoricize solely through the lens of politics, where myth invocation is one of the strategies that the Hindu right has used to rehistoricize the past to claim India as solely a Hindu land and to deny its historical plurality. Rather, as I found, myth telling in the parlor allows for a plurality of ways of being.

First, myth gives Bangalorean women an image of an idealized womanhood to aspire to. They tell these stories not as a codex for normativity but to reflect on themselves, to imagine the women they want to be. Second and perhaps equally important, myth affords Bangaloreans an ecology of imagination that offers the subjunctive as real. Telling myths affords women an anti-charter, *a revocation*, a speaking back to power and a renegotiation of the terms of life toward suturing up new selfhoods. Moreover, unlike the American myth of unity from plurality, Indian Hindu conceptions of the myth lead to the dissolution of unity into a fractious but necessary diversity, where the end point is pointlessness.

These myths do not describe relentless progress toward a perfect society but the fading from view of such a world, freeing women to choose either to find new, innovative, and interpretive readings or to return to the seeming comfort of tradition in which masculinist readings and tellings dominate, but with a difference. In their tellings, the women bring the goddess to life and, in turn, contribute to a genealogy of resistance that insists on the embodied as a constitutive politic of sovereignty over self. But these tellings of myth raise the question of the archive of myth itself: What kind of archive does such a recuperative hermeneutics produce? Rather than render gender's relationship to the mythic archive through the preferred lens of whether it is historical truth (which presumes that there is something inherently needing "correcting" or covering up in gender and sexual desire), I have engaged gender's traces within the mythic archive against and through women's tellings.

As A. K. Ramanujam has said, these womanly tellings run counter to established epistemological expectations. In these tellings, the world of myth is freed from the Christo-colonial encaging of the female imagination, as Bangaloreans emphasize the narrative's nuance and fluid ethical power. In the women's creative tellings, the myths do not offer an unchanging moral pattern by which the present can be judged and on which it can be modeled. Rather, they offer ways to subvert social judgments while still appearing to adhere to them, often in unexpected and often counterintuitive ways, as they emphasize the accident, neglect, and waywardness of the mythical. These tellings form a contemporary female mythopoesis that constructs new female Hindu aesthetic-ethical worlds, inhabiting the cracks in the stories to imagine a different future. For after all, as Stuart Hall tells us, "hegemonies are never completed projects: they are always in contention. There are always cracks and contradictions—and therefore opportunities" (Hall et al. 2013, 17).

Therefore, to me, women in Bangalore *are* intellectual theorists, building aesthetic-ethical worlds in these cracks in the stories, as they polish their nails and banish their wrinkles. These imagined futures built in the fractures of stories are political and social; they often subtly contradict and adumbrate the masculine, heroic, nationalist narrative and serve as interdictions to normative social and ethical expectations. And this work, like their tellings, is not from the center of power outward but from the bottom up and the periphery inward—what we have termed the *edge work of beauty*. This edge work of beauty allows the women to have hope, what I have elsewhere called a "radical hope," in the face of chronic uncertainty and dispossession.

There is no way out of these mythical tellings, for one story leads to another in an endless loop of stories that are nested within one another, one story leading to another. The frame story has stories embedded within it, so even if some argue for a meta-story of stories, even that becomes a story, as does the story in these pages. As A. L. Becker argued in *Beyond Translation: Essays Toward a Modern Philology*, multiple-framed stories create an excess of meaning where the stories resonate with each other, building an amplifying effect that "creates a very thick texture" (1995, 189).

These stories, with their thick texture, act in the world. They become assets and pathways for personal and collective resistance. Tracing Bangalorean women's telling of stories in the parlor alerted me to an alternative understanding of agency. Storytelling prevents the exhausted cynicism of a downward trajectory that doubles as nihilism. It allows women to weave alternate understandings of themselves and the world, and it gives them hope. For, as I learned at the parlor, if you do not tell your story or any story, you lose it—or what might be worse, you get lost outside of it as someone else tells it, often wrongly. Telling stories is how we cement details, preserve continuity, stake a claim, and stay sane within a confounding world. We tell ourselves into being every day.

What Indian women actually do in beauty parlors is this edge work of beauty, this bottom-up and periphery-inward practice, that should be central to building contemporary ethical theory, for it allows for nonheroic participation that paradoxically seeks the future through myth rather than the past. Edge work allows the goddess to emerge despite obstacles. It allows for hidden resistances, for the marginal to become central. It allows for a refusal, for speaking back, and for renegotiating the terms of life.

Rather than assuming that preestablished moral ideas guide action, we, as observers, should acknowledge and explore the ways that women's edge work generates contestations to established values in ways that can be, and have been, overlooked—contestations we may or may not agree with but that are nonetheless powerful. We must acknowledge that in the moment of looking in the mirror, women's experiences and imaginations fuse and a new way of being comes to life.

I was reduced to ashes at the moment of knowledge.
—Irawati Karve, "'All That Is You': An Essay," 1988

You don't have a soul. You are a soul. You have a body.
—Author unknown

Postlude

DREAM

Reflecting Love

It was 3:00 a.m., and the street was dark. The ghostly outlines of the trees emerged from the morning mist, typical of a January morning in the northeastern United States. The streets were empty as I padded downstairs in the cold darkness to check on my sleeping mother. I had awoken suddenly from a happy dream in which she was gardening in our home in Bangalore.

My mother was curled up in her bed, sleeping lightly. She had shrunk over the years and was frail. Yet her indomitable spirit was unbowed despite the depredations of age and illness. She heard me through her sleep, sensing my familiar presence. "Darling, go to bed. I'm okay. Please go and rest. You'll be tired tomorrow," she mumbled, barely awake and yet still acknowledging my concern.

My mother was born and grew up in the twilight of the Raj, as the sun that had shone on the British Empire was setting. She went to a series of British missionary schools and has a cut-glass accent and Victorian phraseology to prove it. She was teaching at Queen Mary's College in Madras when she met and married my father, already a renowned social anthropologist. They chose each other, an act of brave self-determination, breaking intracaste barriers and surprising her parents, since she had previously vowed to be single. She led an unusual life for an Indian woman of her generation, becoming faculty at Delhi University, helping my father build the institution, giving birth to two daughters later in life, whom she raised to be independent because she valued her own independence. She was a committed educator specializing in human and cultural geography, one of the earliest Indian scholars of the field.

She was the family chauffeur, always barefoot, her gorgeous silk saris tucked up behind the pedals. As a child, I remember her driving all over Bangalore and the hills of Berkeley, into the farmlands beyond. She was the first person to map the entire city of Bangalore in the first urban survey of its kind, driving bravely all on her own into the darkness of the exurbs.

My mother, Rukka, as she is known, is a joyous woman with a brilliant smile. She was always well dressed, tall, and elegant when she was by my father's side. She was also the caregiver in the family, caring for my father, us children, and our pets; she did so with a devotion and love that knew no bounds. She was an amazing cook and a stellar gardener, and our garden in Bangalore was the envy of all who knew us. But when I was growing up, I remember she was often exhausted, particularly when extended family came to stay for long periods, as they often did in India, and she took on ever more burdens over and above her work, the family, and her many interests. She never had many friends of her own, since "there was no time," her own desires ungrudgingly set aside to help us achieve our own.

And here she was, some sixty-some years later, dependent on me for most of her care. I knew how she hated dependency, and yet she bore it with a good humor that was astonishing. She made friends with the doctors and nurses in the hospitals that she had to frequent, asking after their families. She smoothed my way, meeting my academic friends and charming them with her stories of life in another time. She taught Indian cooking at the Cambridge Center for Adult Education, first with me and then by herself. She became a television celebrity for her cooking shows and wrote a cookbook in her late eighties and a memoir in her nineties. She listened to me and my sister recount academic gossip as she had listened to my father decades ago and gave me practical advice on how to live life, build my relationship with my spouse, and plant a garden.

After I woke her with my presence that night, she got up to go to the bathroom. I stood in the cool room watching her as she got her cane and carefully made her way from her room. Alert for unusual sounds, I waited at the bathroom door. I watched her look at herself in the mirror and smooth her hair before exiting. She had less of its curly abundance than she once did. She commented, "I need my hat. I feel cold because little hair on my head." "But you have such nice skin, Amma," I told her. She smiled. "A loving daughter's eyes," she commented wryly. "No, you do!" I insisted. And she did, and does. She looked at my reflection in the mirror and then at her hands and said, "So many wrinkles! I feel young, but when I look in the mirror . . ." She trailed off. Then she smiled and said, "That's why they say, 'young at heart'!"

After our midnight sortie to the bathroom, I went back upstairs and lay awake in bed contemplating my mother's life. I remember my mother as she was when I was young. Her bright beautiful smile and her unusual tall strength clad in her colorful silk saris. Her earlobes flashing with the diamond earrings, her parents' gift, that she always wore. Her wrists with the copper bracelet she had picked up in Haridwar on her arm as she gardened, graded papers, or cooked our dinner. And I think of Ursula Le Guin writing of *her* mother: "I see [my mother] rocking, weeding, writing, laughing—I see the turquoise bracelets on her delicate, freckled arm—I see, for a moment, all that at once, I glimpse what no mirror can reflect, the spirit flashing out across the years, beautiful. That must be what the great artists see and paint. That must be why the tired, aged faces in Rembrandt's portraits give us such delight: they show us beauty *not skin-deep but life-deep*" (Le Guin 1992, 165). My mother's beauty is indeed not skin deep but life deep.

But what to make of her misrecognition of herself in the mirror? What do we do when we can no longer align ourselves either with the societal expectations of beauty or with our own embodied forms?

As I look in the mirror, I notice that my hair is graying, and I too am aging. Radhika and Aseema comment on my hair, imploring me to color it. Menaka and Madhu also see the subtle shifts that aging brings to them. So what do we do when practices no longer afford us the outcomes that we rely on? How can we consider aging women's bodies in societies that afford older women no honor and no value?

Every day is composed of a series of mundane caregiving activities for my mother by my sister and myself: of helping my mother pick out her clothes and wrap her sari; of making sure her towels and sheets are laundered and her bed made; of allaying her many anxieties about her medicines running out; of making sure she gets exercise and fresh air; of watching her carefully when she walks and listening for her footfalls; of holding her now thin hands when going to the doctor's offices; of slowing my run to match her careful steps. It is repeatedly spelling her unfamiliar name to countless organizations, always waiting, endless time spent on the minutiae of living. This is our daily and weekly routine.

This routine of care stills time (Kleinman 2019). By nature, I am a rather quick and impatient person who keeps up a frenetic pace of life. Caring for my mother forces me to keep another time, a slower, more deliberate pace. I find pleasure in smaller things, the garden, the sunlight, the sound of birds, the slow pace of writing this monograph. The COVID-19 pandemic stilled time yet further. The cocoon of isolation, the removal of the pressure to be socially and physically present, wrapped itself around us, and caregiving became my entire life. As this came to an end, I tried to explain, largely unsuccessfully, to academic administrators that I needed more time with her, to recognize and rejoice in her life, beautiful and fraught as it is.

Some days are hard, particularly in a society where the elderly are not valued. When people misrecognize her as incompetent, deaf, or, worse yet, cognitively impaired, I cannot escape a sense of unease at the misfit between the assumptions built into the theories and concepts of the body and the life lived in quotidian forces and contingencies. How can one make sense of life, particularly obscured lives? What is the point of theory unless it illuminates them?

Every evening, I light an oil lamp and pray to the gods for my mother's health. Even though it is a Hindu womanly tradition to light a lamp at dusk to invite the goddess Lakshmi into the home, I never did this until recently. But now, I light the lamp every evening and pray with my mother for divine benevolence. Every evening, we partake of the light of the lamp, illuminating our clouded way together, and every evening, my mother touches the lamp and touches my forehead in blessing. And when we tuck her in at night after she has dinner and watched the news, she kisses us and says, "Thank you, darling, for looking after me. I am fortunate to have you all! I'll see you in the morning!"

As the great Indian anthropologist Irawati Karve notes, this is the moment when I am "reduced to ashes," by the stunning knowledge that while the day is filled with my care for my mother's body, the evening is replete with her care of my soul.

Notes

INTRODUCTION

1. The ringtone sang, *Suraj hua maddham, Chand jalna laga, Aasman yeh hai, kyon pighalne gaya?* (Hindi: The sun is setting, the moon is on fire, why does the sky melt into rain?).

2. Gandhari is a prominent character of the epic the *Mahabharata*. She is the princess of Gandhara and the wife of the blind King Dritharashtra, king of the Kurus, the mother of a hundred sons known as the Kauravas. According to the epic, after her marriage, she blindfolds herself to live like her husband and is a devoted wife and pious queen (see Adi Parva Sambhava Parva: *Mahabharata* Book 1, Section LXVII, 139). But the anthropologist Iravati Karve argued that her enforced blindness was a sign of her anger at being hustled into a marriage she did not want to a blind king (Sundar 2007).

3. *Apsaras* are mythical Hindu celestial shape-shifting female spirits. They are beautiful and seductive, eternally youthful, and skilled in courtly music and dance. They live in the court of the king of the gods, Indra, and periodically seduce gods, sages, and men, disrupting narratives and changing outcomes. Depicted as ethereal, romantic, seductive, and mischievous, the most famous among them are Urvashi, Rambha, and Menaka.

4. Teen Deviyaan (Three Goddesses) was the name of a Bollywood hit movie from the 1960s, inspired by D. H. Lawrence's works. It tells the story of a poet who falls in love with three women. But the phrase "teen deviyaan" in Hinduism usually refers to three forms of the goddess: Sri Lakshmi, Parvati, and Saraswati.

5. Now shortened in common parlance in the United States to "cis-het."

6. In the following pages, women as a broad category includes queer and gender-nonconforming people as well.

7. Rashmi Rajagopal, "Prasad Bidapa Talks About His Latest Venture, the Virtual Runway, and the Future of the Industry," *Indulge Express*, June 4, 2020, https://www

.indulgexpress.com/fashion/trends/2020/jun/05/prasad-bidapa-talks-about-his-latest-venture-the-virtual-runway-and-the-future-of-the-industry-25471.html.

8. Suresh Nandi and Sindhu Jain, "India Becomes New Priority for Many International Beauty and Cosmetic Giants," *India Today*, November 15, 1996, https://www.indiatoday.in/magazine/cover-story/story/19961115-india-becomes-new-priority-for-many-international-beauty-cosmetic-giants-834100-1996-11-14.

9. For statistics on the personal care industry and its long-term growth, see https://www.statista.com/outlook/cmo/beauty-personal-care/india.

10. "How Spa Industry Made It Large in India," *Opportunity India*, September 29, 2017, https://www.franchiseindia.com/wellness/How-Spa-Industry-made-it-Large-in-India.10018.

11. Today, the unofficial estimate of Bangalore's population is twelve million, though all counts agree that Bangalore's population will probably be over twenty-five million by 2030.

12. The beauty industry is also called the personal care industry in India.

13. Arunima Mishra, "Beauty and Grooming Industry is Booming in India," *BTMag*, September 14, 2014, https://www.businesstoday.in/magazine/features/vlcc-clsa-everstone-kpmg-ac-nielsen-report/story/209609.html.

14. I am deeply indebted to Brad Weiss and Michael Herzfeld for their help in thinking this question of charter and anti-charter through with me.

15. The *Arabian Nights* as an Orientalist fantasy overtook the spaces of storytelling that were not part of the Christo-colonial world.

16. Recently, storytelling has become a much vaunted craft and subsequently a much reviled trope of twenty-first-century popular culture.

1. ALLURING

1. Women who were considered too thin did not get away either. I was frequently called "stick poochi" (Tamil: stick insect) or "bamboo kaddi" (Kannada: bamboo stick). Passing comments included catcalls on the street as well as shaming remarks in more intimate or even domestic settings.

2. Bangaloreans termed it the "mass molestation."

3. The rise in gender violence in the city over the past decade is startling with increased anecdotal reports of catcalling, groping, touching, and more police reports of overt harassment and even rape.

4. Michael Safi, "Bangalore Police Detain Six Men over New Year's Eve 'Mass Molestation,'" *Guardian*, January 4, 2017, https://www.theguardian.com/world/2017/jan/04/bangalore-police-investigate-new-years-eve-sexual-assault-india.

5. The power of allurement most often drawn from mythical divine women like the apsara Menaka and Shakti goddesses, cast as sirens who lured heroic men to their doom through their beauty, is the central trope of many myths (Kinsley 1988).

6. A version of the goddess who used to be a rural, wilderness, and healing goddess in the village of Banashankari that had become part of the city.

7. The first fifty-one names of the *Lalita Sahasranama* describe the goddess's beautiful form, yet quickly thereafter the poetry turns to the description of her violent conquests

on the battlefield in the slaying of Bhandasura (n. 64–82). Later, the *Lalita Sahasranama* identifies Lalita as both Durga (n. 140) and Kali (n. 751), modeling closely the account of her victories in battle with the accounts of these two goddesses in the *Devi Mahatmya*.

8. Always identified as the Mahadevi, or simply Devi or Durga, the Great Goddess of the Hindu traditions' most memorable image derives from her mythical struggle with the shape-shifting buffalo demon Mahisa.

9. In the Rig Veda Devi Sukta, Durga is believed to say, "I created all worlds at my will, without any higher being, and permeate and dwell within them. The eternal and infinite consciousness is I, it is my greatness dwelling in everything." Devi Sukta, *Rigveda* 10.125.3–10.125.8.

10. The traditions that revere the goddess as the ultimate, nondual reality are known as Śhakta traditions or Tantra for her more esoteric and sexualized forms—as opposed to Vaiṣṇava traditions that revere Viṣṇu and Śaiva traditions that worship Śiva (both male deities). The Srividya Shakta tradition in its most nonheterodox version in South India is mainly practiced by conservative, upper-caste adherents.

11. Our attachment to heuristic expressions like "vernacular," "Brahmanic," "Sanskritic" are not unfounded, as these—as limiting as they may be—have helped us understand how the goddess tradition emerged during the early Puranic period and encapsulated a wide array of goddess/Goddess/Sakta and even Tantra traditions from a variety of ritual and narrative sources and was quickly domesticated and Brahmanized.

12. That he was upper caste and this was potentially a Brahmanic purity project was left unsaid.

13. Madhubala, along with Savitri and Meena Kumari, were early Bollywood film stars. Their style of makeup and sari wearing influenced millions of Indian women.

14. Jayshree's choice of vegetable was straightforward. In these days of iconic sexting, the eggplant emoji has taken on a completely different meaning, one to which I suspect Jayshree is largely oblivious.

15. Known for their fragrant sandal oil soaps.

16. In the 1970s and '80s, I remember my aunts slapping on Ponds cream and Cuticura medicated talc on their faces as part of their toilette and shaking drops of Tata's eau de cologne onto their lace handkerchiefs before setting out to go to work.

17. I thank Professor Gopal Karanth for his pointed reminiscences of hairstyles and beauty influences of the 1950s.

18. Liril girls included Karen Lunel, who shot to instant stardom; actor Pooja Batra; and Bollywood stars Preity Zinta and Deepika Padukone. Viveat Susan Pinto, "40 Years Ago . . . and Now: Liril Girl Showed How to Target a State of Mind," *Business Standard*, October 15, 2014, https://www.business-standard.com/article/management/40-years-ago-and-now-liril-girl-showed-how-to-target-a-state-of-mind-114101501095_1.html.

19. Called crepe jasmine or crepe magnolia, the nandibatlu flower is prized in South India as an Ayurvedic remedy for bodies that are hot. The cooling properties of the flower make them ideal tonics, eye creams, kohl, and hair oil.

20. Commercial "Kajal sticks" and eyeliners have replaced the khol petti or kohl box. The styles recycled with the cat's eye (made famous by silent film stars) have reappeared post Amy Winehouse as the style of choice.

21. One of these famous herbal cosmetic companies that emerged during the consumer and beauty explosion of the 1970s was the brand Shahnaz Husain, which took the Indian cosmetic market by storm. As the brand's page states, Shahnaz Husain's story is "the story of a woman, a first generation entrepreneur, a pioneer, visionary and innovator, who introduced a totally new concept of Ayurvedic Cure and Care worldwide, with universal appeal and application."

22. Mrs. Gowda was referring to Baba Ramdas, the leader of the Pantanjali brand of Ayurvedic remedies.

23. Princy Mascarenhas, "Sephora Launches in Bangalore at the Forum Mall, Koramangala," *Jeromy Diaries*, March 5, 2016, https://www.thejeromydiaries.com/sephora-launches-in-bangalore-at-the-forum-mall-koramangala/#:~:text=Sephora%20opened%20doors%20to%20our,occasion%20and%20inaugurated%20the%20store.

24. In due course, Bharata became the king and the ancestral head of the clan of the cousins who sparked the *Manabharata*. This antecedent story of Shakuntala is embedded in the epic as tracing the royal cousin's ancestry.

2. RADIANT

1. "Anti-Pollution: New Wave in Skin Care," *Times of India*, November 7, 2013, https://timesofindia.indiatimes.com/business/india-business/anti-pollution-new-wave-in-skincare/articleshow/25340117.cms.

2. I am uncomfortable with the usage of "higher" and "lower" castes to indicate their supposed order in the caste hierarchy, but here I use these terms to underline the nature of the caste hierarchy as social order where one's status is based on the community into which one is born.

3. Let me hasten to add that fair skin and skin lightening products are not only dominant in India. African American celebrities in the United States lighten their skin and hair regularly to look whiter. Nigerian pop musician Dencia launched a product called Whitenicious in 2014, which sold out immediately.

4. Neha Mishra and Ronald E. Hall, "Bleached Girls: India and Its Love for Light Skin," *The Conversation*, July 21, 2017, http://theconversation.com/bleached-girls-india-and-its-love-for-light-skin-80655.

5. See Anaka Kaundinya's article "How Fair & Lovely Bottled Up India's Insecurities," *Kajal*, https://www.kajalmag.com/fair-and-lovely-colorism-india/.

6. For a devastating critique of the Fair & Lovely advertisements and the skin lightening industry's effect on Indian women's psyche, see Kaundinya, "How Fair & Lovely Bottled Up India's Insecurities."

7. This easy conflation of race, color, and caste is a fundamental simplification of the pernicious invisible and complicated nature of caste. Although it is all too true that often color and caste overlap in many cases, in many notable cases Dalit castes are actually light skinned (such as those from Kerala) having been more sexually exploited during the colonial era. This complication has been ignored in modern understandings of caste, where it is interpellated comfortably with race, erasing some of the complexities of caste diagnosis and discrimination.

8. The hierarchical classifications in India that intersect with color are often confusing: Jati (type), Varna (literally color but more broadly caste), Kula (clan), Gotra (fictitious lineage descent), language, ethnicity, and religion. Based on some central Hindu texts such as the Vedas and the Suktas, the idea that castes were based on color of Brahman's body has been interpreted and misinterpreted. The mistaken assumption, even among Indians themselves, is that lower castes are darker skinned than upper castes and that Indian colorism and caste map directly onto racist themes and structures.

9. Lower-caste persons are seen as asuddha not only in the embodied sense but in the sense of hygiene. They are seen to clean other people's dirt and not to be able to be cleansed themselves, not having access to hygienic bathing and cleaning facilities, relieving themselves without access to time, water, fresh clothes, and such notions of purity would dictate.

10. These are attributes that one is born with, though of course one can temporarily fall into states of impurity due to biological and social events, such as death, birth, wrong commensality, and so on.

11. Popularized by the Korean beauty industry, the "ten-step method" has been classified as the Japanese method and involves applying various sheet masks followed by location-targeted moisturizing creams such as eye cream, lip balm, and so forth.

12. Jia Tolentino, "The Year That Skin Care Became a Coping Mechanism," *New Yorker*, December 18, 2017, https://www.newyorker.com/culture/cultural-comment/the-year-that-skin-care-became-a-coping-mechanism.

13. On July 7, 2017, eighteen-year-old Aranya Johar published *A Brown Girl's Guide to Beauty* on YouTube, which garnered instant attention.

14. A caste- and class-based epithet to indicate someone who is a street person or a thug. In this case, used to indicate being disheveled.

15. These practices of dusk are fading out as traffic, pollution, and safety concerns, combined with the culture of urban migration into Bangalore and apartment living, makes opening doors to the outside difficult and even dangerous.

16. After watching this procedure, I started observing how many women in Bangalore had removed their sideburns.

17. *Mahābhārata* Book 2, Section LVII, 27: rajasvalā vā bhava yājñaseni ekāmbarā vāpy atha vā vivastrā | dyūte jitā cāsi kṛtāsi dāsī dāsīṣu kāmaś ca yathopajoṣam |||

18. Literary sources depict Draupadi, the wife of the Pāṇḍava brothers in the *Mahabharata*, as leaving her hair loose after she was insulted in public by the Kauravas until their final defeat and death.

19. Spivak raises the question of whether the name Draupadi is a Sanskritization of a more earthy Dopdi—a fascinating speculation.

20. She paid approximately US$5,000 for the oleograph with vintage silk and sequin work.

21. A form of lithography that incorporates color schemes.

22. Rajini Vaidyanathan, "Has Skin Whitening in India Gone Too Far?," BBC *News*, June 6, 2012, https://www.bbc.com/news/magazine-18268914.

3. HOT

1. Ushna understood as "heat" is the inherent property of the liverish constitution, though it can be brought about when the body is out of balance through stress, bad diet, too much medication, or other life factors, symbolizing a pathological fire both inside and outside the body. In such cases, the course of treatment eventually focuses on reducing bile or reducing the heating, in particular. Cooling or sheetala remedies are sought out.

2. Aati kya Khandala? (Will you come with me to Khandala?) is a lyric from a popular song of the same title in the 1998 Bollywood blockbuster *Ghulam*.

3. Last names in India are still caste based and this is also true of Dalit last names—Mala, Madiga, Bhangi, Chamar—are all casted last names that easily slip into epithets. For savarna-casted bodies, the touch of a Dalit person was believed to be polluting and shaming, a humiliation that Dalits have endured and paid for with their very lives for decades, if not centuries.

4. Bile (pittam), wind (vāyu), and phlegm (kapa) represent hot, even-tempered, and cold states of body and psyche—ideas probably influenced by Greek humoral pathology, which is still present in India as the Unani strand of medicine.

5. The priests marked the yoni, the crevice in the rock face from where a stream emerged during the monsoon, with kumkum which they offered as consecrated material (prasadam) to devotees.

6. The Indian constitution makes special provisions for Adivasi and other castes and tribes listed as "scheduled," derived from their listing in the Sixth Schedule of the Indian Constitution, and argues for affirmative action policy that is enshrined in Article 46 of the constitution to overcome social and economic inequality.

7. Helen's biography as a refugee who fled as a child from violence in Rangoon, Burma (now Yangon, Myanmar) in 1943, though little known, resonates with the stories of the beauticians.

8. Her first hit dance number, "Mera naam hai Chin Chin Choo" (Hindi = My name is Chin Chin Choo), solidified her otherness.

9. She means desperate men.

4. WOUNDED

1. The goddess Devi is also known as Shakti. Shakti stands for the feminine divine force that all women carry within themselves.

2. The lingam is the sacred form of Shiva, the male sexual organ.

3. Consecrated food.

4. During the colonial era, British missionaries set up private schools all over the Northeast to cater to planters' and administrators' children and later to the children of army officers and others. As a result of the proliferation of mission schools, many people from the Northeast are fluent in English.

5. See Gardiner Harris, "As Tensions in India's East Turn Deadly, Some Say Officials Ignored Warning Signs," *New York Times*, July 28, 2012, https://www.nytimes.com/2012/07/29/world/asia/after-tensions-in-indias-east-turn-deadly-claims-officials-turned-a-blind-eye.html.

6. Amrit Dhillon, "Indian Troops Ordered to 'Shoot on Sight' amid Violence in Manipur," *Guardian*, May 5, 2023.

7. "9 Killed, Curfew Clamped in Kokrajhar," *Assam Tribune*, July 21, 2012.

8. "PM Announces Rs 300-Crore Package for Assam; Says Riots a Blot on the Nation," *Economic Times*, July 28, 2012.

9. The violence in Bangalore was linked to ethnic strife between Bengali Muslims and indigenous Bodo tribesmen in Assam. In 2012, 77 people had died and over 400,000 people were taking shelter in 270 relief camps, after being displaced from almost 400 villages in Assam.

10. Since 2006, the Indian state has declared regions in the Northeast unsafe as Naxalite territory. The Naxalite rebellion is India's most significant internal security challenge, and the state announced effective "containment" of the threat in 2014, removing the area from the danger of the "Red Corridor" that the Indian state identified as land under Maoist rebellion forces.

11. When the British partitioned Bengal in 1905, they attached the province of Assam to Muslim-majority East Bengal, with Dhaka as its capital. Suddenly, what was a migrant population in Assam was no longer migrant but part of a majority. Seven years later, when Bengal was reunified and Assam became a province of its own, its Bengali population became migrants once again. After the 1947 partition, when East Bengal became East Pakistan, the Bengal-origin Muslim settlers in Assam chose to stay on. But partition also led to a massive influx of Bengali refugees into Assam, Hindus as well as Muslims. This was followed in 1971 by yet another incursion of refugees fleeing from the Pakistan army's genocidal attack on East Pakistan and the liberation war that birthed the new nation of Bangladesh, which together took millions of lives.

12. See "CAA: India's New Citizenship Law Explained," BBC, March 12, 2024, https://www.bbc.com/news/world-asia-india-50670393.

13. "NRC Final List: How and Where to Check Your Name on Assam's National Register of Citizens," *India Today*, August 31, 2019.

14. Utter chaos broke out all over urban India protesting the CAA as discriminatory. The capital city of Delhi led the way with university students protesting and the police and army called out to "keep the peace." Students at Jamila Milia university, a predominantly Muslim university, were arrested and threatened. They raised the slogan "azadi" (Hindi = freedom from), which was last popular during the anti-colonial movements of the Indian independence movement in the 1940s. The contemporary version circulating on social media: "Hum ladke lengey. Azadi! Hum leke rahengey. Azadi! Are sunle Modi. Azadi! (Hindi = We will take the children. Freedom! We will stay. Freedom! Listen, Modi. Freedom!) #CAAProtest #IndiaAgainstCAA #Azadi.

15. Rupa Viswanath's study of colonial Madras presidency in the late nineteenth century detailed similar discrimination that evolved from a caste-state nexus, whereby the policy to spatially exclude and contain Dalit (pariah) residential settlements known as cheris that resulted in land conflicts were resolved by the colonial regime's upholding of local elites' practice of spatial untouchability (Vishwanath 2014).

16. The actual worship of the yoni or sacred vulva is referenced in the sacred text of the Yonitantra.

17. In Tantric literature such as the *Bhagavantam upapurana,* it is suggested that after Kamakhya's death, Shiva became obsessed with her corpse, clinging to it as the only material remainder of his great love. He was angry at her demise, and when Vishnu broke her body into fifty-one parts, Shiva pluralized himself to accompany each of her body fragments. Thus, every Shakti temple also has a temple to Shiva in the form of the lingam (divine phallus) and they are eternally linked in cosmological intercourse, so the fragmented corpse could be read as a sign of renewed life.

18. Nell Hawley's dissertation and her personal communication with the author emphasize the point of Parvati's penance as mirroring Shiva's own. "Does she want Shiva or does she want to become him?"

5. FORTUNATE

1. The pronunciation of this concept varied. Some people used the Sanskritic ending of bhagya(m), whereas others merely used it as bhagya.

2. In thinking of decoration and beauty, the considerations of generations of feminist scholars coalesce; the lived body, the social body, the body politic, the sexual body, the medical body, and the gendered body all blur into one another to produce the *fortunate body,* structured in the image of the divine body and interconnected through a complex network of transactions mediated by the human body in various modalities—including the ritual body from the Brahmanas, the ascetic body from the Upanishads, the devotional body from the Puranas and Bhakti traditions, and the Tantric body (Holdrege 1998, 347). The subtle materiality of the Hindu body leaks through its theological corpus, emerging in the parlor.

3. Although conjugality is still the norm, it is still considered unacceptable that women are more educated or hold better jobs than their husbands, particularly for those marrying within the jati. Women's educational emancipation depended very much on how the men of their jati were educated. This seems to hold true nearly a half century later even though marriages across jati and caste occur more frequently than before.

4. Suhaag raat is the nuptial night when marriage is supposedly consummated. It is the source of great cultural production from Bollywood romantic songs to bawdy jokes. Some bridal henna artists create suhaag raat henna tattoos, with the name of the bride and groom hidden in the bride's henna on feet or hands to encourage embodied exploration. In a culture where arranged marriage is the norm and the couple do not know each other, these kinds of games are supposed to break the ice.

5. Praachi Raniwala, "Unfamiliar Territory for Indian Bridal Industry," *New York Times,* July 16, 2020, https://www.nytimes.com/2020/07/16/fashion/weddings/unfamiliar-territory-for-indian-bridal-industry.html.

6. Johana Bhuiyan, "How South Asia's Bridal Industry Built a WhatsApp Empire," *Guardian,* April 10, 2022, https://www.theguardian.com/world/2022/apr/10/india-pakistan-bridal-weddings.

7. Shubika Sharma interviewed by the *Guardian* started the label Papa Don't Preach for modern Indian bridal wear on Instagram because she found customer interactions "very draining." Because the wedding is such a family moment for South Asians, often her consultancies with the bride would take three or four hours. She started the company in

2011 on a virtual platform but in 2018 expanded on WhatsApp so that she could instantly interact online with her clients and answer their queries. See Bhuiyan, "How South Asia's Bridal Industry Built a WhatsApp Empire."

8. In the Rig Veda Bhaga, "the Generous" is also a common epithet for gods, and in classical Sanskrit, as in contemporary Hindi, bhagavat (H. bhagavān) (possessing fortune, prosperous, holy, divine) is the common word for "god."

9. Bhaga, in some later Vedic treatises—the Brāhmaṇas—has the Allotted Share. Bhaga's blindness may thus be seen as a dramatic representation of fortune's ambiguity: the one who allots prosperity and wealth does so according to an unsighted rule of distribution.

10. Bhagya denotes the "part," the "lot," the fortune that is assigned to everyone at birth. This "lot" may contain good and bad things, but it is viewed as a source of wealth that the person will enjoy during his or her lifetime.

11. This negation of choice has a deep-rooted history. The colonial state criminalized forms of marriage that included elopement, enticement, and seduction, and the law prosecuted these "crimes" to police the sexual morality of Indian women where making available collective traditions from the past (even fictive ones) allow for making sense of the world.

12. "Solah Shringar—16 Indian Bridal Ornaments," *Utsavpedia*, https://www.utsavpedia.com/cultural-connections/solah-shringar-the-grand-makeover.

13. Shilpa Dhamija, "India: The Colossal Rise of the Wedding Industry of the Ultra-Rich," *Luxury Tribune*, January 24, 2023, https://www.luxurytribune.com/en/india-the-colossal-rise-of-the-wedding-industry-of-the-ultra-rich.

14. Dhamija, "India."

15. Wedding planners insisted on four separate ceremonies for Hindu ceremonies—one day for the auspicious bridal turmeric bath and "mehendi" followed that evening by the bride's and the groom's bachelor parties; the next day was a musical evening called a "sangeet" with dancing and drinking, fun and games; the main wedding event called the "muhurat," the auspicious circling of the fire seven times, occurred on the third day; followed by a final day, which was a big reception with dinner. But the four days were often preceded by a week of parties and followed by days of family get-togethers and pujas.

16. Sujata Assomull, "India's Experimental Brides Carry New Opportunity for Luxury," *Vogue India*, April 23, 2023, https://www.vogue.in/content/indias-experimental-brides-carry-new-opportunity-for-luxury.

17. The conjugal fidelity of a married woman toward her husband.

18. In Sri Lanka, she stands alone as a goddess, the "par excellence exemplar of purity, chastity and virginity," and the cult operates both as a system of devotion exalting wifely devotion, and as a medical system for the treatment of demonic possessions (Sinhala = bhutas) that women in particular seem prone to (Obeyesekere 1984, 14).

19. The Karva Chauth vrat is a relic of medieval autumnal military campaigns where women would pray for the safe return of the military menfolk who were away on the battlefield. The karva is an earthenware pot in which the wheat grown in the region would be stored.

20. The women ask each other, "Are you satiated?" to which they reply, "I am satiated by water, not by the love of my husband."

21. The *sindoor bhari maang*, the hair parting filled with vermilion, is the sign of a ritually pure married woman. Radhika associated it with her happiness in marital life and never failed to fill her hair parting with red vermilion.

22. When they see a female deity as sometimes higher than the male, or when they see male and female deities and being next to or sometimes within each other, they do not see an apotheosis of an egalitarian subversion of gender roles. On the contrary, this is the very antithesis of egalitarian individualism toward an underlying genderless unity of the godhead.

23. The Savitri story was the first story from the Indian epics to make an impact in Europe when it was translated.

24. Right when Yudhistira is praising Draupadi for being the ideal wife before she is stripped of her clothes, the Rishi Markandya offers the example of Savitri as the perfect pativrata, the ideal wife.

6. FLUID

1. Saria notes that hijras are one of India's third-gendered or trans populations. They have been an enduring presence in the South Asian imagination—in myth, ritual, and everyday life.

2. Beauty parlor workers and clients said "everyone knew" about gay parlors where yoni massage took place, but when I asked for addresses or contacts, they all became silent, even the nongovernmental organization workers who worked with queer communities. Part of the problem is, of course, the legality and safety of queer people, a problem that persists today despite the legalization of gay marriage and the visibility of gay rights activists in Bangalore.

3. Thirunangai is the self-chosen name for members of the hijra community of Tamil Nadu who have a ritual affiliation with the goddess Angalamman.

4. Blazing up in despair, the desires she told Rama
   Ravaged her heart like a cruel fire. It seemed as if
   the black poison that descended through the hollow, sharp fang
   of a strong snake, newly moulted, were rising through her.
   (*Ramayana Aranyakandam Patalam* 5 72:2900)

5. The origin of the Sanskrit word drāviḍa is Tamil, though in Sanskrit it has been historically used to denote geographic regions of southern India as a whole. It also has been used to refer to the Dravidian ethnic groups of South India and Sri Lanka who speak Dravidian languages. But more recently in Tamil Nadu, Dravida has been used to assert Tamil political identity in opposition to North Indian identity that claims to be Aryan, due to one somewhat questionable historical theory that bands of Transoxanian Aryans migrated to ancient India through the Himalayan mountain passes.

6. The Sanskrit *Ramayana*, also known as Valmiki's *Ramayana*, is believed to be as old as seventh century BCE. It is an epic poem by the poet Valmiki, composed of twenty-four thousand verses in seven kandas or books, that details the adventures of the hero king Rama, his brother Lakshmana, and his wife Sita. Most of the epic poem is about Rama's

exile from his kingdom of Ayodhya, his wandering in the forest, the abduction of Sita by a demon king Ravana to the island of Lanka, and the subsequent war between Rama and Ravana.

7. The Tamil *Ramayana* known as *Iramavataram*, is a twelfth-century Tamil epic poem by the poet Kamban that retells the story of King Rama of Ayodha. Kamban's *Ramayana* is considered one of the greatest works of Tamil literature and enfolds earlier Tamil literary and poetic influences including Sangam poetry, Tamil epics, folk motifs, and the Tamil Alvar saints' devotion to Rama.

8. Safwan Amir (2021), in his dissertation titled "The Muslim Barbers of Malabar: Histories of Contempt and Ethics of Possibility," argues that Muslim barbers in South Asia were frequently the storytellers of the Islamic community.

9. In an article in *Religions*, Safwan Amir (2019) argues that barbers and their intimate connections with hair are subject to ridicule against or around the profession.

10. Vinay Agrawal, "You Can 'Come as You Are' in This Trans Run Beauty Salon," *Gaylaxy*, June 29, 2022, https://www.gaylaxymag.com/exclusive/you-can-come-as-you-are-in-this-trans-run-beauty-salon.

11. Shahmaz Siganporia, "How Drag Became a Medium for Zeehsna Ali to Express Himself," *Vogue*, September 18, 2019, https://www.vogue.in/culture-and-living/content/zeeshan-ali-indian-drag-queen-zeesh-interview-vogue-india.

12. I have used Zeesh's shifting personal pronouns as they wished. Initially they referred to themselves by male pronouns (he, him, and his), then by female (she, her, hers), particularly when performing as a goddess. More recently though, they have taken to the they/them pronoun series, more in keeping with global, cutting-edge gender naming and framing practices.

13. Scott Long, "Bengaluru: No Place for Transgenders?," *Citizen Matters*, December 3, 2014, https://bengaluru.citizenmatters.in/lgbt-transgenders-community-beggary-exploitation-bangalore-6975.

14. One can of course argue that Arjuna is *cursed* to be a woman for a year and so the myth is not an illustration of gender justice.

15. Mohini comes from the verb root *moha*, meaning "to delude, enchant, perplex," or, in short, an illusion.

16. Ardhanarishvara, literally the god who is half-female, is a form of Shiva combined with his consort Parvati representing the androgynous nature of the godhead.

CONCLUSION

1. Kolam are auspicious rice powder floor patterns that decorate the ground in front of the home. The patterns are skillfully drawn by the women of the home, typically every day.

References

Abu-Lughod, Lila. 1991. "Writing Against Culture." In *Recapturing Anthropology: Working in the Present*, edited by Richard G. Fox, 137–62. Sante Fe: School for Advanced Research Press.

Adams, Kathleen M., and Sara Dickey. 2000. *Home and Hegemony: Domestic Service and Identity Politics in South and Southeast Asia*. Ann Arbor: University of Michigan Press.

Agamben, Giorgio. 1998. *Homo Sacer: Sovereign Power and Bare Life*. Translated by Daniel Heller-Roazen. Redwood City, CA: Stanford University Press.

Allocco, Amy L. 2013. "From Survival to Respect: The Narrative Performances and Ritual Authority of a Female Hindu Healer." *Journal of Feminist Studies in Religion* 29 (1): 101–17. https://doi.org/10.2979/jfemistudreli.29.1.101.

Alter, Joseph S. 1992. *The Wrestler's Body: Identity and Ideology in North India*. Berkeley: University of California Press.

Ambrosio, J. 2008. "Writing the Self: Ethical Self-Formation and the Undefined Work of Freedom." *Educational Theory* 58 (3): 251–67.

Amir, Safwan. 2019. "Contempt and Labour: An Exploration Through Muslim Barbers of South Asia." *Religions* 10 (11): 616. https://doi.org/10.3390/rel10110616.

Amir, Safwan. 2021. "The Muslim Barbers of Malabar: Histories of Contempt and Ethics of Possibility." PhD diss., University of Madras.

Amrute, S. 2015. "Moving Rape: Trafficking in the Violence of Postliberalization." *Public Culture* 27 (2): 331–59.

Amrute, Sareeta. 2010. "Living and Praying in the Code: The Flexibility and Discipline of Indian Information Technology Workers (ITers) in a Global Economy." *Anthropological Quarterly* 83 (3): 519–50. https://doi.org/10.1353/anq.2010.0002.

Aneja, Anu. 2019. "Feminist Theory and the Aesthetic Re-Turn." In *Women's and Gender Studies in India*, edited by Anu Aneja, 93–109. New Delhi: Routledge.

Anzaldúa, Gloria E. (1987) 2012. *Borderlands/La Frontera: The New Mestiza*. San Francisco: Aunt Lute Books.

Apffel-Marglin, Frédérique. 1985. *Wives of the God-King: The Rituals of the Devadasis of Puri*. New Delhi: Oxford University Press.

Appadurai, Arjun. 1986. *The Social Life of Things: Commodities in Cultural Perspective*. Cambridge: Cambridge University Press.

Appadurai, Arjun. 1998. "Dead Certainty: Ethnic Violence in the Era of Globalization." *Public Culture* 10 (2): 225–47. https://doi.org/10.1215/08992363-10-2-225.

Appadurai, Arjun. 2004. "The Capacity to Aspire: Culture and the Terms of Recognition." In *Culture and Public Action*, edited by Vijayendra Rao and Michael Walton, 59–84. Stanford, CA: Stanford University Press.

Appadurai, Arjun. 2022. "Haptic and the Phatic in an Era of Globalization." *Glocalism: Journal of Culture, Politics and Innovation* 1. https://doi.org/10.12893/gjcpi.2022.1.2.

Arain, Hafsa. 2023. "Boy Cuts: Female Masculinity and Queer Aesthetics in Karachi, Pakistan." *Journal of Gender Studies* 33 (5): 585–95. https://doi.org/10.1080/09589236.2023.2227121.

Arendt, Hannah. 1998. *The Human Condition*. Chicago: University of Chicago Press.

Arnold, David. 2004. "Race, Place and Bodily Difference in Early Nineteenth-Century India." *Historical Research* 77 (196): 254–73. https://doi: 10.1111/j.0950-3471.2004.00209.x

Aruldoss, Vinnarasan, and Sevasti-Melissa Nolas. 2019. "Tracing Indian Girls' Embodied Orientations Towards Public Life." *Gender, Place and Culture: A Journal of Feminist Geography* 26 (11): 1588–608. https://doi.org/10.1080/0966369X.2019.1586649.

Arumugam, Indira. 2023. "The Sacred Unbound: Insufficient Rituals, Excess Life, and Divine Agency in Rural Tamil Nadu." *HAU: Journal of Ethnographic Theory* 13 (1): 53–67.

Arya, Sunaina, and Aakash Singh Rathore. 2020. *Dalit Feminist Theory: A Reader*. Abingdon: Routledge.

Asad, Talal. 1993. *Genealogies of Religion: Discipline and Reasons of Power in Christianity and Islam*. Baltimore: Johns Hopkins University Press.

Asad, Talal. 2003. *Formations of the Secular: Christianity, Islam, Modernity*. Stanford: Stanford University Press.

Aulino, Felicity. 2014. "Perceiving the Social Body." *Journal of Religious Ethics* 42 (3): 415–41.

Baas, Michiel. 2020. *Muscular India: Masculinity, Mobility and the New Middle Class*. Chennai: Context of Westland Press.

Babb, Lawrence A., Susan Snow Wadley, Joint Committee on South Asia, and American Council of Learned Societies. 1995. *Media and the Transformation of Religion in South Asia*. Philadelphia: University of Pennsylvania Press.

Bacchetta, Paola. 1993. "All Our Goddesses Are Armed: Religion, Resistance, and Revenge in the Life of a Militant Hindu Nationalist Woman." *Bulletin of Concerned Asian Scholars* 25 (4): 38–52. https://doi.org/10.1080/14672715.1993.10416137.

Bacchetta, Paola. 1999. "Militant Hindu Nationalist Women Reimagine Themselves: Notes on Mechanisms of Expansion/Adjustment." *Journal of Women's History* 10 (4): 125–47. https://doi.org/10.1353/jowh.2010.0528.

Bacchetta, Paola. 2002. "Rescaling Transnational 'Queerdom': Lesbian and 'Lesbian' Identitary Positionalities in Delhi in the 1980s." *Antipode* 34 (5): 947–73.
Bacchetta, Paola. 2011. "Gay and Xenophobia in Post-Colonial Hindu Nationalism." *Cahiers du genre* 50: 65–89.
Badcock, C. R. 1975. *Lévi-Strauss: Structuralism and Sociological Theory*. London: Hutchinson.
Baker, Dallas J. 2011. "Queering Practice-Led Research: Subjectivity, Creative Practice and Performative Research." Conference proceedings, *A Scholarly Affair*, 118. Cultural Studies Association of Australasia National Conference, Byron Bay, December 7–9, 2010.
Bandyopadhyay, Anjoli Monique. 1997. "The Religious Significance of Ornaments and Armaments in the Myths and Rituals of Kannaki and Draupadi." MA thesis, McGill University.
Banerjee-Dube, Ishita. 2008. *Caste in History*. London: Oxford University Press.
Banet-Weiser, Sarah. 1999. *The Most Beautiful Girl in the World: Beauty Pageants and National Identity*. Berkeley: University of California Press.
Barthes, Roland. 1977. "The Grain of the Voice." In *Image-Music-Text*, translated by Stephen Heath, 179–89. New York: Hill and Wang.
Barthes, Roland. 1993. *Mythologies*. London: Cape.
Bartky, Sandra Lee. 1988. "Foucault, Femininity, and the Modernization of Patriarchal Power." In *Feminism and Foucault: Reflections on Resistance*, edited by I. Diamond and L. Quinby, 61–86. Boston: Northeastern University Press.
Bartky, Sandra Lee. 1990. *Femininity and Domination: Studies in the Phenomenology of Oppression*. New York: Routledge.
Basu, S. 2015. *The Trouble with Marriage: Feminists Confront Law and Violence in India*. Berkeley: University of California Press.
Basu, Srimati. 1999. *She Comes to Take Her Rights: Indian Women, Property, and Propriety*. Albany: State University of New York Press.
Basu, Srimati. 2012. "Judges of Normality: Mediating Marriage in the Family Courts of Kolkata, India." *Signs: Journal of Women in Culture and Society* 37 (2): 469–92.
Basu, Srimati, and Lucinda Ramberg. 2015. *Conjugality Unbound: Sexual Economies, State Regulation and the Marital Form in India*. New Delhi: Women Unlimited.
Becker, Alton L. 1995. *Beyond Translation: Essays Toward a Modern Philology*. Ann Arbor: University of Michigan Press.
Belier, Wouter W. 1991. *Decayed Gods: Origin and Development of Georges Dumézil's "Idéologie Tripartie."* Leiden: Brill.
Benjamin, Walter. 1968. *Illuminations: Essays and Reflections*. Translated by Harry Zohn. New York: Schocker Books.
Benjamin, Walter. 1999. "Convolute N." In *The Arcades Project*, translated by Howard Eiland and Kevin McLaughlin, 456–88. Cambridge, MA: Harvard University Press.
Berlant, Lauren Gail. 2011. *Cruel Optimism*. Durham, NC: Duke University Press.
Besky, Sarah. 2013. *The Darjeeling Distinction: Labor and Justice on Fair-Trade Tea Plantations in India*. Berkeley: University of California Press.
Beteille, André. 1965. *Caste, Class, and Power: Changing Patterns of Stratification in a Tanjore Village*. Berkeley: University of California Press.

Biehl, João Guilherme, and Torben Eskerod. 2005. *Vita: Life in a Zone of Social Abandonment*. Berkeley: University of California Press.

Biehl, João Guilherme, Byron Good, and Arthur Kleinman. 2007. *Subjectivity: Ethnographic Investigations*. Berkeley: University of California Press.

Biehl, João, and Peter Locke. 2017. *Unfinished: The Anthropology of Becoming*. Durham, NC: Duke University Press.

Biernacki, Loriliai. 2007. *Renowned Goddess of Desire: Women, Sex, and Speech in Tantra*. Oxford: Oxford University Press.

Birkenholtz, Jessica. 2018. *Reciting the Goddess: Narratives of Place and the Making of Hinduism in Nepal*. New York: Oxford University Press.

Black, Paula. 2004. *The Beauty Industry: Gender, Culture, Pleasure*. London: Routledge.

Bloch, Maurice, and Jonathan P. Parry. 1982. *Death and the Regeneration of Life*. Cambridge: Cambridge University Press.

Boris, Eileen, and Rhacel Salazar Parreñas. 2010. Introduction to *Intimate Labors: Cultures, Technologies, and the Politics of Care*, edited by Eileen Boris and Rhacel Salazar Parreñas, 1–12. Stanford: Stanford University Press.

Bounce Salon. N.d. "Our Story." https://www.bouncehere.com/bounce. Accessed June 4, 2025.

Boyer, Dominic. 2005. "The Corporeality of Expertise." *Ethnos* 70 (2): 243–66.

Brandel, Andrew, Veena Das, and Michael Puett. 2023. "Language in Flight: Home and Elsewhere." *Sophia* 63:449–83. https://doi.org/10.1007/s11841-023-00946-3.

Breckenridge, Carol Appadurai. 1995. *Consuming Modernity: Public Culture in a South Asian World*. Minneapolis: University of Minnesota Press.

Brodbeck, Simon. 2013. "The Story of Sāvitrī in the Mahābhārata: A Lineal Interpretation." *Journal of the Royal Asiatic Society* 23 (4): 527–49. http://www.jstor.org/stable/43307676.

Brodbeck, Simon, and Brian Black, eds. 2007. *Gender and Narrative in the Mahābhārata*. London: Routledge.

Brooks, Douglas Renfrew. 1992. *Auspicious Wisdom: The Texts and Traditions of Śrīvidyā Śākta Tantrism in South India*. Albany: State University of New York Press.

Buren, Jane. 1994. "The Engendering of Female Subjectivity." *American Journal of Psychoanalysis* 54 (2): 109–25. https://doi.org/10.1007/BF02821852.

Burke, Timothy. 1996. *Lifebuoy Men, Lux Women: Commodification, Consumption, and Cleanliness in Modern Zimbabwe*. Durham, NC: Duke University Press.

Busby, Cecilia. 1997. "Permeable and Partible Persons: A Comparative Analysis of Gender and Body in South India and Melanesia." *Journal of the Royal Anthropological Institute* 3 (2): 261–78. https://doi.org/10.2307/3035019.

Buse, Christina, Daryl Martin, and Sarah Nettleton. 2018. "Conceptualising 'Materialities of Care': Making Visible Mundane Material Culture in Health and Social Care Contexts." *Sociology of Health and Illness* 40 (2): 243–55. https://doi.org/10.1111/1467-9566.12663.

Butler, Judith. 2000. "Appearances Aside." *California Law Review* 88 (1): 55–63. https://doi.org/10.2307/3481273.

Butler, Judith. 2001. "Giving an Account of Oneself." *Diacritics* 31 (4): 22–40.

Butler, Judith. 2004. *Undoing Gender*. New York: Routledge.

Butler, Judith. 2009. *Frames of War: When Is Life Grievable?* New York: Verso.

Butler, Judith. 2011. *Bodies That Matter: On the Discursive Limits of "Sex."* Abingdon: Routledge.
Butler, Judith, Eduardo Mendieta, and Jonathan VanAntwerpen. 2011. *The Power of Religion in the Public Sphere*. New York: Columbia University Press.
Bynum, Caroline Walker. 1995. *The Resurrection of the Body in Western Christianity, 200–1336*. New York: Columbia University Press.
Bynum, Caroline Walker. 2001. *Metamorphosis and Identity*. New York: Zone Books.
Bynum, Caroline Walker, Stevan Harrell, and Paula Richman. 1986. *Gender and Religion: On the Complexity of Symbols*. Boston: Beacon Press.
Cahill, Ann J. 2003. "Feminist Pleasure and Feminine Beautification." *Hypatia* 18 (4): 42–64. https://doi.org/10.1111/j.1527-2001.2003.tb01412.x.
Caldwell, Sarah. 1999. *Oh Terrifying Mother: Sexuality, Violence, and Worship of the Goddess Kāḷi*. New Delhi: Oxford University Press.
Carman, John Braisted, and Frédérique Apffel-Marglin. 1985. *Purity and Auspiciousness in Indian Society*. Leiden: Brill.
Carroll, Michael P. 1978. "The Savage Bind: Lévi-Strauss' Myth Analysis and Anglophone Social Science." *Pacific Sociological Review* 21 (4): 467–86. https://doi.org/10.2307/1388696.
Cavarero, Adriana. 1993. "Towards a Theory of Sexual Difference." In *The Lonely Mirror: Italian Perspectives on Feminist Theory*, edited by Sandra Kemp and Paola Bono, 189–221. New York: Routledge.
Cavarero, Adriana. 2000. *Relating Narratives: Storytelling and Selfhood*. Translated by Paul Kottman. New York: Routledge.
Cave, Terence. 1988. *Recognitions: A Study in Poetics*. Oxford: Oxford University Press.
Chakravatri, Uma. 1995. "Gender, Caste and Labour: Ideological and Material Structure of Widowhood." *Economic and Political Weekly*. 30: 36, 2248–2256.
Chakravarti, Uma, and Maithreyi Krishnaraj. 2018. "The Formation of Patriarchy and the Subordination of Women." In *Gendering Caste: Through a Feminist Lens*, 63–76. New Delhi: Sage. https://doi.org/10.4135/9789353287818.n5.
Chatterjee, Srirupa, and Shreya Rastogi. 2022. "Television Culture and the Beauty Bias Problem: An Analysis of India's Postmillennial Television Serials." *Media Asia* 49 (3): 213–34. https://doi.org/10.1080/01296612.2021.2010939.
Chatterji, R. 2015. "Conversations, Generations, Genres: Anthropological Knowing as a Form of Life." In *Wording the World: Veena Das and Scenes of Inheritance*, edited by R. Chatterji, 1–20. New York: Fordham University Press.
Chitnis, Suma. 1988. "Feminism: Indian Ethos and Indian Convictions." In *Women in Indian Society: A Reader*, edited by R. Ghadially, 81–95. New Delhi: Sage.
Clark-Decès, Isabelle, and Christophe Guilmoto. 2011. *A Companion to the Anthropology of India*. Malden: Wiley-Blackwell.
Clooney, Francis X. 2005. *Divine Mother, Blessed Mother: Hindu Goddesses and the Virgin Mary*. Oxford: Oxford University Press.
Coakley, Sarah. 2000. "The Eschatological Body: Gender, Transformation, and God." *Modern Theology* 16 (1): 61–73. https://doi.org/10.1111/1468-0025.00115.
Cohen, Colleen B., Richard Wilk, and Beverly Stoltje, eds. 1996. *Beauty Queens on the Global Stage: Gender, Contest, and Power*. New York: Routledge.
Cohen, Gerald Allan. 1978. *Karl Marx's Theory of History: A Defence*. Oxford: Clarendon.

Cohen, Lawrence. 1999. "Where It Hurts: Indian Material for an Ethics of Organ Transplantation." *Daedalus* 128 (4): 135–65.
Cohen, Lawrence. 2007a. "Operability, Bioavailability, and Exception." In *Global Assemblages: Technology, Politics, and Ethics as Anthropological Problems*, edited by Aihwa Ong and Stephen J. Collier, 79–90. Malden: Blackwell. https://doi.org/10.1002/9780470696569.ch5.
Cohen, Lawrence. 2007b. "Song for Pushkin." *Daedalus* 136 (2): 103–15.
Cohen, Lawrence. 2019. "The 'Social' De-Duplicated: On the Aadhaar Platform and the Engineering of Service." *South Asia: Journal of South Asian Studies* 42 (3): 482–500.
Collier, Andrew. 1994. *Critical Realism: An Introduction to Roy Bhaskar's Philosophy*. London: Verso.
Collier, Stephen, and Andrew Lakoff. 2005. "On Regimes of Living." In *Global Assemblages: Technology, Politics and Ethics as Anthropological Problems*, edited by Aihwa Ong and Stephen Collier, 22–40. Malden: Blackwell Publishing.
Comeau, Leah. 2020a. "Garlands for Gods in Southeast India." *Jugaad Project*, June 7, 2020. http://thejugaadproject.pub/home/garlands-for-gods-in-southeast-india.
Comeau, Leah. 2020b. *Material Devotion in a South Indian Poetic World*. London: Bloomsbury.
Conquergood, Dwight. 2006. "Rethinking Ethnography." *The Sage Handbook of Performance Studies*, edited by D. Soyini Madison and Judith Hamera, 351–65. Thousand Oaks, CA: Sage.
Copeman, Jacob. 2019. *Hematologies: The Political Life of Blood in India*. Ithaca, NY: Cornell University Press.
Costonis, John. 1989. *Icons and Aliens: Law, Aesthetics and Environmental Change*. Champaign: University of Illinois Press.
Courtright, Paul B. 1994. "The Iconographies of Sati." In Hawley, *Sati*, 27–43.
Craig, Maxine L. 2002. *Ain't I a Beauty Queen? Black Women, Beauty, and the Politics of Race*. Oxford: Oxford University Press.
Craig, Maxine L. 2006. "Race, Beauty, and the Tangled Knot of Guilty Pleasure." *Feminist Theory* 7 (2): 159–77.
Crawford, M., G. Kerwin, A. Gurung, D. Khati, P. Jha, and A. C. Regmi. 2008. "Globalizing Beauty: Attitudes Toward Beauty Pageants Among Nepali Women." *Feminism and Psychology* 18 (1): 61–86.
D'Alisera, JoAnn. 2004. *An Imagined Geography: Sierra Leonean Muslims in America*. Philadelphia: University of Pennsylvania Press.
Daniel, E. Valentine. 1984. *Fluid Signs: Being a Person the Tamil Way*. Berkeley: University of California Press.
Daniélou, Alain. 1991. *The Myths and Gods of India: The Classic Work on Hindu Polytheism from the Princeton Bollingen Series*. Rochester, VT: Inner Traditions International.
Das, Veena. 1995. *Critical Events: An Anthropological Perspective on Contemporary India*. Delhi: Oxford University Press.
Das, Veena. 2001. *Remaking a World: Violence, Social Suffering, and Recovery*. Berkeley: University of California Press.
Das, Veena. 2007. *Life and Words: Violence and the Descent into the Ordinary*. Berkeley: University of California Press.

Das, Veena. 2014. "Ethics, the Householder's Dilemma, and the Difficulty of Reality." *HAU: Journal of Ethnographic Theory* 4 (1): 487–95. https://doi.org/10.14318/hau4.1.031.

Das, Veena. 2015. "Beyond Trauma, Beyond Humanitarianism, Beyond Empathy." *Medicine Anthropology Theory* 2 (3). https://doi.org/10.17157/mat.2.3.291.

Dave, Naisargi N. 2010. "To Render Real the Imagined: An Ethnographic History of the Lesbian Community in India." *Signs* 35 (3): 595–615.

Dave, Naisargi N. 2012. *Queer Activism in India: A Story in the Anthropology of Ethics*. Durham, NC: Duke University Press.

Dave, Naisargi N. 2014. "Witness." *Cultural Anthropology* 29 (3): 433–56. https://doi.org/10.14506/ca29.3.01.

Deori, Banti. 2016. "A Case of Single Female Labour Migrants Working in the Low-End Service Jobs from North-Eastern Region to the Metropolitan City Chennai, India." *IOSR: Journal of Humanities and Social Science* 21 (12): 20–25.

Dewachi, Omar. 2015a. "Blurred Lines." *Medicine Anthropology Theory* 2 (2). https://doi.org/10.17157/mat.2.2.185.

Dewachi, Omar. 2015b. "When Wounds Travel." *Medical Anthropology Theory* 2 (3). https://doi.org/10.17157/mat.2.3.182.

Dhruvarajan, Vanaja. 1988. "Religious Ideology and Interpersonal Relationships Within the Family." *Journal of Comparative Family Studies* 19 (2): 273–85. https://doi.org/10.3138/jcfs.19.2.273.

Dickey, Sara. 2016. *Living Class in Urban India*. New Brunswick, NJ: Rutgers University Press.

Dirks, Nicholas. B. 2001. *Castes of Mind: Colonialism and the Making of Modern India*. Princeton, NJ: Princeton University Press.

Dissanayake, Wimal. 1996. *Narratives of Agency: Self-Making in China, India, and Japan*. Minneapolis: University of Minnesota Press.

Douglass, Lisa. 1992. *The Power of Sentiment: Love, Hierarchy, and the Jamaican Family Elite*. Boulder, CO: Westview.

Douglas, Mary. 1966. *Purity and Danger: An Analysis of the Conception of Purity and Taboo*. New York: Frederick A. Praeger.

Dumézil, Georges. 1988. *Mitra-Varuna: An Essay on Two Indo-European Representations of Sovereignty*. 2nd ed. New York: Zone Books.

Dumont, Louis. 1980. *Homo Hierarchicus: The Caste System and Its Implications*. Complete rev. English ed. Chicago: University of Chicago Press.

Dumont, Louis. 1983. *Affinity as a Value: Marriage Alliance in South India, with Comparative Essays on Australia*. Chicago: University of Chicago Press.

Dundes, Alan. 1984. *Sacred Narrative: Readings in the Theory of Myth*. Berkeley: University of California Press.

Dundes, Alan. 1997. "Binary Opposition in Myth: The Propp/Lévi-Strauss Debate in Retrospect." *Western Folklore* 56 (1): 39–50. https://doi.org/10.2307/1500385.

Eck, Diana L. 1981. "India's 'Tirthas': 'Crossings' in Sacred Geography." *History of Religions* 20 (4): 323–44. https://doi.org/10.1086/462878.

Eck, Diana L. 1998a. *Darśan: Seeing the Divine Image in India*. 3rd ed. New York: Columbia University Press.

Eck, Diana L. 1998b. "The Imagined Landscape: Patterns in the Construction of Hindu Sacred Geography." *Contributions to Indian Sociology* 32 (2): 165–88.

Eck, Diana L. 2012. *India: A Sacred Geography*. New York: Three Rivers Press.

Edmonds, Alexander. 2007. "The Poor Have the Right to Be Beautiful: Cosmetic Surgery in Neoliberal Brazil." *Journal of the Royal Anthropological Institute* 13 (2): 363–81.

Edmonds, Alexander. 2010. *Pretty Modern: Beauty, Sex, and Plastic Surgery in Brazil*. Durham, NC: Duke University Press.

Eisenlohr, Patrick. 2009. "Technologies of the Spirit: Devotional Islam, Sound Reproduction, and the Dialectics of Mediation and Immediacy in Mauritius." *Anthropological Theory* 9 (3): 273–96.

Eisenlohr, Patrick. 2022. "Atmospheric Resonance: Sonic Motion and the Question of Religious Mediation." *Journal of the Royal Anthropological Institute* 28 (2): 613–31. https://doi.org/10.1111/1467-9655.13662.

Elias, Ana Sofia, Rosalind Gill, and Christina Scharff, eds. 2016. *Aesthetic Labour: Rethinking Beauty Politics in Neoliberalism*. London: Palgrave Macmillan.

Elmore, Mark. 2011. "Bloody Boundaries: Animal Sacrifice and the Labor of Religion." In *Secularism and Religion-Making*, edited by Markus Dressler and Arvind-Pal S. Mandair, 209–25. Oxford: Oxford University Press.

Engelke, Matthew. 2007. *A Problem of Presence: Beyond Scripture in an African Church*. Berkeley: University of California Press.

Engelke, Matthew. 2010. "Religion and the Media Turn: A Review Essay." *American Ethnologist* 37 (2): 371–79.

Englund, H., and T. Leach. 2000. "Ethnography and the Meta-Narratives of Modernity." *Current Anthropology* 41 (2): 225–48. https://doi.org/10.1086/300126.

Erndl, Kathleen M. 1993. *Victory to the Mother: The Hindu Goddess of Northwest India in Myth, Ritual, and Symbol*. New York: Oxford University Press.

Erndl, Kathleen M. 2018. "A Trance Healing Session with Mātājī." In *Tantra in Practice*, edited by David Gordon White, 97–116. Princeton, NJ: Princeton University Press. https://doi.org/10.1515/9780691190457-011.

Etcoff, Nancy. 2000. *Survival of the Prettiest: The Science of Beauty*. New York: Anchor Doubleday.

Evans-Pritchard, E. E. 1940. *The Nuer: A Description of the Modes of Livelihood and Political Institutions of a Nilotic People*. Oxford: Oxford University Press.

Faust, M. A. 1988. "Foucault on Care of the Self: Connecting Writing with Life-Long Learning." *International Journal of Leadership in Education* 1 (2): 181–93.

Felski, Rita. 2006. "'Because It Is Beautiful': New Feminist Perspectives on Beauty." *Feminist Theory* 7 (2): 273–82.

Finkelstein, Maura. 2018. "Ghosts in the Gallery." *Anthropological Quarterly* 91 (3): 937–68. https://doi.org/10.1353/anq.2018.0045.

Finkelstein, Maura. 2019. *The Archive of Loss: Lively Ruination in Mill Land Mumbai*. Durham, NC: Duke University Press.

Finlay, Nyree. 2018. "Personhood and Social Relations." In *The Oxford Handbook of the Archaeology and Anthropology of Hunter-Gatherers*, edited by Vicki Cummings, Peter Jordan, and Marek Zvelebil, 1191–203. Oxford: Oxford University Press.

Flueckiger, Joyce. 2015. *Everyday Hinduism*. New York: Wiley Blackwell.

Flueckiger, Joyce Burkhalter. 2006. *In Amma's Healing Room: Gender and Vernacular Islam in South India*. Bloomington: Indiana University Press.

Flueckiger, Joyce Burkhalter. 2013. *When the World Becomes Female: Guises of a South Indian Goddess*. Bloomington: Indiana University Press.

Flueckiger, Joyce Burkhalter. 2017. "When the Goddess Speaks Her Mind: Possession, Presence, and Narrative Theology in the Gaṅgamma Tradition of Tirupati, South India." *International Journal of Hindu Studies* 21 (2): 165–85. https://doi.org/10.1007/s11407-017-9210-4.

Flueckiger, Joyce Burkhalter. 2020. *Material Acts in Everyday Hindu Worlds*. Rochester: State University of New York Press.

Foucault, Michel. 1977. "Nietzsche, Genealogy, History." In *Language, Counter-Memory, Practice: Selected Essays*, edited by D. F. Bouchard. Ithaca, NY: Cornell University Press.

Foucault, Michel. 1997. "Self Writing." In *Ethics: Subjectivity and Truth*, edited by Paul Rabinow, 207–22. New York: New Press.

Foucault, Michel, and Robert Hurley. 1988. *The History of Sexuality*. New York: Vintage Books.

Foucault, Michel, Donald F. Bouchard, and Sherry Simon. 1977. *Language, Counter-Memory, Practice: Selected Essays and Interviews*. Ithaca, NY: Cornell University Press.

Freeman, Carla. 2014. *Entrepreneurial Selves: Neoliberal Respectability and the Making of a Caribbean Middle Class*. Durham, NC: Duke University Press.

Furman, Frida Kerner. 1997. *Facing the Mirror: Older Women and Beauty Shop Culture*. New York: Routledge.

Galizia, Giovanni, and David Shulman. 2015. *Forgetting: An Interdisciplinary Conversation*. Jerusalem: Hebrew University Magnes Press.

Garlough, Christine. 2012. *Desi Divas: Political Activism in South Asian American Cultural Performances*. Jackson: University of Mississippi Press.

Garlough, Christine. 2013. "Savitri's Stories and Girl Power: Rhetorical Approaches to Feminism(s) in Indian American Ethnic Schools." *Storytelling, Self, Society* 9 (2): 143–68. https://doi.org/10.13110/storselfsoci.9.2.0143.

Geertz, Clifford. 1980. *Negara: The Theatre State in Nineteenth-Century Bali*. Princeton, NJ: Princeton University Press.

Gell, Alfred. 1998. *Art and Agency*. Oxford: Oxford University Press.

Ghadially, Rehana. 1988. *Women in Indian Society: A Reader*. New Delhi: Sage.

Ghosh, Ahmed. 2003. "Writing the Nation on the Beauty Queen's Body: Implications for a 'Hindu' Nation." *Meridians* 4 (1): 205–27.

Giroux, Henry A. 1993. "Living Dangerously: Identity Politics and the New Cultural Racism—Towards a Critical Pedagogy of Representation." *Counterpoints* 1:89–124. http://www.jstor.org/stable/45136433.

Glissant, Édouard. 1997. *The Poetics of Relation*. Translated by Betsy Wing. Ann Arbor: University of Michigan Press.

Glucklich, Ariel. 1994. *The Sense of Adharma*. New York: Oxford University Press.

Glucklich, Ariel. 2001. *Sacred Pain: Hurting the Body for the Sake of the Soul*. Oxford: Oxford University Press.

Godelier, Maurice. 2018. *Claude Lévi-Strauss: A Critical Study of His Thought*. London: Verso.

Gold, Ann Grodzins. 2008. "Deep Beauty: Rajasthani Goddess Shrines Above and Below the Surface." *International Journal of Hindu Studies* 12 (2): 153–79. https://doi.org/10.1007/s11407-008-9059-7.

Golovkova, Anna A. 2020. "The Forgotten Consort: The Goddess and Kāmadeva in the Early Worship of Tripurasundarī." *International Journal of Hindu Studies* 24 (1): 87–106. https://doi.org/10.1007/s11407-020-09272-6.

Goudriaan, Teun, and J. A. Schoterman. 1988. *The Kubjikāmatatantra: Kulālikāmnāya Version*. Critical ed. Leiden: Brill.

Gould, Carol C. 1997. *Gender*. Atlantic Highlands, NJ: Humanities Press.

Grabher, Gudrun. 2019. *Levinas and the Other in Narratives of Facial Disfigurement: Singing Through the Mask*. Abingdon: Routledge.

Gross, Rita M. 1978. "Hindu Female Deities as a Resource for the Contemporary Rediscovery of the Goddess." *Journal of the American Academy of Religion* 46 (3): 269–91.

Grosz, Elizabeth. 1994. *Volatile Bodies: Towards a Corporeal Feminism*. Indianapolis: Indiana University Press.

Guenzi, Catherine. 2012. "The Allotted Share: Managing Fortune in Astrological Counseling in Contemporary India." *Social Analysis* 56 (2): 39–55. https://doi.org/10.3167/sa.2012.560204.

Gunn, Janet. 2008. "Women's Experiences of Hindu Traditions: A State of the Field Review." *Religion Compass* 2 (1): 53–65. https://doi.org/10.1111/j.1749-8171.2007.00055.x.

Gupta, A. 2006. "Section 377 and the Dignity of Indian Homosexuals." *Economic and Political Weekly* 41 (46): 4815–23.

Gupta, Akhil. 2005. "Englishpur ki Kothi: Class Dynamics in the Queer Movement in India." In *Because I Have a Voice: Queer Politics in India*, edited by A. Narrain and G. Bhan, 123–42. New Delhi: Yoda Press.

Gupta, Akhil, and James Ferguson. 1997a. *Anthropological Locations: Boundaries and Grounds of a Field Science*. Berkeley: University of California Press.

Gupta, Akhil, and James Ferguson. 1997b. *Culture, Power, Place: Explorations in Critical Anthropology*. Durham, NC: Duke University Press.

Gupta, Pallavi. 2022. "Broomscapes: Racial Capitalism, Waste, and Caste in Indian Railway Stations." *Ethnic and Racial Studies* 45 (2): 235–56. https://doi.org/10.1080/01419870.2021.1964557.

Guru, Gopal, ed. 2009. *Humiliation: Claims and Contexts*. New Delhi: Oxford University Press.

Guru, Gopal, and Sundar Sarukkai. 2012. *The Cracked Mirror: An Indian Debate on Experience and Theory*. New Delhi: Oxford University Press.

Hall, Ronald E., and Neha Mishra. 2021. "Skin Colour in India vis-à-vis Bleaching Syndrome Pathology: Augmenting Social Work Curriculum Content." *Contemporary Voice of Dalit* 13 (2): 153–64. https://doi.org/10.1177/2455328X211032435.

Hall, Stuart. 1995. "New Ethnicities." In *The Post-Colonial Studies Reader*. New York: Routledge.

Hall, Stuart. 1991. "Old and New Identities, Old and New Ethnicities." In *Culture, Globalization and World Systems*, edited by Anthony D. King, 41–68. Minneapolis: University of Minnesota Press.

Hall, Stuart. 1996. *Stuart Hall: Critical Dialogues in Cultural Studies*, edited by David Morley and Kuan-Hsing Chen. New York: Routledge.

Hall, Stuart, Doreen Massey Hall, and Michael Rustin. 2013. "After Neoliberalism: Analysing the Present." In *After Neoliberalism? The Kilburn Manifesto*. London: Lawrence and Wishart.

Hallam, Elizabeth, Tim Ingold, and Association of Social Anthropologists of the Commonwealth Conference. 2007. *Creativity and Cultural Improvisation*. Oxford: Berg.

Halperin, E. 2019. "Is the Goddess Haḍimbā Tantric? Negotiating Power in a Western Himalayan Sacrificial Arena." *International Journal of Hindu Studies* 23 (2): 195–212.

Handelman, Don. 1998. *Models and Mirrors: Towards an Anthropology of Public Events*. Oxford: Berghahn Press.

Hann, Chris, and Jonathan Parry, eds. 2018. *Industrial Labor on the Margins of Capitalism: Precarity, Class and the Neoliberal Subject*. New York: Berghahn Books.

Haraway, Donna J. 1996. *Simians, Cyborgs and Women: The Reinvention of Nature*. London: Free Association Books.

Hart, George L., and Hank Heifetz. 1988. *The Forest Book of the Rāmāyana of Kampan*. Berkeley: University of California Press.

Hawkins, Simon. 2008. "Hijab: Feminine Allure and Charm to Men in Tunis." *Ethnology* 47 (1): 1–21.

Hawley, John Stratton. 1994. *Sati, the Blessing and the Curse: The Burning of Wives in India*. New York: Oxford University Press.

Hawley, John Stratton, and Donna Marie Wulff. 1996. *Devī: Goddesses of India*. Berkeley: University of California Press.

Hawley, Nell. 2022. "The War That Wasn't: The *Virāṭaparvan*, the *Pañcarātra*, and the Fantasy Life of the *Mahābhārata*." PhD diss., University of Chicago.

Heitzman, James. 1999. "Corporate Strategy and Planning in the Science City: Bangalore as 'Silicon Valley.'" *Economic and Political Weekly* 34 (5): PE2–PE11.

Herzfeld, Michael. 1988. *Anthropology Through the Looking-Glass: Critical Ethnography in the Margins of Europe*. Cambridge: Cambridge University Press.

Hess, Linda. 1999. "Rejecting Sita: Indian Responses to the Ideal Man's Cruel Treatment of His Ideal Wife." *Journal of the American Academy of Religion* 67 (1): 1–32. http://www.jstor.org/stable/1466031.

Hesse-Biber, Sharlene Nagy. 1996. *Am I Thin Enough Yet? The Cult of Thinness and the Commercialization of Identity*. New York: Oxford University Press.

Hiltebeitel, Alf. 1988. *The Cult of Draupadī*. Chicago: University of Chicago Press.

Hiltebeitel, Alf. 1989. *Criminal Gods and Demon Devotees: Essays on the Guardians of Popular Hinduism*. Albany: State University of New York Press.

Hiltebeitel, Alf. 1999. *Rethinking India's Oral and Classical Epics: Draupadī Among Rajputs, Muslims, and Dalits*. Chicago: University of Chicago Press.

Hiltebeitel, Alf. 2011. *Dharma: Its Early History in Law, Religion, and Narrative*. New York: Oxford University Press.

Hiltebeitel, Alf, and Kathleen M. Erndl. 2000. *Is the Goddess a Feminist? The Politics of South Asian Goddesses*. New York: New York University Press.

Hiltebeitel, Alf, and Barbara D. Miller. 1998. *Hair: Its Power and Meaning in Asian Cultures*. Albany: State University of New York Press.

Hirst, Jacqueline Suthren, and Lynn Thomas, eds. 2004. *Playing for Real: Hindu Role Models, Religion, and Gender*. New Delhi: Oxford University Press.

Holdredge, Barbara. 1998. "Body Connections: Hindu Discourses of the Body and the Study of Religion." *International Journal of Hindu Studies* 2 (3): 341–86.

Holstein, James, and Jaber F. Gubrium. 2000. *The Self We Live By: Narrative Identity in a Postmodern World*. Oxford: Oxford University Press.

Hua, Wen. 2013. *Buying Beauty: Cosmetic Surgery in China*. Hong Kong: Hong Kong University Press.

Hudson, Emily T. 2012. *Disorienting Dharma: Ethics and the Aesthetics of Suffering in the Mahabharata*. New York: Oxford University Press.

Hume, David. (1740) 1988. *A Treatise on Human Nature, Book 2 "Of the Passions."* Oxford: Oxford University Press.

Hussain, Salman. 2024. "Hijra, Trans, and the Grids of 'Passing.'" *Sexualities* 27 (8): 1549–67. https://doi.org/10.1177/13634607231157071.

Huyler, Stephen. 1993. "Creating Sacred Spaces: Women's Wall and Floor Decorations in Indian Homes, Mud, Mirror and Thread. " In *Folk Traditions of Rural India*, edited by Nora Fisher, 172–91. Ahmedabad: Mapin Publishing Private Limited and Sante Fe: Museum of New Mexico Press.

Inayatullah, Sohail. 2002. "Reductionism or Layered Complexity: The Futures of Futures Studies." *Futures* 34 (3–4): 295–302.

Inayatullah, Sohail. 2008. "Six Pillars: Futures Thinking for Transforming." *Foresight* 10 (1): 4–28.

Inayatullah, Sohail. 2019. "The Story Creates the Future. 'Futures Through Stories.'" *Critical Muslim* 29:55–69.

Ingold, Tim. 2006. "Rethinking the Animate, Re-Animating Thought." *Ethnos* 71 (1): 9–20. https://doi.org/10.1080/00141840600603111.

Ingold, Tim. 2007. *Lines: A Brief History*. London: Routledge.

Irigaray, Luce. 1993. "Divine Women." In *Sexes and Genealogies*, translated by Gillian C. Gill, 55–73. New York: Columbia University Press.

Iyengar, K. R. S., ed. 1983. *Asian Variations in Ramayana*. New Delhi: Sahitya Akademi.

Jaaware, A. 2018. *Practicing Caste: On Touching and Not Touching*. New York: Fordham University Press.

Jaffrelot, Christopher. 2005. *Dr. Ambedkar and Untouchability: Analyzing and Fighting Caste*. New York: Columbia University Press.

Jantzen, Grace. 1999. *Becoming Divine: Towards a Feminist Philosophy of Religion*. Indianapolis: Indiana University Press.

Jantzen, Grace M. 2004. *Foundations of Violence: Death and the Displacement of Beauty*. London: Routledge.

Jarrin, Alvaro. 2017. *The Biopolitics of Beauty: Cosmetic Citizenship and Affective Capital in Brazil*. Berkeley: University of California Press.

Jones, Geoffrey. 2010. *Beauty Imagined: A History of the Global Beauty Industry*. Oxford: Oxford University Press.

Joy, Annamma, John F. Sherry, Gabriele Troilo, and Jonathan Deschenes. 2010. "Re-Thinking the Relationship Between Self and Other: Levinas and Narratives of Beautifying the Body." *Journal of Consumer Culture* 10 (3): 333–61.

Kang, Milliann. 2010. *The Managed Hand: Race, Gender, and the Body in Beauty Service Work*. Berkeley: University of California Press.

Kannabiran, Vasanth, and Kalpana Kannabiran. 1991. "Caste and Gender: Understanding Dynamics of Power and Violence." *Economic and Political Weekly* 26 (37): 2130–33.

Kant, Immanuel. 1987. *Critique of Judgment*. Translated by Werner S. Pluhar. New York: Hackett Press.

Kantor, Hayden S. 2019. "A Body Set Between Hot and Cold: Everyday Sensory Labor and Attunement in an Indian Village." *Food, Culture, and Society* 22 (2): 237–52. https://doi.org/10.1080/15528014.2019.1573045.

Karve, Irawati Karmarkar. 1961. *Hindu Society: An Interpretation*. Poona: Deccan College.

Karve, Irawati Karmarkar. 1988. "'All That Is You': An Essay." In *The Experience of Hinduism: Essays on Religion in Maharashtra*, edited by Eleanor Zelliot and Maxine Berntsen, 213–22. Albany: State University of New York Press.

Karve, Irawati Karmarkar. 1991. *Yuganta: The End of an Epoch*. Hyderabad: Disha Books.

Kaziga, Ruth, Charles Muchunguzi, Dorcus Achen, and Susan Kools. 2021. "Beauty Is Skin Deep: The Self-Perception of Adolescents and Young Women in Construction of Body Image Within the Ankole Society." *International Journal of Environment and Public Health* 18 (15): 7840.

Keane, Webb. 2014. "Rotting Bodies." *Current Anthropology* 55 (S10): S312–21. https://doi.org/10.1086/678290.

Keane, Webb. 2016. *Ethical Life: Its Natural and Social Histories*. Princeton, NJ: Princeton University Press.

Kersenboom, Saskia. 1995. *Word, Sound, Image: The Life of a Tamil Text*. London: Routledge.

Khubchandani, Kareem. 2020. *Ishtyle: Accenting Gay Indian Nightlife*. Ann Arbor: University of Michigan Press.

Khubchandani, Kareem. 2023. *Decolonize Drag*. New York: OR Books.

Kinsley, David. 1988. *Hindu Goddesses: Visions of the Divine Feminine in the Hindu Religious Tradition*. Berkeley: University of California Press.

Kishwar, Madhu. 1997. *Tantric Visions of the Divine Feminine: The Ten Mahāvidyās*. Berkeley: University of California Press.

Kishwar, Madhu, and Ruth Vanita, eds. 1984. *In Search of Answers: Indian Women's Voices from Manushi*. London: Zed Books.

Kleinman, Arthur. 2019. *The Soul of Care: The Moral Education of a Husband and a Doctor*. New York: Viking.

Kleinman, Arthur. 2020. "Varieties of Experiences of Care." *Perspectives in Biology and Medicine* 63 (3): 458–65. https://doi.org/10.1353/pbm.2020.0033.

Kleinman, Arthur, Veena Das, Margaret Lock, and Mamphele Ramphele. 2001. *Remaking a World: Violence, Social Suffering and Recovery*. Berkeley: University of California Press.

Kleinman, Arthur, Veena Das, and Margaret M. Lock. 1997. *Social Suffering*. Berkeley: University of California Press.

Kranz, Felicitas, and Alumit Ishai. 2006. "Face Perception Is Modulated by Sexual Preference." *Current Biology* 16 (1): 63–68. https://doi.org/10.1016/j.cub.2005.10.070.

Kukreja, Reena. 2021. "Colorism as Marriage Capital: Cross-Region Marriage Migration in India and Dark-Skinned Migrant Brides." *Gender & Society* 35 (1): 85–109. https://doi.org/10.1177/08912432209796 33.

Lamb, Sarah. 2000. *White Saris and Sweet Mangoes: Aging, Gender, and Body in North India.* Berkeley: University of California Press.

Lamb, Sarah. 2018. "Being Single in India: Gendered Identities, Class Mobilities, and Personhoods in Flux." *Ethos* 46 (1): 49–69. https://doi.org/10.1111/etho.12193.

Lamb, Sarah. 2022. *Being Single in India: Stories of Gender, Exclusion, and Possibility.* Berkeley: University of California Press.

Lambek, Michael. 2010. *Ordinary Ethics: Anthropology, Language, and Action.* New York: Fordham University Press.

Lambek, Michael, and Andrew Strathern. 1998. *Bodies and Persons: Comparative Perspectives from Africa and Melanesia.* Cambridge: Cambridge University Press.

Lambek, Michael, Veena Das, Didier Fassin, and Webb Keane. 2015. *Four Lectures in Ethics: Anthropological Perspectives.* Chicago: University of Chicago Press.

Lambert, Helen. 1997. "Illness, Inauspiciousness and Modes of Healing in Rajasthan." *Contributions to Indian Sociology* 31 (2): 253–71. https://doi.org/10.1177/006996697031002004.

Lamont, Michèle, Hanna Herzog, Nissim Mizrachi, Graziella Moraes Silva, Elisa Reis, and Jessica Welburn. 2016. *Getting Respect: Responding to Stigma and Discrimination in the United States, Brazil, and Israel.* Princeton, NJ: Princeton University Press.

Lange, Gerrit. 2022. "Hindu Deities in the Flesh: 'Hot' Emotions, Sensual Interactions, and (Syn)aesthetic Blends." *Religions* 13 (11): 1045. https://doi.org/10.3390/rel13111045.

Leavitt, John. 1996. "Meaning and Feeling in the Anthropology of Emotions." *American Ethnologist* 23: 514–39.

Lee, Joel. 2017. "Odor and Order." *Comparative Studies of South Asia, Africa, and the Middle East* 37 (3): 470–90. https://doi.org/10.1215/1089201x-4279188.

Lee, Joel. 2018. "Who Is the True Halalkhor? Genealogy and Ethics in Dalit Muslim Oral Traditions." *Contributions to Indian Sociology* 52 (1): 1–27.

Legg, S., and S. Roy. 2013. "Neo-Liberalism, Post-Colonialism and Hetero-Sovereignties: Emergent Sexual Formations in Contemporary India." *Interventions: International Journal for Postcolonial Studies* 15 (4): 461–73.

Le Guin, Ursula. 1992. *The Language of the Night.* New York: Harper Collins.

de León, Jason. 2015. *The Land of Open Graves: Living and Dying on the Migrant Trail.* Berkeley: University of California Press.

Lévi-Strauss, Claude. 1955. "The Structural Study of Myth." *Journal of American Folklore* 68 (270): 428–44. https://doi.org/10.2307/536768.

Lévi-Strauss, Claude. 1974. *Tristes tropiques.* New York: Atheneum.

Lévi-Strauss, Claude. 1978. *Myth and Meaning: Five Talks for Radio.* Toronto: University of Toronto Press.

Lévi-Strauss, Claude. 1983. *Structural Anthropology.* Chicago: University of Chicago Press.

Lidola, Maria. 2015. "Of Grooming Bodies and Caring Souls: New-Old Forms of Care Work in Brazilian Waxing Studios in Berlin." In *Care on the Move: Anthropological Perspectives on Work, Kinship, and the Life Course*, edited by Erdmute Alber and Heike Drotbohm, 69–90. Basingstoke: Palgrave Macmillan.

Liebelt, Claudia. 2016. "Grooming Istanbul." *Journal of Middle East Women's Studies* 12 (2): 181–202. https://doi.org/10.1215/15525864-3507628.

Liebelt, Claudia. 2018. "Reshaping 'Turkish' Breasts and Noses: On Cosmetic Surgery, Gendered Norms and the 'Right to Look Normal.'" In *Beauty and the Norm: Debating Standardization in Bodily Appearance*, edited by Claudia Liebelt, Sarah Böllinger, and Ulf Vierke, 155–76. Cham: Springer. https://doi.org/10.1007/978-3-319-91174-8-7.

Liebelt, Claudia. 2019. "Aesthetic Citizenship in Istanbul: On Manufacturing Beauty and Negotiating Belonging Through the Body in Urban Turkey." *Citizenship Studies* 23 (7): 686–702. https://doi.org/10.1080/13621025.2019.1651088.

Liebelt, Claudia. 2023. "Feminine Self-Fashioning in Times of Change." In *Istanbul Appearances: Beauty and the Making of Middle-Class Femininities in Urban Turkey*, 236–74. Syracuse, NY: Syracuse University Press. https://doi.org/10.2307/j.ctv31zqc5j.13.

Lusome, R., and R. B. Bhagat. 2020. "Migration in Northeast India: Inflows, Outflows and Reverse Flows During Pandemic." *Indian Journal of Labour Economics* 63 (4): 1125–41. https://doi.org/10.1007/s41027-020-00278-7.

MacKinnon, Catharine. 1987. *Feminism Unmodified: Discourses on Life and Law*. Cambridge, MA: Harvard University Press.

MacKinnon, Catharine. 2007. *Are Women Human? and Other International Dialogues*. Cambridge, MA: Belknap.

Madison, Greg. 2007. "The End of Belonging: Untold Stories of Leaving Home and the Psychology of Globalization." White paper.

Māhāṇā, Rājakiśora, and Nandini Sundar. 2019. *Negotiating Marginality: Conflicts over Tribal Development in India*. Abingdon: Routledge Press.

Majumdar, Rochona. 2007. "Arguments Within Indian Feminism." *Social History* 32 (4): 434–45. https://doi.org/10.1080/03071020701616803.

Malampalli, Chandra. 2011. *Race, Religion and Law in Colonial India*. Cambridge: Cambridge University Press.

Malinowski, Bronislaw. 1926. *Crime and Custom in Savage Society*. London: Harcourt Brace.

Mani, Lata. 2008. "The Phantom of Globality and the Delirium of Excess." *Economic and Political Weekly* 43 (39): 41–47.

Mankekar, Purnima. 1993. "National Texts and Gendered Lives: An Ethnography of Television Viewers in a North Indian City." *American Ethnologist* 20 (3): 543–63.

Mankekar, Purnima. 1999. *Screening Culture, Viewing Politics: An Ethnography of Television, Womanhood, and Nation in Postcolonial India*. Durham, NC: Duke University Press.

Mankekar, Purnima, and Louisa Schein. 2012. *Media, Erotics, and Transnational Asia*. Durham, NC: Duke University Press.

Marković, S. 2012. "Components of Aesthetic Experience: Aesthetic Fascination, Aesthetic Appraisal, and Aesthetic Emotion." *I-perception* 3 (1): 1–17. https://doi.org/10.1068/i0450aap.

Marriott, McKim. 1976. "Hindu Transactions: Diversity Without Dualism." In *Transaction and Meaning: Directions in the Anthropology of Exchange and Symbolic Behavior*, edited by Bruce Kapferer, 109–42. Philadelphia: ISHI Publications.

Marriott, McKim. 1990. *India Through Hindu Categories*. New Delhi: Sage.

Marriott, McKim, and Ronald Inden. 1976. "Towards an Ethnosociology of South Asian Caste Systems." In *The New Wind: Changing Identities in South Asia*, edited by Kenneth David. The Hague: Mouton Press.

Martínez, Francisco, Lili Di Puppo, and Martin Demant Frederiksen, eds. 2021. *Peripheral Methodologies: Unlearning, Not-Knowing and Ethnographic Limits*. Abingdon: Routledge.

Marx, Karl, and Friedrich Engels. 1967. *Capital: A Critique of Political Economy*. New York: International Publishers.

Masquelier, Adeline Marie. 2005. *Dirt, Undress, and Difference: Critical Perspectives on the Body's Surface*. Bloomington: Indiana University Press.

Mazzarella, William. 2003. *Shoveling Smoke: Advertising and Globalization in Contemporary India*. Durham, NC: Duke University Press.

McDermott, Rachel Fell. 2000. *Mother of My Heart, Daughter of My Dreams: Transformations of Kali and Uma in the Devotional Poetry of Bengal*. New York: Oxford University Press.

McDermott, Rachel Fell. 2008. "The Pujas in Historical and Political Controversy: Colonial and Post-Colonial Goddesses." *Religions of South Asia* 2 (2): 135–59.

McDermott, Rachel Fell. 2011. *Revelry, Rivalry, and Longing for the Goddesses of Bengal: The Fortunes of Hindu Festivals*. New York: Columbia University Press.

McDermott, Rachel Fell, and Jeffrey J. Kripal. 2003. *Encountering Kālī: In the Margins, at the Center, in the West*. Berkeley: University of California Press.

McGrath, Kevin. 2009. *Stri: Women in Epic Mahabharata*. Cambridge, MA: Harvard University Press.

McLain, Karline. 2009. *India's Immortal Comic Books: Gods, Kings and Other Heroes*. Indianapolis: Indiana University Press.

Mencher, Joan P. 1974. "The Caste System Upside Down, or the Not-So-Mysterious East." *Current Anthropology* 15 (4): 469–93.

Menon, Usha. 2002. "Making Śakti: Controlling (Natural) Impurity for Female (Cultural) Power." *Ethos* 30 (1/2): 140–57. http://www.jstor.org/stable/3651819.

Meyer, Birgit. 2020. "Religion as Mediation." *Entangled Religions* 11 (3). https://doi.org/10.13154/er.11.2020.8444.

Mines, Diane P., and Sarah Lamb. 2010. *Everyday Life in South Asia*. 2nd ed., Bloomington: Indiana University Press.

Mishra, Neha. 2015. "India and Colorism: The Finer Nuances." *Washington University, Global Studies Law Review* 14 (4): 725–50. https://openscholarship.wustl.edu/law_globalstudies/vol14/iss4/14.

Mody, Perveez. 2002. "Love and the Law: Love-Marriage in Delhi." *Modern Asian Studies* 36 (1): 223–56. https://doi.org/10.1017/S0026749X02001075.

Monius, Anne E. 2004. "Love, Violence and the Aesthetics of Disgust: Saivas and Jains in Medieval South India." *Journal of Indian Philosophy* 32 (2/3): 113–72. https://doi.org/10.1023/B:INDI.0000020898.04782.7a.

Moodie, Deonnie. 2019. *The Making of a Modern Temple and a Hindu City: Kalighat and Kolkata*. New York: Oxford University Press.

Mookherjee, Nayanika. 2013. "Introduction: Self in South Asia." *Journal of Historical Sociology* 26 (1): 1–18. https://doi.org/10.1111/johs.12008.

Moran, Maria. 2017. "'New Beginnings and Painful Endings': *The Furrow* May 2017." *Furrow* 68 (7/8): 428–31.

Moran, Richard. 2001. *Authority and Estrangement: An Essay on Self knowledge*. Princeton, NJ: Princeton University Press.

Moran, Richard. 2017. *The Philosophical Imagination: Selected Essays*. Oxford: Oxford University Press.

Morphy, Howard. 1998. *Aboriginal Art and Ideas*. New York: Phaidon Press.

Mosse, David. 2020. "The Modernity of Caste and the Market Economy." *Modern Asian Studies* 54 (4): 1225–71. https://doi.org/10.1017/S0026749X19000039.

Mount, Liz. 2017. "Saris and Contemporary Indian Womanhood: How Middle-Class Women Navigate the Tradition/Modernity Split." *Contemporary South Asia* 25 (2): 167–81. https://doi.org/10.1080/09584935.2017.1321617.

Mukherjee, Indrani. 2020. "A Cartography of Angry Indian Goddesses Towards Nomadic Affect." *Indialogs: Spanish Journal of India Studies* 7:11–25. https://doi.org/10.5565/rev/indialogs.150.

Mukhopadhyay, Anway. 2018. *The Goddess in Hindu-Tantric Traditions: Devi as Corpse*. Abingdon: Routledge.

Mulvey, Laura. 1975. "Visual Pleasure and Narrative Cinema." *Screen* 16 (3): 6–18.

Mulvey, Laura. 2009. *Visual and Other Pleasures*. 2nd ed. Houndmills: Palgrave Macmillan.

Munn, Nancy D. 1973. *Walbin Iconography*. Ithaca, NY: Cornell University Press.

Munsi, Urmimala Sarkar. 2016. "Draupadi's Travels and Travails." *Economic and Political Weekly* 51 (50): 12–15.

Munsi, Urmimala Sarkar. 2023. "Becoming a Body." *South Asian History and Culture* 14 (2): 124–39. https://doi.org/10.1080/19472498.2022.2077804.

Murray, David A. B. 2009. *Homophobias: Lust and Loathing Across Time and Space*. Durham, NC: Duke University Press.

Myers, Joshua. 2023. *Of Black Study*. New York: Pluto Press.

Nabokov, Isabelle. 2000. *Religion Against the Self: An Ethnography of Tamil Rituals*. Oxford: Oxford University Press.

Nagarajan, Vijaya. 2018. *Feeding a Thousand Souls: Women, Ritual and Ecology: An Exploration of Kolam*. New York: Oxford University Press.

Nair, Janaki. 2005. *The Promise of the Metropolis: Bangalore's Twentieth Century*. Oxford: Oxford University Press.

Napier, David A. 1986. *Masks, Transformation, and Paradox*. Berkeley: University of California Press.

Narayan, Kirin. 1996. "First Sour, Then Sweet: Women's Ritual Storytelling in the Himalayan Foothills." *Women and Language* 19 (1): 9.

Narayan, Kirin. 2008. "Showers of Flowers." *Jung Journal* 2 (1): 5–22. https://doi.org/10.1525/jung.2008.2.1.5.

Obeyesekere, Gananath. 1984. *The Cult of the Goddess Pattini*. Chicago: University of Chicago Press.

Ochoa, Marcia. 2014. *Queen for a Day: Transformistas, Beauty Queens, and the Performance of Femininity in Venezuela*. Durham, NC: Duke University Press.

O'Hanlon, Michael D. 1989. *Reading the Skin: Adornment, Display and Society Among the Wahgi*. London: British Museum Publications.

Olivelle, Patrick. 2008. "15. Hair and Society: Social Significance of Hair in South Asian Traditions. Collected Essays. 1: Language Texts and Society: Explorations in Ancient Indian Culture and Religion." In *Collected Essays. 1: Language Texts and Society: Explorations in Ancient Indian Culture and Religion*. Florence: Firenze University Press. https://doi.org/10.1400/92588.

Olivelle, Patrick. 2011. *Ascetics and Brahmins: Studies in Ideologies and Institutions*. New York: Anthem Press.

Omvedt, Gail. 2011. *Understanding Caste: From Buddha to Ambedkar and Beyond*. New Delhi: Orient Blackswan.

Orsini, Francesca. 2006. *Love in South Asia: A Cultural History*. Cambridge: Cambridge University Press.

Ortner, S. 1980. *We Will Smash This Prison! Indian Women in Struggle*. London: Zed.

Ortner, S. 2016. "Dark Anthropology and Its Others: Theory Since the Eighties." *HAU: Journal of Ethnographic Theory* 6:47–73.

Ossman, Susan. 2002. *Three Faces of Beauty: Casablanca, Paris, Cairo*. Durham, NC: Duke University Press.

Otero, S. 2020. *Archives of Conjure: Stories of the Dead in Afrolatinx Religions*. New York: Columbia University Press.

Oza, R. 2001. "Showcasing India: Gender, Geography, and Globalization." *Signs* 26 (4): 1067–95.

Packert, Cynthia. 2010. *The Art of Loving Krishna: Ornamentation and Devotion*. Indianapolis: Indiana University Press.

Paik, Shailaja. 2022a. "Dr Ambedkar and the 'Prostitute': Caste, Sexuality and Humanity in Modern India." *Gender & History* 34 (2): 437–57. https://doi.org/10.1111/1468-0424.12557.

Paik, Shailaja. 2022b. *The Vulgarity of Caste: Dalits, Sexuality, and Humanity in Modern India*. Stanford: Stanford University Press.

Pandian, Anand. 2015. *Reel World: An Anthropology of Creation*. Durham, NC: Duke University Press.

Pandian, Anand. 2019. *A Possible Anthropology: Methods for Uneasy Times*. Durham, NC: Duke University Press.

Panjwani, Jyoti. 2000. "Feminist 'Re-Membering' and 'Re-Visions': Vaidehi's 'An Afternoon with Shakuntala' and Mannu Bhandari's 'Swami.'" *Comparative Civilizations Review* 42 (42): article 5.

Parameswaran, Radhika. 2001. "Global Media Events in India: Contests over Beauty, Gender and Nation." *Journalism and Communication Monographs* 3 (2): 52–105. https://doi.org/10.1177/152263790100300202.

Patitsas, Timothy G. 2020. *The Ethics of Beauty*. Maysville, MO: St. Nicholas Press.

Paul, Heike. 2019. *Critical Terms in Futures Studies*. Cham: Springer. https://doi.org/10.1007/978-3-030-28987-4.

Pechilis, Karen. 2023. "Revisiting the Experiential World of Women's Bhakti Poetry." *Religions* 14 (6): 788. https://doi.org/10.3390/rel14060788.

Pinney, Christopher. 2004. *"Photos of the Gods": The Printed Image and Political Struggle in India*. London: Reaktion.

Pintchman, Tracy. 2001. *Seeking Mahādevī: Constructing the Identity of the Hindu Great Goddess*. Albany: State University of New York Press.

Pintchman, Tracy, and Rita D. Sherma. 2011. *Woman and Goddess in Hinduism: Reinterpretations and Re-envisionings*. New York: Palgrave Macmillan.

Pinto, Sarah. 2008. *Where There Is No Midwife: Birth and Loss in Rural India*. New York: Berghahn.

Pinto, Sarah. 2014. *Daughters of Parvati: Women and Madness in Contemporary India*. Philadelphia: University of Pennsylvania Press.

Plemons, Eric. 2017. *The Look of a Woman: Facial Feminization Surgery and the Aims of Trans- Medicine*. Durham, NC: Duke University Press.

Pollock, Sheldon. 2016. *A Rasa Reader: Classical Indian Aesthetics*. New York: Columbia University Press.

Povinelli, Elizabeth A. 2002. *The Cunning of Recognition: Indigenous Alterities and the Making of Australian Multiculturalism*. Durham, NC: Duke University Press.

Powdermaker, Hortense. 1967. *Stranger and Friend: The Way of the Anthropologist*. New York: Norton.

Prasad, Leela. 2006. *Poetics of Conduct: Oral Narrative and Moral Being in a South Indian Town*. New York: Columbia University Press.

Prasad, Leela. 2020. *The Audacious Raconteur: Sovereignty and Storytelling in Colonial India*. Ithaca, NY: Cornell University Press.

Puar, Jasbir. 2007. *Terrorist Assemblages: Homonationalism in Queer Times*. Durham, NC: Duke University Press.

Puett, Michael. 2008. "Ritual and the Subjunctive." In *Ritual and Its Consequences: An Essay on the Limits of Sincerity*, edited by Adam B. Seligman, Robert P. Weller, Michael Puett, and Bennett Simon, 17–42. Oxford: Oxford University Press.

Puett, Michael. 2021. "Creating Worlds, Imagination, Interpretation and the Subjunctive." In *Living with Concepts: Anthropology in the Grip of Reality*, edited by Andrew Brandel and Marco Motta, 181–96. New York: Fordham University Press.

Purkayastha, Bandana. 2021. "Knowledge Hierarchies and Feminist Dilemmas: Contexts, Assemblages, Voices, and Silences." *Producing Inclusive Feminist Knowledge: Positionalities and Discourses in the Global South* 31:23–41. https://doi.org/10.1108/S1529-21262021000031002.

Purkayastha, Bandana, Mangala Subramaniam, Manisha Desai, and Sunita Bose. 2003. "The Study of Gender in India: A Partial Review." *Gender and Society* 17 (4): 503–24. https://doi.org/10.1177/0891243203253793.

Raheja, Gloria Goodwin. 1985. *The Poison in the Gift: Ritual, Prestation, and the Dominant Caste in a North Indian Village*. Chicago: University of Chicago press.

Raheja, Gloria Goodwin. 2003. *Songs, Stories, Lives: Gendered Dialogues and Cultural Critique*. New Delhi: Kali for Women.

Raheja, Gloria Goodwin, and Ann Grodzins Gold. 1994. *Listen to the Heron's Words: Reimagining Gender and Kinship in North India*. Berkeley: University of California Press.

Ramanujan, A. K. 1973. *Speaking of Siva*. Harmondsworth, UK: Penguin.

Ramanujan, A. K. 1991. "Towards a Counter-System: Women's Tales." In *Gender, Genre, and Power in South Asian Expressive Traditions*, edited by Arjun Appadurai, Frank Korom, and Margaret Mills, 33–55. Philadelphia: University of Pennsylvania Press.

Ramanujan, A. K. 1999. "A Flowering Tree: A Woman's Tale." In *The Collected Essays of A. K. Ramanujan*, edited by Vinay Dharwadker, 412–28. Oxford: Oxford University Press.

Ramaswamy, Sumathi. 2010. *The Goddess and the Nation: Mapping Mother India*. Durham, NC: Duke University Press.

Ramberg, Lucinda. 2014. *Given to the Goddess: South Indian Devadasis and the Sexuality of Religion*. Durham, NC: Duke University Press.

Ramberg, Lucinda. 2017. "Who and What Is Sex For? Notes on Theogamy and the Sexuality of Religion." *History of the Present* 7 (2): 175–96. https://doi.org/10.5406/historypresent.7.2.0175.

Rao, Rahul. 2020. "The Nation and Its Queers," *Out of Time: The Queer Politics of Postcoloniality*. New York: Oxford Academic.

Rastogi, Sanjeev, and Ram Singh. 2021. "A Decade of Scientific Publishing in Ayurveda: Journeying Through the Path Less Travelled." *Annals of Ayurvedic Medicine* 10 (4): 310–12. https://doi.org/10.5455/AAM.129815.

Rawat, Ramnarayan, and K. Satyanarayana, eds. 2016. *Dalit Studies*. Durham, NC: Duke University Press.

Ray, Raka, and Seelim Qayum. 2009. *Cultures of Servitude: Modernity, Domesticity and Class in India*. Stanford, CA: Stanford University Press.

Reddy, Gayatri. 2005. *With Respect to Sex: Negotiating Hijra Identity in South India*. Chicago: University of Chicago Press.

Reddy, Gayatri. 2019. "Hijras." In *Global Encyclopedia of Lesbian, Gay, Bisexual, Transgender, and Queer (LGBTQ) History*, edited by Howard Chiang and Anjali Arondekar, 666–70. Farmington Hills, MI: Gale.

Rege, Sharmila. 1998. "Dalit Women Talk Differently: A Critique of Difference and Towards a Dalit Feminist Standpoint Position." *Economic and Political Weekly* 33 (44): WS 39–WS 46.

Rege, Sharmila. 2006. *Writing Caste/Writing Gender: Reading Dalit Women's Testimonios*. New Delhi: Zubaan.

Richman, Paula. 1988. *Women, Branch Stories, and Religious Rhetoric in a Tamil Buddhist Text*. Syracuse, NY: Maxwell School of Citizenship and Public Affairs, Syracuse University.

Richman, Paula. 1991. *Many Ramayanas: The Diversity of a Narrative Tradition in South Asia*. Berkeley: University of California Press.

Richman, Paula. 2001. *Questioning Ramayanas: A South Asian Tradition*. Berkeley: University of California Press.

Roberts, Nathaniel. 2016. *To Be Cared For: The Power of Conversion and Foreignness of Belonging in an Indian Slum*. Berkeley: University of California Press.

Robinson, Hilary. 2000. "Whose Beauty?" In *Beauty Matters*, edited by Peg Zeglin Brand, 224–51. Bloomington: Indiana University Press.

Robinson, Hilary. 2006. *Reading Art, Reading Irigaray*. New York: I. B. Taurus.

Rohrer, I., and M. Thompson. 2023. "Imagination Theory: Anthropological Perspectives." *Anthropological Theory* 23 (2): 186–208.

Roy, Srila. 2022. *Changing the Subject: Feminist and Queer Politics in Neoliberal India*. Durham, NC: Duke University Press.

Sanderson, Alexis. 2006. *Meaning in Tantric Ritual*. New Delhi: Tantra Foundation.

Santayana, George. 1955. *The Sense of Beauty*. New York: Dover.

Santo, Diana Espírito, Marjorie Murray, and Paulina Salinas. 2023. "Ways of Not Knowing in Neoliberal Chile: Notes on a Dark Anthropology." *Social Anthropology/Anthropologie sociale* 30 (2): 1–18.

Sargent, Adam. 2020. "Working Against Labor: Struggles for Self in the Indian Construction Industry." *Anthropology of Work Review* 41:76–85. https://doi.org/10.1111/awr.12199.

Saria, Vaibhav. 2014. "The Perfumed Semen: The Labour of Loving in Rural Orissa, India." PhD diss., Johns Hopkins University.

Saria, Vaibhav. 2019. "Begging for Change: Hijras, Law and Nationalism." *Contributions to Indian Sociology* 53 (1): 133–57. https://doi.org/10.1177/0069966718813588.

Saria, Vaibhav. 2021. *Hijras, Lovers, Brothers Surviving Sex and Poverty in Rural India.* New York: Fordham University Press.

Sarkar, Tanika. 2001. *Hindu Wife, Hindu Nation, Community, Religion, and Cultural Nationalism.* Bloomington: Indiana University Press.

Sarkar, Tanika. 2009. *Rebels, Wives, Saints: Designing Selves and Nations in Colonial Times.* London: Seagull Books.

Sarukkai, Sundar. 2009. "Phenomenology of Untouchability." *Economic and Political Weekly* 44 (37): 39–48.

Sathe, Namrata Rele. n.d. "Queer Counter-Narratives, Feminist Authorship, and the Inclusive Storytelling of Gazal Dhaliwal." In *Women Filmmakers in Contemporary Hindi Cinema*, 215–35. Cham: Springer. https://doi.org/10.1007/978-3-031-10232-5_12.

Satyanarayana, K., and Joel G. Lee. 2023. *Concealing Caste: Passing and Personhood in Dalit Literature.* Oxford: Oxford University Press.

Scarry, Elaine. 1985. *The Body in Pain: The Making and Unmaking of the World.* New York: Oxford University Press.

Scarry, Elaine. 1999. *On Beauty and Being Just.* Princeton, NJ: Princeton University Press.

Schneiderman, Sara, and Louise Tillin. 2015. "Restructuring States, Restructuring Ethnicity: Looking Across Disciplinary Boundaries at Federal Futures in India and Nepal." *Modern Asian Studies* 49 (1): 1–39. doi:10.1017/ S0026749X1300067X.

Schwartz, Susan. 2004. *Rasa: Performing the Divine in India.* New York: Columbia University Press.

Scott, Joan W. 2016. "Storytelling." *History and Theory* 50 (2): 203–9.

Scruton, Roger. 2011. *Beauty: A Very Short Introduction.* Oxford: Oxford University Press.

Sengupta, Saswati. 2020. "Manasā." In *Mutating Goddesses: Bengal's Laukika Hinduism and Gender Rights*, 56–119. New Delhi: Oxford University Press.

Shah, Svati P. 2014. "Queering Critiques of Neoliberalism in India: Urbanism and Inequality in the Era of Transnational 'LGBTQ' Rights." *Antipode* 47 (3): 635–51. https://doi.org/10.1111/anti.12112.

Shah, Svati P. 2019. "Sedition, Sexuality, Gender, and Gender Identity in South Asia." *South Asia Multidisciplinary Academic Journal* 20. https://doi.org/10.4000/samaj.5163.

Shah, Svati. P. 2021. "Impossible Migrants: Debating Sex Work and Gender Identity amid the Crisis of Migrant Labor." *South Atlantic Quarterly* 120 (3): 515–32. https://doi.org/10.1215/00382876-9154884.

Sharma, M. 2006. *Loving Women: Being Lesbian in Unprivileged India.* New Delhi: Yoda Press.

Shukla, Pravina. 2015. *The Grace of Four Moons: Dress, Adornment and the Art of the Body in Modern India*. Indianapolis: Indiana University Press.

Shulman, David. 2006. "The Scent of Memory in Hindu South India." In *The Smell Culture Reader*, edited by Jim Drobnik, 411–27. Oxford: Berg Press.

Shulman, David. 2012. *More than Real: A History of the Imagination in South India*. Cambridge, MA: Harvard University Press.

Shulman, David. 2014. *Tamil Temple Myths: Sacrifice and Divine Marriage in the South Indian Saiva Tradition*. Princeton, NJ: Princeton University Press.

Shulman, David. 2017. *The Presentation of Self in Contemporary Social Life*. Los Angeles: Sage.

Shusterman, Richard. 1999. "Somaesthetics: A Disciplinary Proposal." *Journal of Aesthetics and Art Criticism* 57 (3): 299–312.

Shusterman, Richard. 2018. *Aesthetic Experience and Somaesthetics*. Leiden: Brill.

Simmons, Caleb. 2018. "History, Heritage, and Myth." *Worldviews: Global Religions, Culture, and Ecology* 2 (3): 216–37. https://doi.org/10.1163/15685357-02203101.

Simmons, Caleb, Moumita Sen, and Hillary Rodrigues, eds. 2018. *Nine Nights of the Goddess: The Navarātri Festival of South Asia*. Albany: State University of New York Press.

Skeggs, Bev. 1997. *Formations of Class and Gender: Becoming Respectable*. London: Sage. https://doi.org/10.4135/9781446217597.

Smalls, Krystal A. 2021. "Fat, Black, and Ugly: The Semiotic Production of Prodigious Femininities." *Transforming Anthropology* 29:12–28. https://doi.org/10.1111/traa.12208.

Smith, John D., trans. 2009. *The Mahābharata: An Abridged Translation*. London: Penguin.

Solomon, Harris. 2022a. *Lifelines: The Traffic of Trauma*. Durham, NC: Duke University Press.

Solomon, Harris. 2022b. "Wound Culture." *Annual Review of Anthropology* 51:121–35.

Somers, Margaret R. 1994. "The Narrative Constitution of Identity: A Relational and Network Approach." *Theory and Society* 23 (5): 605–49. https://doi.org/10.1007/BF00992905.

Sontag, Susan. 1972. "The Double Standard of Aging." *Saturday Review*, September 23, 1972, 285–94.

Sontag, Susan. 1975. "Beauty: How Will It Change Next?" *Vogue* Magazine, May 1975. https://archive.vogue.com/article/1975/5/beauty-how-will-it-change-next.

Sontag, Susan. 1975. "A Woman's Beauty: Put Down or Power Source?" *Vogue*, April. https://archive.vogue.com/article/1975/04/01/a-womans-beauty-put-down-or-power-source.

Spivak, Gayatri Chakravorty. 1981. "'Draupadi' by Mahasveta Devi." *Critical Inquiry* 8 (2): 381–402.

Spivak, Gayatri Chakravorty. 1988. *"Draupadi" in Other Worlds: Essays in Cultural Politics*. New York: Routledge.

Spivak, Gayatri Chakravorty. 2010. "Can the Subaltern Speak?" Rev. Ed. In *Can the Subaltern Speak? Reflections on the History of an Idea*, edited by Rosalind Morris, 21–78. New York: Columbia University Press.

Srinivas, M. N. 1957. "Caste in Modern India." *Journal of Asian Studies* 16 (4): 529–48.

Srinivas, M. N. 1962. "Varna and Caste." In *Caste in Modern India and Other Essays*, 20–34. Bombay: Asia Publishing House.

Srinivas, M. N. 1977. "The Changing Position of Indian Women." *Man* 12 (2): 221–38. https://doi.org/10.2307/2800796.

Srinivas, Tulasi. 2018. *The Cow in the Elevator: An Anthropology of Wonder*. Durham, NC: Duke University Press.

Srinivasan, Perundevi. 2014. "Constructing Goddess Worship." In *Inventing and Reinventing the Goddess: Contemporary Iterations of Hindu Deities on the Move*, edited by Sree Padma, 63–87. Lanham, MD: Lexington Books.

Srinivasan, Perundevi. 2019. "Sprouts of the Body, Sprouts of the Field: Identification of the Goddess with Poxes in South India." *Religions* 10 (3): 147. https://doi.org/10.3390/rel10030147.

Srivastava, Sanjay. 2015. "Modi-Masculinity." *Television and New Media* 16 (4): 331–38. https://doi.org/10.1177/1527476415575498.

Srivastava, Simpi. 2020. "Global Production of a Feminine Ideal: Behind the Scenes of Beauty Pageants." *Glocalism: Journal of Culture, Politics and Innovation*. https://doi.org/10.12893/gjcpi.2020.1.10.

Stacey, Judith. 1988. "Can There Be a Feminist Ethnography?" *Women's Studies International Forum* 11 (1): 21–27.

Stoller, Paul. 2021. "Foreword: Between Village and Bush." In *Peripheral Methodologies: Unlearning, Not-knowing, and Ethnographic Limits*, edited by F. M. Martínez, D. Frederiksen, and L. Puppo, ix–xiv. Abingdon, UK: Routledge.

Stonington, Scott. 2020. "Karma Masters: The Ethical Wound, Hauntological Choreography, and Complex Personhood in Thailand." *American Anthropologist* 122 (December 4). https://doi.org/10.1111/aman.13464.

Strathern, Andrew, and Marilyn Strathern. 1971. *Self-Decoration in Mount Hagen*. Toronto: University of Toronto Press.

Strathern, Marilyn. 1979. "The Self in Self-Decoration." *Oceania* 49 (4): 241–57. https://doi.org/10.1002/j.1834-4461.1979.tb01915.x.

Strathern, Marilyn. 1988. *The Gender of the Gift: Problems with Women and Problems with Society in Melanesia*. Berkeley: University of California Press.

Strathern, Marilyn. 1995. *Women in Between: Female Roles in a Male World: Mount Hagen, New Guinea*. Lanham, MD: Rowman and Littlefield.

Sundar, Nandini. 2007. "In the Cause of Anthropology: The Life and Work of Irawati Karve." In *Anthropology in the East: The Founders of Indian Sociology and Anthropology*, edited by Patricia Uberoi, Nandini Sundar, and Satish Deshpande. New Delhi: Permanent Black.

Sundaram, Ravi. 2009. *Pirate Modernity: Delhi's Media Urbanism*. London: Routledge.

Tate, Shirley Anne. 2016. *Skin Bleaching in Black Atlantic Zones: Shade Shifters*. London: Palgrave Macmillan.

Tate, Shirley Anne. 2022. "Beauty." *Canadian Review of Sociology* 59 (4): 547–49. https://doi.org/10.1111/cars.12406.

Taussig, Michael T. 1993. *Mimesis and Alterity: A Particular History of the Senses*. New York: Routledge.

Taussig, Michael T. 2012. *Beauty and the Beast*. Chicago: University of Chicago Press.

Thompson, James. 2015. "Towards an Aesthetics of Care." *Research in Drama Education: The Journal of Applied Theatre and Performance* 20 (4): 430–41, https://doi: 10.1080/13569783.2015.1068109.

Thrift, Nigel. 2010. "Understanding the Material Practices of Glamour. " In *The Affect Theory Reader*, edited by Melissa Gregg and Gregory J. Seigworth, 289–309. Durham, NC: Duke University Press.

Tobler, Judy. 2001. "Goddesses and Women's Spirituality: Transformative Symbols of the Feminine in Hindu Religion." *Journal for the Study of Religion* 14 (2): 49–71. http://www.jstor.org/stable/24764167.

Tolkien, J. R. R. 2008. *Tolkien on Fairy-Stories: Expanded Edition, with Commentary and Notes*. Edited by Verlyn Flieger and Douglas A. Anderson. London: HarperCollins.

Tolstoy, Leo. 1889. *The Kreutzer Sonata*. Berlin: Bibliographic Office.

Turner, Bryan S. 1992. *Regulating Bodies: Essays in Medical Sociology*. London: Routledge.

Turner, Terence S. 2017. "Beauty and the Beast: The Fearful Symmetry of the Jaguar and Other Natural Beings in Kayapo Ritual and Myth." *HAU: Journal of Ethnographic Theory* 7 (2): 51–70.

Ulysse, Gina A. 2002. "Conquering Duppies in Kingston: Miss Tiny and Me, Fieldwork Conflicts, and Being Loved and Rescued." *Anthropology and Humanism* 27:10–26. https://doi.org/10.1525/anhu.2002.27.1.10.

Ulysse, Gina A. 2007. *Downtown Ladies: Informal Commercial Importers, a Haitian Anthropologist, and Self-Making in Jamaica*. Chicago: Chicago University Press.

Upadhya, Carol, and A. R. Vasavi. 2013. "Outposts of the Global Information Economy: Work and Workers in India's Outsourcing Industry." In *In an Outpost of the Global Economy: Work and Workers in India's Information Technology Industry*. Abingdon: Taylor & Francis.

Urban, Hugh. 2011. "The Womb of Tantra: Goddesses, Tribals, and Kings in Assam." *Journal of Hindu Studies* 4: 231–47. https://doi.org/10.1093/jhs/hir034.

Urban, Hugh. 2018. "Dancing for the Snake: Possession, Gender and Identity in the Worship of Manasa in Assam." *Journal of Hindu Studies* 11 (3): 1–24. doi:10.1093/jhs/hiy011.

Urban, Hugh B. 2001. "The Path of Power: Impurity, Kingship, and Sacrifice in Assamese Tantra." *Journal of the American Academy of Religion* 69 (4): 777–816. https://doi.org/10.1093/jaarel/69.4.777.

Urban, Hugh B. 2006. *Magia Sexualis: Sex, Magic, and Liberation in Modern Western Esotericism*. Berkeley: University of California Press.

Urban, Hugh B. 2010. *The Power of Tantra: Religion, Sexuality, and the Politics of South Asian Studies*. London: I. B. Tauris.

Urban, Hugh B. 2019. "'The Cradle of Tantra': Modern Transformations of a Tantric Centre in Northeast India from Nationalist Symbol to Tourist Destination." *South Asia* 42 (2): 256–77. https://doi.org/10.1080/00856401.2019.1570609.

Valeri, Valerio. 1985. *Kingship and Sacrifice: Ritual and Society in Ancient Hawaii*. Chicago: University of Chicago Press.

Vanita, Ruth. 2002. *Queering India: Same-Sex Love and Eroticism in Indian Culture and Society*. New York: Routledge.

Vijayakumar, Gowri. 2020. "Just Work: Sex Work at the Intersections." *Political Power and Social Theory* 37:135–54.

Vishwanath, Rupa. 2014. *The Pariah Problem: Caste, Religion and the Social in Modern India*. New York: Columbia University Press.

Wacquant, Loic. 1995. "Pugs at Work: Bodily Capital and Bodily Labour Among Professional Boxers." *Body and Society* 1 (1): 65–94.

Wadley, Susan. 1983. "The Rains of Estrangement: Understanding the Yearly Hindu Cycle." *Contributions to Indian Sociology* 17, no. 1. London: Sage.

Wadley, Susan Snow. 1975. *Shakti: Power in the Conceptual Structure of Karimpur Religion*. Chicago: Department of Anthropology, University of Chicago.

Wadley, Susan Snow. 2008. *Wife, Mother, Widow: Exploring Women's Lives in Northern India*. New Delhi: Chronicle Books.

Wagner, Roy. 2008. "The Fractal Person." In *Big Men and Great Men: Personifications of Power in Melanesia*, edited by Marilyn Strathern and Maurice Godelier, 159–73. Cambridge: Cambridge University Press.

Walker, Alexander. 1844. *Beauty: Illustrated Chiefly by an Analysis and Classification of Beauty in Woman*. New York: W. H. Colyer.

Wickramasekara, Piyasiri. 2008. "Globalisation, International Labour Migration and the Rights of Migrant Workers." *Third World Quarterly* 29 (7): 1247–64. https://doi.org/10.1080/01436590802386278.

Wolf, Naomi. 2002. *The Beauty Myth: How Images of Beauty Are Used Against Women*. New York: William Morrow.

Wolff, Janet. 2006. "Groundless Beauty: Feminism and the Aesthetics of Uncertainty." *Feminist Theory* 7 (2): 143–58.

Yengde, Suraj. 2019. *Caste Matters*. Gurgaon: Penguin Viking.

Yengde, Suraj. 2023. "Dalit in Black America: Race, Caste, and the Making of the Dalit Black Archive." *Public Culture* 35, 1 (99): 21–41. https://doi.org/10.1215/08992363-10202374.

Young, Iris Marion. 1980. "Throwing like a Girl: A Phenomenology of Feminine Body Comportment, Motility and Spatiality." *Human Studies* 3 (2): 137–56.

Zare, Bonnie, and Afsar Mohammed. 2012. "Burn the Sari or Save the Sari? Dress as a Form of Action in Two Feminist Poems." *Ariel* 43 (2): 69–86.

Index

Abhijñānaśakuntalam (The recognition of Shakuntala) (Kalidasa), 60–61
Adivasi tribal revolt, 85–86
aesthetic practices: Indian medico-therapeutic aesthetic, 34–35; pluralism in, 58–59
afterbirth, as refuse, 109–11
aging, beauty work/beauty care and, 72–73, 138–41, 225–28
alankara (body decoration-beautification), 21, 219
allure: ambivalence of, 34–35; glamor vs., 33–35; goddesses linked to, 42, 230n5; good/bad dichotomy linked to, 55–56; male harassment and, 38–39; modern aesthetics and, 56–59
Amar Chithra Katha (Indian graphic novel series), 12
Ambabuchi Mela festival, 101–2
Amir, Safwan, 239nn8–9
Amman (goddess), 155, 215–24
Amrute, Sareeta, 105
anthropology of beauty, 9–10
Anzaldúa, Gloria, 124, 134
Apffel-Marglin, Frédérique, 81
apsaras (Hindu spirits), 12–13, 33–34, 229n3
Arabian Nights, 24–25, 62
Arain, Hafsa, 192

Ardhanarishvara, 212, 239n16
Arjuna (*Mahabharata* character), 202, 239n14
Arumugam, Indira, 136
Assam: British partitioning of, 235n11; migrants from, 121–23, 128–31, 235n11; violence in, 131–38, 235n9
Ayurvedic Cure and Care, 232n21
Ayurvedic medicine, 9–10; caste politics and, 103–5; medico-therapeutic aesthetic, 34–35

Bachchan, Amitabh, 50–51
Baji Rao Mastani (film), 57–58
Bangalore: beauty culture in, 6–8, 11–16; cosmetics industry in, 154–56; domestic beauty care practices in, 48–49; ethnic violence in, 131–38, 235n9; gender violence in, 38–39, 230n3; growth of, 13; LGBTQ movement in, 186–89, 194–95; marriage culture in, 29–30; modeling agencies in, 13; myth in culture of, 17–20; normalization of haircutting and beauty regimens in, 47; population of, 230n11; public space as threat to women in, 37–38, 230n3; sexual harassment in, 36–39, 96
barbers (*hajama*): Indian women's avoidance of, 46–47; queer culture and, 192; as storytellers, 239n8

Basu, Srimati, 161–62
beauty pageants, 28
beauty parlors: "auntie" parlors, *57*, 94–95; author's early experiences with, 4–5; Bollywood celebrity culture and, 52–54; bridal industry and, 166–69; caste and race politics and, 64–66; "Chinku" girls linked to, 102–6; concepts of beauty and allure in, 35; creative ethics and, 23–24, 220–24; digital parlors, 195–99; in India, 13–16; intimacy of the female body in, 94–99, 116–19, 219–24; LGBTQ community and, 180–82, 192–94; myth and meaning of, 12, 16–20; queer beauty parlors, 179–82, 200–203; rise in Bangalore of, 47
beauty work/beauty care: aging beauty and, 72–73, 138–41; anthropology of, 9–10; in Bangalore, 13–15; body odor in, 99–102; bridal preparations and, 87–91; brightness, hair removal techniques and, 77–80; cast and class hierarchies and, 93; celebrity culture discourse on, 51; creative ethics of, 23–24, 220–24; domestic practices of, 48–49; ethnic/racial stereotyping in, 103–6; fairness and colorism and, 70–72; feminist perspective on, 7–8; glamour and, 53–54; goddesses linked to, 42; as growth industry, 45, 157–58, 177–78; heat and dirt in, 106–11, 116–19; intimacy of the female body in, 94–99, 106–8; Japanese beauty methods, 71, 233n11; LGBTQ community and, 180–82, 192–94; limits of, 93; magic of, 217–24; migrant workers in, 125–26, 128–31, 134–38; myth and, 177–78; pedagogy of beauty and, 54–55; physical impact on workers in, 146–50; queer beauty industry, 179–82, 238n2; race politics and, 76–77; refuse of, 108–11; self-revelation through, 182–86, 219–24; technoscientific processes, 29; vaginal waxing and, 91–93; vulgarity labels in, 111–15; women's stories of, 21–24; wound culture and, 126–28
Becker, A. L., 223
Benjamin, Walter, 25
Berlant, Lauren, 37
Beyond Translation: Essays Toward a Modern Philology (Becker), 223

Bhaga (the Dispenser) (Vedic deity), 158, 237nn8–9
Bhagavad Gita, 19–20
Bhagavantam upapurana (Tantric text), 236n17
bhagya (*masood*) (luck): beauty and, 151–53, 157–60; elements of, 237n10; marriage and, 160–63, 177–78; sola shrungar ritual and, 164–69
Bharathiya Nari, as ideal Indian woman, 28, 44–46
Bharat Mata ("Mother India"), 35, 45, 55, 134–36, 232n24
bir'yun (Aboriginal Australian spiritual powers), 75
BJP government (India), 133–34
Boddy, Janice, 69
bodies and body image: bhagya and, 159–60; body odor, 99–102, 116–17; bridal industry and, 167–69; feminist fortunate body, 236n17; in film magazines, 50–51; heat and dirt from, in beauty work, 109–11, 117–19; impact of beauty work on, 146–50; intimacy in beauty parlors of, 94–99, 106–8; "passing comments" (Indian genre of critique) and, 36–37, 230n1; porosity of, in Hindu tradition, 98–99, 108, 202–3, 206–11, 236n2; queer rights and, 191–92; recognition of, 210–12; rise of image consciousness and, 13–15
Bodos indigenous group, 131, 235n9
Bollywood: bridal industry and influence of, *165*, 166–69; celebrity posters in beauty parlors from, 51–54; Chinese stereotypes in, 104; marriage rituals and, 172–73; royal historical romance genre in, 57–58
Borderlands/Frontera (Anzaldúa), 134
Brazilian waxing, 91–93
bridal industry: growth of, 157–58, 177–78; skin care and, 80; on social media, 54, *84*, 158; solah shrugar ritual and, 163–69
brightness, hair removal techniques and, 77–80
Burke, Edmund, 79
Butler, Judith, 61, 210

care ethics, beauty and, 30
caste system: affirmative action and, 234n6; barbers and, 46–47; beauty parlors and, 29, 96–99; bodily intimacy and, 110–11;

body odor and, 100–102; colonialism and, 235n15; discrimination and, 160; hierarchies in, 232n2; last names linked to, 234n3; neoliberal capitalism and, 177–78; race and color politics and, 65–66, 68–70, 232n7; sexuality within, 102–6; skin and, 98–99; vulgarity labels and, 111–15. *See also* class politics

celebrity culture: Indian women and, 50–51; pedagogy of beauty and, 54–55

Chaubal, Devyani, 50

Chinese, Indian stereotyping of, 1, 95, 100, 102–6, 132

"Chinku" girls, 102–6

Chitnis, Suma, 170

Christo-colonialism, beauty and, 19–20

Citizenship Amendment Act (CAA), 133, 235n14

class politics: bridal industry and, 164–69; caste and, 69–70; fairness and, 67–68; Indian colorism and race politics and, 65–66; LGBTQ culture and, 183–89; marriage and, 161–63; status and, 159–60; vulgarity labels and, 111–15. *See also* caste system; middle class

Clean and Dry Intimate Wash, 92–93

clothing design, Bollywood influence on, 57–58

Coakley, Sarah, 202–3

Cohen, Lawrence, 115, 130, 186

cold (*sheetala*), 100–101

colonialism: Assam and, 235n11; caste system and, 68–70, 234n6, 235n15; heteronormativity and, 183–86; marriage under, 237n11; race and gender politics and, 65; schools under, 234n4

colorism: beauty work/beauty care and, 64–65, 70–72; caste and, 68–70; fairness industry and, 66–68; hierarchical classifications of, 233n8; in Hindu cosmology, 75–76

cosmetics industry, emergence in India of, 13, 46–48

Costonis, John, 9

COVID-19 pandemic, 227–28

"Creating Sacred Spaces" (Huyler), 82

creative ethics, beauty parlors and, 23–24, 220–24

critical realism, beauty and, 11–12

"curated Suhaag (nuptial) look," 157–58

Dalit caste: class politics and, 68–70, 232n7, 235n15; heat and dirt linked to, 106–11, 118–19, 234n3; midwifery in, 109; sexuality linked to, 103–6

"Dark is beautiful" campaign, 76–77

Das, Nandita, 76

Dave, Naisargi, 194

dayabhagya, Hindu concept of, 159–60

De, Shobhaa, 50–51

Deepavali Ausadhi (Deepavali medicine), 48–49

Dencia (Nigerian pop musician), 232n3

depilation, brightness aesthetic and, 77–80

Devadasis (Devi devotees), 81–82

Devi (Mahadevi) (Hindu goddess), 40–43, 231n8, 234n1

Devi, Mahashweta, 85–86

Devy Mahatamya (Glorification of the Goddess) (Markandeya Purana), 41–42

Dewachi, Omar, 146

dharma, beauty and, 19–20

Dickey, Sara, 110

Dickinson, Emily, 210

digital beauty parlors, 195–99

dirt (*asuddha*): beauty work and, 106–11, 116–19; caste and, 110–11; colorism and cast politics and, 69–70, 233n9

dismemberment, beauty work and concept of, 135–38

Dixit, Madhuri, 173

"Dogs, Cats, and Dancers: Thoughts About Beauty" (Le Guin), 6

domestic beauty care practices, 48–49

"Double Standard of Aging, The" (Sontag), 72–73

Douglas, Mary, 94

drag performance artists, 195–99, 211–13

Draupadi story (in *Mahabharata*), 29, 74–75, 83–87, 233n18, 238n24

"Draupadi Vastraharanam" (Draupadi's disrobing) (*Mahabharata*), 83–87

Dravida identity, 190, 192, 238n5

Dumont, Louis, 22–23, 153

Dundes, Alan, 20

vaginal waxing, 91–93

Eck, Diana, 136

edge work, beauty as, 18, 30, 208–13, 223–24

Elmore, Mark, 124

INDEX 269

Erndl, Kathryn, 191
ethical personhood theories: women and, 23–24; women's subjectivities and, 98–99
Ethics of Beauty, The (Patitsas), 210
ethnicity, Indian stereotyping of, 103–6, 132–38
ethnic looks, Bollywood influence on, 58–59
ethnography of beauty, 10–12, 27–28
Evans Pritchard, Hugh, 75
Eve's Weekly (Indian women's magazine), 50–51

Fabulous Lives of Bollywood Wives in 2024, The, 173
Fair & Lovely (Glow & Lovely) bleaching paste, 66–68, 232n6
fairness industry: beauty work/beauty care and, 70–72; Black Americans and, 232n3; Brazilian waxing and, 91–93; colorism politics and, 66–68; race politics and resistance to, 76–77
Femina (Indian women's magazine), 50
feminism: beauty and, 7–8, 236n2; goddesses in secular feminism, 43; incompatibility of subordination with, 105; pativrata and, 170–71; theologians and religious studies scholars, 34
fertility, goddesses linked to, 101–2
fierceness, Hindu goddesses linked to, 34
film industry: concepts of beauty and allure on, 35; influence on Indian women's hairstyle of, 47–48; magazines about, 50–51
filth, beauty work and, 106–8. *See also* refuse, of beauty work
fire (*agneya*), 101
Flueckiger, Joyce, 34
Foucault, Michel, 207
Freeman, Carla, 185

Gaekwad (Baroda princeling), 88–89, 91
Gandhi, Indira (Prime Minister), 85
Gangamma (Hindu goddess), 34
Gauri (Hindu goddess), 74–75
Gell, Alfred, 9–10, 28, 217
gender scholarship: beauty and, 10–12; drag work and, 212–13
gender violence: allure and, 35; "dangerous" woman narrative as justification for, 86–87; in Draupadi story, 83–87; Indian women's experience with, 38–39, 230n3

geography, in Hindu cosmology, 135–38
glamor (glam): allure vs., 33–35; beauty and, 52–54
Glissant, Édouard, 28
Global Industry Analysts, 67
Glucklich, Ariel, 98
goddesses: allure and beauty linked to, 40–43; fairness of, 74–75; fierceness linked to, 34; heat and power of, 101–2; power of, 33–34; queer performances of, 209–11; secular feminism and, 43
Gold, Ann, 137
Grazia magazine, 204
Guenzi, Catherine, 159
guna (moral attributes), 221–24

Hagen culture, 154, 160
haircutting and hairstyling: boycuts, 182–86; henna treatments, 94–96; middle-class Indian women's embrace of, 47–48; *sindor bahra maang* ritual, 171–72, 238n21; smoothness aesthetic and, 80–82, 85; stigma of, for pre-1960s Indian women, 46–47
Hall, Stuart, 223
Hawley, Nell, 83
heat (*ushna*), 95; in beauty work, 109–11, 116–19; in Hindu culture and, 100–102, 234n1; vulgarity linked to, 111–15
Hegel, Georg Wilhelm, 74–75
Heidegger, Martin, 208
Hess, Linda, 170
heteronormativity: in beauty parlors, 180–81; caste and, 155–56; colonialism and, 183–86; neoliberal capitalism and, 66
Hidayatullah (Justice), 170
hijras: in Asia, 179–82, 238n11; queer activism and, 193–94, 200–203
Hiltebeitel, Alf, 85
Hindi-English lexicon (Hinglish), Indian celebrity culture and, 50–51
Hindu cosmology: beauty culture and, 12, 21–24; body odor in, 116–17; colorist hierarchy and, 75–76, 233n8; embodiment in, 159–60; genderless unity in, 238n22; glamor and, 56–57; hijra and, 201–3; Indian women's view of, 74–75; menstrual blood in, 104; myth and, 18; porosity of

bodies in, 98–99; power of goddesses in, 34, 74–75; wedding preparations and, 29–30, 237n15; wifehood and marriage in, 169–71; wound culture, 126–28. *See also* Puranic cosmology

Hindutva ideology: anti-Western criticism and, 92–93; heteronormativity and, 185–86; women's role and, 163, 170–71, 176–77

Hudson, Emily, 19

Hume, David, 124

Huyler, Stephen, 82

identity, beauty as resource for, 62

Indian medico-therapeutic aesthetics, 34–35, 48–49

Indian nation-state: feminine citizenship in, 44–47; homosexuality legalization and recriminalization and, 187–89; model wife ideology in, 170–71; neoliberal economics and, 149–50; women's beauty and allure in, 55–56

India Today, 133

intimacy of female bodies, beauty work and, 96–99, 106–8

Irigaray, Luce, 154

Ishtyle (Khubchandani), 194–95

Jantzen, Grace, 179, 184

Japanese beauty methods, 71, 233n11

Jodhaa-Akbar (film), 57

Karva Chauth vrat, 171–73, 237n19

Kali (Hindu goddess), 34, 41–42, 75

Kalidasa, 60

Kamakhya Devi (goddess), 101–3, 119, 135–36, 155, 236n17

Kamban, 239n7

Kant, Immanuel, on beauty, 8

karmic debt, Hindu concept of, 136–37

Karves, Irawati, 228

Kaundinya, Anaka, 66

Kennedy, Jacqueline, 34

Kersenboom, Saskia, 164

Kesavan, Mukul, 133

Khan, Kareena, 51–54, *52*

Khubchandani, Kareem, 187, 194–95

Kleinman, Arthur, 148

Kohli, Virat, 165

kolam patterns, 215, 239n1

Krishna (*Mahabharata* goddess), 75, 84

Kumari, Meena (Bollywood film star), 231n13

Lacan, Jacques, 177

Lakshmi (Hindu goddess): fairness of, 74–75; image of, 88–91, *90*; marriage rituals linked to, 164; power of, 30, 41–42, 63, 65, 82–83, 155; Sita linked to, 176

Lalitha Sahasranama, 40–42, 230n7

Lamb, Sarah, 161

legacy papers for migrants, 134–35

Le Guin, Ursula, 6, 227

Lévi-Strauss, Claude, 19–20

LGBTQ community: beauty industry and, 179–82; class politics and, 184–86; digital beauty parlors and, 195–99; queer beauty parlors, 194–95; queer rights movement and, 187–89. *See also* queer rights movement; trans culture

Lintas advertising company, 47

liposuction, 142–45

Liril body soap, 47–48, 231n18

L'Oréal, in India, 13

love, bhagya and, 163

MacKinnon, Catharine, 105

Madhubala (Indian film star), 44, 231n13

madness (*pittam*), 101

magical, in anthropology of beauty, 9–10

Mahabharata (Indian epic), 16–20; Draupadi story in, 29, 74–75, 83–87, 233n18; Gandhari character in, 1–3, 16, 229n1; hijra in, 202; Samudra Mathana story, 206–11; Satyavati story in, 115–16; Savitri story in, 174–75

Mahabharata teleserial: advertising during, 47–48; new Indian woman in, 45–46

Mahadevi, Akka, 94

makeup packages: bhagya and, 160; bridal industry and, 166–69, *168*; LGBTQ community and, 196–99, 203–5

male gaze, victimization of men linked to, 38

Malhotra, Manish, 58, 167–68

Malinowski, Bronislaw, 19, 60–61

Mankekar, Purnima, 45–46

Markandeya Purana, 41–42

marriage: beauty as currency of, 154; bhagya and, 159–63, 177–78; ceremonies and rituals included in, 237n15; class politics and, 161–63; educational emancipation and, 236n3; good wife ideology and, 169–71; *maang ka sindor* ritual and, 171–72; negation of choice in, 237n11; solah shrungar ritual and, 163–69; suhaag raat ritual and, 236n4; *vrat* (marital vow), 171–73. *See also* bridal industry; wedding preparations

Marriott, McKim, 22

Masquelier, Adeline, 108

medicalization of beauty, 9–10

Menaka (Hindu apsara), 33–34, 59–61, 230n5

Menon, Usha, 138, 142

menstrual blood, Hindu taboos concerning, 104–6

Merleau-Ponty, Maurice, 207

Meyer, Birgit, 28

middle class: emergence in India of, 13; modern Indian women and emergence of, 46–47. *See also* caste system; class politics

migrants and migrancy: in beauty work, 125–26, 128–31, 145–50; citizenship restrictions and, 133–38; Indian state policy and, 131–38; Indian stereotyping of, 103–6; political economy of beauty and, 29, 115

mirrors, self-representation in, 218–24

misrecognition, in Indian mythology, 60–61

Miss India pageant, 50

Miss Vegetarian Beauty Pageant, 28, 43–45, *44*, 50

modernity, Indian women in context of, 45–46, 50–51

modesty, allure and, 55–59

Mohini (goddess), 206–11

Moolgavkar, Rajibai, 88

moral hierarchy, body odor and, 100–102

Morphy, Howard, 75

mukhathezhuthu (face painting), 215–16

Mulvey, Laura, 1, 7–8

mundane, in anthropology of beauty, 9–10

Munn, Nancy, 167

Muslims: as beauty workers, 111; Bengal partition and, 235n11; glamor and beauty for, 57–59; violence involving, 131–38, 235n14

Myers, Joshua, 214, 217

Mysorean *moggina jadai* hairstyle, 47–48

Mysore Sandal soap company, 46

mythology: allure in, 56–59; beauty and, 12, 16–20, 177–78; body ambivalence in, 207–11; modern Indian womanhood in context of, 45, 60–62, 173–76, 223–24; selfhood discovered in, 210–12, 222–24

Naga ethnic group, 132–33

Narain, Devika, 165

National Registry of Citizens (NRC), 133–34

Navaratri festival (Nine Nights of the Goddess), 42

Naxalbari counterinsurgency, 85–86, 132–33, 235n10

Natyashastra (ancient text), 21

Neeta's Natter (De column), 50–51

Nehru, Jawaharlal, 45–46

neoliberal capitalism: autonomous selfhood and, 118, 162; bhagya and, 155; class politics and, 66, 89; feminism and, 156, 162, 176–77; heteronormativity and, 66; Hindutva ideology and, 176; marriage in India and, 155, 162–65, 171; migrancy and, 131, 150; queer communities in India and, 186–89; women's position and, 177–78

Nuer culture, body art in, 75

Obeyesekere, Gananath, 80

Odyssey, beauty in, 8

O'Hanlon, Michael, 75

oleography, 88–91

Operation Bakuli (Operation Steeplechase), 85

Orientalism, sexual stereotyping and, 105–6

Other, beauty and, 154

Packert Cynthia, 53–54

Padmavat (film), 57

Padukone, Deepika, 51–52, 54–55, 57–58, *165*, *199*

pain, beauty and, 124–28. *See also* wounding, in beauty work

Panchatantra fables, 24–25

Papua New Guinea, skin brilliance in, 75

Parameshwara, G., 37–38

Parvati (Hindu goddess), 40, 74–75, 125, 144, 236n18

"passing comments" (Indian genre of critique), 36–37

Patitsas, Timothy, 210
pativrata (chastity and loyalty), 169–70, 174–75
patriarchy, male gods linked to, 34
Pattini (Patni) (goddess), 170–71
pedagogy of beauty, 54–55
Pinto, Sarah, 109
politics, beauty and, 7–8, 126–28
possession, beauty as, 217–24
posters of celebrities, pedagogy of beauty and, 54–55
power: allure and, 34–35; of Hindu goddesses and apsaras, 33–34; Savriti as symbol of, 173–75
Prasad, Leela, 18
Prasad Bidapa Associates, 12
public space, threat to Indian women of, 37–38
Puranic cosmology, 41–42, 135, 231nn10–11. *See also* Hindu cosmology
purity rituals, caste system and, 46–47

Qayum, Seelim, 112–13
queer rights movement: beauty work/beauty care and, 30, 179–82, 194–95, 238n2; class politics and, 186–89; critiques of, 184–86; hijra activism in, 200–203; in Pakistan, 192. *See also* LGBTQ community; trans culture

race politics: beauty care and, 64–65, 76–77; Dalit caste and, 68–70; ethnic/racial stereotyping and, 103–6
Rai, Aishwarya, *165*
Rajan, Rajeswari Sunder, 43
Rama (*Ramayana* hero), 189–92, 238n6, 239n7
Ramanujan, A. K., 18, 20, 223
Ramayana, 151–53, 174–75, 189–92, 238n6, 239n7
Ramberg, Lucinda, 34, 155
"RamRajya" (rule of Rama), 176
rasa theory, beauty and, 21–24
Ravi Verma, Raja, 88–91
Ray, Raka, 112–13
refuse, of beauty work, 108–11. *See also* filth, beauty work and
Rehman, A. R., 215
representation, politics of, beauty research and, 27–28
Revlon, in India, 13

Richardson, Helen, 104
Rig Vedas, 68
Roy, Srila, 196

sacred narratives, myths as, 20
Sadhana (Indian film star), 47–48
Sahlins, Marshall, 136
Śaiva traditions, 231n10
Sangama, 201
Sanni, Shahmir, 186
Saria, Vaibhav, 201–2
Sarukkai, Sundar, 98
Sati (goddess), 29, 101, 125–26, 128–31, 135–36, 144–45, 150, 173–75
Sati Mata (spirit), 101, 135
Satyavan (*Mahabharata* character), 174–75
Satyavati (*Mahabharata* queen), 116, 119
Savitri (Bollywood film star), 231n13
Savriti mythology, 30, 155, 171, 173–75, 238n22
Scarry, Elaine, 8–9, 137
Section 377 law, 187–89, 201–3
selfhood: beauty linked to, 138–41, 217–24; body intimacy in beauty parlors and, 98–99; composite of, in Bangalorean women, 119; dispossession of perspective on, 61–62; marriage and, 154–56; *pativrata* (chastity and loyalty) and, 174–75; storytelling and, 208–11; transformation of, 212–13
Sephora, 49
sexual harassment, frequency in Bangalore of, 38–39, 96
sexuality and sensuality: beauty and, 29; beauty workers linked to, 102–6; bhagya linked to, 158–59; colorism politics and, 92–93; genital waxing and, 91–93; of goddesses, 101–2; *pativrata* (chastity and loyalty) and, 169–70; policing in beauty workers of, 110–11
sex work, beauty work linked to, 102–6, 113–15
Shaadi Squad (wedding planning company), 165
Shah, Svati, 185
Shahnaz Husain, 232n21
Śakta traditions, 135–136, 231n10
shakti (female power), 34, 41–43, 127–28, 142–43, 230n5
Shaktipeethas (seats of the goddess), 42
Sharma, Anushka, 165

Sharma, Shubika, 236n7
Shikhandi (*Mahabharata* character), 202
Shiva (god), 41, 125–26, 128–31, 144, 236n17
shrungara (beauty rituals), 21, 60–61, 219–20
Shulman, David, 17, 208
shyamoli (dark color), in Hindu cosmology, 75–76
sindor bahra maang ritual, 171–72, 238n21
Sita (goddess), 151–53, 155, 169–71, 176–77, 189–91
skin care: colorism and race politics of, 64–65, 71–72, 76–80; Hindu concept of porous bodies and, 98–99
skin harvesting, 120–23, 145–50
smell, in Hindu culture, 99–102
smoothness, Indian beauty aesthetic and, 80–82
soap industry, rise in India of, 46–47
social media: beauty work details on, 25–28, 35, *54*; bridal industry (India) on, 158, 236n7; colorism and caste politics and, 69–70; fairness advertisements on, *84*
social networks, beauty parlors and, 5–6
solah shrungar (sixteen auspicious decorations) (Hindu wedding ritual), 163–69, 172–73
somaesthetics, 79–80
Somers, Margaret, 61, 210
"Song for Pushkin" (Cohen), 186
Sontag, Susan, 8, 72–73
sowbhagya (marital fortune), 154–56, 164, 177
Srinivas, M. N., 156, 170
Srividya Shakta tradition, 231n10
Star and Style (Indian film magazine), 50–51
Stardust (Indian magazine), 50–51
Stoller, Paul, 137–38
storytelling: beauty and, 18–20, 137–38, 222–24; *bhagya* (fortune), 155; edge work of, 208–11; endless story form of, 61–62; Indian culture of, 24–25, 230n16; by Muslim barbers, 239n8
Strathern, Marilyn, 154
style, generalization in India of, 58–59
suhaag raat ritual, 236n4
Sundaram, Ravi, 126
Surpanakhi epic, 189–92

Tagore, Rabindranath, 1, 8
Tantra traditions, 101, 103–4, 135–36, 231nn10–11, 236n17

Tata, Jamshedji (Sir), 46
Teen Deviyaan (three goddesses), 1–3, 229n4
Tehliani, Tarun, 58
temples, ritual creativity in, 5–6
Thai migrants, Indian stereotyping of, 103–6
Tharwani, Tina, 165
Thirunangai community, 189, 238n3
Thrift, Nigel, 33
TMZ (Indian scandal sheet), 50–51
Tolstoy, Leo, 94
touch, in Hindu culture, 97–99
trans culture: in Bangalore, 195–99; beauty work and, 180–82, 192–95; body image and, 183; queer rights movement and, 186–87
tribal identity, violence and, 131–38, 235n9
Tripurasundari (goddess), 101

ugra (righteous anger, excess), 101–2
Ulysse, Gina, 38–39
Unani medical aesthetic, 234n4

vaginal rejuvenation and waxing, 91–93
Vaiṣṇava traditions, 65, 81, 231n10
Valmiki, 191, 238n6
Value Notes Database, beauty parlor research by, 14–15
vampire facial, 124–26, 138
Vedic literature, bhagya in, 158–59
Vishnu (god), 30, 41, 65, 82, 106, 125, 129, 135, 176, 206–9, 236n17
Viswanatha, Rupa, 235n15
Vogue India, 196–97, 204
vrat (marital vow), 171–73
Vreeland, Diana, 31, 34
vulgarity, beauty workers associated with, 111–15

Wadley, Susan, 158
wedding preparations: beauty work for, 87–91; ceremonies included in, 237n15; Hindu cosmology and, 29–30. *See also* bridal industry; marriage
WhatsApp, bridal industry (India) on, *54*, *84*, 158, *168*, 236n7
Whitenicious, 232n3

"Woman's Beauty, A: Put Down or Power Source" (Sontag), 8
Woman's Day (Indian women's magazine), 50–51
Woman's Era (Indian women's magazine), 50–51
women: bhagya and, 153–60; as embodiment of Indian nation, 35; myth and storytelling by, 20, 222–24; precarity of beauty for, 219–24; single women, in India, 161–63; as social gatekeepers, 154–56; wounding in India of, 141–50
Women of Worth feminist group, 76–77
women's magazines, emergence in India of, 50–51
wounding, in beauty work, 126–28, 131–50. *See also* pain, beauty and

Yama Raj (lord of death), 174–75
Yoni, Hindu concept of, 137